CHRONIC

*Empowerment*

M000266312

A SOCIAL MEDIA
CHRONIC WARRIOR
COLLABORATION

This book is an original publication of ImagineWe, LLC.

If you purchase this book without a cover you should be aware that this book may have been stolen property and reported as "unsold and destroyed" to the publisher. In such a case, neither the author nor the publisher has received any payment for this "stripped book."

**Published by:** ImagineWe, LLC
ImagineWe Publishers
247 Market Street, Suite 201
Lockport, NY 14094
United States
imaginewellc.com

© 2021 ImagineWe, LLC

All rights reserved. No part of this publication may be reproduced, stored in a retrieval system or transmitted in any form or by any means, electronic, mechanical, photocopying, recording or otherwise without the prior permission of the publisher or in accordance with the provisions of the Copyright, Designs and Patents Act 1988 or under the terms of any license permitting limited copying issued by the Copyright Licensing Agency. For permissions, write to the publisher "Attention: Permissions Coordinator" at info@imaginewellc.com.

ISBN: 978-1-946512-47-5 (Paperback)
ISBN: 978-1-946512-49-9 (Hardcover)
ISBN: 978-1-946512-48-2 (Ebook)
Library of Congress Control Number: 2021941970

First Edition: October 2021

PRINTED IN THE UNITED STATES OF AMERICA

We are always looking for new authors of all ages and grade levels. For more information, please visit the website listed above. To shop our selection of books and merchandise you can visit:
www.bookstore.imaginewellc.com

# *In Loving*
## MEMORY

Alicia "Red" Campitelli; July 3, 1985 – May 15, 2021

Anthony Hankinson; alpha-1 antitrypsin deficiency; April 5, 1964–January 23, 2018; Samantha Bowick's uncle

Danny Guy Day Sr.; August 16, 1956 – February 11, 2020; Misti Blu Day's Father

Deanna Marie Jungclaus Orr; amyloidosis; September 16, 1955–November 14, 2014; Samantha Bowick's family friend

Debra A "Debbie" Dowd; January 27, 1957 – November 10, 2015

Jessica Ann Dowd; January 27, 1988 – June 6, 2006

Jimmy (Red) Hankinson; Parkinson's disease; July 3, 1935–January 31, 2004; Samantha Bowick's grandfather

John Michael Cassick; September 3, 1952 – July 27, 2014; Heart Failure; Jessica Cassick's Father

Joy (Sissy) Green; thrombotic thrombocytopenic purpura (TTP); October 22, 1964–October 1, 2012; Samantha Bowick's aunt

Myrtle Gantt Hankinson; heart disease; March 26, 1937–May 25, 1997; Samantha Bowick's grandmother

# CHRONICALLY EMPOWERED-THEMED ADVERTISING

https://imaginewellc.com/

@imaginewepublishers

## IMAGINEWE
### Publishers™

Increase Excitement & Decrease Your
Overwhelm With Our Publishing Services.

- **FULL-SERVICE PUBLISHING SERVICES**
Coaching & Consulting, Professional
Illustration, Editing, Formatting, and Design,
Promotion, Distribution & Sales
- **EDUCATIONAL EVENTS & PROGRAMMING**
- **ONLINE STORE**
- **BLOG**

Dedicated to educating our communities at all ages to initiate diversity and
nclusion, and inspire self-agency and self-confidence around the world.

NOW ACCEPTING
CHILDREN'S BOOK,
NOVEL & MEMOIR
SUBMISSIONS!

## My Medical Musings

*A Story of Love, Laughter, Faith, and Hope;
Living with a Rare Disease*

**WRITTEN BY SAMANTHA MOSS**

COMING IN
2022!

Samantha Moss, was at the height of her successful career, as an Executive
Manager in Financial Services when her health took a negative turn. Despite
many broken bones and a permanent colostomy, she was determined to find
a fulfilling purpose for her life and became the founder of the blog, "My
Medical Musings." This story is full of encouragement for others facing a
sudden change in life's direction, to not give up on finding a new purpose.

## CONTACT US FOR INFORMATION ABOUT ADVERTISING IN FUTURE BOOKS

# Thank You

TO EVERYONE WHO CONTRIBUTED TO AND PLAYED A PART IN THE PRODUCTION OF THIS BOOK. YOUR STORIES ARE REVOLUTIONARY AND INSPIRING. MAY YOU CONTINUE TO SHARE THEM AND RAISE AWARENESS IN ALL DIRECTIONS, GLOBALLY.

-IMAGINEWE PUBISHERS

Do you enjoy writing?
Do you have a story to share?

# BECOME A PUBLISHED AUTHOR!

Our mission at ImagineWe Publishers is to create a simple and convenient way to support authors throughout the publishing process from concept to creation and beyond. We are devoted to educating all people to initiate diversity and inclusion while inspiring self-agency and self-esteem across the world.

## OUR EXPERTISE

**Coaching & Consulting**
One-on-one assistance from concept to completion.

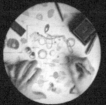

**Professional Production**
Illustration, Formatting & Design

**Promotion & Advertising**
Marketing & Social Media Management

**Professional Publishing**
Launch Event Planning & Book Signings

**Distribution & Sales**
Retail, Wholesale, Fundraising & Educational Programming

IMAGINEWE
Publishers™

# CHRONICALLY *Empowered*

## THE STORY OF THIS SPECIALTY BOOK:

This book is called Chronically Empowered and is a collaboration project with another passionate artist and chronic illness advocate, @thechronicallyhonest, and a whole array of amazing, and powerful chronic illness warriors.

Chronically Honest is an Instagram account that's mission is to share the honest hardships of chronic illnesses through beautiful illustrations displayed with powerful text that describes the image

Our CEO, Jessica Cassick, was caught by surprise when she stumbled upon this Instagram account and it thoroughly appealed to her. This collaboration project is a book created to celebrate Jessica's nine-year Domestic Violence SURVIVOR Anniversary! It is a book of short stories that gives attention to various aspects of chronic illnesses and struggles. Each story falls within a specific theme, and each theme is strategically created to empower individuals facing a range of chronic conditions.

This project is a celebratory collaboration initiative created to spread inspiration and motivation among those suffering chronically. We aim to provide as much joy as tears, in these stories, and to share our mission globally.

Our mission for this book is to create a beautiful, positive, unified, and global feeling of inclusion and empowerment among individuals suffering from the realities of chronic illness. We hope to share the good, the bad, the ugly, and the powerful to inspire hope, resilience, and awareness on the topics discussed in this book.

We are building a book of stories to give hope in times of stress, and to show that even in the most difficult of situations, you are not alone. We welcome you to join us as you read this book. We know that you have a story too and hope that you share it with us, in celebration of your amazing self.

**We accept you as you are, forever.**

# TABLE OF CONTENTS

**12** INTRODUCTION
*CEO's Opening Message*

**18** I AM RESILIENT.
*Stories of chronic illness warriors withstanding extraordinary storms and recovering despite the odds.*

**60** I AM DESERVING.
*Stories of chronic illness warriors learning about how they deserve to be treated.*

**108** I AM CAPABLE.
*Stories of chronic illness warriors achieving exceptional heights.*

**140** I AM WORTHY.
*Stories of chronic illness warriors learning about their worth.*

**174** I AM POWERFUL.
*Stories of chronic illness warriors commanding great things.*

**216** I AM EVER-EVOLVING.
*Stories of chronic illness warriors learning to start over.*

**256** I AM DETERMINED.
*Stories of chronic illness warriors accomplishing things despite their barriers.*

**296** I AM STRONG.
*Stories of chronic illness warriors learning about their strength.*

**334** I AM A WARRIOR.
*Stories of chronic illness warriors paving the way for the rest of us to impact our world.*

**376** CONCLUSION
*Illustrator's Closing Message*

# CONTRIBUTING AUTHORS

DARA KLUGHERZ 20 TARALYNN BIE 26 TOM SEAMAN 32 CHANTAY HAYWOOD 40

SAMANTHA SMITH 44 ANNIE-DANIELLE GRENIER 48 LYNN JULIAN 54

SYDNEY KENDRICK 62 PAMELA BICKFORD 68 TIFFANY KAIROS 74 JENNY JONES 78

JIMMY FREMGEN 84 ANTONIA SCHWARTZ 92 CHEYANNE PERRY SUAREZ 98

AMY EFFENBERGER 110 CASEY STANLEY 112 NATALIE KELLEY 118

JENNIFER DAWN 124 KEISHA GREAVES 126 AMY GIETZEN 132

SANDRA HAMILTON 136 RACHEL SITRO 142 NIKKY BOX 144 REA STRAWHILL 148

KIARA DIJKSTRA 154 LAUREN JAYNE 160 FRANCESSCA PRADO 162

DIANNA CARNEY 168 CHELSEY STORTEBOOM 176 ANDREA NEPH 182

SCOTT NINNEMAN 188 JEMMA-TIFFANY ROSEWATER 194 NATALIE LAUREN 200

DANIELLE MARIE TURCO 206 BRANDON MOUW 210 ALLISON TENNYSON 218

AMY L. BURK 224 LOUISA RÜGGEBERG 230 SAMANTHA MOSS 232

MARIA DE LEON 238 KATYA KOZARY 244 MISTI BLU DAY MCDERMOTT 248

VICTORIA F. BURNS 258 AMANDA OSOWSKI 264 WENDY MEYEROFF 270

ELLA BALASA 276 KAY MIMMS 280 MADELYN SANER 286 AMY COURTNEY 292

JOHANNA VEKARA 298 STACEY LA GATTA 302 KATE HENRY 306 KELLY 312

SARAH GOLDEN 318 KRISTEN LEWIS 324 BECCA BLANCKENBERG 328

EMILY NATANI 336 TESSA HANSEN-SMITH 342 BRANDY HABERER 348

SAMANTHA BOWICK 354 ELIŠKA 360 CYDNI FRIED 366 OLIVER COLLINS 372

JULIA BARTOW 376 JESSICA CASSICK 12

# Chronically Chic®

## BEAUTIFULLY PRACTICAL

Products designed to support and beautify the lives of people with chronic illness.

www.chronicallychicboutique.com

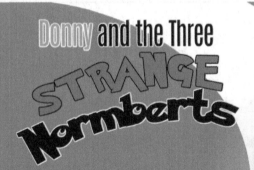

**Donny and the Three STRANGE Normberts**

**BUY NOW!**

WRITTEN BY: NATALIE VAN SCHELTINGA & JENNI LOCK
ILLUSTRATED BY: TONI SCOTT

The Chargimals live in Chargieville alongside the Normberts. The Chargimals live with various health conditions, and the Normberts are the "normal" healthy people. This story is about friendship, reduced mobility, anxiety, and how to overcome obstacles mixed with a little bit of magic.

Brought to you by

The Chargimals

# My Invisible Fear

*Victoria F. Burns, PhD, LSW*

People act surprised when I tell them
How is it possible you have Type 1 diabetes?
Aren't you too old?
You look so fit!
You were so healthy!
You don't look sick!
Other people tell me to think of it as a "gift"
An excuse to embrace eating healthier
I already did
An excuse to embrace less rigorous ways to exercise, like yoga
I miss being able to run
They tell me that I will learn to live with it
That I will get used to it
That I should not consider it as a disability
That eventually I will forget it is even part of my life
That I am "normal"
I don't feel normal
What do they know?
I resent it every day
I didn't ask for this gift
I thought I did everything to avoid it
But the joke's on me
Worst of all is that people don't understand
They tell me "it could be worse"
Of course, it can always be worse
I invite them to walk in my shoes for a day
To embrace my needles
To embrace my counting
To embrace my exhaustion
To embrace my irritability
To embrace my uncertainty
To embrace my frustration
To embrace my isolation
To embrace my resentment
To embrace my fear

# INTRODUCTION

Have you ever had that vibration in what feels like your heart of hearts, or maybe even where you imagine your soul resides? The kind of vibration that sends a pulse through your brain and into your smile? And the kind of vibration that makes you feel what I can only describe as "giddy?" The moment this book became a real, live thing, and even every moment since it began its journey to take on a life of its own within our community, I have felt THAT vibration. I have felt excitement unlike any other, and I cannot even begin to explain how much it continues to grow.

The contributors to this book share my excitement through their faith in and passion for our mission. This project has truly taken on a life of its own, with an ever-growing list of books that are going to be a part of a whole book series. All of these things are a massive gift. Not only a gift that we can thoroughly enjoy, but a gift that anyone and everyone that is a part of this mission can share as well. I've never been a part of something quite like Chronically Empowered, and I am so happy and blessed to say that I am a part of its genesis.

The year 2020 as a whole set ImagineWe Publishers back in our goals. For many, many months it hit hard, but eventually we took a cue from the world and decided to put our productive energy into planning, thinking, and researching to find a way through the heavy year, in order to make 2021 even better than every year before it. This book is one of the many things to be born from our global pandemic of 2020-2021. I am proud to know and be able to work with all of its contributors and I hope you love this book as much as I loved creating it with them.

My name is Jessica Cassick, and I'm a lady of many professions. First and foremost, since 2016, I am the CEO of ImagineWe Publishers. I am the co-founder of Synergy Services Alliance, Inc. (a charity organization that has a foundation in research and economic development in the fusion field of creativity and trauma recovery). I am a college instructor at Niagara County Community College and Buffalo State College where I teach classes in Media Literacy, Public Relations, Speech, Interpersonal Communications, Creativity, and Success. I know, I know...where do I find the time...let alone the energy?! I have absolutely no idea.

All of these professional endeavors interweave the many facets of my passions, talents, and love for academia and communication. But I guess to explain why I literally do so much, I must introduce my disabilities, and "the why" behind why I am connected to the chronic illness community.

In 2011, right before I turned 21, I was stopped at a red light in my small, black, 2-door cavalier and I noticed the SUV pulling up behind me was going a bit fast...too fast. For whatever reason, this teenage driver only appeared to be paying attention, but actually neglected to see and react accordingly to the red light and two lanes of stopped traffic on this January afternoon. I took a deep breath, grimaced, and clenched every part of my body...

(If we were in a tv show or a movie right now, the entire screen would pause...and only I would be unfrozen enough to tell you that this was the very moment that would "ruin" my life and possibly my future... According to my doctors...un-pause!)

As the SUV slammed into the back of my car, my head bounced between the steering wheel and my headrest, my foot left my brake pedal, and my car slammed into the SUV in front of me. My car was filled with a nasty smelling smoke, and my head hurt. I also noticed I couldn't see, and my glasses had flown off my face. As I got out of my car to search for them, the kid behind me came to check if I was okay. I was so distraught about my glasses that I told him to be quiet.

Flash forward a year or two and I was going to a chiropractor, massage therapist, and acupuncturist once a week. I was seeing my pain management doctor for Prolotherapy and steroid injections every other week. I had suffered multiple injuries in my car accident that left me with bilateral partial paralysis. The discs in my neck and back were all jacked

> **"I was only 20 years old, and I had the body and injuries of a 70 year old; I was doing it all while also trying to hold up my life as a single-mom of a newborn baby, and we had just become survivors of Domestic Violence..."**

up. C2-7 and L4-S1 were all either herniated, bulged or straight up torn; multiplied also by degenerative disc disease (which means it's basically going to continue to get worse). I was 20 years old, and I had the internal injuries and bodily structure of a 70 year old; I was doing it all while also trying to hold up my life as a single-mom of a newborn baby, and we had just become survivors of Domestic Violence. Did you know that so many victims of Domestic and Intimate Partner Violence are victims because they have a disability, and this debilitates them to the point where violence and abuse are easier than the exhaustion of trying to leave and risking their lives?

The day my abuser held us hostage in his bathroom, I was sitting on the floor, holding my five-month-old son and hoping and praying, with everything in me, that his cries were fear-based and not pain or injury-based. He was just assaulted moments earlier when my abuser tried to hurt me, and in the process, tunnel visioned right through our poor, defenseless newborn in my arms.

So many people ask that ridiculous question, "why did you stay?" And aside from the fact that I suffered from my own mental

## "Never be able to work again? But my life has barely even started..."

health issues from trauma I faced growing up in a family that came from an intergenerational cycle of violence, this relationship was my own uncomfortable-comfortable-yet perfect, hell. That's the only way I can explain it. The very idea of finding not only the raw physical energy, but the mental energy to leave my relationship and the life I was living, while also being buried in chronic, terrifyingly intense pain nine months out of every year seemed absolutely not worth it. But when my son became a casualty of that violence, my very existence shattered. My comfort zone dissolved, and my purpose and passion for my son's well-being, health, and life shook me to my core. He wasn't going to live this life. He would never know this pain. He would never feel this failure. He would not endure THIS.

This question is the hardest to answer for me. It's the question that brings tears to my eyes every time. All of these things affect me in every cell and part of my being. I'm in pain three quarters of every year, and I think about leaving where I live (Buffalo, NY - one of the coldest places during that time), but I love my family, and this is where we all live.

Last year, right before COVID hit, I was in my worst depression. Nothing was bringing me joy, I didn't feel connected to anything except for agony, and I truly considered whether I needed to take a break from life, in a hospital. The raw fact of the matter is, my pain left me feeling hollow, weak, and I truly didn't know if I could honestly trust my own thoughts, as my desires and daydreams were slowly pulling me into a darkness that was alluring, but breaks my heart as a mother. My disabilities created a HARD life where everything takes so much more energy than someone who doesn't get my stabbing pains in their back, or doesn't break into a sweat doing daily mundane tasks. My pain and disabilities affect me immensely. This combined with my anxiety, PTSD, and depression are why I have so many places to escape professionally. Keeping my mind busy hurts less.

The minute the doctor explained all of my injuries logically and anatomically, I remember not feeling different. Mostly because it didn't REALLY make sense to me. So my alphabet soup in my spine sounds pretty jacked up. I'll just switch to tomato bisque or something, eh? But then he said it, "Your injuries are getting worse by the year, and we think you're too young to attempt surgery. You will never be able to work again. You'll need to apply for permanent disability..."

Never be able to work again? But my life has barely even started? I decided, f*ck that doctor's opinion! I'm only 22, and he can't tell me what I'm capable of! I'm supposed to be intelligent. I'm supposed to be able to handle this. I can't have been dealt a deck that wasn't right for me, and this be my true demise.

So I decided that even though I couldn't

rely on my body, I could rely on my mind to build a future for myself and my son.. I set out on a journey to figure out how to get back into college. I had been academically dismissed multiple times between trying to go to college after being home-schooled and isolated as a teen and then also trying to do it after a house fire, when I was living in a tent. The last time I tried going back to college, my ex wouldn't stop threatening me and yelling at me and attacking me about every male that was in the college building at the same time I was. He was truly insecure and delusional, but I digress. As a result of these failures to stay in college, my grants became student loans that needed to be paid back. To help make ends meet, I flipped a bunch of furniture that I was given after my son and I left the Domestic Violence safe house when we left our abuser. I ended up making enough to pay off the loans and return to school.

I went on to finish my Associate Degree in Business Administration, my Bachelor's Degree in Individualized Studies with a Programmatic Theme in Women and Gender Business Communication, my Master's Degree in Creative Studies (where I launched this company as an independent study, and my charity organization as a master's project) and now I'm finishing my PhD in Creative Leadership for Innovation and Change. I truly love my research. I study the impact that creative problem solving can have in the development of economic and post-traumatic growth on Domestic and Intimate Partner Violence. I am basically creating a program where I take everything that I learned and

monetize it so that I can teach and certify others globally so that they can help survivors worldwide to kickstart their dreams, goals, and find success and financial independence, too. I truly love my research more than I can explain. It also makes my heart vibrate.

If you were to ask me six or more years ago what I love about myself, despite my disabilities, I'm not sure I could give you a positive answer. Over the years, I've just made things work. I've made anything and everything *work.* I've done a lot of research on how I think and what I do, and so many

## "My brain is becoming my money-maker."

times, I've come down to the hypothesis that I think I'm autistic. And it's what makes my brain different from almost every brain across the history of my life. I vividly remember being an outcast in every classroom, because I did my work too fast and then bugged everyone around me because I wasn't being challenged. Growing up I always had to move my desk away from the rest of the class, but because I was so used to it, I moved it right next to the bookshelf so I could read. I think that is why I had the highest accelerated reader score in my class, because what else was I going to do in between staring out the window, dreaming about my future and all the things I wanted to be, do, and know. (If you haven't yet, check out the Eloina Spelloina children's book series. The first book in the series is my grade school revenge on the teacher I couldn't stand in those years for making me move my desk in the beginning, years before I became used to it. She wasn't nice, and she didn't understand that I just wasn't being challenged academically, and I was so miserably bored trying to find things to do when everyone else was doing their school work, and mine was already neatly placed in the turn-in bin.)

Anyway, what I love about myself is that I make things work and I make things happen. I love to solve problems and I love to do it with creative and unique ways that express my "different" brain. It's become this tool at my disposal over the years, that is now turning into my personal arsenal to help those around me. I love to take as many others with me on the journey, as I make things work and help them to succeed in their dreams as well. I love my brain.

The only thing left on my dream career list that I haven't started yet is a new K-12 school. I have a lot of ideas, and essentially most of them are founded in creativity, critical problem solving, no bullying, and a lot of real world projects, applications and entrepreneurship for students of all ages. I imagine a school where my son can go that teaches him all of the basic educational classes, but then also expands his experiences and teaches him how to launch his dreams, create his goals, and be the thing that helps him to grow up loving whoever he turns out to be. I don't want him to feel the way that I did growing up. I would honestly LOVE to create the place to launch him in the ways that I wish that I had access to at his age. I haven't started it yet, but it's on my list!

I pass this advice on the next page on to you from my mother. I grew up with these words being said to me allllll the time, and it's my favorite thing about my childhood.

I truly hope you LOVE this book. Be kind and truthful. Stay safe, as healthy as you can, and always choose happiness. You deserve all these things.

# –Jessica Cassick
## *CEO of ImagineWe Publishers*

"Can't is the only impossible. When you say or think something negative about yourself or someone else, follow it up with two more positives. You are intelligent. You are beautiful and handsome. You are important and full of worth. Opportunities are endless to you. You are only in charge of your own happiness; no one else's. Don't do anything half-assed. Put your everything into everything or don't put anything into it at all. Try your best, that's all you can do. You can do absolutely anything that you set your mind to. And finally, where there's a will, there is ALWAYS most definitely a way."

Dara Klugherz

Taralynn Bie

Tom Seaman

Chantay Haywood

Samantha Smith

Annie-Danielle Grenier

Lynn Julian

# I AM
# Resilient.

**Stories of chronic illness warriors withstanding extraordinary storms and recovering despite the odds.**

# Dara Klugherz

Cleveland, OH, USA

*Student*

**About Dara:**

*My name is Dara Klugherz. I am currently 16 years old and in my junior year of high school. When I'm not doing my job as a student, I spend lots of time with my family, especially my dog who is my main inspiration and best friend. I love to travel and hope to see places all over the world. And mostly, I love to embrace my chronic illnesses. Whether it's through an internship, in a club at my school, or simply on my chronic illness Instagram page, I love to spend my time raising awareness and educating people on chronic illnesses.*

\* \* \*

**IG:** *@kids.with.chronic.illnesses*

*"You'll face pain, tears, hopelessness, loneliness, and fear, but you'll learn strength, resilience, determination, and hope."*

My name is Dara Klugherz and I am a 16 year old high school student. My story really began about nine years ago when I was only around 7 years old.

Since that time, I have been diagnosed with ulcerative colitis and sacroiliitis, along with multiple mental illnesses including depression and social and generalized anxiety disorder. Ulcerative colitis is a form of Inflammatory Bowel Disease, or IBD. Having this disease means that there is inflammation along the lining of my colon, causing a variety of symptoms such as bloody diarrhea, constipation, abdominal pain, urgency, loss of appetite, and more. Sacroiliitis is a consequence of my IBD, although it started much before my IBD symptoms. It is a form of arthritis that has resulted in permanent damage to my lower back, my sacroiliac joint to be exact. For me, sacroiliitis has caused debilitating leg pain that mostly occurs in my thighs, but radiates down my legs as it becomes worse. It's not very common, especially without the ulcerative colitis symptoms, which is part of the reason why it was left undiagnosed for about nine years.

> "However, the pain began evolving, and beforeI knew it, it wasn't going away with sleep anymore."

Beginning around 9 years ago, I would wake up in the middle of the night with a random sharp pain in my legs. I would eventually cry myself back to sleep, and when I woke up again in the morning, the pain would be gone. However, the pain began evolving, and before I knew it, it wasn't going away with sleep anymore. Being a kid, the leg pain was continuously passed over by a variety of pediatric specialists as growing pains, but I think I always knew that it was more than that. My pain was mostly in my thighs, coming and going randomly with no explanation and nothing that ever helped it. It was sharp-- I like to describe it as the biggest knife you can imagine going into my leg, and instead of removing it, more knives kept being stabbed into me. Basically, it was horrible. My legs hurt when I stood up, layed down, sat down, walked, and ran. They hurt through the whole night I was asleep (or screaming in my bed when I couldn't sleep because of the pain). Eventually my parents realized it wasn't growing pains and started to take me to more doctors to investigate. I went to every type of doctor you can think of and more, and they all told me the same thing: I was "faking" it. Again, this wasn't just one doctor, it was nine years worth of doctors telling me I was faking a pain so bad that, at times, I wasn't able to stand up from a chair. As you might imagine, I was more than frustrated by this. I was angry. I was appalled. I felt hopeless.

Fast forward to February, 2019. My legs were still in pain. In fact, they were getting worse and, still, no doctor believed me. So,

# "I went to every type of doctor you can think of and more, and they all told me the same thing: I was "faking" it."

in an attempt to function enough to complete my school work and sports activities, I took Advil at high doses. I then began having bad stomach problems. By stomach problems, I mean diarrhea, abdominal pain, urgency, and blood. I found myself spending hours each day in the bathroom. The diarrhea was so bad that I was even unable to control it while playing in a lacrosse game. I initially thought I had taken too much Advil, but that wasn't the case. A trip to the Emergency Room, a gastroenterologist (GI) appointment, many blood tests, stool samples, a colonoscopy, and an endoscopy later, I was diagnosed with ulcerative colitis. Luckily, there was a silver lining to this mess.

As part of the tests for my IBD, I had an MRI in which my incredible GI doctor noticed something that did not look right with my back. Many more tests and appointments later, I was diagnosed with sacroiliitis, which was the cause of my leg pain. You can't even begin to understand how happy I was to finally receive a diagnosis, even if it did take almost nine years to get there. Giving the pain a diagnosis meant it wasn't "fake" anymore, even though it never was to me.

Unfortunately, getting both of these diagnoses didn't mean that I was cured. In fact, neither of these diseases has a cure. However, there are plenty of treatment options. I know, because I've been through a lot of them so far. I started out on oral steroids to reduce my symptoms enough that I could function properly again, and after a few months I started to do better so I was taken off of them. It didn't take long for all my symptoms to come rushing back, and they were even worse this time. The problem with steroids is that they have a lot of side effects, meaning they aren't something you want to be on long term, so I tried a couple of other medications, including enemas. Enemas are a form of medicine that you take through the rectum. They weren't fun at all and they didn't work, so I went back on steroids. Unsurprisingly, the same thing happened with this round. I started to do better, but as soon as I stopped taking the steroids, I was back to feeling terrible. This time, in an attempt to avoid going back on steroids, I started on a medication called Humira, which is a shot that I had to give myself every two weeks. It started working very quickly, but about as fast as it started working, it stopped working. So, you guessed it, I went back on steroids. Third time's a charm. Well, it actually wasn't for me. When I was put back on steroids the third time, the side effects hit me really hard and they weren't even helping as much anymore. My doctor even had to increase my dose from what I was initially taking, but that didn't really help either. Luckily, my GI doctor was on top of things and by March of 2020, I began a different medication called Remicade, which is now keeping my inflammation under control. Remicade is an infusion, so I have to go to the hospital every eight weeks for about three hours and get an IV with my medicine. It's not the

> **"Despite all the pain, tears, hopelessness, and anger —despite everything—I've managed to keep up my grades in school and join clubs that interest me."**

most fun, but I'll accept a not fun treatment over the pain anyday, and I couldn't be more grateful for it.

So, now that you have an understanding of my journey, and my chronic illnesses in general, you can see that IBD and arthritis are both physical illnesses. But that doesn't mean they only affect me physically. Being undiagnosed for so long, my mental health worsened severely. As I previously mentioned, I felt hopeless. I was constantly ignored and dismissed. I felt alone. After every doctor appointment, I felt more and more like I was never going to get the chance to feel better or even get answers. I had nobody to talk to who truly understood what I was going through. My own friends told me I was faking my pain for attention or to get out of gym class. My doctors and friends, two of the groups of people who should've been there to support me, weren't there for me. The unfortunate reality is that

most people don't believe you when you're undiagnosed with an illness they can't see. It's lonely, terrifying, and depressing. My depression and anxiety were at an all time low. It's something nobody should have to go through. Even diagnosed, I went through so many failed treatment plans, and that only made me feel more hopeless. Thankfully, the infusions I'm on are helping now and I am able to see a brighter future for my health than I had thought possible.

To clarify, "helping my symptoms" does not mean cured. Even though I now have some better days, I will never not be sick, and it hurts knowing that. I can still have a good day and spend the next day camped out in my bathroom. I am now almost always fatigued, even though I get at least ten hours of sleep every night. I always need to know where the bathroom is. Always. I now have to know my limits. I can't run or even walk for too long without risking a leg pain flare up. I had to stop playing on the lacrosse team. Being in high school, I have a 504 plan for accommodations, and although I don't use them often, I am allowed to miss classes as needed for appointments and bad health days, use the bathroom without question, use the elevator, etc. Looking to my future in college, I have to focus on things most people don't necessarily need to worry about. I have to make sure that I can get accommodations similar to what I currently have in high school. For example, for dorms, I need to have proper access to a bathroom. I also have to make sure the campus is manageable and won't cause too many problems for my legs. Things like these may seem little and are what most college students take for granted, but will be huge factors in my college decision, almost as important as academics.

## "Would you trade it all for a chance to have a healthy life?"

Yes, it's rough knowing that this will forever be my life. It's rough knowing that I'll always have to make sure there's a bathroom nearby and not walk as far as I might want.

But this brings me to a question that I think about a lot: Would you trade it all for a chance to have a healthy life? The truth is, as rough as it can be and as much as it makes my life harder, if you were to ask me, here's what I would tell you:

Despite all the pain, tears, hopelessness, and anger —despite everything— I've managed to keep up my grades in school and join clubs that interest me. Yes, I had to stop playing lacrosse, but maybe that was for the better. Maybe that was meant to be. I've still managed to do a lot of the things that normal high schoolers do, but I've done it all in pain, something most high schoolers can't imagine. I've learned my own limits and I've tested them time and time again. I've experienced more in my 16 years of living than many people will experience in a lifetime.

By the middle of my sophomore year of high school, I was becoming friends with other people with disabilities, and I began to realize that I wasn't alone in my chronic illness journey. I took this realization as an opportunity to find my bigger purpose in life. To embrace my passion that I have grown to love more and more, I started a blog in which I began to educate others about invisible disabilities. I have been able to educate my followers on my illnesses, chronic illnesses in general, and experiences that they might not have realized I go through. In addition, I began working with an organization that works with people like me who have IBD, called the Crohn's and Colitis Foundation. I started a program with them that is aimed towards educating young adults about IBD and connecting patients. I dedicate a huge part of my life to bringing visibility to invisible disabilities.

Looking at my life now, I love that I was able to take this dark, painful situation and turn it into an opportunity to find the light. To find my light. I love my strength. I found the strength that I wouldn't have without my illnesses. I love my resilience which makes me unique. The type of resilience and determination that is only really acquired by being shut down and ignored for almost nine years while facing debilitating pain that most people can never imagine. Yes, I have experienced so much pain in my life, but I wouldn't be who I am now without it all. I wouldn't be me. While I have not let myself become any of my illnesses, I've allowed them to become a part of me. A part of me that has made me a better person.

So, no, I wouldn't change it at all. I

wouldn't change it for the easy path because, in the end, this is where I was meant to be.

If I could do anything in life right now, this is exactly what I would want to be doing. I want to be helping other people with chronic illnesses. I want to raise awareness for these terrible, life altering diseases. I want to help people realize that they're not alone because I know that it feels so lonely being sick, but the truth is, they're never going to be alone. And really, I want to help give people the determination and hope that I always needed, but took so long to find - nine years to be more precise.

## "I wouldn't change it for the easy path because, in the end, this is where I was meant to be."

Nine years of pain. Nine years of pretending to be okay. Nine years of wondering what I could've done that was so bad to make me experience this never ending torture. Nine years of being doubted by friends who should've been there to support me. Nine years of being doubted and dismissed by doctors, so much that I began to doubt myself. After every appointment that I went to, I had the opportunity to give up. But no matter how many days I spent laying on the floor, screaming in pain, wanting to feel normal, I never gave up. It took almost nine years, but I finally got answers that I never would've gotten if I had given up. No matter how much I wanted to give up, I never did.

So, if you only get one thing from my story, here's the advice I want you to take:

I know that being sick is hard. Knowing that you're always going to be sick is even harder. But hard doesn't mean it's time to give up, it just means that you have to try harder than you might like. Trying harder means you'll learn more about both yourself and the world. You'll face pain, tears, hopelessness, loneliness, and fear, but you'll learn strength, resilience, determination, and hope. It might feel impossible, but eventually, if you keep trying, things will get better, which is why you can never ever give up. By giving up, you lose your chance to get help and move in the right direction. You also lose your chance to learn and grow. If you give up, you'll lose your chance to become the incredible, experienced, powerful person you were meant to be. I'm in no way saying it's easy or will ever be even close to easy, but in the end, it'll be truly rewarding and you'll be so glad you never gave up. So, don't give up when the pain seems unbearable. Don't give up when nobody believes you. Don't give up when giving up feels like the only option. I promise it'll be worth it in the end.

# Taralynn Bie

Rocky Point, NY, USA

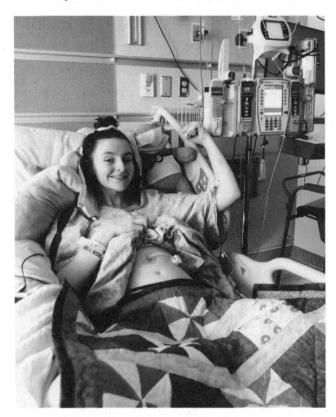

## Manager at Sky Zone, Student & Cat mom

*"Never stop advocating for yourself because by doing so you are also advocating for others. We are all worthy."*

## About Taralynn:

*Hey, my name is Tara, I'm 19 years old and live on long island, New York. I am a chronic illness warrior, suffering from POTS, chronic migraines and gastroparesis. On top of that I'm also a reader, cat mom and a student. I am so honored to have my story along so many amazing warriors. I hope this book helps educate others and show that you are not alone. The rain will end. Thank you for allowing me to share my life.*

\* \* \*

*IG: @taras_story*

*YouTube: Taras Story*

Senior year of high school; what a time. The year of decisions and learning how to be an adult in the real world. Finally able to drive, work and earn your own money, the freedom that you have always craved right there in front of you. At least that's what I was expecting when I went into it.

We all have a day, you know, a day that seems like just another one but actually changes your life without you even knowing. This is where my story starts. I was driving to my new job at a daycare one rainy August morning. I was pulling out of a parklot waiting to make a left hand turn and the next thing I knew I was in the middle of the road with my license plate broken on the street 100 feet away from my car. I think this was the first time my body has ever fully been in a state of shock. I sat frozen with my hands glued to the wheel, eyes bugging out my head. I genuinely had no idea what happened or what to do next. It literally felt like my body just stopped working, like I was outside my body watching what was happening because surely that could not have been me. I was just going to work, I was 2 minutes away from the building, I'm supposed to be there in 5 minutes to start my shift, there is no way I hit that car, this cannot be real. Luckily my mom was not too far behind me, I remember her pulling over and yelling at me to do the same and put on my blinkers. Without her directing me I really do not know what I would have done.

Anyway, that was my day. The one that forever changed my life and gave me no warning at all. I was extremely lucky though, the driver of the other car was totally fine and so sweet. My car took the worst of the hit but nothing that couldn't be fixed. We, meaning my mom because I was too busy sobbing to get a word out, called the police to report the accident but overall it was not too big of a deal. I actually went to work right after because, honestly I don't know why. My stubborn self wanted to and there was no talking me out of it. Was that a smart decision in the grand scheme of things? No, probably not.

A little background on me, I was a relatively healthy kid, I was diagnosed with chronic migraines at age 5 but by age 17 I had a pretty solid handle on them. I was also prone to passing out, but it did not happen often, maybe like once or twice a year. One of the most memorable ones was in my sophomore year of high school. I was playing varsity basketball and had an early morning Saturday practice. The plan was to watch the film of our last game, eat bagels and then have a short practice after. I woke up that morning, felt fine, got ready and my dad drove me to the school like normal. My team and I were sitting outside the gym waiting for our coach when I started feeling nauseous. I sat there and drank water hoping it would pass but it only got worse.

Once my coach got there I asked him if I could use the bathroom, he went and unlocked the door for me and said to meet him and the team downstairs in the film room when I was done. I walked into the bathroom, the light turned on, I looked in the mirror and the next thing I knew I woke up with my head next to the stall and the lights were off (motion sensored lights). I had no idea what happened or how long I was like that. I slowly got up and walked down to the film room in a daze. I vaguely remember telling my coach what happened and then I called my dad and he took me to hospital. I suffered a severe concussion and was "inches away from a brain bleed". After running many tests, the doctors at the ER concluded that I passed out because I did not eat anything before practice. So, like I said before, passing out was not rare for me but it was never something that concerned any doctors, all my tests would come back fine, so I just went on living life.

## "I thought after receiving a diagnosis we finally reached the end and the rest would be easy compared to this."

That whole week of work after the crash is like mush in my brain, I barely remember being at work. Each day I started feeling weaker and weaker. I was constantly lightheaded and overly hot but I continued to go; see, told you I was stubborn. The breaking point came when I passed out at work. The shame and horror I felt that day was unlike anything I have ever felt. Here I am the youngest employee, trying to work at a real job, something I wanted to make a career out of and I passed out in front of everyone. Not to mention I threw up right in front of the entrance on my way out. Ask me about the most embarrassing moment of my life, I do not think anything will ever beat that.

The next month I spent every minute in bed (or in the hospital). I was barely able to move my head without passing out. I was dehydrated, constantly tired and always dizzy but no one seemed to know why.

Now we've reached the big question. Where did everything go so horribly wrong? I guess now is as good a time as ever to introduce myself, so hello my name is Taralynn Bie, everyone calls me Tara, I'm 19 years old, from New York and this is my story.

After seeing well over 15 doctors from around my city and being told that I'm faking multiple times, we finally came across a neurologist who specializes in Dysautonomia, more specifically in Postural Orthostatic Tachycardia Syndrome (POTS). In very basic terms people that have POTS have trouble regulating their blood pressure and heart rate, especially upon change in position, often leading to passing out or feeling dizzy. Before POTS was brought to my attention I had never heard of it, so of course I went right to Google to learn more. Quite frankly I was disappointed with what I found, or did not find should I say. Google did not seem to know that much either and there's not much research or treatment to go along with POTS, but nonetheless the little information I got, gave me something to hold on to, when I had nothing at all. One of the most common ways to get tested for POTS is by having a tilt table test done, which I finally got on October 23, 2019 and just like that my second chronic illness was diagnosed. Many things go into this test but the biggest indicator is how long you last when you are brought to a standing position, while being strapped to a table. My doctor said the average is about 15 minutes before the patient will pass out, I lasted 93 seconds. I never got a full answer on what happened that August morning, but doctors have predicted that I passed out at the wheel and that's the closest thing to an answer I'll ever get.

I thought after receiving a diagnosis we finally reached the end and the rest would be easy compared to this. Boy, was I in for a shock. After the diagnosis I started medicine and physical therapy. I did aqua therapy, which is just like physical therapy but in the pool and I loved it. I was able to do so much more without my heart rate going too high and I felt myself getting stronger. I used a wheelchair 95% of the time because of how unpredictable my passouts were. I also suffered from extreme fatigue, so standing more than a few minutes would literally exhaust me. This also caused me to not be able to attend my senior year of high school in person so I was homeschooled for my final year. I was doing this for about 4 months and I was doing okay for a while. I was learning how to get used to my new life and trying to keep my body happy while still trying to be a teenager. It was during this time that I learned to adapt to life in a wheelchair and all the limitations that go along with it. Like just for example, did you know that some single stall bathrooms, cannot even fit a wheelchair? Like not at all and a lot of places do not have a handicap bathroom. Well, what the heck am I supposed to do now, pee my pants?? Do not even get me started on the looks I would receive, yes I am an 18 year old "healthy" looking girl, using a wheelchair. No, I am not using it for fun, but to many people's surprise I can still walk, not every wheelchair user is paralyzed. Plus it is none of anyone's business so I am not too sure why so many people were concerned with me and my wheelchair use, but I was getting used to it.

Then Coronavirus hit.

> ## "I was stuck and had no choice but to start fresh, but at least this time I had an idea of what I was dealing with."

The world stopped, my treatments stopped, my neurologist that followed my POTS was laid off and could no longer see patients. The physical therapy place I was going to shut down and honestly everything that was going good fell apart at once. I was stuck and had no choice but to start fresh, but at least this time I had an idea of what I was dealing with.

Conveniently in the midst of all that, I also started having stomach issues. I will be the first to admit I'm a picky eater and food was never my friend. I have been eating TUMS after every meal like they were candy since before I could remember. Due to this I have been taken to a gastroenterologist before and have been on medicine to help since I was very young. It started getting serious in the middle of March. Everytime I ate, I would either throw up or be curled in a ball for the next five hours dealing with extreme nausea. On top of that I was just never hungry so I basically just stopped eating. We called my gastroenterologist and let's just say he was less than kind. We had a telehealth appointment and he said POTS is probably just affecting my stomach, which is very possible, and to try a medicine he prescribed me.

After being on that pill for a month, I still wasn't able to eat and was starting to drop weight. At this point I started doing research on my own and came across a chronic illness called gastroparesis, which means that your stomach empties very slowly because the nerves in your stomach are damaged. I noticed that it was common with POTS patients and a lot of my symptoms lined up. We called to schedule another appointment with my gastroenterologist; this is when my doctor asked me if I had developed an eating disorder. I was in shock, now I've had doctors tell me a lot of crazy things, but this took the cake. I respectfully told him no and went through my symptoms with him again and basically begged him to order a gastric emptying scan, which is one of the only ways to be diagnosed with gastroparesis. He agreed reluctantly and on May 21, 2020 the results came back that I had severe gastroparesis. After this he ordered another medicine, said to try it for a month (it didn't work) and that was the last we heard from him.

So there I was with two newly diagnosed chronic illnesses and no one to manage them. Thankfully the next gastroenterologist I saw

**"With my new tube things were going okay, I was definitely nowhere near healthy but I was not done fighting."**

was amazing and truly saved my life. By the time I saw him, it was clear I was very weak and needed help. I was on my fifth month of not eating, I was passing out every few minutes and he saw that right away. I was admitted to the hospital in July, while there he performed a GPOEM surgery on me, in hopes to help the food digest quicker and cause less pain, but by this time my body was too malnourished for anything to help. A week after the GPOEM, I had my first GJ tube placed, finally my body was getting nutrients. That hospital stay ended up being a month long and truly were some of the hardest days of my life.

With my new tube things were going okay, I was definitely nowhere near healthy but I was not done fighting. We started calling a facility in NYC to try to get an appointment with their specialist, but that got cut short. Five weeks after being home with my new tube I started having some problems. A granulated tissue formed around the tube and to be sure it wasn't an infection my doctor recommended going to the ER and having them take a look. So back we went; the doctor there said it looked okay but wanted to do a CatScan to be sure, and thank goodness he did. The scan came back the next morning and showed that my tube flipped and it needed to be replaced as soon as possible. I was admitted and had the surgery the next day. I was discharged a few days later and we returned home and started making phone calls again. Noticing a trend here?

Not even a month later my tube got clogged. Now granted, anyone with a feeding tube knows they get clogged sometimes, but this baby was not budging, so back to the hospital

I went. The only good thing about this was all the nurses and child life specialists started to know me, and let me just say, they were amazing and truly made the life I was living bearable. So having been in the ER all night with no luck of unclogging it, I was admitted for the third time and had a surgery scheduled for the next day to replace it.

As of January 2021 that tube has been working great and I'm super proud to say that December 2020 was my first full month that I did not visit the hospital. It has been a long journey to say the least and I know it is not over yet but I am so grateful for where I am today. I have learned to love myself and my disabilities. I do not treat them like they are flaws anymore, they are just part of me. I love that I am able to teach people what invisible illnesses are and I love how strong my body and mind have been through all this. It is very easy to only see the bad in any situation, but I am here, you are here - reading this right now. That is the biggest win I could ever ask for.

If I could do anything in my life, I would like to work with kids. Having them be around someone that uses a wheelchair or a feeding tube, would teach them that being different is okay and that not everyone's the same. Children have such innocent minds and judgement is something that is taught and learned. If I could teach even one person what an invisible illness is, the world would be a kinder place.

*For anyone reading this that struggles with anything similar to me please know you're not alone. There's a whole community behind you rooting for you to win. You are so loved and can accomplish anything you want to. The rain will end and until it does capture every single rainbow moment life offers you; they are so worth it.*

# Tom Seaman

Wilmington, NC, USA

## About Tom:

*Tom Seaman is a Certified Professional Life Coach in the area of health and wellness, and author of 2 books: Beyond Pain and Suffering: Adapting to Adversity and Life Challenges and Diagnosis dYSTONIA: Navigating the Journey. Tom is also a motivational speaker, chronic pain and dystonia awareness advocate, health blogger, volunteer for dystonia Medica Research Foundation (DMRF) as a support group leader, and is a member and writer for Chronic Illness Bloggers Network, The Mighty, Pateint Worthy, and the Welness Universe.*

\* \* \*

*IG:* @CoachTom12

*Facebook:* @TomSeamanAuthor
@ TomSeamanCoaching

*Website:*
http://www.tomseaman.com/
www.tomseamancoaching.com

### *Life Coach & Author*

*"There is nothing that can't be altered toimprove our quality of life."*

In the Summer of 2001, while pursuing a master's degree in counseling, I developed a painful neurological movement disorder called dystonia. Dystonia is the third most common movement disorder after Parkinson's and Essential tremor but is not well known. Dystonia is caused by miscommunication of chemicals from the brain to the body, resulting in intermittent or sustained muscle spasms/contractions in the part of the body affected. In my case it affects my neck, so it is called cervical dystonia (a.k.a. spasmodic torticollis). The contracting muscles in the neck cause the head to lean/pull to one side or forward or backward. Dystonia is usually accompanied by pain, from moderate to severe, and for some may include a tremor. Performing everyday tasks such as sitting, standing, walking, driving, socializing, working, shaving, brushing your teeth, combing your hair, eating, talking on the phone, etc., become very difficult.

## "By the time I finally got an accurate diagnosis, I was in such extreme pain and disfigurement that I was pretty much unable to do anything on my own."

Currently there is no known cause or cure for dystonia, in most cases. While the symptoms may subside over time, or for a small portion of the dystonia population, a complete remission, dystonia is a condition one will have the rest of their life to varying degrees until a cure is found. The best doctors can do at this time is treat symptoms.

In the very beginning, before getting diagnosed, I noticed that my head would slightly lean to the right when I was sitting and, for lack of a better term, flop to the right when I walked. Thinking it was a musculoskeletal problem, I sought out chiropractic care, where I received neck adjustments and extension traction. After several months, the pain worsened and my neck muscles were involuntarily pulling my head to the right more forcefully. I then saw a few other chiropractors, MD's, an internist, a massage therapist, and physical therapist, none of whom helped. I kept getting worse.

Utterly frustrated, I stopped all care and began researching the internet where I discovered cervical dystonia. After reading everything I could about it, I was convinced this was what I had and then learned, all too late, that some of the treatments I was receiving were ill advised for dystonia. I then sought out a movement disorder neurologist who made the official diagnosis. Like many others with dystonia, I had to originally diagnose myself. Unfortunately, much of the medical community knows little about this disorder and often makes incorrect diagnoses, resulting in treatments that can make symptoms worse.

By the time I finally got an accurate diagnosis, I was in such extreme pain and disfigurement that I was pretty much unable to do anything on my own. My head and neck were turned and stuck about 45 degrees towards my right shoulder, and the disfigurement significantly worsened with any type of movement because of the intense muscle contractions. As a result of my pain and disability, I had to drop out of graduate school, quit my job, and move in with my parents because I had become disabled to the point that I could not function without their help. This was a very difficult pill for me to swallow, having previously been a competitive athlete in several sports my whole life, a full-time student, and an active entrepreneur. The transition from an active, independent person to a disabled person almost completely dependent on others was devastating. I was 30 years old at the time and felt like I was in the prime of my life.

> "Unfortunately, I was not improving at the rate I had hoped and was frustrated that I could not move on with my life."

For about six to eight months, I literally spent my day as follows: wake up, eat breakfast, lie on the floor, eat lunch, lie on the floor, eat dinner, lie on the floor, and then go to bed and try to fall asleep. In fact, I actually ate while laying on the floor. I spent nearly 16 hours a day on my floor in a fetal position in tears half of the time. The pain was so severe that I was unable to shop, cook, clean, do laundry, etc. Everything I could do, or had to do, was with one hand because the other hand was constantly supporting my head and neck to try and alleviate some of the unbearable pain. Over time, I also developed scoliosis due to my body maintaining a twisted posture for so long.

In February 2002, I attended a natural recovery clinic in New Mexico. I have always been one to try a more natural approach to manage my health, so this was my first step towards treatment rather than a more medical approach. Applying the information I learned at the clinic (a very specific exercise, stretching, and massage program), I began showing some improvement about four to six months later. Unfortunately, I was not improving at the rate I had hoped and was frustrated that I could not move on with my life. As a result of my anger and frustration, I gave up on the program and wallowed in despair.

At the urging of friends and family, in January 2003 I went to a neurologist specializing in movement disorders for Botox injections. I also began taking muscle relaxant medications. While Botox is most well-known for cosmetic uses, it has long been used to successfully treat many health conditions. While most people with dystonia benefit from Botox, or one of the other botulinum neurotoxins, and it is often a first line/primary treatment, it did very little to reduce my pain or spasms. I tried a dozen times again in the ensuing years with no success. Medications helped a little. Additional treatments included chiropractic (just for my back this time), acupuncture, and physical therapy, none of which improved my condition.

My frustration and misery skyrocketed, causing me to fall into a deep pit of depression. I became almost completely homebound, began having severe panic attacks, drank alcohol to help reduce the pain and spasms, and had an awful diet. I lost my entire social life. Just grabbing coffee or catching a movie was completely out of my realm of ability at the time. I struggled to wrap my head around this new life where I was so incapable of doing most anything all of my friends were able to do.

## "I was so unhappy and knew of no other way to cope at the time."

Because of my disability and depression, I was very sedentary and no longer cared for my body the way I knew how. I began drinking a lot and eating large quantities of high fat foods throughout the day and night. I went from an athletic 180 pounds in 2001 to a morbidly obese 330 pounds in 2006. I actually don't really know my top weight because I stopped looking at the scale after I hit 310, and I was still rapidly climbing. When my weight was around 240 pounds, I was put on blood pressure medication for hypertension. Having spent the previous six years working for a health education company that focused on nutrition, one can only imagine the depths of despair I was in to choose this type of lifestyle. I was so unhappy and knew of no other way to cope at the time.

## "I suppose my "all or nothing" way of living really paid off in this area."

While I never did anything to change my bad habits, every single day I told myself that the next day would be the day I would begin working on better health. This went on for almost 4 years and I became more depressed, disfigured, and overweight. Thinking back, maybe I didn't feel bad enough or care enough to make changes, but more than anything, I felt so alone and didn't really know what first step to take. I began thinking that I needed something serious to happen to me in order for me to make changes, which is exactly what happened.

In December 2006, I caught a terrible stomach virus and was sick for almost 2 weeks. During that time, my neck was a tiny bit straighter and I lost about 15 pounds. Getting sick really scared me because I rarely get sick. Considering my sedentary lifestyle and poor diet, I thought that getting sick was a sign that I might have developed some other health problem, such as diabetes or some other kind of organ dysfunction. While this was not the type of motivation to change I would have chosen, this was exactly what

I needed to jump start my brain into action.

While I was lying in bed for 2 weeks, all I had were my thoughts. I knew once the stomach virus improved, I had a big decision to make; go back to the way I was living or attempt to make changes to my health. It was a wide-open window of opportunity and I jumped through it. I knew that if I didn't, I would eventually have more serious health problems.

Considering I had already lost about 15 pounds and my neck somehow improved a little while I was sick, I began exercising again and changed my diet. I changed what I ate and when I ate, I cut back on the amount of food I ate, and I walked every day. That's it. No special diet, diet pills, drinks, or any unique exercise program. I just ate properly and walked every day. I started out by walking very short distances and slowly increased it to about 2 miles twice a day. The weight literally dropped off me. My whole life was dedicated to being as healthy as possible. I suppose my "all or nothing" way of living really paid off in this area!

> **"The person I am today is all thanks to the challenges I have faced. A big part of my coping is to not measure myself against anyone else or myself before I got sick."**

When I initially began losing weight in December 2006, I set a goal of being 250 pounds by Summer 2007. I hit this goal in March and by September I weighed 190 pounds, which I have been able to maintain for the last 15 years. I also diligently implemented the dystonia recovery program I learned in 2002 and found about 75% improvement in less than a year.

To date, my neck is significantly better on a more consistent basis, I have much less pain, I am working again (as a life/health and wellness coach), I am socially active, and I no longer take blood pressure medicine because my hypertension is under control with proper diet, weight management, exercise, and other healthy lifestyle choices.

People often say to me that I must have a much better attitude now that I've lost all the weight and have better control of my dystonia. My response is typically, "getting a better attitude is what motivated me to lose the weight and improve my dystonia symptoms." Don't get me wrong; my attitude now is certainly much better and I absolutely feel better, but had my attitude not changed I never would have taken the steps to lose the weight or be so dedicated to my dystonia symptom management program.

People too often look at this concept the wrong way around. Our attitude must change before we can change anything about ourselves. We can't expect that we will have a better attitude after we have lost a lot of weight or made some other significant change. Mental change must occur first. Then we can reap the rewards for our efforts and enjoy our new, healthier mental and physical states. I used to view myself as a victim, which I knew had to change. I basically gave up and let my disorder control me, whereas now, I don't consider myself to be a victim of anything, except what I create in my mind.

## "I believe that we are meant to use our lives to help and serve others..."

Life is certainly much better, but I still have problems with my neck and back that prevent me from doing some activities. However, it is night and day compared to the horror in which I once lived. Every day I have to carefully balance my work and other activities with rest and self-care. I have had to learn to modify my life and embrace the new me with different abilities and interests. I also live with immense gratitude for all I can do. I took so much for granted prior to getting dystonia.

Letting go of the old me and loving myself for who I am today has been one of the most important steps I have taken to live as joyful a life as possible. There are very few days where I do not have fun, challenge myself, and feel proud of myself for my efforts. While dystonia, pain, and obesity have been the greatest challenges of my life, they have been the greatest teachers as well, so I am very grateful for many of the things I have experienced and learned.

The person I am today is all thanks to the challenges I have faced. A big part of my coping is to not measure myself against anyone else or myself before I got sick. I measure my growth based on how far I've come from my darkest days. This is the true value of who I am today.

I used to be someone who essentially lived on a floor, writhing in pain, feeling completely worthless and depressed, in debt and unemployed, morbidly obese, and totally dependent on the help of others. I didn't want to wake up in the morning because I didn't want to face the constant physical and emotional pain. I am now at a healthy weight and in much better control of my dystonia to where I can live a more normal life with passion and excitement. While I need to take medication and dedicate myself to a healthy lifestyle to help control my symptoms, I don't mind doing any of it. The results that come from my hard work and dedication have made me the strong person I am today. This is what I try to stress to others because opportunity has a sly way of sneaking in the back door, so while our challenges in life might be painful, this is often when opportunities for the greatest learning can take place, if we choose to view it this way.

Not wanting others to go through any of the experiences I did, and to help those who are going through similar experiences with their different health issues and other life challenges, I became certified as a professional life coach in 2012. Utilizing this education and the tools I learned from my experience living with dystonia and chronic pain, I now dedicate myself to empowering others to improve their quality of life.

I believe that we are meant to use our lives to help and serve others, so in 2015 I published my first book, Diagnosis Dystonia: Navigating the Journey, which has been recognized by the Michael J Fox Foundation and featured in Pain-Free Living Magazine. This combination autobiography, self-help, education book provides treatment options, coping strategies, skills for daily living, and tools for dealing with the physical and mental challenges of life with a chronic health condition.

In 2021, I published my latest book, Beyond Pain and Suffering: Adapting to Adversity and Life Challenges. This book is broader in scope and provides strategies for managing difficulties we are experiencing at the moment, and for the unpredictable stressors in life, such as financial distress, trauma, pain, diseases and other illnesses, relationship issues, fear, depression, anxiety, and grief, to name just a few. This book offers tools and strategies for how to cope and manage these situations and move beyond the pain and suffering they bring, be it physical, emotional, or both. It teaches how to NOT make the most difficult parts of our life the most significant part of our life. Both books are available on Amazon and at www. tomseamancoaching.com.

In addition to my books, I have written numerous articles that have been published around the world about strategies for living with physical and mental health conditions, as well as other life challenges. I have been a guest on international radio shows and podcasts, and my work was featured in various magazines such as Brain and Life, Pain Free Living, and Pain Pathways. I was the keynote speaker for the first ever National Dystonia Symposium in Canada.

I am also a health and wellness blogger, aspiring motivational speaker, volunteer for the Dystonia Medical Research Foundation as a support group leader, and member and writer for The Mighty, Patient Worthy, The Wellness Universe, and Chronic Illness Bloggers Network.

All of this from a guy who literally lived on his floor for years without any clue what to do with his life and totally reliant on others for practically everything!!

*I have been faced with major challenges throughout my adult life. What helps me jump over hurdles is my belief that everything has a solution. There is nothing that can't be altered to improve our quality of life. Obstacles provide us with opportunities to grow and become better people, and every day I am grateful for the chance to help myself and others achieve their personal best. No matter what we are going through, if we never give up hope and trust that there is a way through our challenges, our lives can be transformed in very meaningful ways!*

# Chantay Haywood

Houston, TX, USA

## About Chantay:

*Chantay C. Haywood is a Houston, Texas native who has been known to push past many challenges in her life while achieving her goals through her faith. With the help of God and her family, she has been overcoming her battle with a rare brain disease. Chantay hopes to bring encouragement to others through her story of strength and resiliency.*

\* \* \*

*IG: @chantay_haywood3*

*"Those days you want to give up – just know you're not alone – stay strong."*

Hello my name is Chantay Haywood, I'm 32 years old. Before my illness took over I was a part of the registration department working 12 hours shifts in the emergency room. I gave everything I had to my job but it took a lot out of me. I remember days after long hours of trying to do everything I could for my patients, when my shift ended I would have to go down to the ER and sign in because I could hardly stand. Talk about embarrassing, and the judgment. When dealing with a chronic illness you're constantly pleading your case and all you want to do is be at home resting after giving all you have to your job.

But before my illness got to where it is now, it started back in 2013 when I was in school for medical billing and coding. I had a teacher who worked for MD Anderson Cancer Center here in Houston, Texas. She started noticing that some days I would look like I was in pain. Well I wouldn't say much about it to anyone but I was having a lot of numbness and pain running down my left leg. Every day she would ask me, "Hey, have you gone to the doctor for that yet?" and I would always respond, "No, not yet."

About two weeks had passed, she came up to me and she said, "I think you need to go to the doctor." So I went to the ER because that day it was hurting me so bad. They told me that I had a sciatic nerve and there was nothing they could do for me, so I just left it alone.

About a year had passed and I was still having the pain but now it was in my back as well. I went to the hospital for back pain. After my CT scan, they came into the room and told me that I have a spinal tumor. I started to have a lot of tests done on my back. All kinds of injections and a biopsy. Then I found out it was something called a vertebral hemangioma.

## "Honestly, if it wasn't for my family and my husband rallying around me with support and love, I don't know where I would be."

These types of tumors are normally found in the vertebrae on accident and are benign. But because mine is so big, it's very painful and it has recently grown and broken a bone in my back, and is pressing on other nerves which is causing so many issues. I went about six years without any tests because nobody knew how to help me and my body couldn't take any more tests. It had become overwhelming. I recall having needles and drills going in my back while I was woken one time too many. I remember screaming for help while they tried to get pieces of my bone. More and more I wanted to die. So I started seeing a pain management doctor because for a lot of days I couldn't get out of bed.

Even now there are a lot of days I can only lay on my side because the pain and pressure is too much for me to sit on my tailbone. Most of the time I wake up already in horrible pain and my husband has to move me to the couch;

many days I want to give up. My body feels weak as the pain tries to take over.

But I thank God for strength. Honestly, if it wasn't for my family and my husband rallying around me with support and love, I don't know where I would be.

So at the beginning of this year my doctor wanted me to see a neurosurgeon. I went to him and had some tests done; I was just praying he would be able to help me, or at least remove it. But then on my brain MRI he found that I have a brain disease called Chiari malformation. This is when your cerebellum is smaller than it is supposed to be or deformed. When this happens it crowds your brain because of too much pressure. Then the lower part of the cerebellum (tonsils) tries to adapt and in turn gets displaced into the top part of your spinal canal.

## "But I'm still here, and every day I get up, I remember I must have a purpose if I'm still here."

The doctor told me that he believed this condition is more important to treat and that it will help me, even with my spinal pain. So on April 21, 2020 I had brain surgery and two bones removed out of my neck which are called (craniectomy and laminectomy). And my life has changed ever since. As of right now I'm not able to work anymore or drive. It's a battle everyday, honestly. God has been my help when I want to give up. I've joined a support group on Facebook that has helped me so much and reminded me that I'm not alone. I've met some of the people who have had the same procedures as me and they have been so supportive. I think it's so important to have a community. I'm still going through tests every so often and trying to make sure that my surgery was a success. I am also hopeful of finding another doctor to help me with the tumor.

But I'm still here, and every day I get up, I remember I must have a purpose if I'm still here. I just hope my story shows strength and resilience. If there was one thing I could do it would be to travel. I know I could do it now but I have fears that I wouldn't be able to enjoy myself. What if I get stuck in my hotel room because of my back pain or pain in my skull that won't let me get out of bed? I want to do many things, like plus size modeling and even YouTube, but lately it's been challenging to push through life. I'm pouring scriptures into myself daily and pray that the Lord helps me hold on.

*That's my prayer for everyone out there dealing with something chronic. Those days you want to give up - just know you're not alone - stay strong, and know that you're greater than your story, that this is just a chapter in your life's book and one day you will look back and see what it was all for.*

*Keep up the fight, Warriors!*

# Samantha Smith

Windham, NY, USA

## Professional Advocate & Running and Nutrition Coach

"Something will always go wrong. Life will always be hard. No one can ever say I didn't work my butt off; and that's the legacy I choose to leave."

## About Samantha:

Samantha received her first diagnosis after graduating college. Living with multiple chronic illnesses meant living in a constant state of trial and error. She was constantly navigating a new normal, all while becoming sicker. She developed a determination to learn what she could about each diagnosis and began attending conferences, along with reaching out to the online communities for support/advice. This began her desire to be an advocate for others like herself. In 2016, Samantha had become sick enough due to a combination of Gastroparesis and other chronic illnesses to need TPN. Thankfully, tube feeds were a success. She was able to wean off of TPN and get strong enough to do the one thing she loved the most; run. Samantha began volunteering and blogging with G-PACT . She is now the president of G-PACT non-profit. She works hard to be a strong patient advocate; lobbying congress, putting together fundraisers, and telling her story. Her story of resilience has inspired others to continue their own journeys, and to find their passion as well. She shares her accomplishments, but doesn't hide the ugly side of living with these illnesses.

\* \* \*

IG: @ibelieve693

I'm not sure who I'd be if I never got sick. I'd like to think I would be the same person, with the same desire for more. I never hated the person I was, but I believe I fell into myself as I learned to live with chronic illness. I found my place in the world advocating for others, even as I learned to navigate the world I never wanted to be in.

I'm not sure when exactly it happened, but early on, I developed an attitude that refused to let me give up no matter what was thrown my way. The harder things got, the more I was determined to prove nothing would stop me. As a new diagnosis rolled in each year, it became harder and harder to keep pushing past the hardships that followed. Multiple hospital trips, central lines, tubes, surgeries, sepsis....the problems continued and tested me in every which way. I was pushed past my breaking point often. My body got beaten down often, and it kept me from living life.

## "I never know how to explain how and why I run."

There isn't a moment that goes by where I don't feel the effects of chronic illness. I make decisions based on my illnesses needs on a daily basis. I do what I can to not aggravate symptoms. Some days keep me down. Some days I thrive. Some days I keep my fingers crossed as I teeter on the edge of a major flare, hoping I won't fall. There are days though, that I don't want whatever might be flaring to make my decisions for me. Those are the days I test my limits and decide just how far I am willing to push them. Sometimes that works

out in my favor, and many times it doesn't. I haven't quite learned my lesson there yet. I'm still quite stubborn.

One thing that's been consistent over the years has been seeing just how capable my sick body is. Every day it does the best it can to let me do what I want to do. It's been through hell and back over and over and yet, it still shows up ready for battle every damn day. Every time I got knocked down, for whatever reason, I was more than determined to make my comeback. Hell, I was planning it before I was even out of the woods. Usually my first question to any doctor was "how soon can I go for a run?" Running is what has continued to keep me going even on my worst days; and it's my first concern when I'm down and out.

I never know how to explain how and why I run. I'm chronically sick. My body is broken more often than it's not, but somehow, I've found a way to run. I found a way to be capable and strong, even though that very thing simultaneously breaks me down.

I found strength in my stride. There's something that happens while I'm pounding the pavement that brings my body and soul to life. It's as if all the pieces fall together with every step and my body finds strength it wasn't sure it had. It was after my worst bout of sepsis that I realized how much running has truly impacted my life; and how much I wasn't willing to ever give it up. In a fleeting moment, my body had had enough, and it was ready to let go. I could feel it in my bones. This was it.

Whether it's divine intervention, medical intervention, or a combination of the two, I held on and clawed my way back. It was then I realized my body fights back because I taught it how. My body has made it through what could have killed me because running gave it the strength to fight back. Nearly losing that solidified my love for the sport, and why I'll never let anything take it away from me.

## "That's something chronic illness GIVES instead of takes: the will to live, and the desire to beat it."

It's not easy for me to do. I get asked a lot how I'm able to. Honestly, I don't really know how to answer that. I told myself that I didn't want my illnesses to hold me back, and I found ways to make it work. Was it easy? Hell no. My feeding tube site would get raw from the movement while on long runs, and my stoma would become raw and bleed. My joints took days to recover. I struggle to hydrate myself because of gastric dysmotility/absorption issues, so I would get easily dehydrated. The summers were BRUTAL on my body. The nerve issues I deal with would cause severe numbness in my feet and legs. I had a few falls because I struggled to feel my foot hit the ground and my leg couldn't support the impact. My electrolyte imbalance was severely affected by dehydration and stress on my body, causing some really tough recoveries.

Even now, years into it, consistent running can be humbling. I've learned that pushing myself isn't always the answer, even though I may want to. I've adopted the motto "rest, don't quit" on the days that just seem impossible.

I realize not everyone is able to do the things they love. They've had to grieve the loss of the life they had before they got sick. I've had to do that too. This isn't what I planned to do with my life. I wanted to go into federal law enforcement. I had so many ideas of how I wanted my life to go, and to put it mildly, this isn't what I ordered. I know I'm one of the lucky ones who is still able most of the time. I think that's why I'm so determined. I've been down and out before, and I don't want to go back there. I know the other shoe could drop at any moment, but I'm not going to sit around and wait for it. I need to make every day something I can be proud of. Even when it hurts, even when I have barely anything left in the tank, I'm going to give my all. That puts a lot of pressure on me to perform, but as long as I'm breathing, it's what I feel I need to do.

That's something chronic illness GIVES instead of takes: the will to live, and the desire to beat it.

After getting sick, I had two choices: give in, or fight. I fought. With some luck, a good medical team, and a whole lot of resilience, I am sitting here typing this to remind YOU, whoever you are, that YOU too can fight back. I know you may be tired. I know it hurts. I feel you. I know it seems endless. It's okay to feel that. It's okay to cry and be mad at the world or God or whoever for what's happened to you. It's okay to grieve the life you won't be able to live, the one you dreamed of. It's going to suck before it gets better. But it will. Take a deep breath and remind yourself who the hell you are. YOU are relentless, and this disease has NO idea who it's messing with.

*Chronic illness
taught me how to fight.*

*It's one hell of a fighter,
but I can take one hell of a punch.*

# Annie-Danielle Grenier

Montréal, Quebec, Canada

## *Rare Disease Advocate*

*"Never stop advocating for yourself because by doing so you are also advocating for others.*
*We are all worthy."*

## About Annie-Danielle:

*I raise awareness, educate and advocate for people living with rare and invisible diseases, having a few myself. I do that mostly as an expert patient, public speaker and through Ma vie de zèbre (My Zebra Life), a blog now turned website that I started in 2013 because I couldn't find much information in French (and none relevant to Québec) about Ehlers-Danlos syndromes, the only diagnosis I had at the time, and I wanted to change that. I'm very active as a patient partner as well, being involved on various committees, doing things like help to change policies, create surveys, educate future healthcare professionals and much more. I'm also a freelance translator (in French and English) and studied in arts and literature as well as in cultural and corporate event organization, worked many years in show business (on stage but also in production) and have a bachelor's degree in psychology. My atypical life experiences give me a different vision that I love to share with people and hopefully inspire, reminding others that illness is not an obstacle to happiness!*

\* \* \*

*IG & FB: @maviedezebre*

*Website: maviedezebre.com*

My name is Annie-Danielle Grenier and I wear two hats: I freelance in the language field, where I do translations, editing and content creation, and I'm a rare disease advocate. But those are my third and fourth careers, as my health has forced me to change multiple times over the years.

I keep needing to adapt, grieve things I can no longer do and rethink what I can do and embrace that instead.

I live with two rare diseases: hypermobile Ehlers-Danlos syndrome and Addison's disease, a type of adrenal insufficiency.

With those come a dozen comorbidities, some of which are rare as well, like gastroparesis or corneal ectasia. My health issues are not only rare, they are considered orphan diseases as they are not well known and don't get much research or funding. Neither can be cured. Most of my issues are also invisible. And yet they're multisystemic and so very complex to deal with!

Hypermobile Ehlers-Danlos syndrome is a genetic condition affecting my collagen. We have collagen in about 80% of our body, so when it's defective, you can end up with problems pretty much everywhere. I have issues with my joints, my eyes, my skin, my cardiovascular and digestive systems, and so much more. Very few parts of my body are not affected in one way or another.

The older I get, the worse my body gets.

As a child I would catch every sickness going around (laryngitis, bronchitis, etc.), but we'd have said I was healthy.

As a teen, I missed a lot of school due to infections and I started getting more severe sprains, but, again, we'd have told you I was healthy...a bit frail maybe, but that was it. After all, I was dancing up to 15 hours a week at one point!

> ## "I went from being that overactive young woman to being bedridden most of the time, fainting by just sitting at the table to eat, unable to read the simplest thing."

I hit a brick wall at 24, when, after a viral infection, I never got better. We learned much, much later that it was POTS (postural orthostatic tachycardia syndrome), somehow kickstarted by the virus. What that means is that my heart starts racing whenever I stand up for a bit too long, especially if I'm not moving, trying to get blood to my brain while it pools in my extremities... and eventually it's like a switch turns off, and my body shuts down to preserve itself.

From that moment back in 2003 my life changed. Back then I was working full time in a hospital to pay bills while freelancing in my field of passion, show business, most of it volunteer internships as I was just starting; all this while going to shows with my friends, and being involved in politics. I would read a few books every week, walk everywhere, did a few dance classes even though it was rough on my knees and had singing lessons through all that as well.

I went from being that overactive young woman to being bedridden most of the time, fainting by just sitting at the table to eat, unable to read the simplest thing. In a constant migraine, pain flares and brain fog.

Having to go back to living with my parents, having to sell my car, losing my job and having to quit all my freelance gigs... having to say no to contracts I had dreamed of getting. And losing all my friends but two.

It took me years, many cycles of hope and disappointment, seeing new doctors, getting tests done, hoping for answers, for treatments... needing time to gather courage and energy after each failure before trying again.

Eventually I found the info I needed (online, of course), went to my family doctor and convinced her to send me to a geneticist, and finally got the hEDS diagnosis. From there, I started to be taken seriously and got the POTS diagnosis, and most important, a treatment. I got better and could do a few more things. I wasn't back to normal, far from it, but I got back some quality of life.

That was in 2010. Since then my joints have gotten worse: from a few sprains as a child or teenager, I now have osteoarthritis throughout my body, many torn ligaments and dislocated joints daily. I can dislocate my jaw eating, or a finger by opening a can of soda.

I also now have Addison's disease. The symptoms started around 2016 and I was diagnosed in late 2018.

Adrenal insufficiency is very similar to diabetes, except it's cortisol my body doesn't produce, instead of insulin. Yet unlike diabetes, I can't prick my finger to check my cortisol levels, I can only go by my symptoms to tell if I'm dangerously low. I constantly need to adjust the medication, replacing what my body doesn't produce, and take more if I live through a stressor, be it an injury, a fever, a big argument or the death of a loved one; all things for which my body would've produced more cortisol if my adrenal glands were healthy. An adrenal crisis, where one's cortisol levels get too low, can be deadly. The synthetic cortisol I take every day keeps me alive.

## "Ironically, I must say I love that about myself... that I still try, that I still get excited on a good day and want to do a hundred different things!"

That new diagnosis was a big adjustment, and hard to learn to live with. But after a few months I started to feel better, and even though I can never forget about it, I now feel in control and back to a better quality of life.

Like many others with complex, multisystemic illnesses, I have many comorbidities. Either they appeared or they were diagnosed over the years, like corneal ectasia which was another one that was hard to diagnose, so I almost lost my eyesight in 2018.

I also ended up in the ER a few times for things that aren't clearly related to my health issues, like gallstones or kidney stones, and had multiple surgeries in the past few years linked to all of those problems.

What all this means day to day is a lot of pain and a lot of limitations, be it from unstable joints or fainting if I stay upright too long, a lot of medical follow-ups and medications to take, needing to be on top of things and managing my health because the healthcare system and my doctors won't do it for me (I have over a dozen specialists involved in my care, from cardiologist to neurologist, GI and pain specialists, etc.). It also means I can't know if I'll feel good tomorrow or what to expect in two years. I could be worse... but I could be better, too!

So through it all, I've ridden the roller coaster of my health and each time I was in a good enough bit, I made the most of it.

I went to China thanks to an international contest in 2010 and was a "pambassador," learning to be a panda keeper.

I took the opportunity to make a stop in Beijing and visited the Great Wall, and it was so emotional for me to be on top of that wall, after climbing all those stairs, when a year earlier I needed my mom to push my wheelchair just to go to the store for a few minutes.

> **"Although I still am not 100% good at this and even after over 15 years, I'll still do too much on a good day and end up bedridden due to this."**

I got back into show business for a few years as well. I was manager and consultant for a few bands, and even got the opportunity to be in the studio for the recording of a whole album. I had the chance to be a stage manager again, at the big stage of a music festival. Just for one night as I was filling in to help...but it felt like being back home. Sadly, I can't do that regularly, but I cherish the memory. If I weren't limited by my health, it's what I'd be doing...well, I'd probably be an artistic director by now, hopefully on Broadway!

When I had to change careers again because I couldn't continue, I went into the language field as a freelancer because it was the obvious choice for me. I'd always loved writing, had done a few classes in translation and linguistics, each of the three times I tried going back to university, and had been doing translations and editing for friends and family since I was a teen. Working from home, at my own pace, seemed like the logical thing. I was worried my brain fog would cause me too much trouble or that I'd be too slow (and when I had my vision problems, it wasn't easy), but it wasn't as bad as I feared and I found ways to adapt. There are months when I can't work at all, others where I do a bit too much for my capacities...but I did find a balance.

I also learned to adapt to my daily life. Be it pace my activities, alternate between mind tasks and physical ones, take regular breaks, listen to my body and stop before I crash... Although I still am not 100% good at this and even after over 15 years, I'll still do too much on a good day and end up bedridden due to this.

Ironically, I must say I love that about myself...that I still try, that I still get excited on a good day and want to do a hundred different things!

I'm also glad for my resilience, glad that I never gave up all those years ago, and each time new symptoms creep up and I need to fight to get a new diagnosis (or to get the right one).

It's also what led me to that other hat I'm wearing, or fourth career. I started writing a blog in 2013, which has now bloomed into a full website, maviedezebre.com, because in my quest for information during all those years, I couldn't find anything in French, or what I could find was from Europe, but it didn't fit with what I was living here in Québec (Canada). Doctors don't always use the same terminology or the same treatments and drugs don't have the same names here. I wanted others to be able to find some information in French related to Québec reality and I wanted to share what my experience was, because as much as I tried to explain it, people struggled to understand what it really meant. It's also why I made a small text-based adventure game, to show what a week in my shoes can be.

> ## "You don't need to have cheated death or be on your last days to focus on the positive, to see that life is beautiful and to make it as good as it can be!"

I'm also on social media with what I call my "zebra persona," where I do most of my advocacy.

I've been working with my cardiologist for a few years now on creating an app for rare disease patients to help manage our daily lives with a complex condition, and I've been asked to be the spokesperson for a new rare diseases clinic that should open soon in our city's university hospital.

I'm more and more involved in patient partnership, which means I am on various committees and help shape policies, future studies, ethics in health, and more. I'm also participating in a few teaching programs for future healthcare workers, from nurses to doctors, including psychologists and dentists. Talking with a first-year medical student and seeing their eyes shine with understanding is so gratifying, and I really feel like this is making a difference and will help change things for the next generation of rare disease patients.

As much as I love my freelance career in languages, I'd love to focus more on advocacy and raising awareness. When I started in psychology when I was 20, it was because I wanted to help people, and this is one way I can do it, albeit differently.

I feel there are two major takeaways from my story.

The first one is not to give up and to trust yourself. If a diagnosis feels wrong, or if you don't have one, keep going, keep trying to get the right diagnosis. It's normal and it's OK to feel completely empty, angry and in despair when you get out of the doctor's office after you've been told you "have nothing." all the tests are normal, or something of the sort. Take the time you need to live those emotions and rest...but don't get stuck there. When a few weeks, or months have gone by and you feel again that need for an answer, that fire to do something, go ahead and don't let anyone stop you! You'll get that answer someday!

The other takeaway is that, as cheesy as it may sound, "seize the opportunity," "it's the little things," "take time to stop and smell the roses," and all those expressions ARE TRUE. My body is not reliable, I can't trust how I'll be tomorrow or even in one hour. So if I have an opportunity, I take it. Yet if I don't feel like doing something, I won't…I'm not talking about house chores here, of course. But there are enough things I can't do even if I want to, that I won't force myself to finish a book I don't really feel like reading anymore or spend time with people who are not nice to me, but I feel "I have to." My energy is limited, so I really assess what's important enough to me to spend energy on.

On the other hand, I take time to notice the positive things in my life, as small as they may be: how the sun shines on my cat's fur, the fun I'm having playing a board game with my spouse, how amazing it feels to be under the covers on a cold morning. And I literally take the time to stop and smell the roses and all other flowers when I take a walk!

You don't need to have cheated death or be on your last days to focus on the positive, to see that life is beautiful and to make it as good as it can be!

**My main takeaway is that illness is no obstacle to happiness!**

# Lynn Julian

Rockledge, FL, USA

## Speaker, Author, Advocate, and Actress

*"I went from wheelchair, to walking again, to running the Boston Marathon. Discover strength through unity. Together, we can achieve anything!"*

## About Lynn:

*Lynn Julian aka CCG Pop Superhero wears more hats than a Hydra has heads. She frees women from the mold that holds them captive and broke the mold of the female Pop Star. She is "Nashville's Version of Fiona Apple". A disabling 2006 stage accident left Lynn in a wheelchair and learning to walk again for 6 years. In 2012, she began acting in short films. On April 15, 2013, Lynn survived the Boston Marathon attack, with brain injury, back injury, hearing loss... and a renewed sense of purpose: running the 2014 Boston marathon. Residing in Boston's Back Bay. Lynn and her Service Dog, Dr. Smallz, find purpose in helping others and hope to inspire us to never give up. She is an author and a speaker, a Patient Advocate; Boston Actress; SEO Consultant and Bombing Survivor. She also consults, in an advisory capacity, as a "patient experience consultant" with corporations, foundations, researchers, politicians and international leaders to form an accurate understanding of chronic illness, rare disease and life with a disability.*

\* \* \*

*IG: @LynnJulian007*

*Website: https://lynnjulian.com/*

## "Who Am I?
### Resilience Is Reinventing Yourself."

I am Lynn Julian...or am I? Now that this performer's days are being directed by chronic illnesses and chronic injuries, replacing film and music professionals, I wonder, "who am I?" "What is my purpose?" This question haunts "Chronic Pain Warriors." "Now that I'm no longer defined by my job, what defines me?" I WAS a professional Pop Musician, and Pop Superhero on 30+ CDs (PopSuperhero.com), until I suffered a disabling stage accident. I WAS a professional actress, in dozens of films (LynnJulian. com), with weekly auditions, until I suffered a brain injury from the Boston Marathon Bombing on April 15, 2013. My resume labels me a Speaker, Author, Consultant, Patient Advocate, Actress, and Activist (Linkedin. com/in/lynnjulian). But, do ANY of those labels accurately portray my everyday life? I'm a funny person, but this is a serious look at a day-in-the-life with chronic illness.

What truly guides my words, actions, mind, and body, are my chronic conditions. I proudly thrive, despite many chronic illnesses, injuries, and rare diseases: TBI (traumatic brain injury causing short term memory loss and body dysregulation); PTSD (post-traumatic stress disorder); hearing loss; chronic migraines (triggered by stress, scents, food, weather, hormones); ADHD; fibromyalgia; arthritis; mast cell disease (severe allergies to scents, foods, dyes, toiletries, environment); hEDS (hypermobile Ehlers Danlos syndrome, a painful connective tissue disorder causing daily partial dislocations of my joints); POTS (postural orthostatic tachycardia syndrome causing dizziness); IBS (irritable bowel syndrome causing daily digestive pain); eczema (painful skin sores); spinal stenosis (chronic neck and upper back pain); sciatica (relapsing low back pain); Lyme disease (relapsing and remitting Lyme, Borrelia fever, babesia, bartonella causing brain inflammation); EBV (Epstein-Barr virus, relapsing due to stress); and more. The chronic fatigue that comes with being a Chronic Pain Warrior left me unable to perform my duties as a Pop Superhero. My new way to be a "Hero" is to advocate! I consult, in an advisory capacity, as a "Patient Experience Consultant" with corporations, foundations, researchers, politicians, and international leaders to form an accurate understanding of chronic illness, rare disease, and life with a disability. Advocating, consulting, volunteering, and creating all give my life a sense of purpose, and make me feel heard, both of which we all need to be happy. My advice, to those newly diagnosed, is to find your passion. What inspires YOU to keep going? That is where you must focus your now limited mind and body. Advocating helps me be the change I wish to see in the world. Volunteering helps me feel good about myself. Acting affords me a creative outlet to feed my soul.

## "You don't look sick!"

I'm often ignorantly told, "you don't look sick!" and asked, "How do TBI and EDS affect you?" How DON'T they? When a condition becomes "chronic," it's always part of you, although it may go in and out of remission. Guess what causes it to "flare-up?" STRESS and WEATHER! Who completely controls stress...or weather? NO ONE. A typical day, for me, may go like this. I wake up and rehydrate with room temperature, filtered water because cold and/or tap water causes a mast cell flare-up. I take several allergy and digestive medications, and anti-inflammatory supplements, then wait an hour before I eat. Breakfast should be caffeine-free, egg-free, gluten-free, dairy-free, allergen and dye-free, and low histamine, in order to avoid a flare-up. That means no coffee; eggs; bacon or gluten-filled breakfast bread. This is followed by a home detox method. I travel with my TB12 vibrating foam roller because it is the best one. It massages my sore muscles and helps drain my lymph nodes. This is followed by physical therapy, stretching, or yoga, including shoulder exercises from the Fern Health App. Once a week, I do coffee enemas, to increase my glutathione, which helps detox. I must make my lunch fresh, as no left-overs or packaged foods are low histamine. That's always followed by walking, or cardio exercise, to help my weakened digestive system process food.

Every afternoon, I plan to work, and, most days, I proudly push through and meet my goals. But...if the barometric pressure falls too fast, I may get a migraine. If I have a stressful meeting or phone call, I may suffer a mast cell flare-up. The first thing people with chronic conditions must learn is to identify their triggers and avoid them. But, you can't control the world around you. So, you learn to give yourself extra time to finish jobs, in case you get a flare-up or migraine. Make tasks flexible, in case you have to reschedule them. If I DO get a migraine, I grab a frozen,

gel ice pack, and my Migraine Rescue Bag. This has everything I need in it: orange or dark glasses to reduce blue light screen glare; CBD and cannabis oil vape pen to reduce nausea, pain, and inflammation; Migrelief essential oils roller/inhaler to reduce nausea and inflammation; ginger chews candy and animal crackers to reduce nausea; bottled water to reduce dehydration. Dinner must be monitored as meticulously as lunch and is followed by foam rolling, squats, 3-5lb, light strengthening exercises...and always more detoxing. My favorite way to detox is soaking in an inexpensive Epsom salt bath while relaxing to music. Histamines are cumulative, meaning they build up in your body to cause flare-ups. So, the secret to my success is detox, Detox, DETOX!

As a Featured Speaker, I teach "The Secret To Being Resilient," which, I believe, is learning to do things differently. In 2020, COVID-19 forced us all to take a crash course in resilience. Coronavirus is a chronic condition that quickly controlled our world, and we scrambled to adapt our lives around it. It immediately occurred to me that those with chronic conditions were already ahead of this learning curve. We learned to do things differently, in order to become resilient, from the day we were diagnosed. We also had to accept, and eventually love, the NEW version of us, with all its weaknesses and needs, in order to be truly happy. After my stage accident, I wasted YEARS trying to go back, and restart my music career. I was a musician, a Pop Superhero, and it was ALL I knew how to be! But, I am too fatigued to do my job anymore. What I finally realized is this: you can ONLY go in one direction...forward. Even

IF I could re-learn to play guitar, keyboards, sing and write music again, I would never perform like the healthier version of myself. We MUST move forward, to survive and thrive in our new body. But, if I wasn't that person, or profession, anymore, who was I? Who did I wish to become? What must I do to become her? Where and how would I find the help I needed to evolve and embrace her? Everyone faced with a life-changing, chronic condition must answer all these questions and more!

## "I was sent home... unable to hold down food...or even walk."

Now that you know TOO MUCH about my current conditions, here's a bit of my backstory/struggles I overcame to transform into the strong, resilient woman I am today. I was born a "performer," entertaining my family as a child, and writing "singer" on my first grade paper when asked, "What do you want to be when you grow up?" Earning a degree in Jazz and Contemporary Music, I worked as a professional musician, and Pop Superhero, for 15 years. During what would become my last performance, the club's stage manager neglected to tape down an electrical cord on the stage floor, a standard OSHA safety practice. (Side Note: I was unable to hold the club accountable, for my accident, for two reasons: the manager had taken a training course on stage set-up and OSHA safety rules do NOT cover "Works For Hire." I have not successfully convinced any Senator to help me change that law to protect Works For Hire: speakers; authors; musicians; actors;

performers.) My foot rolled on the slick cord, flying up in front of me, as I fell backward, knocking myself unconscious. This stage accident left me undiagnosed and bed-bound...for years. I suffered chronic brain fog, migraines, vertigo, nausea, vomiting, neck and back pain, mood swings, tinnitus, light and sound sensitivity. ALL of these are classic symptoms of concussion, which IS a brain injury. Yet, NONE of my doctors diagnosed my TBI, which left me untreated. These medical challenges left my body too weak to walk, unable to lie down to sleep, and too nauseated to hold down food...until I was eventually hospitalized. The lesson? You do NOT have to bleed to have a brain injury...or even hit your head...as I would later learn on April 15, 2013. Causes of TBI can include blunt force trauma, blast force trauma, whiplash, and illness.

After two weeks, I was discharged from the rehab hospital, unable to do physical therapy. Insurance won't pay if you can't do PT. I was sent home...unable to hold down food... or even walk. Determined to take control of my body, my pain, and, eventually my life, I still faced many challenges. After much Google Scholar research, and what felt like an Associate Degree in Neuroscience, I finally figured out I had a TBI! I also deduced that my two-week migraine, while hospitalized, was a "rebound headache" caused by their spinal tap. This is COMMON for patients with EDS. I was VERY frustrated by my medical team's limited awareness about TBI, EDS, the suffering they caused me, and their complete lack of personal responsibility. They told my partner and family I was "throwing up on purpose, for attention" and instructed them "you shouldn't visit her anymore." SHAME ON THEM! After finding the right doctors, the right medications and supplements, and years of daily TBI treatments (physical therapy, occupational therapy, speech therapy, vestibular therapy, ocular therapy, and cognitive behaviour therapy) I began to get my life back...although, in a wheelchair. Five years after my stage accident, I'd reached my goal of walking again...although, with a cane.

## "People who weren't there, always assumed everyone knew a bomb went off immediately and started running. That wasn't what happened."

The following year, the Summer of 2012, I was finally walking unaided...for the first time... again. Unbeknownst to me, mere months later, I'd suffer another brain injury, due to blast force trauma, as an injured survivor of the Boston Marathon Bombing.

I moved to the Back Bay neighborhood of Boston in 2009, to be closer to a large teaching hospital offering the top doctors in Massachusetts. Every year, I look forward to attending the Boston Marathon. Copley Square, the little park at the Finish Line, is my backyard and it felt like the marathon brought half a million people to party at my house. The Boston Marathon was a huge, annual celebration, at every bar and restaurant in the neighborhood...until 2:49 p.m. on April 15, 2013...when the first bomb exploded.

I had healed so much, mentally and physically since my stage accident, that I rarely took my service dog, Lil Stinker, places with me anymore. I only had him with me then because I would be "alone," with half a million new people, until my partner arrived. Even though I'd been walking without my cane for over six months, I was still anxious about going to this international event alone. Doug arrived, rightfully impressed with my location: the ONLY table with a view of the Jumbotron to watch the winners cross the Finish Line of the famous Boston Marathon. There was a HUGE wooden wall behind us that hid the press. Each previous year, we had stood 30+ feet away, near the corner of Boylston and Exeter Streets. This was the nearest sidewalk spot with a direct view of the Boston Marathon Finish Line. Understandably, it was always very crowded... which is exactly why the bombers put the first bomb there. That was the first year I decided to go early and get the ONLY table with a view of the Jumbotron. It had a huge, thick, canvas umbrella, to protect us from the sun...and, later, the explosive shrapnel too.

People who weren't there, always assumed everyone knew a bomb went off immediately and started running. That wasn't what happened. Maybe you've heard of "fight or flight," but it's actually "fight, flight or freeze," and most people froze. No one around me even stood up, let alone ran. I sat there, frozen in fear, dog in my lap. In the first five seconds, my normally calm service dog pawed at my face in panic. I'd never seen him do that and immediately snapped into action. For fear he would bolt away from me, I pressed him into my chest, my arms crossed as if in

## "...Dazed or drunk, they assumed the bomb was a celebratory cannon or fireworks."

a straitjacket. I was now guided by a primal part of my brain, the "Lizard Brain." I was a mama bear protecting her cub. Shocking us, the second bomb went off, ten seconds after the first. Instinct kicked in and I pointed at the bar behind us, telling Doug, "I've got to go." Thanks to my service dog, I was the first one up, but the entrance was blocked by people who didn't realize we were in danger. Dazed or drunk, they assumed the bomb was a celebratory cannon or fireworks. Terrified, crushing my 5lb flailing dog, I shouted, "Move, move, move, move!" frightening them into submission.

Shielding my dog, I shouldered my way through the single-file aisle of the bar, surrounded by panicked people pushing me on all sides. They partially dislocated BOTH my shoulders, which never fully healed due to EDS. They still pop-out every night. Strangers followed me but didn't know where to go. Keep in mind, we didn't know where, or when, more bombs might go off, and assumed one could be in that bar! I ordered everyone to exit through the back door to safety. When all who would listen had gone, we fought our way home, through thousands of people rushing toward the "fireworks." Crying hysterically, I begged them to turn around. We only stopped to let strangers use our phones and alert my building to lockdown.

Once I sat down, and the shock wore off, I finally realized I was in severe pain. The soft couch felt like concrete to my injured back. I heard sounds as if I was underwater, which continued for months. Ringing in my ears, tinnitus, was the loudest sound...and I still live with it constantly today. Normal sounds, and lights, became, and remain, painful. Upon seeking medical attention, and funding to pay for it, I learned tough lessons about "pre-existing injuries." Since I had sciatica previously, even though it was cured, my new low back injury was NOT considered a result of the bombing. The same fallacy was applied to my new brain injury, due to blast force trauma. It was NOT considered "new," even though previous TBIs, and EDS, both make you MORE vulnerable to new TBIs. A doctor even claimed my sudden onset, permanent hearing loss, resulting in hearing aids, was due to EDS...not the bomb that immediately preceded it. Internal, "invisible injuries" are the hardest to diagnose...and even harder to heal. I continue to feel on trial, guilty-until-proven-innocent, trying to validate my injuries to the world. I have no scars to show medical professionals, or the media, as evidence of my injuries. My injuries are invisible... to everyone...but me.

Sydney Kendrick

Pamela Bickford

Tiffany Kairos

Jenny Jones

Jimmy Fremgen

Antonia Schwartz

Cheyanne Perry Suarez

# I AM
# Deserving.

**Stories of chronic illness warriors learning about how they deserve to be treated.**

# Sydney Kendrick

Logan, OH, USA

*Professional Cat Mom & Print and Runway Model*

*"Keep moving forward."*

## About Sydney:

*Hi, I'm Sydney and I'm 23 years old. I have multiple chronic illnesses most of which is due to Classic Ehlers-Danlos Syndrome. I love to read, and I'm a model. I also enjoy nerdy things. And of course, thank you for joining in on my journey.*

\* \* \*

*IG: @clinicallychronically*

Hello there! I'm Sydney and I have multiple chronic illnesses. The main one being Classic Ehlers Danlos Syndrome, and it is a huge part of my life...Pun sort of intended there. It's a genetic connective tissue disease. EDS, is where your collagen is defective. Collagen is the most abundant protein in the body. So, you can imagine that this affects literally everything. When it's defective it causes everything to be overly stretchy and fragile. Yes, this does include the internal organs and even the nervous system! This has caused a lot of problems throughout my entire body, all ranging from orthopedics to gastroenterology and even my nervous system. For me I have issues with my joints dislocating and I have severe gastrointestinal dysmotility. That's where the GI tract is partially or fully paralyzed. When I mean it affects everything, it affects everything. Needless to say, this has caused a lot of issues with food. I love food, but food doesn't love me.

## "It was a pretty scary moment of my health journey. But, also not my only scary moment."

I also have to have yearly scans of my heart and brain. I'm susceptible to things like blood vessels collapsing in my brain causing a stroke, or aneurysms, and even major valves in my heart can collapse. A lot of things can go wrong at any given moment in time. But really, all of this means that I just need to take extra care of my body and that I need to pay close attention to various signs and symptoms of things.

I am, however, most affected in the gastrointestinal tract. I have dysmotility through my stomach all the way through my entire intestinal tract. This has caused me to rely on not only a feeding tube, but also nutrition through a major blood vessel into my heart (Total Parenteral Nutrition). This poses its own set of risks and things to look out for such as sepsis.

My case is a rather severe form of this disease. I've gone from eating on my own, to being fed through my veins. My GI issues began about the time of high school. So, around 2014-2015. It just started off with getting full relatively quickly and some pain with eating certain foods. As well as acid reflux. I had issues with that as well. Looking back on this, this was definitely the beginning of my journey with GI dysmotility.

Things really started to pick up pace after my gallbladder removal surgery. From there, my motility significantly worsened. There were quite a bit of foods that would give me major issues; mostly fibrinous foods and eating large meals. It was at this point that my weight was starting to drop. It was a pretty scary moment of my health journey. But, also not my only scary moment.

A year later, I had my first tube placed. It was an NJ tube. A NJ tube is a tube that goes from your nose to the beginning of the small intestine, NJ standing for Naso-Jejunum. The Jejunum is the first section of your small intestine. This bypassed my failing stomach. We used this tube for tube feeds, as well as occasionally medications. I tolerated it really well and eventually had a surgical tube placed through my abdomen.

My weight stabilized. In fact, at the time, I even regained all of the weight I had lost and then some. But this was rather short lived. I stopped tolerating my tube feeds and had to be placed on a predigested formula and even then, I eventually stopped tolerating that as well. We very quickly realized that I have progressed to the point of having intestinal dysmotility and issues with absorbing the proper nutrition.

> **"I decided that maybe moving in with him will solve some issues. He obviously had trust issues. So maybe, this would fix it."**

Doctors didn't know what to do as I was rapidly losing weight. But I never gave up and I refused to take no for an answer. I was at my lowest weight yet, losing about half of my body weight. My organ function was declining. Even my heart was affected. I was admitted to the hospital to start lifesaving nutrition - Total Parenteral Nutrition, where I would be fed through my veins. Without this radical choice, I would have died later that year in 2019.

An important thing that I want to note about my story is that when I first started my journey, I was with my now ex-boyfriend. We'll call him William for privacy sake. At the beginning, it was amazing. He was there with me through my first two surgeries. We argued every so often, but I figured that was normal. Well, normal enough. Our arguments included his jealousy with me and my relationship with my family, my past decisions with my friends, my relationships with my close friends, and even my illnesses at the time.

When you wear red sunglasses, the red flags become just plain flags. Needless to say, I was blinded by the fact that I was in love. The arguments began to grow closer in frequency. So, I decided that maybe moving in with him will solve some issues. He obviously had trust issues. So maybe, this would fix it. Or, at least that was my thought. Which at the time made total sense? Looking back at it, I should have seen the obvious red flags.

When we would get into these arguments it mainly consisted of him screaming at me for seemingly no reason and for such small things. But with me growing more ill, I thought that this was the only person that would even accept me as a sickly person. I wasn't diagnosed at the time. Yet, I knew deep down that my health would continue to worsen, which ended up being very true.

As time went on and I moved in with him, we were long distance for almost a year. And, honestly moving in with him at first seemed to have helped. But then things began to get worse again. I was getting sicker. I was needed to be in the hospital more often whether that be for doctor's appointments or even procedures. Eventually I wasn't able to work anymore and he got mad over that as well.

It wasn't a healthy relationship. But, my thoughts at that point were, who would want somebody who is as sickly as I am? Even so-called friends that lived nearby agreed. They congratulated him for staying with me. Yet, behind doors I was being verbally abused and now occasionally physically abused.

He would say that it was my fault for being so sick. That I brought this onto myself. It was all because of me. Even after I was diagnosed with my motility disorders, when I was admitted to the hospital to have a feeding tube placed. He even blamed me for having Ehlers Danlos syndrome. Everything seemed to be my own fault.

Needless to say, my mental health declined rapidly. This made my anxiety really bad to the point where I was having panic attacks. Yet I refused to say that it was his fault. I truly believed that it was my own fault. That I was to blame for everything. However, a small part of me believed that this was abusive. So, I brought it up to him. You can guess how that ended up. Not well.

Instead, he blamed me for his treatment towards me and that I deserved it for making him feel that way. Even though I never did anything to deserve such treatment. When he decided that he didn't want to live in the state we were located in, I fully agreed that we should move. Little did he know, this would give me the perfect chance to escape this hell hole of a relationship.

So, we packed everything up. It was decided that I would stay with my family so they could look after me. This was partially true. I was extremely sick at that point. I wasn't tolerating tube feeds anymore and was rapidly losing weight. We arrived at my mother and step-father's place where I would be staying with our two cats, whom he had been abusive towards too.

We were long distance for a while, again. It was all of the same stuff with arguing again. He blamed me when I went septic and was in the intensive care unit. I was too sick to even argue back at that point. I had been dealing with this for 4-5 years. It wasn't until January of 2020 that I finally decided to leave him. I had the two cats and we were in a safe place where he would never be able to touch us ever again. So, I conjured up my strength and did it.

> **"Needless to say, my mental health declined rapidly. This made my anxiety really bad to the point where I was having panic attacks."**

I've been free of that hell hole now for almost a year now. I'm also dating somebody new now that treats me the way I should have been treated in the beginning. My current significant other has even made the effort to learn about my illnesses. He has never blamed me for anything. We have never gotten into an argument and we've been dating now for almost 8 months. I should have done this a lot sooner. I should have left William a lot earlier.

But I'm thankful that I was able to escape when I did. I now realize my own self-worth. I'm worthy of love. I'm worthy to be treated well. I'm worthy to be called beautiful. I am worthy of happiness. I'm proud of myself for that. I love that about myself.

I have since grown adapted to various aspects of my illness from this whole 5-year ordeal. I've grown to be patient with myself. I've grown to not get mad over small and dumb things. If something frustrates me, I'll give myself time to take a brief break and then come back to it later when I'm a lot calmer, and in general I have become a lot calmer about things. Even during very stressful situations like when I needed an emergency blood transfusion.

I've needed to adapt to a lot of things throughout my life. You learn to adapt to new changes rather quickly because you have to. I've now stopped caring about when and where I need to sit down. I'll sit on the floor if I need to. It's pretty funny if you think about it. I also have learned to use mobility aids when I need them. Whether that be wheelchairs, canes, or even my forearm crutches. I've definitely grown a tough skin over the years. I mean, it's not every day that you see a young disabled person with a mobility aid. You receive quite a bit of stares because of it. But when it's either life or death, I mean, I would much rather choose to live. Granted, now I don't eat hardly anything so it's a small challenge to be around food as it's a social aspect in today's society. But, I at the very least do enjoy the smell of food and I love to cook food as well. So, I try to involve myself in that. It's a lot of fun, especially when you have a new outlook on life in general.

I have since doubled my weight and am thriving on TPN. TPN, however, is not without risk. Eventually, my liver may fail as well as my kidneys. You also have a very high risk of getting sepsis. (I have been septic three times since starting TPN.) But I am thriving. I'm living. I'm so thankful for this second chance at life. Or, should I say third chance? As tube feeds have saved my life as well in the beginning.

But you do get used to it. I stopped caring about it quite a long time ago. I guess you can say that I just sort of go with the flow of things.

It's definitely something that I've learned over the years since getting sick. I really love that about myself. I've grown stronger because of it. There's nothing that I can really do about my situation so you grow and adapt to it. You learn your way around various medical things and lingos.

You learn to take medications. You learn your way around tubes and lines. And hopefully slowly, you learn to love yourself despite everything. There's a beautiful quote that I love and more or less live by and that is, "When your body begins to fail you, there is nothing left to do but to embrace it. To wrap your broken arms around a skeleton that has become more of a cage than a body." It's changed my viewpoint that I have of myself. You just accept things the way they are, and you move onwards with life in the best way that you can.

There have been a lot of lessons that I've learned since then. I've grown slowly to love myself and trust that I deserve happiness and that I deserve life. I'm very thankful to even be breathing today. I've learned to have so much empathy towards others and to be calm during stressful and chaotic situations. I really love that about myself.

Someday I would love to get back into performing, or at least to get back into my music. But I would also love to get into public speaking so I can use my experiences to change people's lives for the better. When it comes to music, it is something that I've been putting off for quite some time. Music is extremely important to me. It's helped me get through all of the rough times that I've gone through. I hope that one day I'll be able to start performing again. But with these new sets of wheels, it could be possible. Either way that I decide to go, I want to use either my music or my speeches to change the lives of others. I want to somehow better the lives of other people. To make them not feel alone in their journey. Maybe someday I will achieve my dreams. I haven't given up quite yet. I guess, only time will tell for my future.

I would like to give some advice, now, and this one is for the victims of abuse, the best advice that I can give you if you are in an abusive relationship, please get yourself to a safe place. Whether that be with a close friend or family member. Get out. You are worthy of love. You are worthy to be cared for. You are worthy despite anything that you have gone through, even if you are sick. You can do this. I believe in you. Remember, you are worthy and you do not deserve to be treated the way you are being treated.

All in all, if you are struggling due to illness, whether that be from weight or if your doctors say there are no more options, do not take no for an answer. Keep trying. Find new physicians. Get second opinions.

*If you relate to any of this, it's probably because you or somebody you know has a chronic illness. The best advice I can give is to keep moving forward. To keep going. And with that, I want you to know that I am proud of you. Even if you didn't get out of bed, I am proud of you. If all you did was breathe and drink water, I am proud of you. Keep going. You are strong. We are all strong. I'm alive today because I did not take no for an answer. You got this; we are here with you.*

# Pamela Bickford

Avon, NY, USA

**Senior Editor and Director of Community Outreach & Sales for ImagineWe Publishers, Reiki Practitioner & Caregiver**

*"I am ever-evolving in the dramatic transformation that cancer has brought to my life.."*

## About Pamela:

*Pamela Bickford is a mother, writer, library clerk, and the founder of The Reiki Oiler. She moonlights as an administrative consultant and public speaker. Pamela supports the humane treatment and adoption of homeless animals. She is also an advocate for disability rights in the workplace, autism education, and endometrial cancer awareness. She lives in New York with her husband, 3 cats, 2 rats, 1 Russian Tortoise, and an assortment of fish.*

\* \* \*

*IG:*
*@thereikiolier*

*FB:*
*@TheReikiOiler*

To go forward with my story, I must first take you back to the first moment I learned I had cancer and where I was in my life. It was December 11, 2018. I was at my two-week post-operative appointment after having a partial hysterectomy due to suffering for years with severe anemia and PCOS. I was feeling good and planned to do a little Christmas shopping after my appointment. I was going to ask my doctor if he would approve an early return to my job as a Superintendent's Secretary and Board of Education District Clerk in a public school. It was a job I loved. I was hired in June of 2017, after a nine year career at another school district in another administrative support position. This job was the pinnacle of my career. The various and complex job duties suited me well and I was good at it. The hours were long, but I didn't mind - my daughter was grown and on her own, and my husband worked long hours at his job in the same school district's Transportation Department. I had already made a place for myself, made many improvements to office processes and procedures, and had given new life to the district office and board of education events. I was finally in my element, or so I thought.

So, there I sat in my doctor's office, a smile on my face because I truly felt I had a new lease on life after having my uterus removed, which had caused me immeasurable problems for years. My doctor came in and examined my healing scars. Then he turned back to my chart and said that he had some bad news and some good news to share. He told me the bad news first - that when my uterus and cervix were biopsied - standard procedure when any organ or tissue is removed - some grade three cancer cells were found near the para-aortic lymph vessel. He said that the good news was that it had not penetrated through the wall of the uterus, nor were any cancer cells found in my cervix. He told me that he had already made an appointment for me with a gynecologic oncologist for December 22 and that I needed to make sure I went to that appointment. Then he said he was sorry to have to tell me this news, but he was sure that it was all contained and said that treatments for this type of cancer had come far. He said, "If you are going to get cancer - this is the type to get because it is often curable." Then he put his hand on my shoulder and said I could sit there as long as I needed to but that he had other patients to see, and walked out the door.

I sat there, stunned. My face, I am sure, was as white as the paper sheet I was sitting on. My stomach coiled up into knots. I was not sure what to think. I was unable to cry. I just blankly stared...wondering how on earth I was going to tell my family...my daughter, my husband, my mom, my dad, my step-mom, my autistic brother, my extended family... How was I going to tell my boss and the board members I worked for? What was this going to mean for my career - the one I was just finally settling into and feeling comfortable and successful in? What was this going to mean for my future...for my life? Did I even have a future or would my life be cut short, just when I was finally coming into my own? I mean, cancer is cancer, isn't it? It is an unpredictable and deadly disease. Sure, I know some people who beat it or are living with it. But I also knew far too many who died from it - and many at too young an age.

I very slowly got dressed and walked out to my car, where I sat and stared at nothing again for I don't know how long. It felt like I had entered a place outside of normal time... the place you go in your dreams. Except this was one of my worst nightmares. As I sat there I felt this incredible weight settling over my shoulders. It was a heavy mantle that was mine to bear. And to bear it alone was impossible...I would have to share it with those I loved most.

And then my cell phone rang, and time began ticking again. My heart caught in my throat as I saw it was my mom and she was the first person I told. I hated to do it over the phone, but her call took me by surprise in that vulnerable moment...and I just couldn't talk to her without telling her. But I hated telling her...placing that worry and fear on her shoulders and into her heart. I didn't want to call and tell my husband over the phone because he was driving a school bus...I knew I had to somehow wait for him to get home and tell him in person. So I drove to my daughter's house and she was the second person I told. I hated telling her too. I hated having to put that fear into her...my baby girl who was all grown up into a beautiful young woman. Thank God for her though, because she tells it like she sees it and that day she told me that I was going to be okay. It was the first time that the tables were turned and she became "the mother" and I was the scared little girl. She said she loved me, that I was too strong and stubborn to die of cancer and that WE would get through this. They were words I desperately needed to hear. Telling my husband was awful. He was filled with worry, love, anger, fear - an amalgam of emotions that really had no good outlet. But he held me close and I knew that together, we would get through this somehow. Then I told my dad and step-mom. I have always been my dad's "little girl.". And now I was telling him that his little girl had this terrible disease that kills so many, and telling my step-mom that I had the same disease that took her best friend's life. Delivering the news to the rest of my family, my boss, and a few close friends was equally as difficult.

## "The biopsy, even though done under general anaesthesia, was one of the most traumatic things I had to go through so far in my cancer journey."

I saw the oncologist on December 22. I went with my husband, my daughter and my mother. The doctor shared that he too believed the cancer had been contained in my uterus and the plan was to have a second surgery in February, after I had fully healed from my partial hysterectomy, and he would remove my ovaries, some lymph nodes, and any tissue that looked diseased. I would then get some radiation treatments as a preventative measure. He was as positive as he could be in this situation, and so began the wait for me to heal.

I went back to work the day after Christmas. I had developed a cough from an upper respiratory virus that wouldn't go away. The New Year came and went and things at work were back to normal, relatively. But I kept coughing and people kept noticing and commenting on it. Long story short, I was told by the oncologist that I should see my primary care doctor - that it was highly unlikely the cough was in any way related to my cancer...but something inside me knew differently. I did go through the motions with my PCP...went through all kinds of tests and tried different medications all to no avail. I was getting more and more scared, but trying to not show it. Finally, my PCP sent me to get a chest x-ray on a Thursday. He called me at 8:30 p.m. that same evening to tell me that the results showed enlarged glands and he wanted me to get a CT scan the very next day. So Friday I went for that test. On Saturday, while my daughter and I were at a bridal shower, he called with the test results. My girl and I went outside and I put him on speaker phone. We stood in the cold, with our arms around each other's waists, as he told me that the radiologist suspected that the cancer had spread to my lungs. There were enlarged glands as well as several nodules showing up in both lungs. I would need to get a biopsy to confirm it, but my body had already told me what was going on. He said that sometimes, secondary cancers can develop...so this could be a case of lung cancer on top of endometrial cancer. My PCP was truly hopeful though, and he encouraged me to remain positive, telling me that he has many patients who have lived for years with cancer getting periodic treatments. He is a wonderful physician and has been a true friend and supporter through all of this.

The next step was scheduling a biopsy, which I did, with a doctor who came highly recommended by a friend I have that has lung cancer. The biopsy, even though done under general anaesthesia, was one of the most traumatic things I had to go through so far in my cancer journey. Waking up from that procedure, I remember begging the nurse's to kill me because I could barely breathe and could not stop coughing and crying for over an hour. It was horrible. There are no other words for it.

I went home the same day, but the week that followed was probably the worst week I have experienced. I was scared and depressed and anxious. It was February break week at school, but I had to be at work by 8 a.m. the day after my biopsy for a special board meeting. Luckily, being break week, things were slow and not many people were around to see me dissolve into tears over and over, as I waited to get the results that would prove what I already knew. By this time, I had long been "sleeping" on my reclining couch at night, because it was too uncomfortable for me to be in bed. Coughing kept me up all night. I could not carry on a normal conversation or take a deep breath without coughing.

The following Monday, my husband, daughter and mom all trooped into the office of the pulmonary/lung oncology surgeon who performed the biopsy. He confirmed that my cough was due to swollen glands that were right below my trachea. He also confirmed that I had 10 -12 cancerous nodules in each lung. This meant my cancer was considered to be at Stage 4, because it had spread so far from its original site in my uterus. Surgery was not an option because I would have no lungs left. That was a difficult appointment to endure, but the doctor was so kind, and while the news was hard for all of us to hear, that doctor gave me hope. He looked me straight in the eye and told me that I was young, in relatively good health, and he told me that I could beat it. He advised me to start a daily walking regimen and to practice purposeful breathing - to use my lungs and keep them functioning. Because the cancer had spread, the surgery to remove my ovaries and lymph nodes was off the table. My only option at that point would be chemotherapy. So back I went to the gynecologic oncologist a couple days later and got scheduled to begin treatment on March 6, 2019.

Over the course of nine months, I received 12 chemotherapy treatments, once every three weeks. As I began to move forward with treatments, I finally felt like I was "doing something" to help save myself. During this time, I also began on a journey of self-contemplation, reevaluating my life, my spirituality, my values, my goals, my talents, and thinking about what would I most regret not doing with my life were I not able to beat this cancer? The thing that kept rising to the top was my writing. Almost from the beginning of my knowledge that my cancer had most likely spread to my lungs, I began sharing my journey, bit by bit on Facebook. Almost like a blog. And people came out of the woodwork, liking and commenting on my posts. They felt my writing was truly inspirational.

Now, I have always been a helper of others...taking care of others is a specialty (taking care of myself always seemed to fall to the wayside). My grandpa nicknamed me "The Goodwill Ambassador" because even as a toddler I was always spreading good cheer and wanting to help others however I could. I didn't need anything in return - just a smile and a thank you was plenty. It made me feel so good about myself. Cancer made me realize that in order to continue being able to take care of others, I was going to have to put myself first and do all that I could to enable myself to return to a state of relative good health.

**"As I moved further into remission, I knew that I had to recreate myself and how I move through this world."**

This inward turning, this time of self reflection and taking strong action to help my body, resulted in a transformation of how I wanted to BE in this world. As the chemo did its work, I in turn, worked with the chemo - through exercise during treatments. While the drug literally dripped into my veins I walked for miles in figure eights or marched in place to get my blood flowing, my heart pumping, and helping to force that medicine throughout all the cells of my body. In my last few chemo's I was even alternating five minutes of walking/marching with three minutes of jogging in place! I don't know where my energy came from, I don't know why I was able to respond so well to the chemo, but I can only think it was a combination of divine intervention, positive thinking, and exercise. As I walked, I talked to the medicine, I talked to the cancer cells and to my healthy cells. I talked to God/the Universe/my guardian angels/my spirit guides. I meditated. I also received Reiki treatments while getting chemo. All these things and more, gave me strength and made me feel powerful in the face of my cancer. The scans all showed that what I was doing to help my body, this combination of western, holistic, and personal medicine, was working. It was what enabled me to achieve remission.

I continued to push forward through other life obstacles that occurred, as I moved further into remission. COVID-19 hit the U.S. and caused everything to shut down. Then I had the previously postponed cancer-related surgery to remove my ovaries. And then, I unexpectedly (and wrongfully, I believe) lost that job I loved so much. All of this happened within days of each other.

As I moved further into remission, I knew that I had to recreate myself and how I move through this world. I have a God-given talent for sharing stories through my writing, and even more, the chronic illness and other trials I have faced throughout my life have set me up to be able to empathize with a diverse group of people and problems. I knew that I needed to use all of that to help others going forward.

I sought out a Reiki teacher and studied, learned and practiced my way through Levels 1 and 2. Now I am nearing the time I will earn my Level 3, Master/Teacher certification, with Reiki and be able to teach and attune others to this marvelous way of living. I also began using Young Living essential oils to help support my overall health and wellness. The oils complement my Reiki practice and bring so many benefits to a session with my clients. Additionally, I am writing a book about my cancer journey that I hope will serve as inspiration to others.

I am ever-evolving in the dramatic transformation that cancer has brought to my life. I will never again not listen to or pay attention to my own needs at the expense of my health. I will use the worst life has thrown at me and turn it into something positive, meaningful, worthwhile, and helpful to myself and others. I will use my experience to be an advocate for others who experience unlawful treatment in the workplace, while dealing with chronic illness or disability.

Most of all, I will continue to send love and healing energy to myself and to all the world, through Reiki. Even knowing my cancer could recur, I don't focus on that and I won't worry about it. I am a chronic illness warrior - deserving, empowered and changed in a good way, by my experiences.

# Tiffany Kairos

Medina, OH, USA

## About Tiffany:

*Tiffany Kairos is a blogger, advocate, and founder of The Epilepsy Network (TEN). She passionately shares her journey about life with epilepsy and is devoted to helping others with conditons to find their voice and become catalysts in the mission to spread awareness about chronic illnesses. Articles that she has written can be found on her website located below as well as on Huffpost, Mayo Clinic, The Mighty and many more.*

*\* \* \**

*IG:*
*@tiffanykairos*

*Website:*
*www.tiffanykairos.com*

*Co-Founder of The Epilepsy Network (TEN),*
*Epilepsy Advocate & Blogger*

*"Asking for help doesn't make you weak – it reveals strength."*

My name is Tiffany Kairos. I am a blogger writing about navigating life with epilepsy, and an advocate and the founder of The Epilepsy Network (TEN). I've lived with epilepsy for over ten years.

Epilepsy is a neurological disorder in which brain activity becomes abnormal, causing seizures.

I was diagnosed after experiencing a seizure while driving and crashing into a tree. Thankfully, my only injury was whiplash.

After my diagnosis, I had to stop working due to the fact that I could not control my seizures and it became too great a risk. My husband and I lost our home, and we had to begin our lives all over again. I struggled with depression all the while struggling with relentless seizures.

## "Starting over takes courage and strength. Not just in a physical sense but emotionally, too."

On the surface, you might never know that I live with a chronic illness. People see me smiling. They see me active. But, that's the nature of my illness. I don't know when I am going to get hit with a seizure. I might feel great one moment and the next, I need to rest in order to bounce back.

I'd like to think that I'm a pretty good judge of character. Following my diagnosis, my friends were quick to offer their unwavering support, calling and paying visits. However, over time calls and visits began to shrink. Texts would grow smaller and smaller. My friends gradually faded out of the picture one-by-one. I can't read people's minds, just as they can't see my unwell brain. Was I a burden to them? Were they afraid of my condition? Perhaps it's a mix of both, but I'll never really know.

Starting over takes courage and strength. Not just in a physical sense but emotionally too. I was immensely grateful for the love and support that was given to me from my husband and family, like a life jacket to save me from sinking. Encouraging words, lending an ear to talk to, offering advice and even a shoulder to cry on if needed.

Inspired by such a tragedy, my husband and I began researching my condition in order to better understand my life and the lives of others affected by epilepsy. We created an online community and organization - The Epilepsy Network (TEN) and also, I created a personal blog about my journey living with epilepsy (tiffanykairos.com).

Navigating life with epilepsy can be a challenge but it has helped me grow stronger than I ever imagined that I could be. I had to recognize and acknowledge my limitations. As an independent person it was tough to come to the conclusion that I would need to ask for help for things that I could do by myself before diagnosis. With time and loving support, I came to understand that asking for help doesn't make you weak - it reveals strength.

I, who once denied help from anyone and was adamant about doing things on my own, found solace in reaching out to others when in need and accepting offers extended to me. Looking at it in a whole new perspective, I felt empowered asking and receiving help rather than denying it.

Following my diagnosis, I made the decision to no longer drive since I still have continual seizures and I want to ensure the safety of others and myself. This can make things difficult when needing or wanting to get to and from places, such as grocery shopping, meetings, a friend's house, etc. Thankfully, in this day in age, you can do just about anything online, even shop for groceries! Which is what I do to help me take care of what I need or want done.

> **"Navigating life with epilepsy can be a challenge but it has helped me grow stronger than I ever imagined that I could be."**

I often think about what I would want to do in life if I could be doing anything in addition to blogging and advocating. I know that with my ambitious zest for life, I would most certainly like to either act in or direct television programs/movies educating people about epilepsy and seizures.

# Those reading this right now, remember this...

Take it one step at a time. Start each day with the mission to be the best you can be and do the best that you can do. Do what you need to do. Listen to your doctors. Remember to focus on all things that lift you up and make you happy and not focus on any doubts or fears you may have.

# Jenny Jones

Oklahoma City, OK, USA

## Medical Social Worker

*"You are not alone in your struggles."*

## About Jenny:

*Jenny lives with two rare diseases – Familial Adenomatous Polyposis and Short Bowel Syndrome. Her chronic illness began when she was a child. The odds were against her but with the support of her family, pediatric GI specialist, and school personnel, Jenny surprised everyone to not in her spare time raises awareness and funds for her rare diseases through her Blog, Vlog, and Shop. only survive her illness but also achieve her dreams. Now, Jenny is a Medical Social Worker and Jenny enjoys life the most by spending time with those closest to her, her dogs, and educating others about Familial Adenomatous Polyposis and Short Bowel Syndrome.*

\* \* \*

**IG:** *@LifesaPolyp*

**YouTube:** *@lifesapolyp*

**Website:** *www.lifesapolyp.com*

I'm Jenny and my story starts when I was about eight years old. I have a hard time remembering my childhood due to the medical trauma I would start experiencing just two years later. I remember being healthy until I started having chronic stomach pain in the 3 rd grade. My parents took me to my Primary Care Physician (PCP) as there was no improvement to my stomach pain. Our insurance at the time required a referral to see a specialist. My PCP refused to refer me to a GI specialist though, stating I was "just a whiny child" and there was nothing wrong with me. As soon as my parents were able to change from an HMO insurance plan to a PPO plan, my parents found me a GI specialist. She was very thorough and took a family history from my mother of GI issues. As soon as she learned that my mother and grandfather both had Familial Adenomatous Polyposis, she scheduled me for genetic testing and an EDG and colonoscopy. She suspected I had Familial Adenomatous Polyposis too. The EDG found that my stomach was pre-ulcerous from stress that was causing my stomach pain.

Familial Adenomatous Polyposis is a rare genetic disease that is caused by a mutation to the APC gene and causes 100s to 1000s of precancerous polyps to develop into cancer. These polyps will turn cancerous if the colon is not removed in time. There are several extra colonic manifestations of Familial Adenomatous Polyposis as well including bone growths, Desmoid tumors, supernumerary teeth and high risk of other GI cancers and other cancers throughout the body. Through my genetic testing, EDG, and colonoscopy it was confirmed that I had indeed inherited Familial Adenomatous Polyposis from my mother. My polyps were biopsied and one doctor stated the polyps had already started to turn cancerous while another doctor stated the polyps had not started turning cancerous yet but would at some point.

### "...my small intestine had wrapped around itself and my surrounding organs resulting in discontinuation of blood circulation to my organs."

My GI specialist recommended removing my colon and so I had my first surgery at age 9. My surgeon preferred for me to have a permanent ileostomy, however, my parents advocated for me to have a temporary ileostomy with a J Pouch creation to allow my ostomy to be reversed. However, I experienced complications. Within a couple of weeks, my incision became infected and the Children's ER had to surgically reopen my incision, flush it, and pack it. The medical personnel did this without any sedation or effective pain management, as morphine does not control pain for me at all. It was the worst pain I have ever experienced in my life.

Within another week, I was in excruciating pain and was taken back to the Children's ER. The ER doctor ordered an X-ray, which didn't show anything to be wrong, so he sent me home telling my parents I was "a whiny child with nothing wrong" with me. The ER doctor did not call my GI specialist to alert her that I was in the ER with abdominal pain. The next morning the pain had not improved so my parents took me back to the Children's ER. This time a different ER doctor performed Barium X-ray instead of only an X-ray and discovered my small intestine had wrapped around itself and my surrounding organs resulting in discontinuation of blood circulation to my organs. My GI specialist was alerted this time that I was in the ER. The ER staff and my GI specialist couldn't believe I had lived through the night. I had emergency surgery and it was discovered that the lack of blood supply had killed part of my small intestine, including my J Pouch. My ileostomy stoma was relocated from my left side to the right and I no longer qualified for my ostomy reversal. I was diagnosed with the rare disease, Short Bowel Syndrome due to further removal of my small intestine. Two days later I required another surgery to remove my dead J Pouch.

Short Bowel Syndrome results due to the dysfunction or removal of intestine and causes malabsorption of nutrients as severe, chronic diarrhea is typical. Some individuals require a feeding tube and TPN in order to obtain the required nutrients.

The following year I had another surgery in an attempt to complete a Straight Pull Thru as I did not have enough small intestine remaining for another J Pouch to be created. The Straight Pull Thru was not completed at this time as the surgeon did not believe it would be successful. Either during this surgery or in an additional surgery soon after, I required surgery to remove abdominal adhesions. I was severely underweight after this year of surgeries and my GI specialist advised I would require a feeding tube if I didn't gain weight. After a lot of effort and following a high fat diet, I gained enough weight to reach 100 lbs and no longer required a feeding tube.

I was physically healthy for the next several years but my mental health greatly suffered. I had undiagnosed medical PTSD from all of my surgeries. I also transferred to a new school for sixth grade after being homeschooled for a year due to my health issues. The first semester at this new school was great but the second semester was full of bullying. I became so depressed and full of anger between the PTSD and bullying that I became suicidal and homicidal until my mid high school years. I hated having an ostomy and I hated everyone I thought had wronged me medically and in school. My parents offered to obtain mental health services for me but I refused.

While in high school, my GI specialist referred me to another specialist to determine if I would be able to have my ostomy reversed into a Straight Pull Thru. This new specialist advised that if I could create a reservoir in my lower small intestine by doing kegel exercises with a ballooned catheter inserted into my anus for a year, I might be able to have my ostomy reversed. I was desperate to have my ostomy reversed. I absolutely hated my body and my ostomy. At age 15, I was finally able to have my ostomy reversed into a Straight Pull Thru.

When I was 16, I requested to start seeing a mental health therapist and she recommended I start on an antidepressant medication. Between receiving counseling and medication management, I finally was able to start processing the medical trauma I had experienced.

The first few years following my Straight Pull Thru were difficult as I was experiencing severe, chronic vomiting and excessive diarrhea. I was unable to maintain my weight and my electrolytes were dangerously low. I required weekly GI appointments and labs resulting in frequent hospitalizations for IV fluids to replenish my electrolytes. My GI specialist later told me that she never knew if I would survive from one appointment with her to the next appointment the following week. I underwent extensive medical testing at my hospital that included tests such as x-rays, barium x-rays, nuclear tests, CT scans, intestinal scopes, etc.

> **"In spite of all of my health issues and surgeries, I was able to graduate not only high school on time but I also went on to earn a Master's in Social Work."**

During this time, it was found that I had a hole in my small intestine. I was placed on a NPO diet where I couldn't drink or eat anything for what seemed like weeks. I received TPN and hyperbaric treatments for 2 hours for 20 sessions to heal the intestinal hole. My GI specialist started me back to drinking and eating slowly. First, I could only have an ounce of ice chips once an hour, then one ounce of water once an hour. Once I was allowed to start eating meals again, I could only have plain eggs for breakfast and plain chicken with rice for lunch and dinner. In spite of all the months of testing, nothing could be identified to explain my vomiting, excessive diarrhea, and electrolyte imbalances. Exploratory surgery was the last option and it finally allowed it to be revealed that I had adhesions creating a stricture around my small intestine causing vomiting and excessive diarrhea. The adhesions were removed in another surgery.

It was a long recovery period after this surgery, as I continued to have dangerous electrolyte imbalances for the next 5 years. I even went to an out-of-state hospital for additional medical testing to determine any other possible causes for my electrolyte imbalances other than my Short Bowel Syndrome. No other culprits were found. I required a massive amount of daily medications, supplements, and quarterly hospitalizations to maintain my electrolyte levels. My health finally started to stabilize after those 5 years. I continue to have EDGs and a lower intestinal scope to monitor for precancerous polyps throughout my GI tract. Years of malabsorption have caused degeneration in my neck that causes chronic pain and limited movement. I am also being followed by a nephrologist due to cysts on my kidneys that she believes developed due to my chronic dehydration. My Short Bowel Syndrome causes me to use the restroom a minimum of 20 times a day and I continue to take several medications daily to manage my symptoms and electrolytes.

I have chronic nausea and abdominal pain, particularly when I eat or drink, that are due to adhesions worsening. I anticipate I will require more surgeries for adhesion removal and/or the Whipple procedure due to precancerous polyps that continues to grow in my duodenum.

## "Not only did I experience medical trauma but I also was very isolated in my rare diseases."

In spite of all of my health issues and surgeries, I was able to graduate not only high school on time but I also went on to earn a Master's in Social Work. I graduated from high school, college, and graduate school all with honors. I wanted to originally be a veterinarian but I was unable to provide medical care to animals due to medical PTSD. I decided the next best thing would be to help others with chronic health conditions. I felt incredibly alone as a child and teen in my physical and mental health struggles that I didn't want others to go through the same things I had experienced. Not only did I experience medical trauma but I also was very isolated in my rare diseases. I didn't know anyone outside of my family with Familial Adenomatous Polyposis. In high school, I started attending meetings with the United Ostomy Associations of America support groups. I met several other individuals with ostomies but none had my disease. However, in high school I also started attending the Youth Rally as a camper and finally met one other person with Familial Adenomatous Polyposis outside of my family. The Youth Rally is an organization that provides an annual summer camp for teens with bowel or bladder diversions for community support, disease education, and independent living skills. In college, I volunteered for two years as a counselor for the Youth Rally.

I would love to specifically work with children with cancer or ostomies. However, I am unwilling to relocate in order to work for major cancer centers. Instead, I started volunteering and working with a local hospice. I absolutely loved hospice work but the travel became too much for my body and health. The stress of traveling worsened my Short Bowel Syndrome and I was no longer able to physically function. I took a brief break from working to recover and for the last 10 years, I have been working full time with dialysis patients to help educate, counsel, and provide resources. My employer has been understanding and cooperative with my health needs allowing me to take the time I need to recover from the work week so that I may work the next week.

I have been amazed at myself that I have been able to accomplish so much in my academic career as well as maintaining full time employment. My GI specialist was never sure if I would be healthy enough to achieve these accomplishments but she supported me in all my endeavors. She supported me so much that she actually kept me as a patient for over 20 years until I was age 30. By the time I turned 30, she was ready to retire and send me to an adult GI specialist.

In 2012, I expanded my horizons by starting an anonymous blog about living with Familial Adenomatous Polyposis and

Short Bowel Syndrome – Life's a Polyp. I was finally becoming less ashamed of my health and body. As my confidence in myself grew, I identified myself as the author of Life's a Polyp and increasingly became more open about my health experiences. The aim of Life's a Polyp is to raise awareness about Familial Adenomatous Polyposis, Short Bowel Syndrome, chronic illness, ostomies and other bowel diversions. The reach continues to grow from a blog to include a Youtube channel and a shop. I started a fundraiser with my first t-shirt design featuring Familial Adenomatous Polyposis to open a research fund for Familial Adenomatous Polyposis through the National Organization for Rare Disorders (NORD). Now, Life's a Polyp Shop features designs to highlight Familial Adenomatous Polyposis, rare diseases, and chronic illness in general and all proceeds are donated to the NORD Familial Adenomatous Polyposis Research Fund. My latest Life's a Polyp venture is writing a children's book about Familial Adenomatous Polyposis to help children learn about Familial Adenomatous Polyposis and what it can entail.

I am thrilled at the direction my life has taken. I have been able to use my own medical trauma to help others learn to cope with their chronic health conditions. I love that my confidence and self-love have grown to allow me to share my experiences with others in the hopes that I may further help another person. Without my health conditions, I would not be able to help others in such a manner.

One of my goals in life is to let others know they are not alone in their struggles. As a child with a rare disease, I felt completely alone but now with technology advances we no longer have to be alone with our illnesses. The internet and social media have afforded us connections with others that never would have been possible. These connections are powerful. Not only are we no longer alone, but now we have sounding boards to share our insights into our health conditions. This is particularly important with rare diseases as doctors are not always familiar with a rare disease. Being able to gather information from others helps us to further advocate for ourselves with our medical care teams. I have learned over the years the importance of self-advocacy.

I am no longer afraid to ask my doctors to prescribe me medications I want to try for my symptom management or medical tests and treatments I want completed to monitor and treat my conditions. Having a cooperative, collaborative relationship with one's doctor is essential for optimal care. Not only are my doctors knowledgeable but they are also willing to listen to me and my requests. Sometimes doctors run out of ideas of treatments to try and can benefit from our assistance in researching our conditions and possible treatment options. My adult GI specialist and I went through several trial and error attempts to discover the best medication management for my chronic nausea and pain. Although I continue to have chronic nausea and pain, both are now at tolerable levels. This would have not been achieved though if I was not able to connect with others with my health conditions and discuss new options with my doctors.

# Jimmy Fremgen

Sacramento, CA, USA

*Writer & Advocate*

## About Jimmy:

*Jimmy Fremgen's career as a congressional and legislative aide spanned 5 elected officials, three legislative bodies, two coasts, and one nuclear weapons agreement. From 2012-2016 he worked as Senior Policy Advisor to Congressman Elijah E. Cummings and the House Oversight Committee. Prior to turning to politics Jimmy was a high school history and civics teacher. He is a small business owner and community organizer who is passionate about healthcare access, civic education, and empathy. He lives in Sacramento, CA.*

\* \* \*

*IG: @jimmy_Fremgen*

*"It [is] this feeling of helplessness that we were fighting to erase."*

## The Empathy of Helplessness

From the sidewalk I could see it. Seven feet and five inches of metal and plastic, slender gray legs splayed in a broad stance with a portal between them. The confrontation loomed as each person ahead shuffled forward and slipped between the blast-resistant doors at the horseshoe shaped driveway of the Rayburn House Office Building.

Security checkpoints—an unpleasant but compulsory part of my employment.

As Senior Policy Advisor for Congressman Elijah E. Cummings, metal detectors (or more accurately, magnetometers) were ubiquitous in my routine at the United State Capitol. Checkpoints were at the doors to the office buildings, at the underground tunnels to the Capitol, at the entrance to the parking garage. If I had a meeting in the Capitol itself and decided to grab some fresh air on the way? I'd clear two checkpoints on the 200 yard walk from door to door. If I wanted flatbread tacos from the National Museum of Native American History, I'd weigh whether it was worth clearing security twice rather than hit the cafeteria connected underground to my building.

## "I was Iron Man."

For me the issue tended to lie with their operators, the ones who find it hard to believe that the perfectly normal(ish) looking 24 year-old man in front of them actually had a pacemaker.

I was 14 when I had sat swinging my gangly legs from the examination table at University of California, San Francisco's Pediatric Heart Clinic. I had grown up regularly visiting a cardiologist for a heart condition discovered at birth, Hypertrophic Cardiomyopathy. Thanks to some recent palpitations that left me gasping for air as I succumbed to tunnel vision, I had been promoted to my first electrophysiologist.

Dr. Collins was a woman in her mid thirties with olive skin and a salt-and-pepper pixie cut who had sought to set me at ease even as she ordered a battery of tests. Results in hand, she pulled up a stool to explain them to my parents.

"If you look at the scale from white to black, with white representing perfectly healthy and black being on the edge of death—I'm concerned that Jimmy is in one of the darkest shades of gray."

I would need an implantable cardioverter defibrillator (ICD)—pronto.

I was worried that this might impact my plans for Spring Break. The next week I was scheduled to leave for Mexico with my church youth group to build houses in the slums above Tijuana. I had plans with my friends! I HAD to go.

Not to worry, the staff assured me. Though I had found myself on the wrong end of the heart-health scale, it would take "at least a couple months" to work it out with my insurance company. Apparently life-preserving heart surgery is expensive and subject to negotiation.

For three months, my dad's employer-funded insurance plan bartered with the hospital while I finished freshman year of highschool and slid into summer. While they debated, I nervously analysed each heart flutter, wondering whether this would be the one that pushed me further down the scale I'd heard described.

In July of 2003, Dr. Collins made an incision above my left pectoral and used her fingers to create a scar tissue pocket under the skin. Inside she placed the heavy metal box half the size of a deck of cards to track my heart rhythms and fire off powerful shocks as needed. From the top of the device, two insulated "leads" were fished through my body into the chambers of my heart and anchored to the muscle with tiny corkscrews.

I was Iron Man.

Now if my heart beat dropped below 60 beats-per-minute (bpm) I would receive miniscule jolts of electricity that would fill in the missing beats until my own heart (hopefully) took over. I was told that this would be imperceptible. If my heart raced beyond 222 bpm, the device would charge its capacitors and deliver a direct shock to the inner walls of my heart, jolting it (hopefully) back to normal. I was told this would be very memorable, akin to being kicked in the chest by a horse—if I hadn't already passed out.

Leaving the hospital, I received a list of the new rules that would dictate my mechanically enhanced lifestyle. No more contact sports seemed a blessing and maybe a chance to get out of P.E. class. No skydiving—no problem. Microwaves hadn't been a concern for pacemakers for at least a decade but I should take care to avoid powerful magnetic fields from metal detectors, department store theft detectors and hydroelectric dams. The horrifying scenario of having my ICD forcibly removed from my body by an MRI or fried by an electrical generator seemed like a good enough reason to take this seriously.

## "This was an experience worth avoiding."

Though these warnings seemed to be aimed at the septuagenarians that made up the primary demographic of the pacemaker market, I was terrified. For the first few months I rankled the eyebrows of security guards by darting through theft scanners like I was smuggling jewels. I was probably the only person in America that was happy when the TSA went to body scanners to look under my clothes rather than endure the anxiety attack that came with going through a metal detector. ("What's that bulge in your chest young man?" "Oh nothing officer, just my pacemaker.") I was relieved when it turned out that rollercoasters weren't such a big deal and intramural soccer was survivable. This guess-and-check approach has limits though—you couldn't pay me to get inside an MRI machine.

I'm not sure how extensive the training is to operate a magnetometer, but it seems to imbue the police officers, TSA agents, security guards, and high school seniors that run them with a certain degree of skepticism when you try to negotiate your way around them.

## "The officers seemed extra impatient, their voices riding on the din as they tried to manage the entitled lobbyists and the staffers in the cattle pen on the doorstep of democracy."

Nervousness manifests in me as quippy humor, and over time I harnessed this coping mechanism to build relationships with many of the Capitol Police Officers that worked the security checkpoints. Instead of going through the magnetometer, I would walk around the line and submit to a pat down, the invasion of personal space well worth the peace of mind that came with avoiding an involuntary defib shock. This was more of a courtesy than formal policy, but once I found an understanding crew, I would come and go through that door as much as possible before they rotated to a new post in three months. The officers manning the entrance at the Rayburn Horseshoe made me feel safe. This was my door.

I slid into the doorway, the full weight of the steel panels and bulletproof glass inside the door slamming against my shoulder, the harsh midwinter wind adding to its heft. From the back of a throng of lobbyists and visitors, I craned to scan the officers on duty. I looked for familiar faces and that slight head nod that would release me to duck under, skip the line, and get my physical inspection. How long has it been since the last rotation?

I was 21 the first time I got defibrillated. I had bound up the stairs to my second floor apartment, backpack stuffed with imitation "Magna Cartas" by 7th graders at my student teaching assignment. Late for my own grad school classes, I'd stopped at 7-Eleven on the way home to slug down an unholy "dinner" of meat off the rollers and a Dr. Pepper Slurpee.

Stepping inside, I felt light headed and reached for my pulse. I'd later learn that my heart was racing to 233 bpm, so fast and erratic I couldn't track it. My mind snapped to my worst fear, that I would pass out and die alone on the floor of my living room. Forcing myself off the couch, I staggered to the door, and as I grasped the handle, felt like I got hit by a bus. A blinding light rolled across my vision and I collapsed. When I regained consciousness, I was breathless and on my hands and knees, half out the front door of my apartment.

This was an experience worth avoiding.

Described by one critic as an "architectural natural disaster," the lobby of the Rayburn House Office Building has all of the grandeur you could expect from a government building hastily constructed during the 1960's. Any attempts to evoke splendor with tall ceilings and engraved wisdom on the walls of its lobbies had been upstaged by the post-9/11 installation of metal detectors and stanchions to corral the masses.

This morning was particularly busy. It was 8:22 a.m. with hearings scheduled to start at 9:00 a.m.. Commuting staffers were being joined by lobbyists arriving from their offices on K Street to tag out the homeless "line standers" they'd paid to camp out since early morning for today's proceedings.

The officers seemed extra impatient, their voices riding on the din as they tried to manage the entitled lobbyists and the staffers in the cattle pen on the doorstep of democracy. They watched the clock, anticipating when lobbyists would be settled into their seats, perfectly framed in the wide shot on C-Span, with staffers having scattered to search for coffee via the catacombs.

We shuffled closer, leather soled shoes revealing the Seal of the House of Representatives emblazoned onto the rugs beneath. Reaching the X-ray, I removed my overcoat and emptied my pockets, transferring my cell phone, Blackberry, keys and wallet into my messenger bag for more efficient scanning.

Congressman Duncan Hunter burst through the door to my left, entering through the exit door while bellowing "Hey guys!" toward the officers s he bypassed the cacophony. Most people are jealous of the power, prestige and name recognition that comes with being a Member of Congress—I wanted it so I could skip security.

As the officer screened the lobbyist in front of me, the metal clasps on his expensive overcoat triggering the alarm both times, I tried to get a read on his demeanor. Mr. K Street, now a flagged security risk, was making a show out of his rush to get to the hearing while the officer tried to wand him down.

## "He bellowed the command, one hand outstretched toward me, the other reaching for his sidearm."

I watched the way the officer methodically went through the full security process while lecturing the impatient man on procedure. As he bent to wand the lower half of his hostage, I noticed the single gold chevron on his navy blue epaulet.

A rookie.

My heart dropped and bounced off the floor, returning full of anxiety.

I quickly took off everything that could possibly have metal in it or hide a weapon—suit jacket, belt, watch, tie clip, all went into the basket for the X-ray before I stepped in front of the opening. I didn't want to be perceived as hiding anything.

The officer, finally done with Mr. K Street, beckoned me through the portal of the magnetometer.

I leaned forward cautiously, "I have a pacemaker.

The officer looked at me, a bit puzzled, and waved me forward again.

I raised my voice to be heard over the beeping of the other security checkpoint and the chatter of the windblown public.

"I have a pacemaker. I can't go through."

I presented my ID and a medical card from the Sergeant at Arms that identified me as a congressional staffer and placed me in the same category as pregnant women: exempt from screening by metal detector. I held both up to show to him.

There was a pause between us, he turned and made eye contact with a sergeant nearby, before turning back to me, smiling and giving me an understanding nod.

Crisis averted.

Relieved and thankful that he finally understood, I smiled and in one fluid motion slid under the rope and popped back up. Bounding forward to go around the magnetometer and submit to my pat down, I looked up to make thankful eye contact with the officer.

"Sir, STOP!"

He bellowed the command, one hand outstretched toward me, the other reaching for his sidearm.

I frze as the room came to a stop. Lobbyists engrossed in their smartphones, chattering staffers, officers that had barely been paying attention, all of them looked up as the officer and I locked eyes.

To the officer, I was everything he had been trained to watch for. A lone wolf, raising objections, refusing to be screened, rushing the checkpoint. I was a threat.

When I'd tried to explain myself prior, I had struggled to be heard over the racket. Now, as I stammered to clarify my actions, the only noise in the lobby was the churning of the X-ray machine belts and coats rustling as people craned to see what was happening.

I slowly climbed back under the rope line and again stood in front of the magnetometer.

My ICD is constantly watching for a deadly rhythm. When one is identified, it is analyzed for about eight seconds, considering whether a shock is warranted as it charges the high voltage capacitors. If a shock is still needed, the device delivers up to 35 Joules of electricity directly to the inner wall of the heart to save it from a deadly rhythm.

> "I have a pacemaker, it is dangerous for me to go through here. I'm happy to do a pat down, but I don't want to go through."

When an ICD malfunctions, it can take a healthy heart rhythm and force it into something much more malicious. This happened to my mom once, when her ICD began malfunctioning and fired off 11 times before the paramedics finally deactivated the device. From my childhood bedroom, I had heard her begging for relief, not caring if she was in a deadly rhythm.

Fearing this scenario, I shakily explained, "I have a pacemaker, it is dangerous for me to go through here. I'm happy to do a pat down, but I don't want to o through."

I looked around at the other officers, pleading with my eyes for them to intervene.

I was keenly aware that I was becoming a spectacle. I'd be what people talked about on their way to coffee today. The officer looked at me, impatient with my objections."You'll be fine," and beckoned me through.

## "I took a deep breath, stepped forward, closed my eyes, and waited for the heavy thump and blinding light that would arrive with dosed electricity straight to the heart."

The problem with going through a magnetometer with an ICD is that when you walk through, the magnetometer blasts magnetic waves to detect metal. To an ICD this static looks like imminent heart failure. Repeated interference confuses the sensor but if you walk through the magnetic field once and it doesn't trigger the magnetometer, you're fine.

With this in mind, desperate to get out of there, I stepped through.

The shrill alarm of the machine sounded. "Go back through please."

I thought about the eight seconds it takes for the ICD to charge up to deliver a shock and walked back through. Tick tock.

I removed my badge, placing it on the conveyor, the only thing I was still wearing that might have metal in it. People around me had resumed clearing security through the other checkpoint but I could see that I was still the star attraction.

"Again," the officer motioned toward me.

My anxiety was climbing and my heart rate with it, surely not dissuading my ICD from sending a defibrillation my way. How many seconds had it been?

BEEEEEEEEP!

My shoulders sank. The officer was getting impatient, my fearful anxiety was quickly turning to anger. I was not in the mood to ride in an ambulance today.

"Sir, are you sure you don't have any metal in your pockets?" he asked skeptically.

I made a show of patting down my pockets, drawing it out as long as possible before walking back through, attempting to count to eight. I had resigned myself to it. I was going to get shocked.

I stood in front of the aperture, all but disrobed. Stripped of my overcoat, suit jacket, belt, keys, wallet, and my dignity.

I took a deep breath, stepped forward, closed my eyes, and waited for the heavy thump and blinding light that would arrive with dosed electricity straight to the heart.

Nothing came.

No shock, no thump, and no beep.

"Thank you sir, have a nice day," the officer disinterestedly intoned. I couldn't believe it. After all that, I was okay?

## "It was a feeling I needed to bottle up and save."

With a combination of rage, relief, and humiliation I leaned over the X-Ray belt and scooped up my belongings, crushed by the bins that had continued to come through during the delay. Slinging my bag over my shoulder, I balled everything else into the overcoat, desperate to get out of there and not caring about the creases I was putting in my suit.

It was a reminder, not just of a need for more training for the Capitol Police—which they received after a lieutenant heard about and reviewed video of the encounter—but to have more empathy for others around me. The officer had made me feel small and helpless when I failed to conform to his expectation of normalcy.

It was a feeling I needed to bottle up and save. As a young, white man from the suburbs above San Francisco, I'd rarely felt the irascible heat of discrimination and barely brushed against cultures that weren't familiar. As a congressional staffer serving inner city Baltimore, I had to remind myself that it was this feeling of helplessness that we were fighting to erase.

Arriving at my desk with my mind still swimming, I smoothed out my jacket, stowing my keys and wallet in the appropriate pockets.

I had barely collapsed into my chair before my phone rang.

"The congressman needs his briefing memo and talking points for the gun trafficking event," the congressman's scheduler relayed to me."Meet him in the Rayburn Horseshoe in five minutes."

I glanced over the requested documents for typos that would result in an unwanted furious phone call and printed. Rising from my desk, I went to the printer and placed the documents into a manilla folder, passing this semester's college interns on my way.

Walking to the door I reached for my overcoat and flashed back to the events of a few minutes prior, the heat of my anxiety returning as soon as I remembered that the horseshoe shaped driveway was on the other side of security.

I paused, placed my coat back on the hook and smiled.

This time, I'd send an intern.

# Antonia Schwartz

Berkeley, CA, USA

**Student**

## About Antonia:

*Antonia Schwartz is a senior in high school living in Berkeley, California. sHE WAS DIAGNOSED WITH crohn's Disease the summer before her junior year. Due to her illness, she dropped out of her Arts high school where she had been dancing 17+ hours per week, only to struggle through a normal school day.*

\* \* \*

*IG: @antoniaschwaan*

*"Contribute to change."*

In the middle of the night, the Monday before my senior year of high school, I awake with an almost indescribable ache all over my body. It's impossible to tell where the pain is coming from – everything hurts. I am used to a lot of terrible pain, but as I cry in bed from the aches, I know that this is on another level. I gather all the strength I have, walk a few feet to my bedroom door, then cling to the doorknob, grabbing it fiercely because of the pain. Slowly, I make it to my kitchen cabinet, grab the pain pills, and quickly sit down. I collapse in the chair with the unopened bottle, my knees against my chest, heaving to catch my breath. I take the pills, and after a long break sitting at the kitchen table, I drag myself back to my bedroom and slowly drift back into slumber.

I wake up the next morning with no change, and grab another dose of extra-strength Tylenol and chug it down with a glass of water by my bedside. Then I drag myself to the couch to tell my mom I need to go to the hospital.

I sit in the emergency room for hours, inhaling the sterile smell of my surgical mask against my pale face and crusty lips. After successive visits from first responders, my dad comes to send my mom home. The earlier pain medication starts to wear off and he watches me cry in pain while nurses try to process my request for medication. My chest shakily expands and contracts, while I frantically try to breathe in a way that somehow might throttle back the pain signals my body is sending to my brain. I glance over to my dad and see him rise from his seat to yell for help through the hallway, desperate to see this pain disappear. I hear him yelling at the nurse that he will leave and buy his own meds at Walgreens, before someone reassures him and rushes off.

The pain meds finally arrive and we steadily climb the care ladder, from resident to head gastroenterologist on call. Then it's blood work, contrast, CT scan, COVID-19 test, and finally, I'm admitted to the hospital around dawn the next morning. Looking over all the tests done in the ER, the gastroenterologist sees the acute inflammation present in the terminal ileum of my intestine from Crohn's disease.

\* \* \*

Flashback to just over a year prior, and I'm in an emergency room with a fever and in pain. I was immediately admitted and endured a variety of traumatic tests before I was diagnosed with Crohn's disease, an autoimmune disease that causes my immune system to overreact and create inflammation of the intestinal tract. After my first hospitalization, I spent junior year getting test after test, while juggling my school work and constantly missing class due to symptoms, sometimes several days a week. A little over half way through my junior year, the COVID-19 pandemic hit the United States, which added additional stress about entering medical environments. Because of my immune suppressant medication, I was at higher risk for COVID-19, and was stuck at home over the summer break. But, instead of being bored out of my mind, I had an infinite amount of time to find out what was causing all my pain that persisted, despite the tests that said my Crohn's was in remission. I tried not to do it alone. I saw doctor after doctor, but every visit led to nothing new. Each time, it felt like a gust of wind bursting through my chest, snuffing out what little hope and energy I still had left.

> **"I am overwhelmed and frustrated—after months of trying new things and miscommunication with my doctors, I can not believe I am back in the hospital with a Crohn's flare."**

Sadly, my experience wasn't unusual. Along the way of seeking help from others, many chronic illness patients are doubted, either about severity or even the existence of the pain itself. I faced multiple so-called experts who suggested that my experience was psychological. At one point in my journey for answers, I was referred to see a holistic medicine physician who had me try an absurdly severe diet. I am not kidding, I could only eat six different foods for three weeks. When we agreed that the diet didn't seem to help, he tried counseling, including one session where he tried to strategically counsel us in family therapy but ultimately left my whole family frustrated. Then, he just suggested that I stop my internet searches. The same searching had given us multiple ideas on what to rule out, and new ideas that other physicians welcomed with wide-eyed positivity because they hadn't thought of them before. My experience with help that didn't help left me feeling even more lost. I felt misunderstood and forgotten by the healthcare system. But despite feeling lost, these experiences truly made the warrior spirit inside me grow more dedicated to get to the bottom of my own health journey.

\* \* \*

Now, lying on the bed in the ER, I am overwhelmed and frustrated -- after months of trying new things and miscommunication with my doctors, I can not believe I am back in the hospital with a Crohn's flare. I can hear the nurses closing one door and opening another, while their PPE brushes against their clothes. After spending the entire night in the ER, I was finally brought to my room at around 5:30 a.m.

First, I am booked for the next morning's 7:30 a.m. slot in surgery for an endoscopy. After a brief attempt at some sleep, the prep for the procedure begins. Despite my advocacy, my prep was poorly planned, and in order to speed up the prep process, my team decided to insert a nasogastric tube, a nasal tube stretching from my nose into my stomach.

A nurse shows me the tube and then moves quickly to insert it before I have any time to think. I feel my mother's strong grip on my hand as the heat from her body melts into my shivering skin. The tube goes up through my nose, like a COVID swab, hitting each narrow wall in my nasal cavity. Then it hits my throat. I try to cough it out by reflex while the nurse reminds me to take a sip of water to help get the tube down my esophagus. After a few seconds, it's in. Each time I try to speak, the tube rattles around in the back of my throat from my vibrating vocal cords. But it's in, and the prep liquid is flowing. I don't know why, but I immediately burst into tears. I am scared, overwhelmed, and in pain, but determined to get better. There is no other way.

I arrive at pre-op where an anesthesiologist meets with me to see if I have any more questions. As she talks, I realize that I know her from an earlier scope. She gives me what looks like a smile of recognition, a friendly face doing her job with love and kindness. Then, she rolls me into the operating room and places an oxygen mask over my nose and mouth. Breathe in. And out. People move around me, but I just stare at the ceiling and try not to focus on anything in particular. In. Out. I get dizzy, and everything starts to slow. Then the lights start to fade, and I black out.

In recovery, I start to gain consciousness, but struggle to open my eyes. It takes all my energy in that moment to slowly lift my eyelids, millimeter by millimeter. A nurse notices my movement and quickly grabs my mother so she can be by my side. Results of the scope roll in each hour and finally the gastroenterologist on call arrives -- he explains that there is inflammation in my small intestine and suggests a biologic drug called Remicade. This drug has worked wonders for my younger cousin who also suffers from Crohn's disease, so I'm excited to see if it might do the same for me.

As the nurses prepare to add the medication into my IV, I feel new tickling sensations going down my arm. I look and realize there is saline dripping from my IV. The nurses notice too and quickly take the IV out. They struggle to place a new one, but they have to do it as soon as possible, before the medication goes bad. Nurse after nurse comes in, and each time I can feel the needle pierce through each layer of my skin into the muscle surrounding the veins. They prod me once and they miss. They prod me twice, and they miss. This continues until, once again, tears flow from exhaustion and overload. Finally, a nurse practitioner walks into the room with an ultrasound machine to help her aim the needle into one of my dehydrated and frail veins. She advises me to put headphones on and listen to a song to help me relax. As I take myself out of the moment, the nurse is finally able to place the IV. She pricks my skin one last time, advancing the needle into the vein, careful not to make it blow through the other side. She leaves the catheter inside my arm and secures it. At this point, I am emotionally and mentally exhausted -- because of the medication, I quickly slip into a slumber that will last for hours.

The next morning I wake up and know my hospital experience will soon be over. For the first time since being admitted, I am not in full-body pain. I rise from my bed with hope in my eyes -- for the first time in over half a year, I have a real glimmer of a future with some normalcy. A few hours later, I walked out of the room where I had been confined for days. I gather my things, open the large hospital door, and put one weak foot in front of another. I use every last exhausted muscle to walk out, even using my baby toes to balance myself, as I walk down the hall and pass the nurses station. I feel such immense gratitude and love for the nurses that took care of me while I was ill. Nothing can express how much it means to have a kind face come into your room when you're at your worst. But coupled with this gratitude is a kind of resentment -- I am unable to erase any of the terrifying memories. No person lives through experiences of feeling helpless and frozen without lingering fears.

* * *

That hospital visit was just one chapter in what is now a long story. It's been nearly two years since my first hospitalization, and I still have terrible memories that pop up into my head where I struggle to snap myself back to reality. On my seventeenth birthday, my gastroenterologist handed me a flyer about post-traumatic stress disorder -- it is now clear to me that my medical experiences have left me with trauma. Medical trauma is something that is woefully under-researched and medically misunderstood. I want everyone to know that it is okay to see a medical facility as a place for healing, but it is also okay to fear it. People can experience pain, injury, serious illness, unpleasant medical procedures, and frightening experiences while in a medical environment. This is especially the case for people suffering from a chronic illness; PTSD is most often triggered by past events and chronic illness patients must repeatedly face their trauma in order to receive life-changing, or even life-saving, medical care. In fact, I know that an overwhelming number of children with injuries and chronic illnesses show signs of post-traumatic stress. As I learned more, I started to feel less alone in my experiences once I finally found a community of fellow warriors

**"Over the last year, I have grieved the life that I used to live and grieved the future life that I will never have."**

The most important thing that Crohn's disease has taught me is a major lesson in the meaning of community. I have learned that the community is not always physical or visible -- through social media, I came across hundreds of different accounts dedicated to battling chronic illness. On these forums, participants speak about the physical and mental effects of pain, and just reading them left me feeling so much more understood. One Instagram post by a poet named Dhiman said: "So, trust the process, trust your strength, you will grow stronger as you make your own way." Another of my favorite users, "The Chronically Honest," uses art to defy typical influencer norms and tell her unique story. One of her posts depicts herself getting an infusion with the caption "It is hard when something is out of your hands, yet others make you feel like you should be trying harder to change it." Posts like these let me understand that my situation is not uncommon within the chronic illness community. They let me understand that what others think isn't always right. That this is my body and my life. That others will never understand, so how could they possibly know how it feels or what to say?

> **"Now, I realize that the way I can help others feel the same is through contributing to change."**

Over the last year, I have grieved the life that I used to live and grieved the future life that I will never have. Crohn's disease stole the future that I had imagined, of stage lights, tutus, and pointe shoes. If this were not my reality, I know I would still be pursuing a professional dance career. Now, instead of training in a pre-professional dance conservatory, I take walks in my neighborhood and focus the energy I have on my academics. This journey has put me on the path of pursuing health sciences in college and then pursuing medical school. Achieving small accomplishments, like walking over twenty minutes through the neighborhood, and realigning my vision for the future has made the warrior spirit inside me evolve. I love myself for this; my battle with Crohn's disease has made me a dedicated, resilient warrior.

Now, I realize that the way I can help others feel the same is through contributing to change. It may be uncomfortable to tell my story, but I am ready to sacrifice my comfort in order to comfort others, offering a light to those silently suffering from chronic illness.

My name is Antonia Schwartz. I am eighteen years old and about to start my life after high school. But even at such a young age, putting my story into a book is not as simple as, "here you go, this is it." It is a scary act to sacrifice and tell my personal tale to the world. I decided to tell a story that gives the most raw version of the most frightening time of my life. I am proud of my bravery. Despite the fear and shame of Crohn's disease, I am ready to share. I hope that doing so will inspire courage and resiliency in the world of those suffering from any chronic illness. Even if only one person reads my story and feels a sense of community and comfort, this will make it worthwhile.

# Cheyanne Perry Suarez

Easley, SC, USA

*South Carolina Division President/Publisher @ IWP & Psychology & Neuroscience Writer*

*"I had my whole life ahead of me and dreams that my illness could not prevent me from accomplishing."*

## About Cheyanne:

*Cheyanne was born and raised in sunny Florida, but currently resides in the state of South Carolina with her husband and red-headed Persian cat named Weasley. She graduated with her bachelor's degree in Psychology from North Greenville University and is now the President and main publisher of the SC division of ImagineWe Publishers. Despite health challenges from her chronic diagnoses, she strives to live her life as fully as possible. In her spare time, she enjoys knitting, reading, writing, and blogging on her website listed below.*

\* \* \*

*IG:*
*@hospitalprncss*

*Website:*
*www.hospitalprincess.com*

Long, black skid marks painted the road. Smoke emanated from under a bent, damaged hood. The sudden impact had forced both vehicles to an abrupt halt. Only six blocks away, a police officer knocked on the door of a quaint, seagull gray house in a modest neighborhood. His professional uniform was no consolation for delivering the unfortunate news to a young woman who, up until that very moment, was still reveling in the car-crash passion of newlywed bliss. The officer led her to the scene.

Minutes later, she stood amongst the rubble solemnly watching as the emergency crew prepared her husband for transport. It was assumed he fell asleep behind the wheel. The predicted outcome was grim. Her face appeared almost stoic as the EMTs performed their duties, yet inside her emotions were crumbling. Wailing emergency vehicles echoed from the street. With both hands clutching her stomach, she cursed the sound for deafening their sacred vows—for allowing 'til death do us part to come too soon.

## "On a dreary December day, the remnants of death drenched my black funeral clothes."

Despite numerous miscarriages, the young newlyweds were unknowingly parents the day of the accident that killed my biological father. The shattered glass compared to our family's future—broken, with pieces missing, but with a slight glimmer of hope reflected in the kaleidoscope of ambulance lights and the morning sun. I was their miracle baby.

* * *

I toddled through the cemetery holding a bouquet of yellow memorial roses. Before I could arrive at my father's gravesite, I was distracted by a looming figure in the distance."Ghost, ghost!" I babbled with the vocabulary of a small child. Lifting my hand, I felt inclined to wave at the friendly apparition. My mother walked alongside me. The fearful apprehension in her demeanor was palpable upon noticing there was nobody else visibly present. She grabbed my arm to coax me, her spirit-seeing two-year-old daughter, to the car with the intention of never stepping foot in another cemetery. But as I grew older, I did not lack for funerals to attend or gravesites to visit.

* * *

On a dreary December day, the remnants of death drenched my black funeral clothes. The pastor, with spittle flying from his mouth, monotonously droned on about "better places" and how the Lord "giveth and taketh away." I was too juvenile to grasp the complexity of the situation. All I understood was that the man I knew as my father, the man who cared for me for the first five years of my life, had passed away. I would not come home to daddy's surprise whisker kisses or weekend cartoon binges in front of the television while we devoured Bavarian cream chocolate donuts. It was as if someone had taken half of my pulsating heart from my chest and left it in the casket with his vacant body. I was inconsolable. Once again, my mother stood alongside me. She squeezed my tear-splattered palms. Although I didn't realize it then, strength and resiliency reverberated from her hands to mine.

* * *

I sat in a red upholstered chair in the therapist's office. Anxiously twiddling my thumbs, I was not thrilled about the shrink's efforts to coerce me into divulging my deepest, darkest secrets—even if it was play therapy. No amount of Monopoly board games or dress up skits could make me forget what was wrong. This was not a "get out of jail free card." My thoughts turned to the emotions behind the behavior that brought me to counseling. When my mom found me, I was in the fetal position crouched between the washer and dryer. I recalled the shaking vibrations of the machines as I tried to hide from the realization that everyone I loved would unexpectedly die. However, I couldn't hide from reality.

New beginnings developed from my anxiety. As I healed from my emotional wounds, my mom passed the hours by conversing with the office's receptionist. They became fast friends, and much to my mom's reluctance, she was set up on a blind date. Almost every consecutive evening for months, she was that of a giddy school girl. I rested on the bed in the spare room we were staying in at my grandmother's house, playing with a Polly Pocket set until my mom

pressed the red end call button on her stone-age Motorola flip phone. Eventually, after outings to the bowling alley and dinner dates to Sonic for hamburgers, I traded in my dolls for toy cars because I had a new father and brother. The four of us were happy, content. I could finally rest in security...until I couldn't.

* * *

"Go, go, go, go, go," my parents screamed as I rounded the bases. The attention was nerve-wracking, but I knew how blessed I was to have family cheering from the sidelines. Still, I was that pre-teen who internally cringed at their fanatics.

Perspiration dripped from my forehead and it wasn't solely from the hot Florida sun. As I slid into home plate, I sprinted off of the field to the porta potty. I turned my head away from the stench, but my efforts were futile. Mere seconds passed and I added to the putrid smell as my guts escaped me. I skipped breakfast that morning, had yet to attempt lunch, and I was pretty sure last night's dinner cleared my gastrointestinal tract within an hour. I was shaky, queasy, and my stamina was rapidly depleting. I was running on fumes. Literally. I exited the stall wiping my face with my #8 jersey. My mom noticed my distress. While my dad remained with me, she drove to the convenient store nearby and returned with a chocolate peanut butter protein bar. The chalky texture in my mouth was repulsive, but I ate it anyway. I took my position as catcher dreading what would likely happen next.

At the start of the inning, the ump yelled,

"BATTER UP!" The pitcher threw the ball. My stomach churned, stars clouded my vision, and a dizzying sensation encompassed my body. I staggered to the bathroom again, which is where I seemed to spend the majority of my time lately.

All too often, I was the girl running off of the softball field to be sick. To ensure I finished the game, I didn't eat, yet the alternative was just as bad. I vomited. Embarrassed by the outcome, I left the field. When I arrived to my house, the orange clay washed down the shower drain along with my softball career.

\* \* \*

The man in the white coat interrupted my counting of the ceiling tiles, anything to distract my mind from the tedium of the appointment. The doctor informed me of the results of the extensive testing I had endured. He uttered the phrases "Ehlers Danlos syndrome," "postural orthostatic tachycardia syndrome," and "gastroparesis." Suddenly, my life made sense. From dislocating my elbow as a child to the intermittent bouts of diarrhea and throwing up so forcefully that my family compared me to the exorcist with my ability to projectile vomit six-feet across the room, the strange manifestations that had been plaguing my body had a name. My collagen was faulty, which meant my digestive tract was partially paralyzed and my nervous system was not regulating bodily functions that are supposed to occur automatically. The doctor pulled out his prescription pad. He rewrote my life's plans, editing them with medical diagnoses that have no cure.

However, I was not keen on fulfilling that script. I had my whole life ahead of me and dreams that my illness could not prevent me from accomplishing.

\* \* \*

The algebra teacher scribbled a list of equations on the whiteboard, but my focus was fixed elsewhere. A group of students were huddled around their desks laughing and carrying on, clearly not eager to resume school after break. The boy who occupied the seat beside mine questioned, "How can you be so pale when we just got back from summer vacation?" Hurt, I did not respond. Unbeknownst to him, my pasty complexion was due to chronic illness. I pretended to concentrate on the lesson, but I was really thinking about how the persistent ache in my bones was a reminder that my high school experience was not meeting my expectations. High school is generally depicted as late study nights, an abundance of friends, and ceaseless fun during the four years that determine success. However, my fairytale daydreams were the opposite of what I envisioned. Instead, most of my courses were completed online. I barely had enough energy to attend one period, and that class wasn't necessarily pleasant when I came home crying on the first day.

If it's true that a guy picks on a girl he has a crush on, then I guess this was love at first sight...at least for one of us. My first date with the "mean kid" was to the movies to see The Hobbit. My family invited him to dinner afterward. He used that opportunity to request their permission to begin a relationship with me. Impressed by his gentlemanly etiquette, they warned him that with my extensive heath issues, I was not like other teenage girls. They suggested he pray about the decision. The Lord must have answered yes because we were official before my curfew.

* * *

Strangers at the shopping mall gawked as we pulled into the parking lot. We were on another date. Three months into the relationship, I had a temporary feeding tube placed in preparation for the surgical tube that would be inserted into my abdomen. The tube was threaded through my nose, down my throat, and into my small intestine. A piece of tape secured it to my cheek. Aside from the physical discomfort similar to that of choking on a giant spaghetti noodle, I was humiliated. The tube was a visible representation of the illness I diligently worked to conceal. We strolled hand-in-hand and he made me feel beautiful regardless.

As I adjusted, the tube was not as terrible as I imagined it to be. Although its care and upkeep was occasionally burdensome, receiving proper nutrition offered me the slightest glimpse into the life I yearned for. We took advantage of my newfound energy with beach trips and family gatherings—ensuring I allotted time in my schedule for homework. I even crossed the stage as high school valedictorian at my senior graduation. When the fun-filled dates were over, I stuck my head out of the passenger seat window. My blonde hair fluttered in the breeze. I was invincible.

* * *

I swallowed the capsule and a diffuse redness appeared on my neck. In the background, I heard, "Walgreens pharmacy, please hold." My mom had called to inquire about my medication. My heart was pounding like a subwoofer in my chest. A thick sticky mucus lined my airway followed by an incessant nagging cough. To our surprise, the reaction I was having was not a side effect. Once my eyes grew puffy and my skin became itchy, the symptoms were relieved by a dose of allergy medication.

> "The thirty-two staples lining my abdomen was the evidence that my perceived invincibility was transitory."

The offending treatment was discontinued, yet my reactions rebounded. I was having severe, life threatening reactions triggered by all foods, hypoallergenic formula, water, medications, chemicals products, makeup, lotion, soaps, and more. My family could not cook in my presence without airborne food particles causing a reaction. When the reactions progressed to anaphylaxis, I learned how to administer an EpiPen.

I spent eight months of that year in the hospital. Apparently another Ehlers Danlos comorbidity had reared its ugly head. The specialist blamed my mast cells. As he elaborated further, he explained that we all have mast cells, but mine are defective. They are easily activated to release reaction-inducing chemicals. I was officially diagnosed with mast cell activation syndrome after a series of blood and urine tests. Because traditional therapies were unsuccessful, I was discharged on an intravenous infusion of continuous Benadryl.

* * *

My eyes fluttered as I awoke from my anesthesia nap. The thirty-two staples lining my abdomen was the evidence that my perceived invincibility was transitory. I had a jagged scar spanning from beneath my breast bone to my pelvis. Before surgery, I had been transported to the hospital via ambulance for a suspected bowel obstruction. The agonizing attacks had been repetitively occurring for months. My skin stretched taut from the distension of my belly and I struggled to catch my breath. I was claustrophobic in my own body. Imaging revealed that my colon had twisted. The emergency room physician wheeled my gurney to surgery immediately. I was under the knife for six hours. Stressed and disheveled, the surgeon emerged from the operating room to greet my family in waiting. He was unable to salvage my bowel because the tissues were too fragile, so my colon and a portion of my small intestine were removed. Most of what I remember of that two week admission into the intensive care unit are fragmented memories of hypovolemic shock. I slept constantly. When I was awake,

I submitted homework assignments online in my drug-induced stupor and desperately prayed for normalcy.

* * *

"If you do nothing, it is not going to end well," the transplant team stated bluntly. I was never the same after the bowel surgery. It was the catalyst for worsening intestinal failure and stimulating an immune response. The symptoms were not fully explained by just Ehlers Danlos syndrome. Every three to four weeks post-op, I was admitted with small bowel obstructions, high fevers that mimicked sepsis, and bleeding intestinal ulcerations that required several blood transfusions. I no longer tolerated tube feeds, and had to transition to IV nutrition. My health was declining at a startling pace. If I did not improve, I would need a liver and small bowel transplant.

To be proactive, the oncologist jammed a screw-like contraption into my bone to remove a sample of marrow. They were frantically searching for the source of my unusual maladies. The good news was that it was not cancer, but rather, a condition known as hemophagocytic lymphohistiocytosis (HLH) or "cancer's cousin." The immune cells in my body were damaging my organs and healthy cells. Simultaneously, my geneticist contacted us with results from bloodwork I had weeks ago. The mystery was solved. The genetic sequencing panel showed two compound heterozygous mutations in the gene TTC7A—a gene that encodes for a protein imperative to the integrity of the bowel and immune system. The mutations gave reason for problems with my immune system, as well as why I suffered from bowel obstructions and intestinal ulcerations.

Having answers did not bring about complete solutions. Approximately one-hundred people in the world have these mutations. The prognosis is unknown. One of the few approved treatments is a medication previously tested on zebrafish. The information on human studies is scant. Nevertheless, I swallowed a capsule each morning that seemed to be helping. With hope as an active ingredient, my family and I had closure despite the uncertainties of the future.

* * *

On a chilly November afternoon, both of my parents pushed my wheelchair down the aisle. I tightly grasped my bouquet adorned with lace and blush colored rose petals. The attendance was small and the smiles of the guests were disguised by masks, but the stipulations and restrictions from the COVID-19 pandemic did not detract from the day's significance. The mountains, a symbol of strong, tenacious love, emerged from behind us. It was his turn to profess his vows. He began, "From the first day we saw each other, I was drawn to you." He continued, "I vow to always try to make you happy and to make you feel like the princess that you are…I love you with every part of my being."

I restrained happy tears."My love, my best friend, my confidant," I said. My voice trembled with emotion, "I am exceedingly grateful to be here, alive, proclaiming these promises to you." I paused. On many occasions, considering the events that had transpired, I wondered if I would live to the day of my wedding ceremony. I clumsily flipped the page of my vow book and read, "In some ways, I remain a version of that fifteen-year-old girl with stars in her eyes, and you, that rambunctious boy who sat next to her in math class. It has been an honor growing up alongside you. I promise to love you from this day to the end of my days."

"You may kiss the bride," my dad, the officiant, proclaimed. There were cheers and laughter and hope all around. I gazed toward the heavens with peace in my heart. No matter how soon 'til death do us part rings true, I've lived my happily ever after.

On many occasions, considering the events that had transpired, I wondered if I would live to the day of my wedding ceremony. I clumsily flipped the page of my vow book and read...

"In some ways, I remain a version of that fifteen-year-old girl with stars in her eyes, and you, that rambunctious boy who sat next to her in math class. It has been an honor growing up alongside you. I promise to love you from this day to the end of my days."

# Life's a Polyp

My journey with Familial Adenomatous Polyposis
and Short Bowel Syndrome

 lifesapolyp.com     lifesapolyp    cafe press .com/lifesapolyp

# CHRONICLES OF ZAZZLES'

## CONNECTIVE TISSUE ISSUES

**Buy Now!**

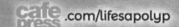

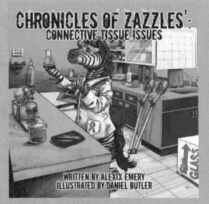

WRITTEN BY ALEXIX EMERY A.K.A ROBIN POWERS
ILLUSTRATED BY: DANIEL BUTLER

Zazzles is a beautiful zebra who loves to rhyme, solve problems, teach, and do science things. She grew up suffering from many things, but never let it stop her from achieving her dreams. Find out about how Zazzles adapts to her Connective Tissue Issues in this very first children's book in the Chronicles of Zazzles series!

**RAISING EHLERS DANLOS SYNDROME EDUCATION & AWARENESS FOR CHILDREN**

Blog, Vlog, Chronic Illness Resources, and More!

# PRINCESS CROWNS AND HOSPITAL GOWNS

🌐 hospitalprincess.com    📷 @hospitalprncss    ⓕ @hospitalprincess    ▶ @hospitalprincess

**BUY NOW!**

WRITTEN BY: CHEYANNE PERRY SUAREZ

ILLUSTRATED BY: DANIEL BUTLER

Pearl is a pufferfish who loves to swim, but she is not an ordinary fish. After learning about her illness, she is teased and taunted by the other kids at school. Find out how a new friend, with a similar diagnosis, proves that although they are not ordinary (like all the other fish) they sure can be EXTRAordinarily unique! Together they conquer their limitations and find new ways to race through the things they love to do.

CHRONICALLY Empowered

Amy Effenberger

Casey Stanley

Natalie Kelley

Jennifer Dawn

Keisha Greaves

Amy Gietzen

Sandra Hamilton

# I AM
# *Capable.*

**Stories of chronic illness warriors achieving exceptional heights.**

# Amy Effenberger

Las Vegas, NV, USA

**College Student**

"*You are a strong, determined human being who can accomplish anything you want to.*"

## About Amy:

*I'm Amy and I run the blog BowelBee (linked provided below). I created this blog in 2020 to help others like me. I hope to be that person that someone can turn to when they need some comfort. I absolutely love to pain and began creating pieces for people with chronic illnesses to relate to. I'm a 19-year-old college student who is just trying to do some good in the world. Talk to me about Harry Potter or Greys Anatomy and I'll be your best friend. Feel free to reach out to me anytime when you need someone to talk to. I absolutely love meeting anyone in the IBD or chronic illness community.*

\* \* \*

*IG: @bowelbee*

*Website: www.bowelbee.weebly.com*

I am Amy Effenberger. I am a college student. I am determined to graduate early, and despite my illness to still succeed. Currently, I am working towards a degree in biomedical science and will be graduating in Spring 2022. My future profession will be as an Emergency Medical Technician, but I would also like to continue my advocacy and raise awareness of Ulcerative Colitis. I was diagnosed with this disease in April 2018. Ulcerative Colitis (UC) is an autoimmune disease classified as Inflammatory Bowel Disease. Essentially it means that my immune system is attacking my large intestine. When this happens, ulcers form in the intestine and they start to bleed. This is why oftentimes, patients with this illness have blood in their stool.

While living with this illness, I have had to adapt in various different ways. The biggest difference is that I now have to follow a gluten-free diet. Gluten was found to be my main trigger food, the food that caused me to flare up. As a result, I cut it out of my diet and my health began improving immediately. This change is still something that I struggle with since it meant removing a ton of delicious food. Most gluten-free alternatives are not quite the same. However, I have been experimenting with new recipes in order to adapt.

When I was diagnosed, my disease wasn't as intense as others who have the same illness. I didn't need surgery. My disease wasn't severe. Though that doesn't make me any less of a Warrior. I didn't need surgery, but I spent months not knowing what was going on and a day in the emergency room. My disease wasn't severe, but any level of severity of the disease is difficult to deal with, even moderate.

If I could be doing anything in my life, I would be doing the same as I am now. Advocating. That's what I want to do for this disease and other chronic illnesses. Chronic means forever, so we should be forever advocating. I would also be working as an EMT already, but that is beside the point. The main point is that I would like to be doing more advocacy at the moment.

## "I am a warrior who is trying to help other warriors."

I was able to push through this time of my life. That is something I am proud of and love about myself. It can be a really difficult time for so many, as it was for me. I love that now, I can help others who are just starting to go through all of this. I am able to help them in their worst time because I know exactly what it feels like. I can tell them about the nights spent in the bathroom, I can tell them about the clenching of your stomach just to feel better. Because knowing that someone understands their pain, means everything to them. That is why I started my blog (BowelBee), to be that person for them.

I am a warrior who is trying to help other warriors. Despite my illness, I am able to live my life the way I want to. My advice for you is to remember that you are a strong, determined human being who can accomplish anything you want to. No one can take this from you. Embrace it. Embrace everything there is about it. You are capable and you are a warrior. You are a strong, determined human being who can accomplish anything you want to. Embrace your illness and rise even higher. We are determined.

We are warriors.

# Casey Stanley

Worcester, Worcestershire, UK

## Entrepreneur

*"Find a path where you can find the beauty in life."*

## About Casey:

*Life changes with such a condition as mine, and at times it feels like everything can seem to fall apart. It is hard to find the person you are. So hello, my name is Casey, and i am 22 years old. I love all things crime dramas, Harry Potter and Star Trek. I also have a life-changing condition called Fibromyalgia.*

\* \* \*

*IG: @auniquefibrolife @auniquefibromyalgialife*

*Facebook: @auniquefibromyalgialife*

*Website: www.auniquelife.co.uk/*

My name is Casey Stanley and I'm 22 years old. I used to be a Software Developer, creating websites and applications for companies. Unfortunately, my newfound career didn't last long. The symptoms from my chronic illness became too much. I couldn't physically drive to work or even get out of bed some days. I simply couldn't work any longer and had to hand in my notice. It was a very difficult time for me. I was fresh out of University and beginning a new chapter in my life. The world I had built up, my world, was simply crashing down around me. I had just started a brand-new career that had so much potential, but I couldn't work. I had a mortgage and bills to pay but couldn't just go out and get another job. It was difficult, but I was determined to make something out of myself. So, I decided to become self-employed. This way, my job worked around me instead of working me into the ground. I could actually work from the comfort of my bed and not spend hours driving every day. It was a way to prioritise my health, to get my symptoms under management. This is when my business, A Unique Life, was formed.

## "It's a struggle, trying to shift and adapt to your new normal."

I have a condition called Fibromyalgia. It results in widespread pain, fatigue, and a host of over 200 other symptoms. It's very difficult at the moment to perform daily tasks, such as showering or cooking food. I rely heavily on my family and loved ones to help me, as a lot of the time I am bed-bound. These limitations in physical capabilities really have an affect on your mental health. It's a struggle, trying to shift and adapt to your new normal. So while I was adapting and trying to come to terms with my illness, I decided to write a blog. It was quite therapeutic for me, and I loved connecting and helping others. Over time, I have found such a community online, and I really wanted to bring that into the streets. I wanted to bring awareness to a closer community, so I decided to start an online shop. Selling products helped to keep a roof over my head as well as brought that all-important awareness to my condition, as well as so many others. Growing my business was a great way to help me mentally, and helped keep my mind off my physical symptoms.

It's great that I managed to find something that I can do. It helps to have something to focus on, to feel like you're doing something. It's hard at times, and I really push myself. Sometimes I push myself a little too much and end up going into a flare. These are the things I need to work on though. That special balance between work, family, home life and rest. It's a struggle to get this balance right, even for those who aren't chronically ill. It really has helped with my mental health in the long run though. Being able to share my stories, connect with others and simply help them. Adapting to having a chronic illness is hard, it's a big learning curve, but it's something that needs to be worked on, little by little, every day. I'm glad that I have found something in my life that I feel like I can do. There are many creative people in our chronic illness community. They often sell their items on sites like Etsy. It's amazing to see all these small business and truly talented people. I often think about what I could be doing with my life. Creating a great career in the Computing field, or being a forensic scientist, something I always wanted as a child. The thing is, with what I'm doing now, I'm helping people. I don't know whether fate is real, but with everything that has happened in my life, I often think that maybe this is something I was supposed to do. Even if it isn't, it's something I can do. I can help people, share my story and spread awareness, all these opportunities have happened because of my illness. I am happy doing what I'm doing. It's a great job, and although I could think about what I could be doing, I might not be able to help people the way I do with this job. I may have ended up hating those careers. I will never know. The only thing I can do is focus on the present and what is happening now, and I'm happy with what I'm doing.

> **"People really don't realise the mental impact that chronic illness has on a person."**

# #morethanourillness

Many of us within the chronic illness community have a job that adapts to our illness, many are lucky enough to have sympathetic employers who help them to do their job. There are, however, many out there who are in the same boat that I was in. Many people in the chronic illness community struggle to hold down a job. They had a job, sometimes a career they've been in for years. It's hard enough to deal with all the symptoms, hospital appointments, and judgements from others. It's even harder when you are financially insecure. Many of us live from paycheck to paycheck. When our health affects our work, it's a very hard place to be in. It's another thing that adds to all the stress you're already experiencing in your life. It was hard for me to lose my job, my health, my friends. People often judge you - employers, doctors, family, friends, strangers. This is why I wanted to spend my time spreading activism. I want you all to know that I understand. Chronic illnesses result in losing a lot of things in life, but we need to find our strength.

As someone who went to University for a Computing degree, I decided I would make my own website, and subsequent shop. There are many people out there who are good at painting, drawing, making teddy bears, clothing, the list goes on. You need to know your strengths, to look inside and see what you want to do. See what you can do. It can be hard to do a lot of things, maybe there is something that gets your mind off the pain, something that calms you. Is it possible to make a business out of those strengths?

It may be hard to find what you want to do. A new direction in life. I know it's hard not to focus on what you have lost. I know it can be hard to look for the positives in life. But you can do it. People with chronic illnesses are strong. We go through so much everyday, things most people don't see, but that's why I know that if you relate to anything I have said so far, that you can get through it. Financial insecurity is horrible. It eats at you everyday, but life is worth it. You are worth it. You will get through this. Just take each day as it comes and you will be able to find something that not only helps you financially, but it will make you feel like you are doing something positive to help the world.

People really don't realise the mental impact that chronic illness has on a person. The constant pain, the constant brain fog, fatigue, IBS, TMJ, and a host of over 200 other symptoms are sometimes often separate. The mental impact of it all is very underrated. It's hard to understand how your life has changed so much. Most of the time, your brain is telling you one thing, while your body is telling you another. It's hard to adjust, getting frustrated at what you could do and what you can't do. It's an adjustment period. It's also a time of grief. It's not really talked about enough, but you often grieve the person you used to be and what your life used to be like. Depression is usually a major part of a chronic illness. It's hard to focus on a future when you feel like

you've lost so much. As I'm still adjusting seven years later, I really want to help those who are newly diagnosed. I never had anyone to help me all those years ago, and I want to be that person for people.

> ## "My life so far has been quite a struggle. I struggle everyday, but there is beauty in life."

Not only is it important to share awareness of invisible illnesses such as Fibromyalgia, I like to bring awareness to all types of chronic illnesses. I have t-shirts on my website not only focusing on the illness I have, but also more general ones around chronic illness awareness, migraine awareness and being a spoonie. I hope to expand my collection of t-shirts, to slowly include all types of chronic illnesses. At the moment, I have two projects on my business Instagram to spread awareness of other illnesses. My first project is called #morethanourillness, where I share the person behind their illness. Anyone with a chronic illness can take part. I share people's names, illness/es and then more about who they are as a person. Whether they like crime dramas or walks on the beach. We are all more than our chronic illness. We are people who have likes, dislikes and experiences. I hope this project helps to not only bring more awareness to the kind of people we are, but also helps to share the amazing accounts you can find. So whether you have Endometriosis, POTS, or Fibromyalgia, you can find a person you can connect with. Finding a person you can connect with is so important, so my second project is sharing the stories of others. Posting photos of people who have bought one of my t-shirts. I share their experiences with their illness, and anything they would like the world to know.

With everything seeming to fall apart, with how much your life changes with such a condition. It's hard to find the person you are. As I like to share the people behind the illness. It's important for those who have been recently diagnosed to find those things they love in life, the things they love about themselves. I am a big crime drama fan, having watched them for as long as I can remember. I am also a big Harry Potter and Star Trek fan. I feel like the things I love make me the person I am. I like that I'm not the same as everyone else. Hence the name of my website, A Unique Life. I like being unique, being a nerd or a geek. I love being different, liking things that others may not. It makes me, me. Everything that has happened to you, everything you watched as a kid, or still do now, makes you, you. It's a beautiful thing to be the person you are. If we were all the same, the world would be a very boring place.

My life so far has been quite a struggle. I struggle everyday, but there is beauty in life. I've been able to do something worthy. To fight for disability rights. To spread awareness of not only my condition, and that of thousands of other people around the world. I get to meet amazing people every single day. Talking to all of you about what you have been through. Helping anyone I can. I feel less alone being part of this community, and I hope anyone that becomes a part of it can feel that too. I hope my business expands. I hope there will be a day when people can park in the disability bay and not get judged by the way they look.

*I hope my t-shirts start conversations. Meaningful conversations about chronic illness, invisible illness and disability. I hope it can bring awareness to those who have never heard of these conditions. So if they ever come across anyone with a chronic illness, they have the understanding and compassion to make them feel comfortable. I also wish to help people who are newly diagnosed, to find a path where they can find the beauty in life. Don't forget that there is a light at the end of every tunnel.*

# Natalie Kelley

Portland, OR, USA

**Chronic Illness
Mindset Coach**

"*Acceptance is scary, but acceptance is beautiful at the same time.*"

## About Natalie:

*Natalie Kelley, the founder of Plenty and well, is a chronic illness mindset and lifestyle coach and host of the Plenty and Well Podcast based in Portland, Oregeon. After years of struggling, she was diagnosed with ulcerative colitis in 2017 at 21-years-old. She had begun her blog and brand a few years prior as a way to share about health and wellness, but after her diagnosis she changed paths to discuss life with chronic illness and provide support for others. After a life altering flareup in 2018 and a hospital stay, Natalie realized her purpose ran deeper than just sharing wisdom on social media. She obtained her holistic health coaching certification which led her to where she is now. She offers womxn with chronic illnesses 1:1 coaching as well as hosts her group program, The Path to Empowered Acceptance, which aims to help individuals find acceptance, confidence and joy on their journey through mindset tools and self-awareness.*

\* \* \*

*IG:* @plentyandwellwithnat

Sitting here, at my desk, running my own business, and loving every second... it's something my newly diagnosed self could never have believed.

I wouldn't have believed I would find acceptance and joy. I wouldn't have believed I would find my purpose and my calling because of my illness. I wouldn't have believed I would be able to, one day, live on my own while running my own business.

I wouldn't have believed that I did it. I started thriving despite the ways life tried to cut me down again and again and again. I did it.

I'm Natalie Kelley, CEO of Plenty and Well, founder of the Path to Empowered Acceptance program, and chronic illness mindset coach, and this is the story of how my ulcerative colitis diagnosis rocked my world, broke me to pieces, and forced me to rebuild myself.

## "My friend Parker was the victim of a random act of violence..."

Sometimes I think about the past five years of my life and my hands begin to shake. My heart beats faster. Tears spring to my eyes. Five years of grief and loss and heartache and turmoil. Five years of fighting and breaking and growing and learning. Five years of trying to calm the shaking hands, beating heart and watery eyes when I tell my story. And although this is a story of my chronic illness journey, my true 'story' begins before my diagnosis, on November 16th, 2014.

November 16th, 2014 flipped my world on its head. I can still remember it as if it was yesterday. Being woken up in my freshman year dorm by a call: "Natalie. He died." All I remember next is screaming "No no no no no" over and over and over. I ran to my resident advisor's room, pounding on the door, shaking uncontrollably, crumbling on the floor.

Dead. Died. Gone.

My friend Parker was the victim of a random act of violence on November 16th, 2014. Ripped from our lives too early for no reason. Taken by someone else's selfish actions. This was my first experience with grief and that grief tore me apart, still does at times. I tried to pick up the pieces, but the thing about grief is it always leaves you a little broken and beaten. Leaves you a little more weathered. Ages you a little quicker. Over the following months I tried to cover up the cracks in my heart – with drinking, with silence, with fake smiles, with control.

Control is how I mainly dealt with the feeling of complete disarray in my heart, brain, soul. Control – over my body, over my food, over my appearance. Maybe if I ate less or ran more it'd numb me just enough to not feel the ache. Slowly I slipped down, down, down. Trying harder and harder to numb the pain with my obsessive behaviors. Months of self-destruction passed, and I finally sought help – from friends, family, a counselor and a nutritionist. I began talking about my pain and healing my relationship with my body.

But as time went on, I started feeling sick. Very sick. My mind was getting healthier, yet my body was hurting – physically now, not just with the aches of grief. My memories from sophomore year to right before my senior year of college are riddled with moments of pain and confusion. Lying on the bathroom floor writhing in pain after a few sips of a beer in Ireland. Leaving sorority meetings and class early because of stomach pain. Racing home to use the bathroom in the middle of runs.

> **"The stomach pain, the bloat, the blood, the fatigue. But with graduation so close on the horizon and a colonoscopy already scheduled for that summer, I ignored it."**

Stomach pain was my version of normal, or so I thought. I thought I caused it. I thought my eating disorder had messed my insides up so much that they were simply getting back at me. Or perhaps my body was just transitioning from deprivation to normal amounts of food. Little did I know the biggest shock of my life was about to be handed to me. I finally realized it was time to get answers when I was traveling with my family in Europe in July of 2017. I had never felt so sick in my entire life and would end up curled on my bed, in our apartment, crying, by the end of most days.

I remember being half awake after my colonoscopy, munching on the post-procedure snack my mom had packed me and my doctor saying "you have ulcerative colitis" as if it was no big deal. It didn't register until I was in the car on the way home. I remember staring out the window thinking, "I have a disease. I am sick. I will always be sick." I had an incurable disease that would never go away.

I had known I had felt sick for quite some time. But feeling sick and being sick seemed so much different all of a sudden. I was about to enter my senior year of college, I was about to run a marathon, I was about to map out the rest of my life, yet I had just had my entire life flipped on its head once again.

For those first nine months after my diagnosis it was pretty smooth sailing. I managed to stick to the Specific Carbohydrate Diet even while in college. My friends, professors and bosses were all very accommodating and compassionate when I needed to change plans, miss class or leave work early when I felt sick. I successfully ran my first marathon. I kept up my good grades, I made memories with friends and I finished up my leadership positions within my sorority. It was almost as if I could just eat my special food, pop my pills and simply ignore ulcerative colitis.

That is, until it decided to give me a wakeup call. About two months before my college graduation my symptoms started coming back. The stomach pain, the bloat, the blood, the fatigue. But with graduation so close on the horizon and a colonoscopy already scheduled for that summer, I ignored it.

I wanted to soak up the last eight weeks of college with my best friends and squeeze every last ounce out of it. I didn't want to worry about doctors or new medications or more medications or an even stricter diet. I was 22 with my whole life ahead of me. I didn't want how sick I felt to become my reality, so I naively thought pushing it aside would be the answer. The week of graduation, after little sleep, high stress and a lot of running to cope with my emotions about graduating, I could tell things were getting worse. My family came to visit a few days before the ceremony and I could barely get up off of the couch; my fatigue was so severe. I tried to rally the best I could and join in on the fun, but each day felt like I was walking with legs that weighed ten times their actual weight.

"Maybe it's just the stress," I, once again, naively tried to convince myself.

## "But then it did get worse. Far worse."

Fast forward a few weeks of being home - my symptoms were still very present, but I kept pushing. I was studying for my personal training certification, dedicating all of my time to building my own business and, ultimately, trying to figure out how to transition to adulthood.

I was finally forced to slow down when I got a nasty cold that simply wouldn't let up. No amount of sleep, liquids or elderberry syrup was doing the trick. I remember the moment I felt it in my stomach. I was sitting by the lake trying to distract myself from how sick I felt, and it was like someone punched me in the gut. Out of the blue a solid, never-ending pain just struck. When I got home I told my mom, "I think I have the stomach flu," because I was still trying to pretend my ulcerative colitis wasn't getting worse.

But then it did get worse. Far worse. I woke up in the middle of the night a couple of days later with the most horrifyingly intense pain and nausea. I remember sobbing in a ball wishing I could just cut myself open and rip my insides out of my body. As the days turned into almost two weeks of being bedridden, unable to even drink water without writhing in horrific pain and crying, my mom finally rushed me to the ER. I was admitted into the hospital and after a colonoscopy we found out my mild ulcerative colitis had progressed to a severe case. My entire colon was inflamed and covered in ulcers. I remember being told the news and feeling like I would never get my life back.

I spent five long nights in the hospital, fighting to get better, fighting to keep hope, fighting to stay positive. But it was hard. Disheartening. Scary. Crying less than ten times a day was a success. Walking one lap around the hospital wing was a success. Brushing my hair was a success. Those five nights changed my life. They pushed my greatest limits and made me stronger than I could have ever imagined. They made me realize that I needed to embrace my diagnosis and I needed to change my lifestyle beyond simply what I was eating. I needed to respect my body more, rest more and realize that yes, I was sick, but I would be able to feel healthier if I changed my mindset about my sickness.

So, the moment I was let out of that hospital room I stopped avoiding my diagnosis and instead started speaking out about it. I shared my story, I got vulnerable and I began committing to my own healing, so I could help heal others.

## "There were moments in that hospital bed I thought I would never be where I am today..."

I always see that hospitalization as the starting point of the rest of my life. Five days that broke me, but also, finally, took the blindfold of denial off of my eyes. Five days that showed me that I was given this illness in order to find passion and purpose so I could help others. My program, Path to Empowered Acceptance, is the blueprint of the learning, growing and healing I did from the day I got out of the hospital. It's a blueprint for the acceptance, confidence and true optimism I was able to find.

Looking back at the years since being out of the hospital it makes me almost cry happy tears. There were moments in that hospital bed I thought I would never be where I am today - running my own business, helping other women with chronic illnesses and connecting with the most amazing chronic illness community on Instagram. Of course,

there are ups and downs, good days and bad days. There are days where the anxiety and fear still hit me and days where the grief over what I thought my life would be washes over me like a tidal wave. That grief is hard because it's so different from the grief I felt when I lost my friend Parker. It's grief, but grief over losing myself. Or what I thought I would be.

But if there's anything I've learned in the past years it's that I have to embrace the new me and my new future and I'm in a place where I know I truly have, and it's the most beautiful gift to share those lessons with others. There are ebbs and flows in this journey of mine and I've learned to take them as they come, because healing and acceptance are like a game of chutes and ladders - sometimes life and illness gets hard and you slide down a chute, but when you have mindset tools you can use, it's easier to climb back up the ladders of life once again. I've learned to soak up every second of the good moments and give myself grace during the hard ones. I've learned to stand up for myself, be my biggest advocate and put myself first.

## "If someone asked me if I would get rid of my diagnosis if given the option, I wouldn't."

Sometimes I just sit and think back over the past years of my life. It's a blur - of pain, tears, loss, grief and confusion. But it's also a blur of indescribable growth, change and self-discovery.

Each day I get to wake up and get to use my story to help other folks with chronic illnesses. I get to connect with chronic illness warriors around the world. I get to use the pain and grief I've endured to help heal others' pain and grief, even if just a little bit. I get to take my own healing journey and turn it into a program that helps others find acceptance, confidence and joy. And I couldn't be more grateful.

If someone asked me if I would get rid of my diagnosis if given the option, I wouldn't. I've thought about that a lot and I truly wouldn't change it for the world. I believe I was put on this path for a reason and if breaking and rebuilding myself is what I needed to do in order to build up the broken, then I'm grateful.

And sometimes I wish I could go back to my newly diagnosed self, wrought with grief and pain, yet completely unaware of the continual grief she would be faced with, and slip a little note under her door, but since I can't do that I'll tell you all what I would tell that past version of myself. Keep going, even when it feels impossible. Keep believing in your journey and your growth and your healing. Keep going and keep believing even when you crumble on the floor and cry. One day you'll find acceptance, but only after you finally realize you deserve acceptance. Acceptance of your illness, your new self, and this new life. Acceptance is scary, but acceptance is beautiful at the same time.

Acceptance is being able to find optimism while still validating your struggles. Acceptance is being able to advocate for yourself. Acceptance is feeling confident despite being different from others your age. Acceptance is freedom. And acceptance is for you. Acceptance is something to be proud of. And I am proud. Proud and joyful and passionate and always a little broken, but mostly proud. Proud of how I took my broken pieces and I built something beautiful in order to build others up. Proud to have built a business as I rebuilt myself and proud of the way my community has healed themselves just like I healed myself.

# Jennifer Dawn

Manitoba, Canada

## About Jennifer:

*Jennifer Dawn, 39 years old. Diagnosed at 32; years after advocating for myself to get onto disability. Being young and not looking ill I proved my Illness after hiring a 3rd party representative. Chronic pain doesnt define me. My smile, empathy, listening ear and laugh do.*

\* \* \*

**IG:**
*@Furbabyslove*

*Empath*

*"Don't suppress your feelings. Feel your them."*

My name is Jennifer Dawn. I first realized I was capable of learning differently at 14 years old when I had to become ambidextrous to write papers in school. You see, my chronic pain started in my right hand and I am right hand dominant. The pain moved from my right hand up into my shoulder then down into my lower back. With the compensating; my left hand, shoulder then knees and finally ankles all experienced the classic triggers of Fibromyalgia. The year I was no longer able to work because of the agonizing pain was the year I was finally diagnosed at age 32. I was determined to graduate from University after having to prove my symptoms. I had two Pain Doctors tell me, "You will just have to deal/live with this," but it was completely demeaning having the top in the specialty tell me that frustrating news.

## "I smile despite my pain..."

I wear yoga/exercise pants and I know how to use my pinkies to lower and pull up my pants before/after the washroom. Dry shampoo is a good friend. I wash my hair every four to five days waiting for a good day to be able to wash, dry and comb my long hair. My arms get fatigued in the shower so I use shampoo and conditioner at the same time. I do meal prep, that way when I have painful days I still have something to eat that is healthier than processed foods. The Gut Biome is important with Fibromyalgia. I R]recommend the elimination diet to figure out what foods and drinks trigger you. Exercise if and when you can. If something hurts, stop, and don't say I have to do three more reps. Also, use props to help modify and be able to do some yoga or light strength training. Practice Qi Gong, meditation and deep breathing. Don't suppress your feelings. Feel your feelings. If you need to cry, cry! Sometimes a nap helps too! I have told my GP I am laughing because it's better than crying. He then went and got me pain medication.

My smile, long hair and my empathy. I have been the mentor and I have been mentored. I smile despite my pain and I walk away from ignorant people that don't accept my chronic pain. It's wiser to walk away then fight with fools. You can't compare yourself to others. People experience pain differently and what works for someone might not work for you. Fibromyalgia is like a jigsaw puzzle; each piece is different. I have been the mentor and I have been mentored. The fibro fog you have to have a sense of humour to deal with it sometimes.

I am a Christian and my Faith helps me know that I am determined to live. Telling myself I am capable and that I will be healthy, helps me know that one day I will complete my long suffering and I have accepted that it might be in Heaven when that happens. I have HOPE tattooed to my wrist, that way every morning I wake up and know "Hold On Pain Ends."

Tacking horses and mucking out the stalls. The last time I brushed a horse I did one side then my hands were in agony. The owner said, "Well, come on, what about the other side?" Seeing my eyes, he knew to complete the grooming.

# Keisha Greaves

Cambridge, MA, USA

**Founder of Girls Chronically Rock**

_" If you want to do anything badly enough, you can."_

## About Keisha:

_Keisha Greaves, the founder of Girls Chronically Rock, has always been passionate about fashion. Born and raised in Cambridge, MA, Keisha has a bachelor's degree in Fashion Design and Merchandising and an MBA. At age 24, she was diagnosed with Limb-Girdle Muscular Dystrophy, and her life changed. Today, Keisha is a motivational speaker who talks about spreading awareness of Muscular Dystrophy, balancing life with chronic illnesses, raising money for causes, advocating for disability, and other related topics. Keisha has been featured in several media outlets like Good Morning America, The Today Show, ABC News, and more! One of her proudest moments is when she was featured in Today Style Heroes 2018. She was featured with other celebrities like Gabriella Union, Drew Barrymore, Debra Messing, Mindy Kaling, and more, for her inspired clothing line._

\* \* \*

_IG: @girlschronically_rock_

_Website: girlschronicallyrock.com_

## Living with LGMD

You'd be surprised what you take for granted. Those things you don't even think of but are naturally a part of life. Like now, in COVID times, when we aren't allowed to hug, or even see, our friends.

My feet were planted on the low-cut grass in the outfield, my usual spot. A girl from the opposing team took her stance to bat. She squatted and furrowed her brow with focus. When the pitcher released, her bat met the ball with a powerful smack. It whizzed far to a place where I knew I could reach it. I squinted my eyes and leapt towards the ball, making the best (and only) catch I'd gotten all season."OUT!" My fellow teammates cheered in excitement as I smiled from ear to ear. It was time for our turn at bat.

## "Having this job was a dream come true."

Afternoons in elementary school were spent this way, on the softball field swinging my bat and gleefully whizzing from base to base until I stole home. Stealing bases turned into stealing glances at crushes as I ran between floors for classes at my rather large high school. Before I knew it, I found my second home at Framingham State University where I spent my days in fashion and merchandising classes, sewing bold pieces for the runways (leather polka-dot blazer combos and tulle lined mini-dresses are some of my favorites), planning Fashion Club events and making tons of friends along the way, especially in Black Student Union. My nights were equally eventful as my girls and I got dressed up to

Beyonce blasting in the background and made our way to parties and events.

I loved to sew, modelling my designs for the likes of Kimora Lee Simmons and Betsey Johnson – my favorites. My admiration for Kimora came during the peak of the Baby Phat age. Her line was bejeweled and her clothing was embroidered with her signature Siamese cat logo – often in gold. I loved that she was a boss that had it all. She managed her business and clothing line and never tried to hide the fact that she was a mother. Betsey was the funky that I needed in my life. Her style was bold and unexpected. I adored her for her layered prints and the creativity that embodied her inner child. I'd always been recognized for my style, a casual yet chic mix, and in part, I owe it to those two. I adapted my looks in my own ways, oftentimes pairing a creative tee with a blazer or strutting around campus with an eye-popping dress, eighties-inspired dress, extra tulle with a dash of cheetah print. I was living my life on my terms and I was loving it. I was Keisha Greaves: agile, loving, creative daughter, sister and friend.

After college graduation, I found myself back in my home town of Cambridge, Massachusetts to earn my MBA. While in school, I put my bachelor's degree in Fashion Merchandising to work. I was an independent merchandiser for a company, travelling from store to store to ensure that brands were represented accurately in their respective places in department stores and boutiques. Having this job was a dream come true. It was something I loved to do, and the flexibility allowed me time to still make it to my classes and study for my second degree.

One day, I'd been walking around the

supermarket with my mother and sister. We'd been chatting and shopping, basking in the quality time of the necessary task, when out of nowhere I tumbled onto the floor. It took everyone by surprise, including myself. As I sat on the cold grocery ground, my legs had seemed to have left the rest of me. It felt like they'd betrayed me, and it seemed that the rest of my body was upset about it. It became dead weight. I couldn't lift myself. It was the most confusing experience I'd ever known. My mind told my limbs to do something that they just wouldn't do. I needed my mom and sister to help bring me to my feet.

I chalked it up to needing to lose weight and did my best to brush it off. I was sure

# "They both asked me the same: sit on the table and raise your leg. Both times, I couldn't."

that was the issue. Until it happened again, and again, and again. My legs felt weak and I was always on edge that I would be on the ground without warning or my consent. Then, my arms followed suit. I remember lifting my arms to reach for a snack in the kitchen cabinet. That feeling of perplexity and frustration from the grocery store returned as I struggled to make my hand meet the box. It happened again during my regular exercise time, too. I popped in my "Walk Away the Pounds" DVD. Following Leslie Sansone to step up, step down, slide, then – I couldn't reach. I couldn't understand it. I felt like I was fighting against a ton of weights pushing it back down. Something wasn't right. My mom

and I agreed that I should go see a doctor.

We made an appointment. And then another. They both asked me the same: sit on the table and raise your leg. Both times, I couldn't. I felt like something was wrong, but I still told myself that I just needed to lose weight, but the looks of concern on their faces as they helped to lift it up for me caused concern and worry. After seeing an orthopedist, I saw a neurologist and then the real work began: testing (and a lot of it!) The EMG required sticking a needle in my legs and moving them about the muscles to see how they react (and I had to do that one not once, but twice!). I was asked to keep still and calm as I was pushed into a tight tube for my MRI. The EKG had me hooked up to a bunch of pads and wires. The entire process was draining and uncomfortable, but the biggest test confirmed my diagnosis: the muscle biopsy. It was a surgery that I was wide awake for. On my back, in the cold operating room, they injected my leg with anesthesia. I made sure not to move as they sliced open my right leg and extracted a chunk of my muscle. It was weird to be awake during this time. If it hadn't hurt so much, I probably would have tried to reach out and touch the muscle sample as they prepared it for diagnostics. They closed everything up, gave me a pair of crutches and sent me on my way.

I thought I'd be going to class that evening, like usual, but the pain and grogginess of the surgery proved otherwise. I was bummed to have to share the process with my teacher; before I did, none of this seemed real. But it was certainly becoming all too real.

About a week later, I got a phone call that would change my life as I knew it. Dr.

Wang's voice was firm. She declared that I had muscular dystrophy; Limb-Girdle Muscular Dystrophy to be exact. The phone call lasted a couple of minutes. She'd share more about it when we met next in person.

I hung up and rushed to Google. I had to know what this was, what it meant, and

## "I began to shut everyone out – sinking into my new reality and the onslaught of feelings that came with it."

what on earth I would do. I learned that this particular type impacts the body from the shoulders down to the legs. I learned that most of the folks with MD are males and they usually are diagnosed as a baby or during adolescence. I learned that it's progressive and that there is no cure.

I was in a mix of disbelief and confusion."How long am I going to live?" I questioned."Will I have to be in a wheelchair?" I wondered. I shook my head "What if she's wrong? This can't be my life. It has to be something else," I finally decided.

I began to shut everyone out – sinking into my new reality and the onslaught of feelings that came with it. I was a very private person, keeping most things to myself and only displaying a bubbly personality with lots of laughter. I didn't feel much like laughing now, so I buried myself, away from most.

My immediate family were my support. I'd read that a healthy diet and exercise could help

keep my new situation at bay so my cousin and I joined Weight Watchers. I spent time with my mother and sister. My mom accompanied me to doctor's appointments. I made it to class, sometimes on my own, other times with a cane. I continued to work as a merchandiser, as long as I was able. I lost 36 pounds and I felt like I would be able to somehow conquer this thing!

I only realize now that I was still in denial about it for a few years after I received that phone call. I thought I could diet and exercise it away, ignoring the reality that it was a progressive and all-encompassing disease. Though I walked with a cane many days, whenever I had an important meeting or interview, I'd tell the manager I'd recently sprained my ankle or had gotten into a car accident. I never wanted to verbally acknowledge what was happening.

I confided in a close friend about what I was experiencing. He encouraged me to let the cat out of the bag. Hesitantly, I opened up my laptop and just started spilling out my thoughts onto a page. It wasn't until I was stroking the keys non-stop, that the truth finally set in my heart.

"Wow, I have muscular dystrophy," I thought. Then, I said it to myself. I have muscular dystrophy. It was like a weight was lifted from my mind. I read what I wrote back to myself and with the new acceptance of truth, I thought maybe it was time to share it with the world.".... I told my employer just last year that I had MD and am waiting on a response. It took a weight off my shoulder to be honest with my boss. I feel so relieved. My condition has progressed since then. I am regularly tired, need the use of a cane, still have issues walking and not getting tired and occasionally need a wheelchair. You don't know how it feels until it happens to you. I often feel like it controls my life...."

I posted it on my Tumblr page and shared the post on Facebook where all my friends, family and acquaintances would learn about the secret that I'd been holding onto for years. They read my post and supported me with tons of positive feedback and "thank you" for finally sharing my experience.

It felt warm. My family – my blood relatives and my Facebook family – continued to be a light and checked on me as the symptoms progressed. It was really nice, but after a while, I started to feel like they really didn't get it. They didn't know what it was like to fall constantly or not be certain if you can even move day by day. They didn't realize that I had to call ahead to go to the club at night, to ensure that they had a functioning elevator so that I could make my way up to groove to the music.

I started reaching out to others in the disabilities community via social media and began cultivating a new sense of family. Others who "got it." It felt like I was finally understood and even better, that I was not alone.

Now, five years later, I only know that I have LGMD. The doctors can't put their fingers on what subtype yet, but they know that at some point this thing could affect my heart. Echo-cardiogram tests are pretty regular for me, to let them know that my heart is still in working order. It's certainly scary but it has become "my normal."

Living with LGMD is still new to me. Every day, I wake up not knowing how my legs are going to feel or if I'll feel them at all. I don't know what pain I'll have as I try to leave my apartment. I walk gingerly, hoping not to fall, afraid that I won't be able to pick myself back up. It's made me realize my internal strength despite the weakening of my limbs. I didn't think that I would have so much strength to continue on after my diagnosis in my early twenties, but I somehow figured it out – and flipped it into a motivating organization. I have the power of resilience and positivity. If I didn't have it before, I developed a strong sense of empathy, really understanding that people everywhere struggle with things that the outside world cannot see. I am one of them.

I look back and feel like I took things for granted: stealing bases on the softball field, running up and down the stairs with friends in high school, sewing my one-of-a-kind designs to strut around in and dress my models. But there's no way I could have known. My new normal doesn't include any of that. Instead, it includes a lot of time with my Personal Care Assistant (PCA) who helps me get in and out of bed, the shower and around town. It includes plenty of trips to the doctor and physical therapy. And sometimes, lots of stares from people wondering what a young millennial is doing walking around town with a limp and a cane.

That's all okay. My new life is my life. I've accepted my new normal. I've regained my bubbly personality and have become a source of positivity and support for others in the disabled and diseased community through my organization and clothing line, Girls Chronically Rock. My smile has returned, knowing that I am still fulfilling my dreams. My path looks a little different than I envisioned but I am happy. I still hang out with friends at bars and restaurants and enjoy my favorite foods and reality TV. I have no problem belting out my favorite Beyoncé songs. I am a business owner who loves the work that I do. I'm happy. I'm loved. I'm whole. I won't take where I've come from for granted. Not one bit!

There's no cure or pill that will fix it. My MD isn't going anywhere. It has its way of controlling some of my life, but it isn't who I am. I'm still Keisha Greaves: loving, creative daughter, sister and friend. I've even gained a few more titles: graduate, survivor, entrepreneur, speaker and advocate. This didn't take my life, it gave me purpose behind all that I do. Pressing on after my diagnosis is the hardest thing I've ever done, but I'm much stronger for doing it. My will and support of my family keeps me going.

In a way, I guess that's how everyone is experiencing life right about now. As of the time that I'm writing this, no cure or vaccine for COVID has been created and when I flip between the news stations, it seems that it isn't going anywhere anytime soon either. It does, similarly, have its way of controlling our lives – mandatory stay-at-home orders, masks and other protective equipment, forced distance between family and friends, and then some. Post-pandemic, we'll all have gained some new talents, skills and titles – becoming a little bit more survivor and superhero. My advice is to allow it to give you purpose, and set your true priorities into perspective. This might be the hardest thing we have ever done, collectively, but how we support each other is what will keep us going.

*I want to remind you to never underestimate the power of your desire. If you want to do anything badly enough, you can. Everyday, I ask myself "How do I decide I want to live?" My PCA helps me from my bed, gets me ready for the day then I conquer it, with a smile. That's how I choose to live now, each and every day.*

# Amy Gietzen

Buffalo, NY, USA

**Professional Scleroderma patient, Patient Advocate and Public Speaker.**

*"Trust your instincts and never give up!"*

## About Amy:

*Amy Gietzen was born and raised in Buffalo, New York. Amy is both a scleroderma patient and Patient Advocate, who's mission includes the raising of awareness of Scleroderma on many levels. Amy's diagnosis came at an early age of just 19 years old. Her journey followed many twists and turns. Realizing her needs as well as young adults living with scleroderma might be different, she started to advocate for young adults and travel to various colleges and hospitals, support groups and conferences to speak about her journey and educate clinicians. In 2016 Amy created a virtual outlet for patients to connects, with The Scleroderma SuperStarz on Inspire and continues to provide support through her virtual meet ups called SYNC and through her work with SPIN (Scleroderma Patient-Centered Intervention Network) and The Steffen's Foundation, based out of Albany NY. In 2020 Amy was a recipient of National Volunteer of the Year award from the Scleroderma Foundation, and The Ernst DuPont Award from The Steffens Foundation.*

\* \* \*

*IG: @sclerostarz*

*FB: @StayingAlivewithScleroderma*

Hi my name is Amy Gietzen and I am from Buffalo, New York. I am a Patient Advocate for the Scleroderma National Foundation. I also run a Virtual Support Group for young adult patients called SYNC ( Scleroderma Young Adults Needing Connection). I am a Public Speaker and sit on various boards to help the scleroderma community educate and spread awareness. I have a rare, chronic, autoimmune disease called Scleroderma. Scleroderma is a progressive disease that affects your skin, connective tissue, and internal organs. It happens when your immune system causes your body to make too much of the protein collagen, an important part of your skin.

As a result, your skin gets thick, hard and tight, and scars can form on your lungs, heart, and kidneys. Your blood vessels may thicken and stop working the way they should. This leads to tissue damage and various other symptoms that can lead to death. There is no known cause or cure for scleroderma. Scleroderma isn't contagious or infectious, meaning you can't get it from other people.

> **"Of course I was hoping that all of these tests would come back completely fine and my diagnosis would just be a big mistake!"**

I have spent the majority of my adult life SICK. When I say sick I am not speaking about a common cold or even appendicitis.

My last year as a teenager was when I was diagnosed with Systemic Scleroderma.

Being told as a late teen that you have a debilitating, most likely terminal illness that has no known origin or cure was more than a shock. It was like I was pushed in front of a moving train. Following my initial diagnosis, I had a series of tests and procedures. It started with routine blood work and a chest x-ray. The blood work was to check to be 100% sure that I indeed have Scleroderma. You would think that they would have done this blood work prior to telling me I had this rare, crippling disease but hey I'm not the person with the MD, so what do I know. They do a blood test to check your ANA. ANA stands for Antinuclear Antibodies. 95% of patients with Scleroderma have elevated ANA levels in their bloodstream. I was also told I need to do a PFT (Pulmonary Function Test) and a chest X-ray. Those two tests check your lung function and they check to see if there's any scarring on the lungs or Pulmonary Fibrosis yet. Lastly I had to have a Barium Swallow test done. This test is to check your esophagus and mouth and also to evaluate your ability to swallow in different physical positions.

Of course I was hoping that all of these tests would come back completely fine and my diagnosis would just be a big mistake! Unfortunately for me that did not happen in the slightest. My ANA was positive with high levels, my PFT was abnormal for a woman my age and my chest x-ray showed the start of scarring around the outer edges of both of my lungs! All bets were off and it was 100% true, I had Systemic Scleroderma and there was nothing I could do to make it disappear."How could this be happening?" I was a healthy, active, young woman."What did I do wrong to develop this disease?" Those questions and about a hundred more would race through my mind on a daily basis. I could not go on with my life living in the dark. I wanted some answers!

About a month after my diagnosis I hit the books hard! I wanted/needed to know everything I could about this disease that by now was affecting my skin on my face, my hands and fingers, my lungs, my throat and how I swallowed and ate food. I wasn't going to just let this disease take me for a wild ride. If I was going to be living with Scleroderma I most certainly wanted to be in the driver's seat controlling the speed and direction of this disease and how it would ultimately affect me both emotionally and physically.

## "I had literally found the medical jackpot."

There was absolutely not a thing regarding Scleroderma and how it is treated on the internet! The most I could find was about 2 sentences basically stating that Scleroderma was a very rare disease that means "hard skin" and is mostly found in women in their late 40's and is terminal."Wow" I could not believe my eyes. I could not find anything. No treatment options, no research, not even a clinic locally that I could go to for treatment. This went on for about one week. I was determined to find something, or anything factual about Scleroderma, most importantly I needed to find somewhere in the US where they treated this disease and could help me, because locally I could not find a single soul that could even spell it correctly let alone

prescribe me medications and order tests. My current doctor was good, but he only saw elderly women with Scleroderma and his way of treating this disease was to treat me symptomatically. Don't get me wrong, that is a great way to treat patients, however I was a 20 year old woman by then and I wanted to STOP progression, not just be treated when I had a symptom.

By the end of the seventh day of my failed attempt at research. I was ready to give up entirely. Then I came across a hospital located in Pittsburgh, Pennsylvania. At this hospital was a doctor who specifically specialized in Scleroderma and had done Scleroderma research for over 40 years! I had literally found the medical jackpot. Let's just say after that, the rest is history.

Fast forward about 15 years later, I am still going to see that doctor I found in Pittsburgh and I am still researching and learning about Scleroderma and what I can do as a patient to have the best quality of life possible. 16 years total is a long time to be living with Systemic Scleroderma and as crazy as it may sound, I consider myself pretty lucky to have made it this far."Why you ask?" Scleroderma can very well be a deadly disease. I have limited hand, fingers and wrist motion, arthritis and stiffness daily, difficulty walking, bending, kneeling and for the most part moving. I also have Pulmonary Fibrosis, heart palpitations, dry eye and mouth, acid reflux, GERD, CREST, and Raynaud's Phenomenon. But I still, most definitely consider myself lucky. For starters, it definitely could and may very well be much much worse, symptom-wise, and to be frank, I could not even be alive right now to be writing this for all of you to read.

## "Although I am faced with obstacles daily that try to break my spirit. I will not let this disease dictate my life path and the stops I make on the way."

I have found with this disease you have to take the good with the bad and a positive attitude and outlook on your life goes a long way. I can't change what has become my life or go back and erase being diagnosed with Scleroderma and honestly I really don't think if I had the opportunity to I would! I have learned so much about myself, that had I not been diagnosed with this disease, I don't think I would have ever known. I have met some truly amazing and inspiring men, women and children over the years, whose lives have touched mine and have forever changed my heart. I have been afforded some incredible opportunities to travel and advocate about this disease and to me, being able to share my passion for educating and raising awareness about Scleroderma, has really changed and shaped me into the strong, capable, passionate person I am today.

For those of you reading this who are newly diagnosed and scared out of your mind, who are alone and struggling to live in constant pain and have no support system. Or even for those of you who are 100% healthy and are just reading this article to pass the time. We all are given moments in our lives when we have a choice to make, a choice that can change our lives for the better or worse. Most of us will choose life for the better. Living my life with Scleroderma wasn't a choice I got to make and it most certainly was not the kind of choice that you would think would change your life for the better, but in my case that is exactly what happened.

Scleroderma had exposed all of my insecurities and my weaknesses and forced me to face my mortality. Scleroderma has given me a new outlook on my life and taught me to savor the time and the people in my life that I love and care about and to live in the now. Although I am faced with obstacles daily that try to break my spirit. I will not let this disease dictate my life path and the stops I make on the way. I just might have to take a few more stops than I would have liked to but life is all about rolling with the punches and making the most out of the life you are given, and that is just what I intend to do and a hell of a lot more!

My one token bit of advice for others living with this disease, is to listen to your body and don't accept no for an answer. Too many times doctors have told me that I don't know what I'm talking about or that there is nothing they can do. If I just accepted my fate and didn't try to find other avenues of treatment, I'd be dead by now! Trust your instincts and never give up!

# Sandra Hamilton

Stanmore Middx, UK

## About Sandra:

*Fighting a battle with relapsing Non Hodgkins Follicular lymphoma since 2007. Passionate that no-one suffers needlessly with wasted chemotherapies. I started Cure Cancer at UCL Cancer Institute to help find a cure for terminal cancers and personalized treatments. Our charity buys and installs the latest research equipment for UCL Cancer Institute.*

\* \* \*

*IG: @curecancer_at_ucl*

## CEO of Sandalex Investments Ltd. & Founder of Cure Cancer at UCL Cancer Institute

*"Take my hand... follow me through my stem cell cancer journey to give hope and clarification to others..."*

My name is Mrs. Sandra Hamilton, CEO of Sandalex Investments Ltd. (a Property Developer Management Company), and founder of Cure Cancer at UCL Cancer Institute - Aesthetician.

I was diagnosed with Non-Hodgkin's Follicular Lymphatic Lymphoma in 2007. Being told that you have cancer is both shocking and terrifying. The treatments that were available were painful courses of different chemotherapies and if everything failed, there was stem-cell therapy.

## "Having tried all the existing treatments, sadly the outlook for me was bleak."

NHL: Follicular Lymphatic Lymphoma is a cancer of the lymphatic system. Follicular lymphoma develops when the body makes abnormal B lymphocytes. These lymphocytes are a type of white blood cell that normally helps us fight infections. Each year in the UK 15,000 people are diagnosed with NHL and 6000 will die within 12 months of being told . In the under 30's age group, it is the second most common cancer behind Leukaemia. This cancer is sometimes containable but not curable. Having undergone different chemotherapy treatments almost every 6 months since 2007 my body craves sleep almost 12 hours a night. Just going for a walk can leave me exhausted. I worry more about the impact on my family as they can only watch.

In 2011, Cure Cancer at UCL Cancer Institute was born, and I have been tirelessly fundraising for the cancer institute situated in the Paul O'Gorman Centre ever since. Our ethos is that 100% of the money raised at our events goes towards the purchase and installation of medical research equipment to the institute.

Winning the 2012 Community Hero Award was a proud moment, and a chance for me to reflect on all that has been achieved since my diagnosis.

Having tried all the existing treatments, sadly the outlook for me was bleak. So back in 2015, I had to have stem-cell therapy at UCLH. Without the funding for new research in order to develop new drugs, thousands of people like me will soon run out of options.

## "I try to be myself and some say I am an absolute trooper soldiering through with a smile on my face despite it all."

Raising money whilst undergoing chemotherapy and radiation treatments and trying to run two businesses has not been easy. In this tough economic climate, it is so difficult to ask people to dig deep and to part with their hard-earned cash. But I am lucky to have the phenomenal and unrelenting support of my family and friends.

In January 2015, I started a six month journey to undergo high dose chemotherapy with Rituximab and stem cell therapy in the HCA facility at University College London Hospital. Thankfully due to the machinery that supporters of Cure Cancer have helped install at the UCL Cancer Institute, I was able to have a much more targeted and specific treatment!

## "My strength of character is not just to roll over and give up."

I try to be myself and some say I am an absolute trooper soldiering through with a smile on my face despite it all. I send everyone my best wishes and thanks to all they have done to support, and help me and the charity. I am always thinking of how I can assist the charity, and look to see if something positive can be gained from my experience and make the process worthwhile. I decided that the best way to do this was to have my treatment documented. This is to highlight the realities of this cancer treatment and its effects for future patients and their families so that they can gain a better understanding of what to expect. The documentary highlights the basic and clinical research that goes on at both UCL and UCLH and will provide a useful public information resource. In our desire to complete this documentary, Sassy films came on board to film my journey. I

and the charity as a whole wish to thank Sassy Films for all their assistance and support.

If I had to choose one thing that I love about myself despite my illness it would be my tenacity. My strength of character is not just to roll over and give up. My stubbornness, when told you have 3 months to live, to endure.

With knowledge comes understanding and lessens the fear of the unknown. Thinking about life outside of my illness, if I could be doing anything in my life, it would be travelling the world, and at the same time looking for an entrepreneur to donate an empty property so I can have sustainable income for the researchers at UCL Cancer Institute.

*If you are reading this, and worried or uneasy about the future before you, whilst everyone handles the news YOU have cancer [or any diagnosis], differently. Take a breath, reevaluate your life, make the most of your time left and go to your grave saying "I tried."*

*Take my hand... follow me through my stem cell cancer journey to give hope and clarification to others.*

Rachel Sitro

Nikky Box

Rea Strawhill

Kiara Dijkstra

Lauren Jayne

Francessca Prado

Dianna Carney

# I AM
## *Worthy.*

**Stories of chronic illness warriors learning about their worth.**

# Rachel Sitro

Weehawken, NJ, USA

## About Rachel:

Rachel is a 27 year old who was diagnosed with moderate-severe Crohn's Disease at the age of 23. She is passionate about helping others with chronic illnesses and in her spare time finds joy in baking healthy treats.

\* \* \*

*IG:* @Rachelpalumbo3

*Customer Service Manager*

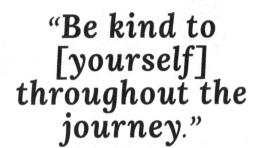

## "Be kind to [yourself] throughout the journey."

My name is Rachel. I am 27 and suffer from Crohn's disease. I was diagnosed at the age of 23. For those who don't know what Crohn's disease is, it is an incurable chronic illness that affects your intestines/gut which affects you in other aspects as well, these include skin issues, fatigue, emotional well-being, etc. My illness affects me daily. I am always thinking and planning out every "normal"' daily task. I am always thinking of the times I can eat, how to plan out leaving the house, where the bathrooms are at every store, and if I am going to be able to have access to my "safe" foods when out and about. I previously was employed working remotely (due to my illness) as an Account Executive for an organic tanning brand, but before the pandemic hit I unfortunately lost my job. I am currently finding it difficult to find a job that caters to my illness and needs.

> ## "As the years went on with my illness, I have learned how to speak to people about my needs and advocate for myself if I need rest or am unable to go somewhere or do certain things."

As the years went on with my illness, I have learned how to speak to people about my needs and advocate for myself if I need rest or am unable to go somewhere or do certain things. Recently, after failing 3 biologics in 4 years I needed surgery. This has taught me about resilience and how to continue to persevere with my illness despite feeling weak, because with a chronic illness there is no giving up. Every day is a fight, and it's a fight that most people do not see. Continuing to have courage and strength to move forward every day is something that I've learned. Despite my illness, I love that I am empathetic of others, especially those fighting battles with disease, and those that continue to be strong while most people do not understand their battles. In my life, I hope to have a family one day. I hope to teach my children to be strong and empathetic to others and I hope that they in return will be empathetic to me and my daily battle. I hope to do more for others with chronic illnesses and I hope to teach others fighting similar battles to never give up hope, and to continue to stick up for yourself even when you feel like others do not understand, and to always move forward with strength.

It is not easy and the battle is never over, but I hope that others will be kind to themselves throughout the journey.

# Nikky Box

London, England

## CEO of Innabox Ltd & Illustrator

"*Each day I try to put a little bit of light into the world that may help somebody who is suffering.*"

## About Nikky:

*My name is Nikky, and I'm a 33-year-old illustrator from London. Symptoms of bloating and pelvic pain started in my teens. 14 years later, I received my Endometriosis diagnosis. I run a small business, Innabox @ innaboxdesign from home with my two cats, where I share my third story through my art. I want to empower and help others while raising awareness for chronic pain and conditions. Let's turn our pain into power!*

\* \* \*

**IG:** *@innaboxdesign*

My Name is Nikky Box and I'm an illustrator and small business owner (Innabox) from London. My first official diagnosis was of a chronic UTI in November 2018. I then went on to receive a heavy diagnosis which dramatically changed my life: Severe Endometriosis.

I am a young woman at just 32 years old, yet I have battled and struggled with my conditions throughout the 'best years' of my life. You don't get your 20's and 30's back, so to think of what has been taken from me is devastating. Endometriosis and my chronic UTI affect my life in every way possible. Relationships, sex life, friendships, my career, my home, my confidence... Everything. Watching others live their life to the fullest, whilst you are left in the background hurts.

Chronic UTI's are not widely heard of. In fact, there aren't many doctors/professors to treat the condition at all. I was lucky enough to come across Professor James Malone Lee who has written the book 'Cystitis Unmasked.' He challenges the ideology of the IC diagnosis and has vastly opened many people's eyes to embedded infections. As a sufferer of this awful condition, I cried happy tears when I met the professor. I couldn't believe that my excruciating pelvic, vaginal, and bladder pain possibly had an end to it. However, once I discovered I also had stage 4 endometriosis, this added additional complications but also provided me with answers to more of my widespread pain. I do not miss the days before treatment started (I am currently 2 years in) where I was screaming on the toilet in agony

*"Before my diagnosis, I always tried to keep up with your general abled-person, with all of their energy and accomplishments. I couldn't understand why for a very long time, I was not able to do the same as them."*

with tears running down my face and blood trickling down my legs.

Chronic illness is like a jigsaw puzzle, you keep trying to put all of the pieces together until collectively, you have your answers. Having tons of symptoms can make things extremely complicated and feel like you are never going to get a diagnosis or help. Through my own research and 14 years of pain, I decided to seek an endometriosis specialist. He diagnosed me within ten minutes of my consultation with him and I can honestly say that it was one of the worst days of my life. Although I had suffered for an unacceptable amount of time, I wasn't ready to hear that I had a severe illness that was sticking around for life. I was unaware that endometriosis could cause the amount of damage that it has done to my body and millions of other women/people. How could I be facing a bowel resection and a possible stoma bag? I was in pure shock.

Before my diagnosis, I always tried to

keep up with your general abled-person, with all of their energy and accomplishments. I couldn't understand why for a very long time, I was not able to do the same as them. It's truly hard without a diagnosis to limit yourself and understand that you deserve to rest. I often fell into the category of lazy or unfit. Or that's how I felt. I decided to work part time after past full time jobs seemed impossible for me to keep up with, but I still found myself struggling and fainting at work. After some self reflection and big changes in my personal life at the time, I decided I would try doing what I had always loved, designing! I had no clue where to start but look at me now! Running my own business has given me freedom to work the hours I am capable of, under my own roof. Well, my parent's roof! I don't think I would have survived anywhere but home due to my millions of toilet breaks per day!

## "Yes my illness is invisible, but if you look really closely you will notice that those little imperfections are all part of my conditions."

Let's talk about mental health for a second. The embarrassment of running to find toilets when I'm out with friends so that I don't poop myself. The grief I felt when I was diagnosed or the fact I can't carry out activities that I used to do easily anymore. The intrusive thoughts and much more that we face on our worst days can ruin us if we let them. I was crushed when receiving my endometriosis diagnosis and my health declined mass amounts due to the state of my mental health. It's so important to find ways of coping and making sure that self care is a priority in my life. I have learned that I must come first. Putting other people first is a thing of the past as I simply just do not have the energy. Being in pain every day is something you can't imagine if you haven't experienced it. The tears, the rolling around on the floor, all of the "fucks" and "shits," kicks and punches to furniture, and more just to get through. It can put you in a very dark place.

I have overcome a lot of confidence issues and anxieties along my chronic illness journey and one thing I do love about myself is my resilience. Despite the hard times, the daily fight with my health, I still manage to run a business, maintain a relationship, help others on their own journeys and just keep bloody going each day! I have always been a fighter, I don't give up easily and I am stubborn as hell. In this circumstance, it seems to have helped me! I am extremely empathetic so everything has fallen into place for me recently regarding my path in life. I find my work brings comfort to others also going through similar situations and being able to help others by telling my own story just feels right to me. I turned my pain into power!

I used to be a very shy girl, with little to no confidence or self worth. If anything, chronic illness has shown me what I am made of. I have actually gained more self confidence from sharing my experience with chronic pain and building up a thriving small business through the pain. I no longer have to play hide and seek. Hide from the world and try to fit in whilst seeking approval from everyone. It was exhausting and I am exhausted enough!

My appearance has always been important to me, like it is for most women, but it took me a very long time to embrace my endo belly, fluctuating weight and pimple prone skin. I would get caught up worrying over every aspect of how I looked until I actually understood it. Yes my illness is invisible, but if you look really closely you will notice that those little imperfections are all part of my conditions. To me, it's just another part of my story to tell now and nothing to be ashamed of. For many years I thought my endo belly was down to bloating from my misdiagnosis of IBS. My skin and weight must have been my fault for what I was eating and nothing to do with hormones at all! Not everything is within our control and I think it's important to remember that. We can do everything right as chronically ill people and still end up in some kind of flare.

I am so happy that I get to do what I love every day. Creativity flows through me and is my self care. It nourishes my soul and I would be lost without it! It's my outlet and I am proud to say that I actually wouldn't see my life much differently in terms of what I am achieving with my business, but I am working on manifesting my own home with a dream studio to work from and more life adventures. I potentially could take my business anywhere... Who knows, maybe in the future I will be travelling the world! I wouldn't rule it out. I know I am capable of healing and getting to that place, or at least back to a place where I could manage my illness easier. If I managed to walk 100 miles in 5 days once along the Camino de Santiago in Spain, I can do it again! But one step at a time; I have a pretty big surgery ahead of me yet!

Each day I try to put a little bit of light into the world that may help somebody who is suffering. I love to zone out drawing on my iPad Pro and it means the world to me that people can relate to my work or feel seen through it. I know from my own battle that the worst feeling in the world is being totally misunderstood and feeling alone. Having someone to talk to can really make a difference so I try to provide that starting point for people to open up a conversation about the condition I may be drawing about. This year alone I have helped a couple of my friends also get their endo diagnosis!

For anyone reading this who relates to my story, my advice to you would be to trust yourself. You know your body and you know when something isn't right. Never give up, this is your life and you deserve to be living it, not simply existing. I feel like there are a lot of gaps in the system that need filling, so take your research to your doctor and educate them!

# Rea Strawhill

Vienna, Austria, Europe

**Online Content Creator**

*"No matter what happens in life, never forget that you are loved, appreciated and worthy as you are."*

## About Rea:

*Hi! I am Rea, and I have ME/CFS. My illness, also known as Chronic Fatigue Syndrome, started after an infection with mononucleosis when I was 18. I struggled with my health for years, but no doctor could explain what was wrong with me until I got my diagnosis almost 8 years later. All of my experiences motivated me to become an advocate for myself and for others and to raise awareness for this severely misunderstood illness. Along my journey, I realized that there are so many stereotypes out there about illness and disability that are not true! Since then, it has become my mission to provide information about these misconceptions and crush some these false stereotypes! It would be a pleasure if you would follow me along on this journey.*

\* \* \*

*IG: @rea.strawhill*

*Website: www.reastrawhill.com*

## How I Regained My Confidence After I LostMy Health

I am Rea, a seemingly normal 27 year old Austrian woman, and today I am telling you my story. I was born in 1993 in upper Austria, I was always a good student and I loved music and theatre. I lived a relatively normal life, but in 2011 my life changed forever. I graduated from high school, entered university and I also became very sick with mononucleosis. So far, none of these things seem particularly life-changing. Many young people graduate from high school and go to university, and many young people experience mono at some point in their lives. But in my case, it was different, because the illness never really went away. And I would struggle for years, not knowing what was wrong with me. Until I stumbled upon my diagnosis seven years later, in 2018.

I will never forget the day when I read about "Chronic Fatigue Syndrome" for the first time. I was sitting on the couch and I was just scrolling through Instagram. I was looking through the stories of an Austrian newspaper when a headline caught my attention."Chronic Fatigue Syndrome: When Exhaustion Becomes Permanent."

I suddenly felt a cold chill. I clicked the article and I felt as if a stranger had described my whole life experience.

At that time, I was going through the most difficult time I had ever experienced before, and I had no idea what was happening. I was a teacher at that time in a middle school in Vienna. In that year, I became the head teacher of a new first class and I was thrilled. The moment I met these kids, I took them into my heart. I was so happy to be a part of their lives and I was thrilled for all the things that we would learn together. I was happy in my career and looking forward to the following years. But there was one thing wrong with me that I couldn't quite figure out: I was getting sick all the time. And I was constantly exhausted and tired for seemingly no reason.

Back when I started University, I wasn't feeling great, but it was also not that bad. I had a part-time job, which was very flexible, and I organized my days in a way so that I could get enough rest, without really consciously knowing that I did that. But I got sick a lot, and I felt exhausted very easily. I felt like something wasn't quite right. I went to see doctors, and the only solution that was found: allergies. I got treated for my allergies, but it didn't really help. Apparently, nothing else was wrong with me, so I tried to eat healthy, get enough exercise and keep going.

Then I started my job as a middle school teacher. In my first year, I was getting one flu after the other."That is normal in the first year, your immune system is getting used to being in contact with children all the time" or "You are just getting used to this new routine, your body will get used to it," are the things that people explained to me. I often went to see my doctor because I needed sick leave, explaining to them that I constantly felt fatigued, I had sleeping disorders and

I just couldn't get rid of this sore throat, and I was starting to get worried. "You are very stressed. Try this antidepressant" - and I did. But nothing got better. Every day I had to fight to even make it out of bed. At some point, I went to see a psychiatrist to treat my sleeping disorder, and I started psychotherapy.

The years went by, but my problems didn't get better. I waited and waited, but my body didn't get used to this environment and routine. I still caught one flu after the other and my fatigue was just numbing. My days practically consisted of working, eating and sleeping. I had no more energy for anything else.

It went on like this for a while, until 2018, when I got hit by two infections right after the other, and my body just collapsed. I had no more energy. I had so many symptoms that nobody could explain. I constantly felt feverish and dizzy, I was in pain, the fatigue was unbearable and I just couldn't get better anymore. But according to my GP there was nothing medically wrong with me.

I was in so much despair. No doctor had any answers, apart from "You're probably stressed." People assumed that I must hate going to work, or that I was looking for a way out, when the opposite was true. I wished for nothing more than going back to work, to be there for these kids I felt responsible for and do my job that I loved so much. I felt extremely misunderstood, like nobody really listened to what I had to say. And then I read the article. I didn't want to accept it at first. The illness that was described in the article sounded horrifying, and they mentioned that there was no cure. I didn't want that. I preferred to listen to my psychiatrist, who told me that after a few weeks of antidepressants I would be fine again, and able to go back to work. That sounded much better than what was described in that article!

But weeks went by and nothing got better, and I couldn't get that article out of my head. I read it again and finally contacted the doctor that was mentioned, a specialist with lots of experience with Chronic Fatigue Syndrome. So, I made an appointment. "It's probably not that, but it doesn't hurt to rule it out," I thought.

A few weeks and a bunch of tests later, and I had my diagnosis. What I had was not depression. It was ME/CFS.

The diagnosis hit me hard at first. I felt as if I had lost everything. But there was also a feeling of relief: I finally knew what was wrong with me. After years of being belittled and misdiagnosed, I finally had found a doctor who took me seriously. And I had an explanation for what was going on with me, and why my body reacted the way it did.

In the following months, I learned more and more about ME/CFS, and the more I learned about it, the more shocked I was.

Chronic Fatigue Syndrome, or Myalgic Encephalomyelitis, is a neurological disease that is still very unknown, although it is anything but rare. In Austria alone, an estimated 25,000 people suffer from this illness, around the world there must be millions. It is listed in the International Classification of Diseases (ICD) under the code G93.3, but most people I meet, even doctors, have never heard about it before, until I tell them about it. As of now, there is no cure for this illness.

Living with ME/CFS feels like you're living in a cage, but that cage is your body. Sometimes I have to remind myself that I am 27, because I am living in a body that feels much older.

Many people describe it like having a constant flu that never really goes away. No matter how much rest you get, how many hours you sleep, you never wake up rested, and every day you experience symptoms like pain, dizziness or brain-fog in varying forms. Some people who are severely affected are even bed bound.

And then there's PEM: Post-exertional malaise, the key symptom of ME/CFS: a worsening of symptoms after too much activity. This symptom is really the worst, and it can hit you with a vengeance. Imagine, one day you feel a little better, and you feel motivated and happy. So, you do stuff: whatever it is that you feel like doing that day. But then suddenly it hits you: you did too much. You wake up the next day, feeling like you got hit by a bus. You used too much of your energy, and now you have to pay. It can be relentless. I had to learn to adapt to this, to ration my energy and not go over my threshold. The key is to find a balance between doing enough, while not overdoing it – which is way harder than it sounds.

The thing I realized soon, is that most people who have not experienced chronic fatigue, cannot relate to the feeling at all.

Many people say things like, "Well I'm also tired all the time, but I still go to work" or "When I'm really tired I go for a run and then I feel better!"

> **"People assume the worst things about you: that you are lazy, that it is "just in your head," that what you have is not a serious illness, but a bad case of hypochondria."**

To them I explain the following thought experiment:

Imagine having an old phone, with a broken battery that doesn't properly charge anymore. You constantly have to charge it and as soon as you remove the cable, the battery dies quicker than you can look.

Now imagine this broken battery is your body. Instead of charging to 100% when you sleep, it might charge to 20%. And these 20% last for a very little while, until you are exhausted again, forced to rest and preserve the little energy you have.

Imagine having to live your whole life on 20% energy. Suddenly you realize that every little activity costs energy. Getting up from bed. Showering, brushing your teeth, grocery shopping, cooking food, cleaning the house, spending time with friends... You learn that your energy is the most valuable currency that you have and that you need to ration it properly. Otherwise you might run out and be unable to do anything for a couple of days.

Living with ME/CFS is hard, but the hardest part about it is not the symptoms you have to live with. It's the disbelief and the stigma of living with an unknown, invisible illness.

People assume the worst things about you: that you are lazy, that it is "just in your head," that what you have is not a serious illness, but a bad case of hypochondria. And the worst thing is, that many doctors, who should know better, seem to think the same. I have experienced medical gaslighting so many times in my life, and it has seriously damaged me and taken a toll on my self-esteem. I still sometimes wonder, if what I am going through is even real, and if my experiences are maybe really "all in my head." The fact that my illness is pretty much invisible, at least at first glance, doesn't help. To most people I just look like a normal, energetic young woman. They have no idea how I feel on the inside.

## "Maybe my pain is real, and it's not just in my head."

Suddenly, there is this need to explain to other people, even strangers, why you cannot do certain things. People who doubt, if you're really that sick. People who question if your experience is even real. We constantly need to prove to other people that we are not making this up. People think that you lack discipline, and you could just get better if you tried harder. That it has something to do with a weak personality. But that is such a false stereotype.

In my heart, I am full of motivation to do many things in my life. But I have to set priorities because I simply cannot do all the things I would like to do.

It can be frustrating to constantly have to say no to things you would love to do, because you don't have any energy left. It feels like I am an active person with an active mind, trapped in a body that is constantly exhausted, hurting and in need of rest. Resting when all you want to do is anything but rest, is one of the hardest things that does take lots of discipline. In the years of living with this illness, I had to fight hard, to regain my confidence. I realized that I grew up with so many stereotypes about chronic illness, and that none of them were true.

Loving myself with my chronic illness is a constant process that takes work every day, and sometimes I'm still struggling with it. I realized that in order to overcome these insecurities, I needed to start to dismantle my internalized ableism, and since I began that process I learned so much.

I learned that even though I am sick, I am allowed to feel good in my own body. I am allowed to enjoy my good days without having to feel guilty. I learned how to stand up for myself. I learned not to let anyone take away my worth. I learned that my experience is valid. I learned that my life has worth, no matter how much I am able to accomplish. I learned that I am ok the way I am. I learned that I am allowed to be me, and that having a unique personality while being ill is ok. I learned that I don't have to fit into a certain stereotype in order to be taken seriously: I deserve to be taken seriously, the way that I am. I am an expressive person that loves to laugh and have fun, and having a chronic illness doesn't take that away from me.

## "You know your body best, you live in it every day and you are the only one, who truly knows, how it feels."

I came to realize that I have not lost everything. I may have lost my job and part of my health. But I gained so much as well. I gained new confidence, new experiences, new strength and new self-love that I have never had before.

Would I get rid of my illness if I could? Yes, in a heartbeat. Having ME/CFS is the hardest thing I could have ever imagined and I would love it, if I could just switch it off. There are so many things that I would do if I was able to, such as making music every day, going hiking, seeing concerts, and most importantly, having a career again. I miss being healthy. But that does not mean that my illness hasn't taught me valuable lessons about life and about myself, that I am endlessly grateful for. I learned to advocate for myself and for others, and I am proud of that. I would say that I am now a stronger person than I ever was.

So yes, I have lost a lot. But I have also gained so much that is forever valuable to me. If this story seemed familiar to you and you are now wondering: "Maybe my pain is real and not just in my head," then you are probably right. Especially women are being told so many times that we are being "hysterical," that we are "just stressed" and need to "chill a little," that everything is ok. It took my years to realize that I was not ok. I had to learn to stand up for myself and fight for my diagnosis, and I am glad that I did. Because finally knowing what was wrong with me, was such an important step in my journey. So, if anyone ever says to you "It's probably all in your head," don't listen. You know your body best, you live in it every day and you are the only one, who truly knows, how it feels. Nobody has the right to invalidate you. Always know that what you are going through is valid. And no matter what happens in life, never forget that you are loved, appreciated and worthy as you are.

# Kiara Dijkstra

Albany, Western Australia

**Part-time Student**

*"I'm not perfect, but I'm much improved."*

**About Kiara:**

*Hey! My name is Kiara, but you might know me as @chronically.m.e. So I guess this is the awkward part where I'm supposed to say stuff about me. I'm a twenty year old Australian and I'm studying Psychological science and Sociology part time. I'm christian and a Ravenclaw (although these are two totally different categories). I have chronic fatigue syndrome, fibromyalgia, depression, and anxiety. I've been chronically ill for five years. I've learned so much since my diagnosis and while I still struggle sometimes, it's been so amazing sharing my story. I hope my story makes people feel less alone. Or maybe my story helps someone support their chronically ill friend. That's what I hope for.*

\* \* \*

*IG, Podcast & Tik Tok:*
*@chronically.m.e.*

Hey, I'm Kiara, I'm 20 and I live in Australia. I'll introduce myself properly a bit later, but for now what you need to know is that I'm sick. Chronically ill, actually.

*flashback music* It all started in 2016 when I was 15. Two years prior I had been extremely athletic but that all vanished in an instant. My head was so heavy, it felt like there were a ton of bricks on my forehead, I needed my hand to support my pounding head. I still remember the chair I was sitting on while being engulfed in this all-powerful fatigue. My whole body felt drained, as if each cell was operating on 2% battery. That night my health put limitations on me for the first time.

> **"As my ability slipped away, I had to grieve the life I had, and the one I dreamt of. The things I rooted my identity in had been stolen, so where did that leave me?"**

My life slowly crumbled away over those next few months, and my identity along with it. I was forced to give up all the things that I valued: CrossFit, religious studies, fun subjects at school and all social events. Health was something I always took for granted. But now that was gone too. It was terrifying not knowing what was going on in my own body. I felt alienated from it. And I couldn't articulate to others what was happening to me because I didn't know myself. We went to the doctor, after about a month of this. But we weren't given any answers, only empty promises.

As time went on, I started to fear the future. I felt trapped in my own body, in this nightmare situation. As my ability slipped away, I had to grieve the life I had, and the one I dreamt of. The things I rooted my identity in had been stolen, so where did that leave me? What's worse, other people had to grieve for me, and I had to watch them. I remember instances where I laid down exhausted and had Mum leaning over me, crying. Still my family struggles to accept that I may be like this permanently. My sister still prays for my healing at the dinner table.

Time ticked on in 2016. We saw almost every health-related person in my area. I spent most of my time on a mattress in the living room. I'd get out of bed and go straight there. I started counting months of illness instead of weeks. I now count in years. Months and months of medical experimentation proved futile. It was incredibly disheartening, trying your absolute hardest without results. It felt like my fault, like if only I tried harder, then I'd get better; a few doctors insinuated that. Eventually I received a Glandular Fever diagnosis. It felt wrong to be so relieved. But it was something I could hold onto even if it didn't explain all my symptoms.

I missed out on a lot these past years. But it wasn't all horrible. I graduated grade 10 with only A's and B's. I was so proud of that, and the award of recognition I got, because there were times I wondered if I would graduate at all. It felt like I got a bit of my old self back, even if I sacrificed so much to get there. In the next years I completed a Certificate 2 in Skills for Work and Vocational Pathways in eight weeks instead of a year, received the highest grade in my childcare class in grade 11, a Certificate 3 in Assistant in Nursing, a Certificate 3 in Aged Care, a Certificate 4 in Pathways to Nursing, HD's and D's in all my uni units. I'm really proud of all these achievements.

## "I'm proud of all I've accomplished academically and the battles I've won."

However, while it looks great on paper, during those years I suffered mentally. When I was fifteen, I became depressed. I felt unlovable and helpless. The things I used to get praised for I could no longer do. I lacked purpose. There were days in a row where all I did was cry. Screaming because I didn't want this life, I wanted another one. I stopped saying 'Good morning' because I hated each day. I ignored my basic needs like warmth, urination and food for as long as possible. I felt so alone because nobody could understand. So, for everyone reading this, whether you're going through similar situations or not, you are not alone, and I know how hard you have to fight just to survive, even if other people don't recognise that. I used to hate the expression 'there's a light at the end of the tunnel' because it brushed past

how much pain I was in, at that moment. But I promise you: things get better if you hang around long enough to see it. My mental health got dangerously low. But now, I am studying, managing my fatigue and mental health, I have great friends and family, I'm no longer scared to talk about what I'm going through, and I'm absolutely loving life. If I can do that, you can too. Remember you are loved. You are valued and needed. And I am begging you: Please. Stay.

It took a long time for me to be able to manage my mental health. I started antidepressants, which I'm still on, after receiving a diagnosis and starting counselling. Two years later I was diagnosed with anxiety. Two years after that: an eating disorder. And even though those times were filled with incredible suffering, there were still pockets of joy. Through all of it I learnt that I am strong. I am really, really strong. I've lost my entire identity and built it again. I've felt so worthless I thought my life wasn't worth anything, yet I survived and found purpose. I've had doctors tell me I was making it up, lost friends, and had people say the movie that made me feel undeserving of life was the greatest movie ever. I've had to watch, powerless, as my ability to study diminished and am now slowly building it back up. My body tried to fight itself and lost, although that's more of an ongoing battle. I've had my closest friends tell me awful things without realizing they applied to me and still managed to be resilient. I used to be so scared to talk about what I was going through but now I have an Instagram page dedicated to it! (@chronically.m.e). I've had my dreams break and become unattainable and still come back spitting blood. I've been diagnosed with depression, anxiety and an eating disorder and am still fighting. It sometimes feels like I'm being dumped by wave after wave, but my point is you get through. You persevere and fight until things become okay again. My chronic illness forced me into a lot of situations I never wanted to be in, but by the grace of God I got through. Life is never perfect or easy, especially with a chronic illness, but the good days slowly become more frequent than the bad.

I'm proud of all I've accomplished academically and the battles I've won. I wonder, though, if I could have avoided those battles if I hadn't pushed myself so much. Looking back, it was essential to me to be good at something, but a lot of the time I was utterly miserable. Yeah, academia was hard, but I think there's something more admirable about listening to your body. Regardless of fearing being useless. It takes more strength and self-control to not do what you want, than overexerting yourself does. It's not acknowledged as a success but maybe it should be. It's hard to place greater importance in long term rewards rather than instant gratification. Almost all the messages regarding disabled and chronically ill people are inspirational and achievement based. But where does that leave those who can't do everything? Like me when I couldn't do anything I wanted to. What about those, like me, whose ambitions and abilities don't match?

Anyway, it's probably time for that introduction I promised. Hi, my name is Kiara, I'm 20, Australian, and I have Chronic Fatigue Syndrome (CFS), Depression, Anxiety, Misophonia, Binocular Vision Dysfunction, Fibromyalgia and have recovered from an eating disorder. I can't remember receiving the CFS diagnosis because it wasn't one definite moment. I think it was around two years after first getting sick. It was over multiple doctors' appointments. Before you know you're receiving treatment, you assume you've got it. Sometimes they read out a list of symptoms and you just say 'yup' to the ones you have, which for me was almost all of them. It felt so great to finally feel like I understood what was happening to me. There was something tangible that I could use to explain to other people and connect with people like me. It's weird wanting a diagnosis, but a diagnosis gives meaning, explanation, resources and community.

Maybe I should explain. The things that affect me the most are CFS and Fibromyalgia. I'm able to identify CFS symptoms more easily, and it affects me more, however, it's important to note that a lot of the symptoms overlap.

Anyway, CFS is a neurological disorder that causes inflammation of the brain stem and affects all body systems. A symptom of this, unsurprisingly, is the overwhelming, constant, debilitating fatigue. A kind of fatigue that doesn't go away with rest and that causes another symptom, Post Exertional Malaise (PEM). PEM causes immense fatigue after an activity. If you run a marathon, obviously you'd be tired afterwards because you exerted a lot of energy. With CFS the window of energy/ activity you have before it causes fatigue is extremely small. It makes simple tasks difficult or impossible. Showering, driving into town, dressing, cooking -everything- is now extremely taxing. Even the basic tasks to keep yourself alive and functioning take energy. It also means you don't have energy for anything else.

The way I like to explain it, is if you have $100, $50 is a lot because that's half of your total. But if you were a millionaire you probably wouldn't even notice the absence of $50. Able-bodied people are millionaires when it comes to energy. But people like me, people with CFS, live on an extremely tight budget. You're forced to choose where you're spending your energy. There are constantly activities that I can't do so that I can survive or do something else. For example, I'm frequently forced to prioritise appointments over parties.

And the fatigue is so much more than regular tiredness. It's like a cloud of smoke that engulfs your whole body. This fatigue is ever present and doesn't disappear with rest. Your muscles become weak. You get muscle pain and aches, joint soreness or stiffness. Your brain seems to operate like a 1980s computer with super slow internet. It's hard to think straight, you can't remember words and it's hard to articulate your thoughts; especially when you're particularly fatigued. You get these enormous headaches and migraines daily. At worst, some, including myself, get nerve pain where it's difficult to move your limbs. You never wake up refreshed, you go to bed each day not knowing if you'll be better or worse the next day. It's going through the stress of not knowing your body every day. You can imagine how debilitating and isolating it is when you can barely do things to keep yourself alive. For some it's like COVID lockdown daily, not knowing when it'll end. Socialising or employment are things you can rarely do. The horrible thing is you get desensitized by it. Day by day, you force yourself to function so that the pain becomes a part of you, something you don't register as much. But one day it can all come crashing down. It's scary knowing that this may very well be the rest of your life. That's not to say I don't experience joy or have fun, but there's this constant extra weight to carry.

Obviously, my illnesses take a lot out of me emotionally. I'm still learning how to manage these feelings. It helps to take it day by day, being grounded and practicing gratitude. I also encourage professional help. Physically, my illness affects me enormously. Every aspect of my life has been influenced. It's changed my career path multiple times, my abilities and identity. Currently, I'm able to study part-time online (Psychological Science and Sociology). But that may change. I'm not sure what I want to be, but I love the idea of activism, advocacy or Occupational Therapy. I live with my parents, I'm not able to help with chores, employment is off the table for now and I sleep about as much as

## "Self-love and appreciation used to seem like an unattainable goal."

a koala. I don't have the life of an average teenager. My social group is smaller than some and I'm not at all active like I used to be.

Adapting to my limitations has been a real process. Five years have passed since I first became sick. I was in denial about my situation for years. I was angry and scared. But now I'm learning to appreciate myself in every individual moment. Whatever I need or feel at any specific time. Looking at my emotions and symptoms as constantly changing really helps. Listening to my body and giving myself what I need is difficult but important. For me it means extra rest, going to bed early and afternoon naps. Scheduling appointments or social events with days in-between so I can recover. Budgeting, or pacing my energy, have been so critical in managing my illness. Not pushing myself beyond my limits, not going at 100% means I don't experience PEM or flares as much.

So, most of the time I'm at a stable level of fatigue, instead of being so incredibly exhausted almost all the time. I allow myself to feel every emotion, and rest without guilt. I don't compare myself to others, I let myself cry and appreciate who I am as a person. Meaning I can exist without self-hatred and start actually looking after myself. I limit exhausting activities and use a wheelchair when shopping or going long distances. I also adapt my goals and expectations to be accessible for me. I study part-time online, because it suits my needs better. I've altered my expectations of employment and I leave parties early. This was impossible at the beginning, and it takes practice. I'm not perfect, but I'm much improved.

Self-love and appreciation used to seem like an unattainable goal. Now I (try to) accept myself regardless of productivity or emotions I'm feeling. I love my caring nature and my love for studying. I know how hard it can be living with chronic conditions, and how it makes you hate your body and yourself. But you are not alone. There is a massive online community of people who go through the same things as you, which has been so incredibly helpful for me. It's scary and daunting but I know you can make it through. Focus on small appreciations and individual moments. You're doing absolutely amazing and I am so proud of you. Your struggles are real. Listen to your needs, your worth is inherent and not based on accomplishment. You are loved. And you are never alone.

# Lauren Jayne

California, USA

## Chronic & Mental Illness Advocate

*"It would have been so easy to just give up and believe the voices in our heads telling us we are worthless, but we all have something to offer the world, no matter how unlikely it seems."*

**About Lauren:**

*My name is Liz, and I'm a chronic and mental illness advocate. I have fibromyalgia, POTS, and I deal with mental health issues. After being diagnosed with fibromyalgia, I decided to start an Instagram page to provide support to other like myself. I know how hard it can be when you're initially diagnosed with a chronic illness and I want others in our community to know they're not alone.*

\* \* \*

*IG: @heylozzy*

My name is Loz and I'm a chronic and mental illness advocate. I have fibromyalgia, a disorder characterized by widespread musculoskeletal pain accompanied by fatigue, sleep, memory and mood issues. I also have (Postural Orthostatic Tachycardia Syndrome (POTS), which is a disorder causing most of your blood to circulate in your lower body when standing up, and in response, this causes a major spike in heart rate which leads to symptoms such as lightheadedness, nausea, fainting, and rapid heartbeat, which are only relieved by lying down again.

## "I came to understand that the negative self-talk that was ingrained in my head was all wrong."

Because of my conditions, I am severely limited in how active I can be and thus have been forced into quitting my job. The impact of this was huge and I lost all sense of self-worth. It seemed that I was no longer worthy of anything and I began to feel I was just a burden on the people around me. After years of feeling helpless, I decided that enough was enough and I had to do something to take back control of my life.

Beginning with therapy, I came to understand that the negative self-talk that was ingrained in my head was all wrong - I began to realize that life didn't have to be over; and that I should feel worthy of happiness again. This led to me creating an Instagram page to help others, and at the same time help myself, to realize that I have something to offer to other people who are going through similar chronic illnesses. With hard work and consistency, I grew my page into something meaningful and have been very fortunate to have found lots of opportunities through my social media presence, which all started from simply wanting to connect with other people experiencing the feelings that I was going through and to try to support each other. It would have been so easy to just give up and believe the voices in our heads telling us we are worthless, but we all have something to offer the world, no matter how unlikely it seems.

**These are my tips for realizing self-worth:**

1. Stop comparing yourself to other people. Everybody's journey is unique and comparing your life to somebody else's will cause you to wonder if you are doing something wrong.

2. Embrace opportunities! You never know what something could lead to and if it does not work out, learn from and embrace your mistakes.

3. Take time to understand yourself, learn what your body can do and what it can't do. Learn how to practice self-care. When you have a flare or a down day - analyze what caused it, incorporate ways to prevent it from happening, and think about how to fit your flares around your lifestyle. For example, if I do something in the morning which will likely cause a pain flare-up; I will keep my afternoon free to recover.

4. Practice self-development. If you are good at something, keep doing it and hone your skills. Then let the world see! It's okay to showcase your talent and this is great for your self-worth.

5. Sharing your journey with others can actually really compound your positive mind-set. Helping people is a big way to feel worthy.

# Francessca Prado

Essex, MD, USA

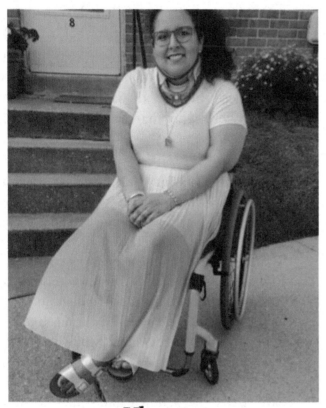

**Vlogger**

## About Francessca:

*Hi, my name is Francessca Emily. I am from Maryland, born and raised. Maryland is on the Eastern Coast of the United States. We are known for our Baltimore Orioles, Chesapeake Bay Crabs and home of Old Bay Seasoning. I live with my Mom, Mary, and two of the sweetest most loving and intuitive Doodles ever, Zoey and Zayla. Zayla is my service dog-in-training. I am a Pisces, born in March and I'm twenty-six years old. I have been disabled for over sixteen years. I am also an Origami Owl Designer. And this is my story.*

\* \* \*

**IG:** *@thedizzyzebra*

*"Keep fighting and then fight some more."*

When I was born, the doctors told my mom that I was going to have many health issues, one of which was Turner syndrome. The geneticist even pressured my Mom to have an abortion but Mom insisted that she waited all her life for me and what if they were wrong! I was born a perfectly healthy viable baby. I lead a full and happy, productive life up until age ten.

It was New Year's Eve 2006. My cousins invited my Mom and I up to Harford County to see their hotel suite and hang out for a few hours. I thought it was so cool and begged Mom to go. When we got there, I was so excited because they had a huge hot tub. To be honest, at ten years old I thought it was a swimming pool. They let me get in the hot tub (and swim!). After only a few minutes in the hot tub though I was as limp as a wet noodle. I had fainted. My cousin carried me to the floor and laid me on the towels, where my Mom and cousins stayed close by while I recovered. Once I recovered, she helped me to dress, got more fluids into me and then my cousin carried me to the car.

## "As my Mom always says, 'Come on, let's hurry up and wait.'"

My Mom has POTS so she recognized the symptoms. She was never told POTS was hereditary so she really wasn't sure that is what was happening but she kept it in the back of her mind. As time went on, she watched and realized the symptoms I was having were beginning to look all too familiar.

Although these issues began in December 2006--- I was not diagnosed with POTS until August 2007 at the age of 11. One thing that we have discovered throughout the years is the medical world doesn't move very fast. As my Mom always says, "Come on, let's hurry up and wait."

However, my health issues didn't stop with the diagnosis of POTS. In the years that followed other serious health issues developed. Since then, I have been diagnosed with a plethora of rare illnesses such as Postural Orthostatic Tachycardia Syndrome (POTS) which causes fainting and a host of other autonomic symptoms, Ehlers Danlos syndrome (EDS)—a connective tissue disorder that causes dislocations and subluxations, mast cell activation syndrome—a blood disorder that causes severe allergic reactions and anaphylaxis, thoracic outlet syndrome (TOS), thrombocytopenia —low platelets, hyperacusis—which causes super sensitive hearing and pain, interstitial cystitis (IC—which causes irritation and painful spasms in your female parts), anemia, gastroparesis (GP)—which I will explain in more detail below, migraines that cause language disturbances, low lying tonsil (not quite Chiari), and a pineal cyst... and sadly the list seems to just keep growing as more things develop.

These diseases come with a long list of symptoms, many of which alter the quality of life and make life quite difficult on a daily basis. For instance, I am not able to eat hardly anything, especially solids, due to gastroparesis. I have four safe foods and most are in liquid form. I cannot eat meat at all. For those who aren't aware, gastroparesis means "paralyzed stomach." Food sits like a rock at the bottom of the sea and it doesn't move…it just sits and sits and sits. This causes severe pain, cramping, nausea, diarrhea and vomiting - sometimes all at the same time.

## "I was literally begging God and my Mom to put me out of my misery."

When this happens it also affects the mast cells and POTS, as they react not only to physical symptoms but also to emotions, causing my blood pressure to plummet and mast cells to flare. When this happens, it causes me to faint and get extremely weak. It doesn't matter whether I am lying down, sitting or trying to stand---I will faint. POTS is not choosy as to "when" it happens. The mast cells cause me to have severe reactions like hives, itching, flushing, and anaphylaxis. At the present time, this happens on a daily basis despite daily infusions and medications. I have to calculate my every move so that I don't eat something or put myself in a situation where I would be in danger of a mast cell flare. For me, the environment, medications, emotions and exercise can throw me into a mast cell reaction.

So, I have to be careful of EVERYTHING. This has been my longest flare to date and has by far been the worst since it has caused me to be bedridden since May 2020. These illnesses affect me physically, cognitively, emotionally and figuratively. They also in turn affect family members; for me it's my Mom. Life isn't easy but you learn to take the punches and roll with the tide. You learn to adapt and persevere.

A few years back in 2011, my head pain was at its all time worst. I was literally begging God and my Mom to put me out of my misery. Every single minute of every single day for over a year and a half was filled with severe debilitating head pain. Pain so bad that it would literally stop me in my tracks and throw me to my knees. I would fall to the floor clutching my head, screaming, crying and writhing in pain.

One night I wanted to die so badly. I couldn't take the pain. My Mom laid on the bed next to me, she was holding me as I cried out for help. I just wanted it to be over. I told her that I hated God. I screamed every obscenity and bad thing I could say. I couldn't understand, "why" he gave me this pain and why he was punishing me.

My Mom tried so hard to console me and get me to listen but I just wouldn't. I couldn't understand why God wasn't listening and hearing my pleas. At one point, my Mom was at her wits end in trying to talk sense to me. She asked me to look at her. She said, "How do you know it's not the Devil who's making you hurt so bad? Think about it, the Devil wants you to think it's God. If the Devil can get you to believe it's God then you will hate God. And if you hate God the Devil has EVERYTHING to gain, including your soul!"

She told me to think about it.

"If the Devil turns you against God, who benefits?"

> **"So, I began to think of ways to change my present situation. I told myself I could handle this situation one of two ways. I can choose bitterness like before or I could make the best of a very terrible situation."**

It ALL made perfect sense! If the devil won, I would have turned my back on God and that's EXACTLY what the Devil wanted. How could I even think my God would desert me or make me go through this alone??

Needless to say, THAT incident was a huge turning point in my life. From that moment onward my beliefs changed and my faith grew in our Lord. I turned my life and my faith completely over to God. I knew he was there for me and he would never forsake me. That night I cried myself to sleep as my Mom held me.

The next morning as we were leaving for an appointment. My Mom backed out of the parking spot and as she pulled forward something made her glance up at the sky. Up in the sky right in front of us before our very eyes was a cloud in the shape of an angel. We both cried and we were very emotional. She told me that after I fell asleep, she asked God to please show her a sign that things would get better. And there it was!

After seeing the angel, we knew things would improve. And it did, my head pain slowly dissolved and stayed away up until a week ago. Because of that night, my faith plays a huge part in who I am today, how I feel about my illnesses and how I live my life. I try to not let my illnesses define me, however...I really haven't known life without being sick.

I think I have some great qualities. I'm caring, funny (so I'm told), creative, crafty, love to write, and love my Mom, family, friends and dogs, Zayla and Zoey. And something I haven't shared till now is that I can speak to spirits. Yes, I am a medium. I've always had the ability but as a child spirits scared me and so I pushed it aside. However, a few years ago I began to embrace my gift and spirit hasn't stopped talking since.

I am currently bedridden and have been since May 2020. Basically, it has been a tough situation but I have found and learned ways to adapt. When I was first diagnosed back in 2007, I became so bitter and angry at God. I blamed God and didn't understand why I was so sick. I blocked out most of those memories but I still remember bits and pieces---fragments of a shattered life. I would faint even laying down. I couldn't even lift my head without losing consciousness. I didn't want to become bitter again and I knew that things needed to change. So, I began to think of ways to change my present situation. I told myself I could handle this situation one of two ways. I can choose bitterness like before or I could make the best of a very terrible situation. I prayed to God and asked him to help me feel useful again.

Growing up, like most teens, I felt like the world was out to get me. After I became ill, I felt betrayed by God. I grew up in a loving home, I was a good person, I prayed and went to church...but I just couldn't understand "why" God made me so sick. What did I do wrong? I decided this time I wasn't going to let my illness win and I was going to make the best of a very bad situation. It was going on month six of being bedridden. Something HAD to change before I slipped into a deep depression. I wasn't able to do much physically but I did spend a lot of time on my phone and it made sense to me, why not use it to my benefit.

So...I took a gamble and spent twenty dollars to enroll as an Origami Owl Designer. What did I have to lose right? Next, I chose my webpage and a cute catchy title. I decided to add a little spin on my name and called my page, "Frantastic."

I had a goal in mind in the first month and that was to earn my Origami Owl kit and a spot on the Disney LaunchSquad.

I went into this endeavor with realistic expectations and a few goals. You get what you put into it right? I knew I wasn't going to get rich and that was okay. It was really important to me to know what it felt like to work. After all, I have been sick all of my life. So, I set small goals for myself and I did this all from my couch where I had spent the last nine months because I was too sick to stand without fainting. In fact, I got many chuckles because that was my little slogan when I would do a Facebook Live event. I always say, "Live from da couch!" and I would show off my new pajamas. I kept it real and I think people liked that about me.

> **"Keep fighting and then fight some more. Never give up because today's pain and discomfort may not be tomorrow's. Always look for the silver lining!"**

Being the quiet "Disnerd" that I am, I originally joined Origami Owl because I wanted to be part of the Disney Collection. However, as time went by, I discovered so much more. As an Origami Owl Designer, I have found purpose, a work family, positive affirmations, work experience, and my life. It gave me a new lease on life and helped me to see things in a more positive light. It's taught me to look at my glass as half full instead of half empty.

I'm not better by a long shot. In fact, currently my health has taken a turn for the worse; but I'm still persevering and trying to stay in a good headspace. I wanted to share my story because all of my life I wanted to help others and although I didn't get to become an oncology nurse that I once dreamed of as a kid, I realized I can still help others by sharing my testimony.

I'm not successful by any means. I don't hit my sales goals every month but I keep pushing forward, don't beat myself up over it and I don't give up. My accomplishments aren't like other peoples but they are MY accomplishments. I'm proud of myself and what I've been able to achieve while bedridden. I earned my Origami Owl kit and my spot on the team. I learned so many life lessons and I am determined to stay strong and not let these diseases win! They do not define who I am. And I will never let anyone make me feel like I am less of a person. I am worthy of happiness. As sick as I get...I keep reminding myself that I am in control. And I am not going down without a fight. If you can remember anything from my testimony, I hope you will remember these words —

"Keep fighting and then fight some more. Never give up because today's pain and discomfort may not be tomorrow's. Always look for the silver lining!"

As they say, "When life gives you a thousand reasons to cry, think of a thousand reasons to smile." There is always a silver lining, you just have to find it. Find something that makes you smile. Maybe it's a pet. I know my dogs bring so much unconditional love, so many cuddles and comfort to me. Maybe it's music or singing or watching your favorite show. Maybe it's something else, maybe it's journaling, writing, being near family, your BFF or prayer. Maybe it's all of the above---whatever it is, do it for you and know YOU ARE WORTH IT!

And remember!

You can do anything if you put your mind to it, you just need to think outside the box and maybe try it a different way.

Like me,
Francessca.

Signing off,
live and from the couch!

# Dianna Carney

Plymouth, MS, USA

*Freelance Writer & SEO Content Creator*

*"A label doesn't take away your power."*

## About Dianna:

*Dianna was born in New York City. After the tragic day of September 11th, Dianna's family permanently relocated to an island in Boston Harbor where she spent the rest of her childhood. In 2016, Dianna was first diagnosed with adult-onset asthma, which lead to multiple more diagnosis including Systemic Lupus Erythematosus and Alpha-1 Antitrypsin Deficiency. Dianna now resides in a Boston Suburb with her partner and family of fur babies. She spends her days cuddled with her dogs, writing, and creating YouTube videos.*

\* \* \*

*IG: @diannabyday*

The first chronic illness I was diagnosed with was adult-onset asthma. In a few years, my doctors and I recognized that this diagnosis was, in fact, a symptom of a larger ailment - lupus.

## "Part of being human is recognizing you have limits and flaws."

To sum up a complex illness into a few words, lupus is when the body's immune system recognizes itself as a threat. Attacking oneself comes in many forms, from random fevers and bouts of exhaustion, to multiple lung infections each year and, at its worst, failing organs. Although a cure doesn't exist, taking immunosuppressants can help trick your body into not attacking itself. Whether in pill or even chemo form, immunosuppressants help calm one's body down during these attacks. In 2020, I was prescribed prednisone six times and had three emergency room trips due to low blood oxygen levels. My immune system loves to bully my lungs!

Part of being human is recognizing you have limits and flaws. For some of us, it's easier to point out those imperfections than others. If you're anything like me, then putting yourself down isn't just a habit - it's a hobby that you could consider a guilty pleasure. Around the time I turned 16, I had fallen into the practice of sitting in front of my floor-length mirror at night after finishing my homework. I'd start by picking apart my face, and finally, I'd settle on a single feature I wanted to change. Next, I'd spend hours obsessively watching YouTube tutorials and studying how-to articles about contouring, makeup application, and techniques to hide my flaws. As I got older, those how-to articles shifted into "how to diet without anyone noticing" and "how many hours a day I needed to work out to burn off that bagel I had for breakfast."

My middle school years, although filled with self-hatred, also showed me how strong my body was. All of those times I didn't feed it, all the times I pushed myself too many extra miles on the treadmill - my body never let me down.

Fast forward to my chronic illness diagnosis. Within the blink of an eye, my entire perception changed. When I was told something was wrong with me, I labeled my body weak. From that moment on, I identified as fragile.

## "I've always been an optimistic person, striving to see the positive in everything, but there were times I couldn't find the energy to take care of my own basic needs, never mind stay smiling."

Yes, part of being human is having flaws, but what if I was...broken? That single thought played on repeat in my mind longer than I care to admit.

Over the next few years, my attitude would bounce between being optimistic regarding my diagnosis to the extreme contrary, feeling alone, depressed, and beaten down by my own body.

I've always been an optimistic person, striving to see the positive in everything, but there were times I couldn't find the energy to take care of my own basic needs, never mind stay smiling. I found myself having to call out of work because I physically couldn't drive, never mind make it through an eight-hour shift. Or when I had to excuse myself halfway through a work shift to take my emergency medication due to a flare up; those were the times I felt isolated even when surrounded by my friends.

## "All those times I'd felt so alone was an illusion I'd built out of my own fears."

I found myself missing who I was and what I was once capable of; trekking through the forest, running in 5k races, and going on adventures that didn't need to be planned around doctor's appointments or medication refills.

This made me begin thinking- why do I feel so isolated by a medical diagnosis when I've been the same person the entire time? A label doesn't take away my power - it's a tool to help me understand myself more, therefore allowing me to take my power back while simultaneously gaining control over my life and my future, once again.

I saw my body as limiting me to what I was capable of, and I blamed my diagnosis on why I couldn't - wouldn't - become the person I wanted to be.

But then I remembered the last time I felt limited by my body - when I was suffering the most from an eating disorder. In the past, the only way I found myself able to recover was by changing my mindset.

My first step to accepting my body and loving myself was through sharing my truths. The simple act of telling others about my chronic illnesses and not being embarrassed by the labels changed my life. I hadn't realized how much I'd held back from others; it's hard not to feel like you're dragging others into your personal life and becoming a burden when talking about your medical history.

As soon as I began speaking up, I found myself surrounded by people who not only cared about me but wanted to help me, whether by being a shoulder I could lean on (sometimes quite literally, chronic fatigue is no joke, folks!) or by giving me suggestions and recommendations.

All those times I'd felt so alone was an illusion I'd built out of my own fears.

My chronic illness has made me realize how strong I am. Now I see my diagnoses as a reminder of the power I have within me. Sure, my body is attacking itself, but that just means I'm a fighter.

# Wildling Apothecary

## MISTIBLUDREAM.COM/SHOP

# GARDEN
## of Blu

**BUY NOW!**

### WRITTEN BY MISTI BLU DAY MCDERMOTT

A memoir about being lost in the dark, living with chronic illness, grief, and depression while discovering self-worth and growing through it all. There is a moment in life where we can make the decision to break generational patterns and bloom, despite our circumstances and roots. Some flowers bloom in the dark. Misti shares her vulnerable story and collective writing (starting at the age of 15), hoping to shed light on mental health, self-care, chronic illness, loss, and trauma.

501(c)(3)

# SYNERGY SERVICES ALLIANCE

HELP US TO EMPOWER
SURVIVORS OF DOMESTIC &
INTIMATE PARTNER VIOLENCE
TO IMPROVE THEIR:

- *Economic Development,*
- *Financial Independence,*
- *Self-Esteem, Self-Efficacy & Self-Discovery*

SYNERGYSERVICESALLIANCE.ORG

# ADAM'S WAY

WRITTEN & ILLUSTRATED BY:
APRIL RADDER

**Buy Now!**

*RAISING SPINA BIFIDA EDUCATION & AWARENESS FOR CHILDREN*

A young boy born with spina bifida, determined to be a hockey player, defies the odds against his disability and bullying in this true story of courage, determination, and success. This is a story of how that young boy overcame obstacles, strived for success and accomplished the goals he set out to achieve. Adam's Way is a book that will not only teach children about never giving up but adults as well.

WRITTEN IN SUPPORT OF

174

Chelsey Storteboom

Andrea Neph

Scott Ninneman

Jemma-Tiffany Rosewater

Natalie Jezierny

Danielle Marie Turco

Brandon Mouw

# I AM Powerful.

Stories of chronic illness warriors commanding great things.

# Chelsey Storteboom

New York, NY, USA

**Associate Director, Musical Theater at 92Y & Podcaster**

*"Give yourself grace."*

## About Chelsey:

*Born and raised in Langley, British Columbia, Chelsey Storteboom moved to New York City in 2010 to attend the American Musical and Dramatic Academy, @amdaofficial. She performed in musicals across North America and abroad before returning to NYC. She is now the Associate Director of Musical Theater at the 92nd St. Y. Since being diagnosed with Rheumatoid Arthritis in 2020, Chelsey has become a chronic illness advocate and podcaster. Her podcasts, My Immune System Hates Me!, features chronic illness sufferers who breakdown their illness, diagnostic process, treatment, and wellness journey. Her goal is to educate her listeners and raise awareness about chronic conditions in order to help others with their diagnosises.*

\* \* \*

*IG: @chelseyboom*
*@myimmunesystempod*

*Website: www.chelseyboom.com*

## My Immune System Hates Me!

Imagine this: You're a musical theater educator living alone in New York City during the peak of a pandemic. You've been quarantined for 6 weeks, teaching dance classes from your 150 square foot studio apartment. Your downstairs neighbor hates you because of all the singing and jumping jacks you've been doing on their ceiling. You leave your house once a day for a walk and visit the grocery store once a week. The only conversations you've had are with faces on a screen. The threat of losing your job is being dangled in front of you, as well as losing your mind in isolation. You're afraid of getting COVID, afraid for the safety of your friends and family, and afraid of this pandemic's effect on humanity.

And then your joints start to hurt. Not just hurt, they become immobile.

This was me. Chelsey Storteboom. A 30-year-old woman who has been dancing her whole life, suddenly can't move her arm. A singer who can't open her mouth. Cool, thanks universe.

I had just finished teaching a jazz class when the left side of my jaw started to hurt. I thought it was a bit strange that only one side of my mouth was achy, but I went on with my night. As the hours passed, the pain got worse and worse while my mouth became harder and harder to open. Then, the same pain and immobility started creeping into my left shoulder. I decided not to worry, I'll feel better in the morning.

## "I can't do my hair, I can't get dressed, I can't eat breakfast, I can't—"

I didn't feel better in the morning. In fact, I felt much, much worse.

I opened up my telehealth app to get in touch with a doctor. I explained to him where the pain started and how it had progressed.

"It's a tooth infection," he said.

"Are you sure? My teeth don't hurt. And what about my shoulder?" I probed.

"Any time there's pain in the jaw, it's a tooth infection," he declared."I'll send you a prescription for an antibiotic."

I huffed as I hung up the phone. I knew he was wrong, but it's hard to argue with a medical professional. There was no way I was going to take that antibiotic, so I resigned myself to loading up on Advil. I had the day off, so I let myself wallow and decided not to worry about being productive.

The next morning, I woke up in excruciating pain. I couldn't put a shirt on or brush my hair without bursting into tears."What's wrong with me," I wondered worriedly. I've dealt with injuries before; sprained ankles, pulled groins, torn hamstrings, floating ribs. At least with those, I could pinpoint what caused them and seek treatment. This was not like any injury I'd had before. This came from out of nowhere.

My boss called to talk through our class plan for the day. When she asked how I was, I couldn't hold back. I immediately started sobbing and explained my mystery ailment to her.

"I can't do my hair, I can't get dressed, I can't eat breakfast, I can't—"

"So, here's what you're going to do," she interrupted, "You're not going to teach today. I can't have you teaching a class shirtless, with only one functioning arm, messy hair, and tears in your eyes!" I laughed at this. "I'll cover your classes. You have got to get to an Urgent Care and figure this out."

So, I did.

Let me remind you that this all happened in April 2020, when New York City was the North American epicenter of the COVID-19 pandemic. Bodies were being stored in refrigerator trucks, a hospital ship had just pulled into the harbor, people were dying in their homes because the hospitals were flooded

## "She listened to my complaints and assessed me. Her conclusion: some pinched nerves."

But I braved the plague and went to a clinic.

After a quick assessment, the doctor told me I had a pinched nerve in my jaw which then affected the nerves in my shoulder. She thought maybe I had been grinding my teeth at night and prescribed me some muscle relaxers and extra strength ibuprofen. I took the meds but felt no improvement.

By the next week, things started to get weird. My left shoulder and jaw were back to their usual pain-free mobility, but now my right shoulder and jaw were no good. As time went on, the pain bounced around my body. My shoulders, jaws, hands, fingers, wrists, ankles, and feet were all affected.

As more and more doctors told me I was suffering from a pinched nerve, I began to Google my symptoms. Were these symptoms of COVID? Diabetes? Arthritis? Cancer?! I knew it wasn't just a targeted injury, something in my body was malfunctioning.

In July, COVID cases had started to dip and restrictions were being lifted. Retail stores were open, restaurants were offering outdoor dining, and salons were fixing people's COVID cuts. I finally felt courageous enough to visit my primary care doctor in person.

She listened to my complaints and assessed me. Her conclusion: some pinched nerves.

Gee, thanks, that was definitely worth risking my life on the subway for. She recommended I see a dentist for my jaw and a physical therapist for my shoulders and hands. She prescribed me some pain meds and sent me on my way.

I knew it wasn't a structural issue, but I decided to book an appointment with my chiropractor. I had an old back injury that was acting up and thought maybe I could bring up the joint pain. She's an old tap dance student of mine so I trusted her to assess me. Plus, she's manipulated my spine in ways to help with acid reflux, so I figured it was worth a shot!

The day of my appointment, my right hand was twice its usual size. I began explaining the migrating pain I had been feeling and told her about all the doctors that kept diagnosing it as a pinched nerve.

"A pinched nerve does not cause this kind of swelling," she said, acknowledging my balloon hand."You need to get tested for Lyme disease and rheumatoid arthritis."

## "Why does my immune system hate me so much?!"

"Arthritis?" I objected, "but I'm too young for that!"

"You're thinking of osteoarthritis," she rolled her eyes, "rheumatoid arthritis affects all ages."

After my adjustment, I emailed my doctor to demand some blood tests. Writing sharp emails has always been one of my special skills; if you sell me a faulty product, you better believe I'm sending you an email for a refund! This time, it was my body that was faulty so the email I sent was extra spicy!

My doctor reluctantly sent in test requests and let me tell you, I have never been so excited to have my blood drawn! I could feel myself getting closer to an answer. I couldn't wait to solve this mystery, cure it, and get back to normal.

I have never missed work or school due to illness, but since April, I have skipped eight days of teaching. Eight times I had

been scheduled to teach a class and couldn't. Eight times my coworkers had to pick up my slack and scrambled to cover for me. Eight times I sat crying on Zoom (with my camera off of course), unable to move while I watched these kids dance around their messy bedrooms. I was so excited to be pain-free again.

Of course, it's never that easy.

My test results came back positive for rheumatoid arthritis.

RA is an autoimmune disease where the immune system attacks healthy cells by mistake, causing inflammation. Joints are the most commonly affected area and most of the time, pain occurs in the same joints on both sides of the body. The inflammation also causes swelling, which can render joints immobile. As the disease progresses, the tissue damage can cause brittle bones and deformity. There is no cure.

Duh, of course I had RA. Google predicted this long ago. My symptoms were exactly as the internet described them. I don't often recommend Googling your symptoms, but the search engines got an A+ this time.

Why does my immune system hate me so much?! Day and night, she was bullying me, beating away at my joints until they were battered and bruised. She wasn't protecting me from some intrusive enemy, she was attacking the very body she lived in!

I booked an appointment with a rheumatologist who gave me pamphlets for all my drug options. She ordered more blood tests and x-rays so we could monitor the disease progression.

After reading through the pamphlets, balancing all the side effects, and checking in with Dr. Google, I settled on my drug of choice. I started on a steroid and a DMARD (Disease Modifying Anti-Rheumatic Drug). I would eventually be able to wean off of the steroid, but I'll be on the DMARD long-term.

> ## "Your body may not be capable of what it used to be, so don't push it. If you need to spend the day in bed, do it, and don't feel guilty about it."

My immune system wasn't bullying me at all, she was just confused. She needed to be powered down. My immunosuppressant drugs were rocking her to sleep so I could get on with my life.

After about 6 weeks on medication, I was starting to feel like myself again. No more shoulder pain, no more swollen hands, and I could finally open my mouth again. I'm not completely back to normal; I'm sometimes sore after knitting a while. I use a tool to open jars because of my weakened hands, and my jaw clicks, but these are merely annoyances.

But that's not where my story ends.

I became fascinated with my immune system and how she works. Why did she turn on me? Why did she malfunction? And why my joints? Why not my skin, my thyroid, my colon? I turned to Dr. Google for answers. When I wasn't satisfied with the results, I turned to my go-to mode of passing time, podcasts.

I searched all over for a podcast that would explain my immune system to me. I wanted to hear real people with autoimmune diseases describe their experiences. I wanted to hear about their diagnostic process, their angry emails to doctors, their journey to recovery.

All I could find were people telling me what diets to try or how helpful meditation is. I decided if I can't find a podcast, I guess I'll make my own.

I pulled out my microphone (I'm a singer, of course I just happen to have a microphone lying around) and wrote a script. I had no idea what I was doing, but I knew it needed to be done.

The next day, I had my first episode ready for distribution.

I decided to reach out to people with chronic conditions and invite them on to my show. I was going to provide a platform for people to describe their experiences, in hopes that it would reach other sufferers. I had experience with RA, but what about other autoimmune diseases, invisible illnesses, genetic diseases, and mental illnesses? I wanted to cover everything I could. I wanted to give a thorough look into how these types of illnesses present themselves and how to manage them.

I want to build a community. I want to build a stockpile of resources for the chronically ill. I want a place where we can gather and compare solutions, products, doctors, and treatments. I want to bring awareness to these conditions so that they're no longer as difficult to diagnose. I want to make this process smoother for others.

The moment my podcast went live, I became an advocate. Suddenly, people from all over the world began to reach out to me, either to say they related with my story, or to tell me their own story. I always ask them "What is your advice for others?" Overwhelmingly, the responses have been to speak up to your doctor. They are experts in medicine, but you are the expert of your body. You know your body best and when something doesn't feel right, don't rest until you have the answer.

## "If I can survive an autoimmune disease diagnosis in the middle of a pandemic, I can do anything."

The other piece of advice that comes up a lot is to give yourself grace. Your body may not be capable of what it used to be, so don't push it. If you need to spend the day in bed, do it, and don't feel guilty about it.

I'm proud of the woman I have become since April 2020. I've learned so much about my body, about empathy, and about change. I know that whatever obstacles life throws at me, I'm capable of getting through them. If I can survive an autoimmune disease diagnosis in the middle of a pandemic, I can

do anything.

Imagine this: You're living your life as you always do, when suddenly, your jaw hurts. Within a few hours, the same pain shows up in your shoulder. As the pain gets worse and migrates throughout your body, you search for a cure. Doctors dismiss you and you're at your wits' end. You turn to Dr. Google for the answer and what pops up? An episode of a podcast about chronic illness. You click the link. You hear from someone who also suddenly started feeling a mystery pain. She too has been dismissed by doctors and was at her wits' end. But then she tells you her diagnosis. You send an angry email to your doctor, demanding blood tests. The results come in and you begin to heal.

# Andrea Neph

Tulsa, OK, USA

*Client Success Manager*

*"I am here to be your safe space, your shoulder to cry on, your ear to vent to, or just someone to support you on your journey."*

## About Andrea:

*Andrea Neph has battled endometriosis since she started her mensural cycle at the age of 12. As of 2021, she will have had nine surgeries for her condition. She shares her story as much as possible to provide other Endo Warriors with support, resources, and all of the love she can manifest from a far. When people ask why she continues to fight, she acknowledges a pain-free life is too foreign to process, but she won't stop fighting to make sure her daughter Lucy never has to. Andrea lives in Owasso, OK with her husband of 10 years, her 8-year-old son Ezra, and her 6-year-old daughter, Lucy.*

\* \* \*

*IG: @momminwithendo*

I'm Andrea. A wife. A mother of two. A digital campaign manager. And an #EndoWarrior.

The Mayo Clinic describes endometriosis (en-doc-me-tree-O-sis) as "an often painful disorder in which tissue similar to the tissue that normally lines the inside of your uterus — the endometrium — grows outside your uterus. Endometriosis most commonly involves your ovaries, fallopian tubes and the tissue lining your pelvis. Rarely, endometrial tissue may spread beyond pelvic organs."

However, endometriosis is ranked as one of the 20 most painful conditions. And it sucks. Symptoms include but are not limited to painful periods, painful intercourse, pain between periods, excessive bleeding during or in between periods, painful ovulation, infertility, exhaustion and fatigue, nausea, and – of course – endo belly. Some doctors call this bloating, but if you know, you know.

> **"I cried. I was still crying when I called my dad, knowing he thought I was making it all up, but desperate for someone to be on my side."**

At the beginning of 2019 I signed away my uterus. It had been a long time coming and I had discussed it ad nauseam with my friends, my husband, and my endometriosis groups on social media. I put it off as long as I could but after three surgeries in 13 months, I accepted what doctors had been telling me for years: it was time to say goodbye to my baby-maker.

I cried, hard, and for days after I signed the consent form. There is a big difference between talking about getting rid of the organs causing you pain, and signing a form saying that a doctor can remove everything inside you that makes you a woman.

My uterus and I had some good times. I mean, things started off rough when it decided to shed its lining for the first time when I was 45 minutes into a four-hour deep-sea fishing trip with my dad, my brother and my papa.

Then it started landing me in the emergency room multiple times a year with excruciating pain. Doctors would always assume it was my appendix, run me through a CT Scan, determine it was in fact NOT my appendix, and send me home with pain meds and absolutely no answers.

I was actually the one who figured out what was going on. After a lot of research, I approached my OBGYN at the age of 16 and told her I was pretty sure I had endometriosis. She put me on birth control and things got better for a while.

When I was 21, I had been to my doctor several times trying to express in G-rated language how much pain I was in and how unhelpful she was as my medical advocate. She finally said I needed surgery.

When I went in for my pre-op appointment, excited to finally figure out what had been causing the pain I'd been in for the better part of a decade. My doctor walked in and said, "Actually, I think you have a hernia," and asked me to come back for an ultrasound.

I cried. I was still crying when I called my dad, knowing he thought I was making it all up, but desperate for someone to be on my side. He had his colleague make a couple calls and the next week I saw the woman who changed my life.

> **"Many women with endometriosis never get to have biological children, and I know how incredible it is that I had two perfectly healthy pregnancies and gave birth to two perfectly healthy children."**

My doctor is one of the best doctors I have ever met. As I began explaining my eight-year health ordeal, I cried. I told her that I felt crazy, and everyone thought I was making it all up. She was very calm, very compassionate, and performed an ultrasound. She hovered over a black blob and said, "You see that? That's a seven-centimeter cyst on your right ovary." She scheduled me for surgery the following day.

Things got a lot better after that. My uterus finally made up for all the hell she'd caused when I became pregnant with my first child at the age of 25. We had a really good time growing Ezra, and then again growing Lucy, who I became pregnant with when Ezra was six months old. She and I were quite the team baking those little buns with her as my oven.

I got to watch her stretch and transform my body in magical ways. She kept my babies safe and warm throughout my pregnancies with no issues, and then alerted me when it was time to go to the hospital to bring my little pea pods into the world.

From the time Lucy was born in 2014 to the time I signed off on my full hysterectomy in 2019, I had four surgeries to remove endometriosis and large cysts and quite frankly, it just wasn't working for either of us anymore.

Endometriosis continued to grow all over her, along with a few other organs, getting worse with every surgery. I was in pain and exhausted all the time, making it hard to be the mother I wanted to be with the two children she helped me bring into this world.

So in February 2019, I finally said goodbye to my uterus, my ovaries, and my fallopian tubes. Praying that this would bring an end to my pain, I had my sixth surgery for endometriosis and said goodbye to having the big family I always wanted.

When I was trying to get pregnant, there was a moment in the middle of a Bass Pro Shop where I had an all-out breakdown. I had been dealing with my endometriosis for about 10 years at the time, and I knew there was a chance that having a biological baby wasn't in the cards for me.

At the time, everyone I knew was finding

themselves pregnant. A family member who only wanted one child was pregnant with number two. A teenager I used to babysit was due that summer. A co-worker who wasn't trying found herself expecting. Everyone was pregnant and it all seemed by accident. I, on the other hand, took my temperature every morning, logged my menstrual cycles, cut out alcohol and caffeine, and laid upside down for half an hour every time my husband and I had sex. It wasn't fair.

Fast forward to 2019 and I had two beautiful, healthy children who are the lights of my life and the songs of my soul, and yet I felt like I did in the middle of that Bass Pro Shop.

I always pictured myself with five children. My dream was to be like the family in The Family Stone, with all my children and their families coming home for Christmas, watching old movies, gathering around the dinner table, and being surrounded by love and laughter. After my second C-section just 15 months after my first, I was told I had to wait until my daughter was at least three before we could start trying again.

In the meantime, my endometriosis got worse. In 2018, when my doctor told me that I would need a hysterectomy within the next year, my husband and I decided to try to get pregnant as long as we could until the inevitable happened. Five months into trying, an ultrasound that I had hoped would eventually show baby number three showed an ovarian cyst larger than 6 centimeters. Within a week I was back in the operating room. We decided then that I would have a hysterectomy in February 2019.

Now, I am one of the lucky ones. Many women with endometriosis never get to have biological children, and I know how incredible it is that I had two perfectly healthy pregnancies and gave birth to two perfectly healthy children. I just didn't feel like I was done.

Two of my most favorite people in the world were pregnant when I had my hysterectomy - my cousin, who is like my sister, and my very best friend. I was over the moon excited for them - they were the ones who hosted my baby shower, sent gifts, stayed with us after the babies were born, and supported me through it all. They deserved this happiness more than anything.

I was also grieving.

I grieved the children that I would never carry. I grieved that I would never be pregnant again. Had I known that my last pregnancy was going to be the last time I felt a baby kick from the inside, the last time I saw a little kidney bean on the ultrasound with a fluttering heartbeat, the last time I would know the excitement of going into labor and showing up at the hospital knowing that our lives and our family would never be the same again - had I known, I would've written everything down, taken more pictures, enjoyed each kick and hiccup, and sat in silence inhaling every beautiful and incredible moment of growing a life inside of me.

It took time to process and accept that my vision for my family was going to be different than I dreamed, and while I was so excited that two people I loved more than anything were going to experience the amazing miracle that is pregnancy and childbirth, I also grieved.

After my hysterectomy, it didn't get better. After three CT scans in 18 months that all came back clear, I went back under in September 2020. My OBGYN found endometriosis on the back of my pelvic walls, on the tissue where my ovaries once were, and all over my bladder. I was both devastated and relieved. Devastated that my hysterectomy – and the menopause symptoms that followed it – didn't bring me any closer to living pain-free; relieved that I was not crazy after fearing it was phantom pains or all in my head.

Five weeks after my seventh laparoscopy for endometriosis, my urologist performed a hydrodistension to make sure that endometriosis was not on the inside of my bladder. Fortunately, it was not.

Finally, in February 2021 I was able to see a Nancy Nook approved doctor. People in the endometriosis community say that excision is the gold standard of surgery. That is great and all, but there are only 200 surgeons who perform excision, and many don't accept insurance. I would have loved to trade in my seven laser surgeries that are only 10% effective for an excision surgery that is 80% effective; alas, the excision surgeon in North Texas did not accept insurance and my family could not afford to pay out of pocket.

Then I found a doctor that was less than two hours from me in Oklahoma City, and he accepted my insurance. To say I felt like I hit the jackpot is an understatement. After running a hormone panel – the only doctor to ever run this blood test but not the only doctor to ever prescribe me hormones – he determined which hormones I should be on, sent in my prescriptions, and scheduled my excision surgery for March 18th. It might as well be on December 25th, as excited as I am.

## "I started MomminWithEndo and women have reached out to me on all social platforms to find more information, to offer support, or just to have another prayer warrior in their corner"

I am in pain every single day. I sit around a four (on a scale of one to ten) but there are days it gets up to six or seven and I can't get out of bed. Sometimes it's a full on 10 and feels like I'm in labor and I lay in child's pose, rocking back and forth and making sounds that can only be found out in nature.

You will always find me with a cart when I'm at the store, even if I'm only picking up a few items, because if the pain increases, I need something to lean on. You will never find me at the mall because I gave up after having to take multiple rests walking around what most women consider the most magical place on earth.

People ask me what my goal is - with

all the surgeries, medications, hormones, therapies, and everything else – what is my actual goal? It's not to be pain free. I would love that, I dream of it and pray for it, but honestly, my goal is that if my daughter hits puberty and is affected by this genetic condition, that she doesn't have to have nine surgeries. That she doesn't have to go through eight doctors. That she doesn't have to spend countless nights in the emergency room, feeling like nobody believes her or that the pain is in her head. I do this for my daughter. I will continue to have surgery after surgery if it means she just has to have one. I will continue to try different hormones and medications and therapies and whatever else, if it means my daughter starts at square 123 instead of square one.

When I was 13, 17, and 21 – I felt so alone. Nobody really knew what endometriosis was, there was limited education and resources. Half the time I felt like I was one of three people in the world with it, instead of knowing that I was one in ten women who have endometriosis. Thanks to Nancy Peterson and her Nancy's Nook, there is a support system out there for our people to find each other and pour love and compassion into one another.

I started MomminWithEndo and women have reached out to me on all social platforms to find more information, to offer support, or just to have another prayer warrior in their corner. I love that I can offer a safe and judgement free space for people who feel alone, unseen, or ignored.

If I could do anything, I would pour light and love into all people suffering with a chronic illness. I'd love to speak publicly, start a support group, or another organization bringing awareness to endometriosis and chronic pain, so nobody ever feels alone. I've suffered from depression most of my life, and the mental toll that chronic illness takes on a person is devastating; it has been reported that half of people with endometriosis have had suicidal thoughts. Nobody should feel alone, so anything I can do to help someone feel less alone, that's what I want to do.

For anyone who suffers from chronic pain, chronic illness or endometriosis, I see you. I know your pain and I know it's real, even if everyone else makes you feel otherwise. I know you're in pain most of the time, and when you're not huddled in the fetal position trying to find a moment or two or relief, you're exhausted and trying to find a few hours of rest before you have to face the world. I am here to be your safe space, your shoulder to cry on, your ear to vent to, or just someone to support you on your journey. That's what we should all be to each other – we're all in this together.

# Scott Ninneman

Dunlap, TN, USA

**Tax Preparer/Bookkeeper & Blogger**

*"If you're going through hell, keep going."*

## About Scott:

*Scott Ninneman is a daytime bookkeeper and tax preparer by day, and a writer at night. Scott is the voice behind the blog Speaking Bipolar, where he writes about battling mental and chronic illness. He is an active volunteer in his community. His other passions include poetry, gardening and hiking.*

* * *

*IG: @speakingbipolar*

*Website & Blog:*
*https://speakingbipolar.com/*

## "If you're going through hell, keep going."

That's one of my favorite quotes by Winston Churchill. It epitomizes the struggle of life with mental and chronic illness. Those wise words keep me going every day.

My name is Scott Ninneman, and I am a chronic and mental illness warrior. During the day, I work as a bookkeeper and tax preparer. When I'm not at work, I care for my elderly parents, am an active volunteer in my community, maintain the blog, Speaking Bipolar, and write content for various websites. I don't always get everything done, but I'm determined to try my best.

I've been blessed with a few chronic health conditions, but I'm only going to talk about two of them today.

As you can probably guess from the name of my blog, Speaking Bipolar, I have bipolar disorder. In addition, I have the auto-inflammatory disease Familial Mediterranean Fever (FMF). The two together can carry quite a wallop.

Familial Mediterranean Fever is a genetic disorder that causes your body to develop periodic fevers and create excess inflammation. Episodes of fever, called attacks, generally last up to 72 hours, but can leave you miserable much longer. You can also experience attacks one right after the other.

As the inflammation builds in your body, it crushes your vital organs such as your heart, lungs, liver, and kidneys. This squeezing induces severe chest and abdominal pain. The fever makes you feel like you have the flu and usually comes with widespread body pain. It has left me with neuropathy throughout most of my body making it uncomfortable for me to stand, sit, or even sleep at night.

Familial Mediterranean Fever is a rare disease affecting less than 1 in 1,000 people (up to 1 in 200 in some communities.) There is very little information available to help you cope with it. I dedicate a portion of my blog to talking about the disease. While I can only share my personal experiences, I hope they help others with the condition.

The blessings of chronic illness...

Earlier I said I was blessed to have a few chronic health conditions. That may sound like a strange thing to say about having an illness. However, living with chronic illness has taught me to be a better person. I'm more empathetic to what other people are feeling and attuned to their emotions.

Of course, living with chronic illness has its negative side as well. For me, the most painful thing was giving up physical activity such as hiking and gardening. It's also frustrating when I'm limited in the time I can spend with friends and family. Between pain, fevers, and general fatigue, there's seldom any energy left after my work hours.

Yet, in the good weeks, I do what I can. I volunteer, care for my family, and love to write online. Besides writing about bipolar and chronic illness, I also write poetry and short fiction.

## "...life didn't stop just because I was sick."

I haven't always been happy-go-lucky in terms of my illnesses. Before they diagnosed me with bipolar disorder in my mid-twenties, suicidal ideation was my constant companion. After a few years, I wrangled the bipolar into submission, but then in my late 30s, I started to experience unexplained physical symptoms.

It took 10 years for me to get the right diagnosis of Familial Mediterranean Fever. Those years living with constant pain and fatigue almost got the best of me. I endured a multitude of tests with normal results, leaving me thinking I was losing my mind and that life wasn't worth living. After they diagnosed me, all I wanted to do was feel sorry for myself and shut down.

Step-by-step, I learned that life didn't stop just because I was sick. There were so many things I could still do, and it was up to me to figure out what those things were. Ever since, I've been determined to use my experiences to help others. I may not be the best example, but I try to do what I can. Those times when I mess up, I try to be open with my readers about my poor decisions and how I feel about them.

I will not pretend it doesn't suck to have a chronic illness. There is nothing I would like more than to be healthy again. However, this is the life I have right now, so I'm determined to do my best with it. I'm a firm believer that life is 10 percent what happens to you, and 90 percent how you choose to react to it.

I choose to be happy and positive. I choose to focus on the things I can still do. Even if that number declines from year to year, there are still many options available to me. As long as I have any ability, I'm going to do what I can and make the best of my life while helping others.

Chronic illness on stage...

Chronic illness can disrupt your life in sudden and unexpected ways. For example, let me tell you about a night I gave a public book reading and how my illnesses interfered.

I'm not a fan of public speaking, but I don't mind public reading. Concentrating on the written material means I don't have to look at the audience. That's important for an introvert like me.

> *"...when it feels impossible to draw any more breath into your exhausted lungs, ]that's what I felt on stage."*

Since my bipolar disorder diagnosis, I've thought of my brain as a separate entity. That distinction made it easier to cope with the troublesome voices I was constantly hearing. It wasn't me. It was that crazy brain of mine.

With the Familial Mediterranean Fever diagnosis, I distanced myself from my body as well.

"My body hates me," I tell people.

Since FMF literally crushes your vital organs, it's accurate to say my body is trying to kill me. It makes sense why I'd want to distance myself from it.

Before I went up to the stage to read that night, I knew it was a bad idea. Sharp pains in my abdomen hurt so much, I had to rub it for relief. Various belts were slowly wrapping tighter around my midsection. While still in my chair, breathing required increased effort, but I pushed the doubt from my mind and climbed the stage when they announced my name.

The first couple of paragraphs went fine.

I got this, I told myself.

My body laughed wickedly deep inside. The belts got tighter.

With each new breath, the amount of air coming in was less than what went out.

I had many paragraphs left to read, but it was becoming ever clearer my air would run out long before then.

Have you ever run too far? In high school, we had this horrible test every year called the Twelve Minute Run. The requirement was to run the entire twelve minutes and reach a certain distance in that time. Failure to reach the goal meant weeks of additional gym time until you could take the test and pass.

As you can imagine, many students collapsed or tossed their cookies on Twelve Minute Run Day. Big, yellow garbage cans lined the running track, but often not close enough. It's surprising how few barfing teenagers can fit comfortably around a bin.

It was the worst kind of medieval torture, and something I hope the school no longer requires.

That feeling, when you've run too long, when it feels impossible to draw any more breath into your exhausted lungs, that's what I felt on stage. Inflammation was compressing my lungs too tightly to breathe properly.

I'm a very stubborn person.

Somewhere, my mom is yelling out a sarcastic, "No, not you!"

Face it, Mom, I get it equally from you and Dad.

Once I start something, I'm determined to finish. Tell me I can't, and I'll prove you wrong, even if I almost die trying.

## *"I was angry my body was making it impossible to hide my illness."*

With five paragraphs left, I squeezed my free hand into a tight fist and kept reading. Peering at the page, those paragraphs seemed to grow before my eyes to Faulkner-length. The situation was becoming hopeless.

Each word became more difficult as I took longer and longer pauses at every punctuation mark and then after every couple of words.

At one point, as if someone else were talking, I told the audience, "I'm having trouble breathing."

Panicked faces looked back at me, but no one seemed to know what to do. I pressed on.

Try as you may to fight it, a lack of oxygen induces anxiety. Anxiety brings with it sweating, shaking, and even less incoming air.

Picture it: my voice getting weaker, my hands shaking, and my face undoubtedly red and sweaty.

The tension in the room was palpable as the reading became meaningless and all eyes were watching me to see what would happen next.

Through jagged breaths, I finished every word of my reading, but those last sentences held no meaning. When I looked up, the room was spinning and hazy.With every ounce of energy in my body, I slithered from the stage and back to my chair.

Sitting down, intense anger washed over me. I was angry my body was making it impossible to hide my illness. It devastated me that I'd given a terrible reading and embarrassed myself in front of everyone.

If my body were a separate entity, I would have dragged it outside and pummeled it with whatever blunt instrument I could find. Unfortunately, we're inseparable, so all I could do was be angry. A deep, searing, destructive anger.

My study group is a compassionate circle of friends. While they don't all understand chronic illness, they try to be supportive. I would've preferred to be invisible and disappear from the room without notice. Instead, I put a smile on my face and forced myself to let my friends comfort me.

The price for pushing myself that night led to several days in bed, but I don't regret it.

Living with a chronic illness is a constant adventure. Relatively fine one moment, you can be a helpless mess the next.

The only option is to keep fighting.

Will I accept another reading assignment? Probably. This is not the first time I stopped breathing on stage, and probably won't be the last. I survived the embarrassment of the past, so why stop now?

There may come a time when I have to stop, when the anxiety and lack of oxygen is too intense. When that happens, I'm sure my stubbornness will give in, but that day is not today.

Today, I choose to keep fighting.

Living with chronic illness...

Through trial and error, I learned the best way to cope with my illness was to only work three or four days a week. That requires me to keep my expenses low and to use much of my down time for rest. This balancing act allows me to continue supporting myself. In addition, living with bipolar has taught me to be conscious of my mental health as well.

I don't believe that chronic illness has lessened me. I love the person I've become, and a lot of that is because of living with illness.

If you know me in real life, you know that I'm rarely seen without a smile on my face. I'm usually laughing or coming up with something funny to say. In reality, my smile is often hiding the pain and fatigue I'm trying to conceal from the world.

Since I know the things hiding behind my smile, I am quick to pick up on how other people are feeling. I immediately sense pain, depression, and fatigue in others. I feel their emotions regardless of their expression. I consider that empathy a gift.

Chronic illness has also taught me to be more patient and kind to others. When a person is rude to me, I can see past the action and imagine what events might trigger their rudeness. It's made me more forgiving and taught me the ability to let most things roll off my back.

Before illness, my dreams used to be traveling the world as a full-time writer and eventually settling down on a quiet beach somewhere warm. It's unlikely I'll reach either of those goals, but I'm happy with my peaceful life in the mountains of Tennessee. Travel gets more difficult with each passing year, even before the pandemic, so I may never realize that goal. However, life has taught me that the unexpected is often possible, so I'm keeping it as a dream.

Advice for other warriors...

There is an abundance of advice I could give to others living with a chronic condition. In fact, it's the subject I most frequently write about online. To condense my knowledge, I can sum up much of it into three key points.

One, it's vital you take responsibility for your own health. No matter how great your care team is, no one knows you the way you know yourself. It's up to you to make sure you are taking care of yourself and that you are tracking the way medications and treatments are affecting you. It also means that you might have to stand up for yourself to make a medical professional understand what's happening with you.

Taking responsibility for your care includes learning as much as you can about your condition and treatment options. If there's no information out there, then write your own as you go along.

Two, it's imperative to take time for yourself. Self-care can feel selfish, especially if you have others you're caring for, but it's not something you can skip. If you don't take care of yourself first, you're no good to anyone else.

Three, it's okay to feel sorry for yourself sometimes. Just like you mourn any other loss in your life, it's okay to mourn the loss of your health and any new limitations. Staying in that darkness can be a dangerous trap, but the occasional pity party is healthy. Take the time to cry and eat ice cream and scream into a pillow. Letting out that stress will help you endure the other days.

Life with chronic illness doesn't have to be solely about sacrifices. If I've learned anything, it's that I still can live a full and productive life. The key is learning what things work for you and which things don't. Since many chronic illnesses are progressive, this means you need to be constantly reevaluating. Yet, even if things get worse, there are always things you can do to make the world a better place.

For me, I do my meager part by volunteering in my community and writing online. For you, the possibilities are endless. The secret is to keep looking for the things you can do and put behind you the things you can't.

No matter how you move forward, the most important thing is to always keep fighting. Remember,

## "If you're going through hell, keep going."

# Jemma-Tiffany Rosewater

Columbia, MDw, USA

## Writer/Author & Hyperacusis Advocate

*"My goal is to become an advocate and author."*

## About Jemma-Tiffany:

*Jemma is the fonder of the Hyperacusis Awareness movement and has lived with hyperacusis since she was six years old. She also has several other medical conditions, and a including a significant visual impairment. Her childhood has been very different than most kids. She has been unable to attend social events, go to the store or most public places, listen to music, wash dishes, go on vacation, or even take showers because the noise causes her extreme physical pain and lingering migraines.Most of the time she would (still does) stay in her soundproof bedroom, closet, or grandma's underground basement. She experiences pain on a daily basis just from noises like airplanes, or phones ringing. Unfortunately growing up most Doctors didn't believe her pain and often thought that she had an emotional or psychological condition. Due to the rarity of hyperacusis and the lack of research, she was often subjected to sound exposure treatments that increased my pain and worsened her condition. Her goal is to help raise awareness about hyperacusis and other rare disorders/chronic pain conditions, put in place laws to accommodate those with hyperacusis, and push for more research to be done on hyperacusis.*

\* \* \*

**IG:** *@jemma_rosewater @Hyperacusis_awareness*

# Growing Up with Hyperacusis

## My Early Years

My name is Jemma-Tiffany. At age seven, I started having awful migraines that would last for months at a time and were exacerbated by normal sounds. I became unable to attend school and was put on home and hospital instruction. My mother took me to a lot of different doctors but none of them knew what was going on, they said that I had chronic migraines with extreme sound sensitivity. I became unable to go to the store, attend parties, go to restaurants, or even watch TV on a normal volume due to the physical pain these things caused my head and ears. Around this time I was also diagnosed with glaucoma and became legally blind. I was born with cataracts so I already had low vision.

## Late Elementary School Years

In the beginning of third grade my mother took me to see an audiologist; she felt like my sound sensitivity was more extreme than normal migraines. The audiologist said that I had a rare disorder called Hyperacusis, unfortunately many of the treatments that he had me do for my Hyperacusis only intensified my pain. In third grade they started me off at school which was very painful for me. The pain eventually built up to where I was lying in bed for about a month and ended up on home and hospital instruction again. Except now my Hyperacusis was worse; the sound of wind blowing or birds chirping was physically painful and I was no longer able to go outside. My mother took me to see many different doctors and therapists, unfortunately many of them did not believe me about experiencing physical pain from sounds.

Many of the doctors thought that my condition was a psychosomatic/emotional disorder. Even the few doctors who did believe that I experienced physical pain still forced me to do desensitization and sound exposure therapy. These plans only increased my pain level which led to me being even more sensitive to sound. I felt so misunderstood and alone and it was so frustrating being in pain and having no one believe me. In fourth grade, I was transferred to another school that had a specialized program for students with emotional disabilities.

## "All of the noise from attending school had caused a long-term increase in my hyperacusis."

Unfortunately, many of these students would scream and bang loudly which was excruciatingly painful for me. The pain just continued to build up day after day and eventually I was no longer able to continue attending school and once again ended up on home and hospital instruction. Fourth grade was also when my mother and grandma first

**"I started going to school at a special program and although it was quieter than some of the schools I'd been to in the past, it was still extremely loud and painful."**

realized that I was having seizures, because I banged a plate against the table, fell down, and peed in the bed. The first neurologist my mom took me to told her that it was just drama, but she didn't believe him. We went to see another neurologist who did an EEG, and then diagnosed me with epilepsy.

All of the noise from attending school had caused a long-term increase in my hyperacusis. I was no longer able to eat in the kitchen. The sound of the refrigerator humming caused throbbing pain on my forehead and the sides of my head above my ears. The sound of silverware clanking together felt like I was being stabbed in the temple and ear. I could not even sleep in my own bedroom because I was able to hear the sound of traffic from the road which sent throbbing pain to my forehead. My parents sound-proofed my bedroom and I slept in a closet inside of it with both of the doors closed. Whenever the people would come to mow the grass or blow the leaves my mother had to drive me away because the sound from the power tools felt like I was being punched on the forehead and ears. I spent most of my time either in my grandmother's underground basement or my closet. I have to watch all of my TV shows on volume one and am unable to listen to music. When my friends come over we just hang out in my bedroom and talk softly. I was receiving home and hospital instruction at an office building and this was working quite well for me. It was quiet and I was able to learn without it being extremely painful.

In fifth grade they decided to have me go back to school again only this time they said they would put me in a separate room by myself. The room they got me in was right next to the music room! The sound of the drums was so painful for me I felt like I was being beaten in the head and ears. The pain once again continued to build up and I could no longer attend school anymore and ended up on home and hospital instruction once more. I spent most of my time in my closet or in my grandmother's underground basement. Although I was in less pain as my environment was much quieter, I was under a constant high level of stress and fear, as many of my doctors were wanting me to do sound exposure therapy. I felt miserable because no one understood my Hyperacusis; no one understood what it was like to experience pain from every sound. I was so afraid they were going to make me do exposure therapy, as they were always talking about it.

### The Darkest Years

In sixth grade they started me off in the very beginning of the year on home and hospital instruction, but it was in a louder building. This increased my pain level and I thought that I just couldn't take it anymore. I knew that something really bad was about to happen to me and people were going to start making me do desensitization. Having experienced the physical pain of this in the past, I tried to prevent myself from having to go through that pain again, and I attempted suicide. I ended up in a psychiatric hospital. The doctors there thought that I was just being manipulative and they did not believe that I experienced physical pain from sound. They thought that my Hyperacusis was something that I was making up. They forced me to go to group therapy and eat meals with the other children who were nonverbal and would often scream and bang. I was in more pain than I have ever been in my life, even more pain than the time I fell and fractured my wrist. I felt like my head was going to explode, my ears felt like they were on fire, and oftentimes I wanted to cry because the pain was so bad. They tried to convince my parents that I was just being manipulative and that my Hyperacusis was purely a behavioral problem and that I did not experience real physical pain from sound. My mother did not believe this, however she and my family did implement the behavioral plan that they sent home with me when I was discharged. I went to a day program for about a week after being discharged and the doctors there decided to take me off of home and hospital instruction.

I started going to school at a special program and although it was quieter than some of the schools I'd been to in the past, it was still extremely loud and painful. Every day I was in extreme pain and the adults in my life did not believe me at home or at school. At home my parents tried to implement the behavioral plan which mostly involves me doing things in the kitchen or on the main level. I refused, as I was in so much pain and people thought that I was simply being uncooperative. Every day I wanted to die because the pain was so bad. Finally I decided to do a lot of research on my own to try to find out more information about Hyperacusis. I wrote a research paper to my doctor and after about six months of me refusing to do the plan and trying to explain to them that it was causing me extreme pain they finally got rid of it. Unfortunately, I still continued to attend school. Not only did attending school cause me pain while I was at school, but I had lingering pain on the weekends and days off. I often missed at least one day of school every week due to the pain from sounds. My migraines were awful and the Hyperacusis was not improving at all.

I still wanted to kill myself because I was in so much pain and I didn't know if it would ever end. My mother decided to take away my headphones and start forcing me to take showers that summer. The sound of the shower water running sent throbbing pain through my forehead on the side of my head. The sound of the water hitting the bathtub sent sharp pain into my temples and ears. I cried every time I had to take a shower because it was so painful and the pain lasted long after the shower

**"I was still in extreme pain every day; small sounds still hurt me."**

was finished so even though I showered only every other day I was still in heightened and elevated pain in between. Without my headphones to cover my whole ears I only had my earplugs. This further elevated my pain level and I continued to make frequent suicide attempts. I was never able to escape from the pain. Finally my mother stopped forcing me to take showers and my father was willing to run my bathwater.

Starting in the seventh grade, whenever there was extremely loud noise for an extended period of time, I would have uncontrolled body movements that my mom said looked like I had been slapped. I was diagnosed with hyperekplexia (exaggerated startle reflex to sound). I was still in extreme pain from attending school and even though I was not allowed to wear my headphones at home, thankfully my mother would allow me to wear them at school. I spent all of middle school wanting nothing more than to die, to somehow escape from this pain. I just wanted the pain to go away and no one understood. I made another major suicide attempt in eighth grade. I ended up in the emergency room although I was able to convince the psychologist on duty to let me go home. Things did begin to improve slightly after this when my doctors and parents agreed to look at some of the more recent research on hyperacusis and different therapies that did not involve sound. I started using different electrical nerve stimulation devices which helped reduce my pain level a little. I was now able to sit in my bedroom without any hearing protection, as well as sit in the upstairs bedrooms when it was quiet without hearing protection, without exacerbating my pain.

I was still in extreme pain every day; small sounds still hurt me. This was when I found out about Hyperacusis Research, a nonprofit organization dedicated to finding a cure to Hyperacusis with pain. Their research was what started to help my parents and doctors to understand more about Hyperacusis. I reached out to President Bryan Pollard of Hyperacusis Research and shared many of their research articles with my parents and doctors. I also found an online support group on Facebook called Hyperacusis Support and Research. This was so helpful for me as I was finally able to talk with other people who had Hyperacusis with pain and were made worse by sound therapy and had similar experiences with doctors and family members who did not understand.

## A Light in the Tunnel and the Spark that Ignited my Advocacy

In ninth grade they had to shorten my schedule as my pain was just too intense from all of the noise to do a full day of school as I had several classes in a noisier part of the building. I also received home and hospital instruction for math class, which was helpful. Although my mother is more understanding, she still continues to believe in auditory gain theory that if I am overprotective then it will make my Hyperacusis worse. I continue to follow Hyperacusis Research and show this information to my parents and doctors. In 10th grade, I had a project where we had to create a bill proposal for government class. My proposal encouraged the state of Maryland to create a Hyperacusis school program.

I took it much further than a school project though! Shortly after, I began to call congress about Hyperacusis. I also reached out to the Maryland State Board of Education and strongly encouraged them to create a Hyperacusis school program in my lifetime. In February of this year, for the first time, I spoke publicly. I did a presentation in front of the Howard County Department of Special Education and made several recommendations. I told my story of struggling as a student with Hyperacusis. I described what it is physically like for me every day. Hyperacusis Research has continued to publish more peer reviewed articles in medical journals about Hyperacusis. With the confidence of the medical research articles, experiences in contacting government officials/ legislative advocacy, and the empowerment that I got from speaking publicly, I realized that there were ways that I could make a difference for people with Hyperacusis. I started doing just that! I reached out to a researcher, Paul Fuchs. He is researching pain and Hyperacusis at Johns Hopkins. I shared some of my questions and thoughts about his research. I also reached out to NORD, National Organization for Rare Disorders. When the COVID-10 quarantine began I was in a lot less pain, as I could stay in my closet and soundproof bedroom all day. In addition, I am able to participate in a lot more things now, because everything is virtual. I can control the volume and mute the sound.

I have reached out to Dr. Fan Fang-Zeng who is researching pain Hyperacusis and told them about my situation. I have decided that I want to dedicate my life to raising awareness and advocacy about Hyperacusis, getting accommodations in place for people with Hyperacusis, and helping to inform the medical community about pain Hyperacusis. I have now started a Facebook page as well as an Instagram business page and YouTube called Hyperacusis Awareness to help educate policymakers and doctors in the community...

I am now in the 11th grade, doing distance-learning, which has been the best school year I have ever had. I am a part of several organizations including YARR (Young Adult rare Representatives), through the EveryLife Foundation for Rare Disease, International Pain Foundation, Rare Youth Revolution, and of course Hyperacusis Research. As part of my movement to help people with hyperacusis I have started a Patient Education and Support Program, as well as a hyperacusis education and accommodations virtual training. My goal is to become an advocate and author. I am already working with an editor and in the process of self-publishing my novel, called Alien Princess.

# Natalie Jezierny

Park Ridge, IL, USA

*Professional Binge Watcher*

## About Natalie:

*My name is Natalie Jezierny and I'm from the Midwest. I've always had a passion for writing since I was little. I'm so glad to be able to share my story with the world. On my Instagram, I post updates about my health, spread awareness, and help others to advocate for themselves. I enjoy meeting new people and helping them through their own situations. Throughout my journey, I have learned so much, and have had the opportunity to grow as a person. In my free time, I enjoy spending time with my family and friends. I love being around the people who make me feel supported and happy. I hope you enjoy my story, and are able to learn something new today!*

\* \* \*

**IG:** *@spooniesrus*

*"Trust the process. It might not seem like it now, but you will get there."*

My name is Natalie Jezierny. I'm 15 years old and currently a sophomore in highschool. I became sick back in 2018. Since then, I've had multiple diagnoses after many years of fighting for one. My main diagnosis is my autoimmune disease; which we believe triggered everything else I have. Lots of these illnesses have comorbidities, meaning they go hand in hand. If you have one, you have a high chance of developing the other. I was undiagnosed for four years leaving me with terrible deviations in my hands that I'm working on getting back to normal. However, the damage might be permanent. I have postural orthostatic tachycardia syndrome (POTS), juvenile rheumatoid arthritis (JRA), irritable bowel syndrome (IBS), chronic fatigue syndrome (CFS), amplified musculoskeletal pain syndrome (AMPS), and gastroesophageal reflux disease (GERD).

POTS is caused by a dysfunction in the autonomic nervous system. It controls your heart rate and blood pressure causing dizziness, tachycardia, fatigue, circulation issues, and more. JRA is an autoimmune disease that causes my body's immune system to attack its own tissue and joints. This causes intense joint pain, swelling, fatigue, hair loss, and much more. AMPS is an overactive reflex that causes constriction of blood vessels. The symptoms I experience are allodynia (pain upon touch), fire waves and shocks, and random pains. CFS is an extreme state of fatigue that never gets better with no explanation. This causes me to be tired no matter how much sleep I get. I also experience hot flashes, nausea, shortness of breath, body aches, and generally feeling unwell.

IBS is a spastic state of the colon. Whatever I eat causes intense abdominal pain. GERD is a digestive disease where bile or stomach acid irritates the food pipe lining. This gives me chest pain, sour taste in my mouth, and burning of the stomach. To sum it up, all of this makes me feel like I have the flu every minute of my life. To manage these conditions, I take lots of medication, engage in physical and occupational therapy, use splinting, and apply heat compression. This helps to some extent, but the symptoms are always there. One day I woke up sick, and never got better.

## "Adapting isn't easy. It's really shitty. You grieve who you used to be, the potential you could've had, and all the wasted time gone."

My illnesses affect my everyday life. Day to day tasks become impossible. Getting out of bed is a chore. There's no energy to be spent and definitely none to be wasted. If there's something I want to do, I have to rest for days in hopes I'll be able to accomplish it. I need help with tasks most teens can do on their own. I like to be as independent as I can be, so accepting help can be hard. A big change of mine has been having to switch to homeschooling since becoming sick. If I sit up at my desk for two hours, I end up with heavy symptoms. Such as, sweats, nausea, fatigue, can't speak, trouble breathing, and chills. This is something most people don't understand. How could something as simple as sitting up do this much damage? Sometimes just standing is enough to trigger a flare. CFS is one of my illnesses that impacts me the most. It's stolen my ability to do anything without rest. Wake up and take a shower, rest. Make lunch and eat it, rest. Spend time doing something with my family, rest. No matter what you do, it takes energy you don't have. Majority of the time, I do school from my bed. It has prevented a lot of CFS flares. It is not ideal, but it's what's best for my health.

My illnesses have left me immunocompromised and stuck in isolation. I can't see my friends or my family. Back when I was able to see people, there were many times I had to cancel at the last minute. Sometimes, people understand it as I don't want to see them or didn't feel like coming. In reality, it's due to pain or fatigue. I truly wish I was able to go out like kids my age. Instead, I just watch them all have fun while I sit in bed. My illnesses have caused me to lose friends, but also showed who really cared: the people who will come visit you when you're stuck at home and who will cheer you up on a bad day.

Countless doctors appointments, failed treatments, and side effects play a large role in my life. I'm not able to do things I used to be able to do. One of the biggest symptoms I experience is brain fog. Some of the symptoms are confusion, trouble speaking, and slurring words. Other times, I can't even speak. It is very hard to have conversations or memorize things. Flare days are when my illnesses amplify and impact me the most. I'm not myself. I lay in bed all day and try every remedy known to man. Heat, ice, pain medicine, braces, splints, and distraction. No matter how many of these things I try, nothing helps. Unfortunately, it is just something you have to wait out. Being patient is hard. Flares can last one day, a month or two, or even a year. You just never know. When I notice a flare starting, I try to rest right away. This can prevent it from getting worse. It could also prevent the length of the flare. Fighting a flare and doing schoolwork is one of the hardest things I've ever had to do. The days feel like they never end, and the homework just piles on. Even with accommodations, there's days I don't want to use them because even if I use an extension on this assignment, then I'm just going to get another one tomorrow.

## "I'm very passionate about helping others advocate for themselves as well."

Adapting isn't easy. It's really shitty. You grieve who you used to be, the potential you could've had, and all the wasted time gone. You wake up everyday and no matter how many things you did right, you're still sick. You're always going to be sick. It's like you're living a nightmare each day. You watch everyone else around you live their life and have fun while yours just passes by. This is something that never gets easier. You think to yourself, "I wish

I could do that." In reality, if you did do that, you could end up hospitalized. I've had a hard time adapting to this bad hand of cards I was dealt. You are starting over; a new life thrown at you that's completely different than the one you were living. You try to relearn how to do your daily activities. Plan how you are going to manage the many doctor's appointments a week. Worry about your future and if you will be able to afford your healthcare. Being someone who takes almost 20 medications daily (not to mention the injections, mobility aids, copays, and emergency room costs), it's scary to think about not having affordable healthcare. These are things chronically ill people need to live. It's not optional and most definitely shouldn't be negotiable. Along with all of this, you start to look for accommodations that will help you. Since I'm in school, we have a plan going. I deal with memory loss, so quizzes and tests are out of the question most times. Something I strongly recommend if you're in school is to get a 504 plan. A 504 plan is a plan developed for a child with a disability. They are entitled to the appropriate accommodations. This helps ensure their ability to succeed. Working with my teachers to help me succeed has been amazing. Something as simple as a teacher's copy of notes instead of writing them myself helps. All the small things add up. This can help you get by, make things a little more enjoyable, and hopefully prevent flares as well. As far as home life goes, you learn what you need to change and add to make your routine more accessible such as using a shower chair, needing mobility aids, and asking for help.

I've always loved my ability to be

> **"After going through a couple bad doctors, finding the right team who believes me is the best gift. I wish I could provide that for others. I want to be able to help people like they've helped me."**

empathetic and help people. I think it's one of the most important traits to have. You can really put things into a different perspective. It's helped me understand others better, even when I'm not in the exact same situation as them. I'm able to give support and advice to almost anyone. It's easy for me to see what they are going through when I've been through it myself. I'm very passionate about helping others advocate for themselves as well. I hate seeing them go through the process of diagnosis testing, and watching them get treated badly by doctors infuriates me! I want to be an outlet for them because I know how it feels to have the world crashing down on your shoulders. My health account is a place people can come to be understood, which is the main reason why I started it. I love meeting new people and hearing their stories. It's pretty much an instant connection. When you find other people who are in the same boat as you, you're automatic friends. I always try to give advice on how to handle these situations. I started something called

Sunshine Mail. After receiving many cards from sweet followers it encouraged me. I know how much joy the letters I got gave me. I wanted to be able to do that for others. I got the supplies I needed and started getting to work! I created a google form where people can fill out their information. This helps me get to know them better and what illnesses they have. Sunshine mail is a handmade card of encouragement. I also include fun stickers. I love seeing the smiles on their faces when they receive the card. It makes me happy knowing I can make someone's day just a bit better. Everyone is going through so much, little acts of kindness can go a long way. It's always important to think of other people.

If I could be doing anything in my life it would be pursuing a career in the medical field. I love learning about anything medical. I enjoy researching my conditions to see if there's other options for treatment. But for now that will have to remain a hobby. After going through a couple bad doctors, finding the right team who believes me is the best gift. I wish I could provide that for others. I want to be able to help people like they've helped me. To give back and be the person who validated you and made you feel heard. In an ideal world, I would've loved to be in pediatrics! I love working with kids, and I feel I would be able to relate to them well. Getting diagnosed with these life changing illnesses at a young age is hard. You have barely lived and now you have to dedicate a lot of your time to your health. The way you get treated by a doctor can make or break your day. I would have loved to make kids' visits more enjoyable.

## "Being undiagnosed is HARD. Being in pain everyday is HARD. Not being validated by doctors is HARD. Being dismissed by family members is HARD."

Even for healthy ones just coming in for a checkup, it can be scary for them. The way my pediatric doctors have treated me is a way I will remember forever. It was almost always a positive experience. My doctors tell me all the time I'd make a good physician. Hearing them say that means so much.

Unfortunately, I'm too sick to work in the medical field. CFS has left me bedridden for most of the day. I know I wouldn't be able to make it to work everyday if that was my profession. However, I genuinely love the social media platform. I'm able to connect with others, raise awareness, and share my story! This is something I plan to do until I can't anymore. Throughout my journey, I have met so many amazing people all because of my health-related Instagram. I will keep using my voice until change is made, until treatments are found, until no-good, crappy doctors get their act together and are held accountable for their actions. The day our healthcare system is changed will be the highlight of my life. Each day I'm filled with joy to meet new people on this platform. My story might be someone else's survival guide. When I first got sick I wished I had someone to guide me through it the way that I'm guiding other people through it right now. Just knowing people are out there dealing with the same issues you are is comforting. If this community has shown me one thing, it's that you are not alone. I have hope that together as a community we will do amazing things.

A huge piece of advice I'd give to someone relating to my story is to trust the process. It might not seem like it now, but you will get there. Being undiagnosed is HARD. Being in pain everyday is HARD. Not being validated by doctors is HARD. Being dismissed by family members is HARD. You will eventually find the right team who treats you like you should be treated. You will find people who are there for you no matter what and who provide you with support and advice. You will find medication that works for you. It might take some tweaking of dosages and trial and error, but in the end you will find answers. Never stop advocating for yourself. You know your body better than anyone. If you feel something is wrong, speak up! Your condition is just a chapter your doctor learned about in med school, but you're the one living it. They don't know what it's like, which is why it is so important to advocate for yourself. Doctors can be so dismissive and cruel. Show them you aren't going to take their crap. It's no cure, but it's a routine to get you by. You will slowly learn to adjust to this new life. That might mean giving up something you used to do, or making some changes in your usual routine. You're starting over. Learning to live with chronic illness can be tough. Cut yourself some slack. You can find happiness despite the circumstances and that's the most important thing to remember. As Alise Morse Earle said, "Everyday might not be good, but there's something good in every day." No matter what, bad days are inevitable. It can be frustrating asking for help, but there's no shame in needing it. Taking care of your mental health is super important when being diagnosed as the news can have a huge negative impact, especially when trying to deal with the change of it all. Even though you might think you don't need it now, seeing a therapist can help dramatically. Having a professional help you deal with the stress can take some weight off your chest. The less stress, the better.

# Danielle Marie Turco

Woodbury, NY, USA

## Certified Lifestyle Coach & E-RYT 500 Yoga Instructor

*"Life is way too precious to waste energy on anything that does not bring [you] happiness."*

**About Danielle:**

*Danielle is a certified life coach, yoga instructor and blogs about her life journey on her website and Instagram. Thanks to yoga, she continues to grow in her spiritual journey and has also begun to do some motivational speaking. Danielle is currently in the process of writing and publishing a book about keto and autoimmune disease. This book is being published by ImagineWe Publishers and you can find updates about this book on my social media.*

\* \* \*

*IG: @ketolupie*

*Facebook: @ketolupie1*

*TikToc: @ketolupie*

*Website:*
*www.ketolupie.com*
*http://laxinforlupus.org/*

I was diagnosed with lupus and antiphospholipid antibody syndrome in the winter of 2000. I was 27 years old and pregnant with my son. My pregnancy was horrible. I was beyond exhausted, every piece of my body hurt (including my hair), my balance was terribly off and I felt so sick. I knew this couldn't be normal. While reviewing my blood work at a routine visit my OB very matter-of-factly stated, "Oh and you have lupus." She said they would monitor me, but everything would be ok and not to worry.

I had never heard of lupus and had a million questions. The doctor was very dismissive and sent me on my way. I spent the rest of my pregnancy under the care of her group and trusted them. That was a mistake. By my third trimester I was rapidly gaining weight, filling up with fluid and my blood pressure kept rising. The group was consistent in telling me, "All of this is normal and everything will be fine." Three weeks before my due date the baby hadn't moved in hours. He was normally very active so I became concerned. I called the office and they had me come right over. I saw an OB I had never seen before. She took one look at me and knew something was wrong. After her evaluation she told us I was pre-eclamptic and needed to be induced immediately.

My delivery was like something out of a horror scene. I began to hemorrhage and all hands were on deck. I had never seen so many people in a room at one time for one patient. Thankfully, they controlled the bleeding. My beautiful baby and I were going to be ok.

Two days later my husband took us home.

About four days after the birth of my son something started to bother me in my leg. The doctors sent me for an ultrasound. They found a blood clot in my leg. I was told this was normal after giving birth. I was put on Coumadin and checked daily to make sure the clot didn't travel to my heart. At this point I trusted no one and began a search for a rheumatologist to explain lupus to me and what the rest of my life would look like.

I found someone amazing upon a friend's recommendation. He did a ton of bloodwork and a very extensive evaluation at my first visit. He was so kind and understanding. I was sent home with so many resources and information to keep me busy until my next visit where we would go over everything. I was like a sponge absorbing every piece of information I could get my hands on.

## "No one knows what causes lupus. We do know lupus and other autoimmune diseases run in families."

At my next visit I received my diagnosis, lupus and antiphospholipid antibody syndrome. He explained how these diseases have been affecting me for years and the roles they played during my pregnancy. Then, he put me on a baby aspirin daily and Plaquenil. I was not happy about the Plaquenil and refused to take a medication that may or may not work."What are these two diseases I have been diagnosed with?" was the question I kept asking myself. Antiphospholipid antibody syndrome is when your immune system produces antibodies that make your blood sticky and more likely to clot. It is as if your blood begins to clot against itself. We produce antibodies to protect the body against invaders, such as viruses and bacteria. Antiphospholipid syndrome is usually caused by an underlying condition, such as an autoimmune disorder (in my case lupus), infection or certain medications. You also can develop the syndrome without an underlying cause or pre-existing conditions.

## "I decided to put every minute of my day into finding out how to make myself healthier."

Antiphospholipid antibody syndrome can affect any or multiple organs of the body. Depending on which organ is affected by a blood clot and how severe the obstruction of blood flow to that organ is, untreated antiphospholipid syndrome can lead to permanent organ damage or death. A few common complications of this syndrome include, kidney failure, stroke, cardiovascular problems, lung problems and numerous pregnancy complications.

Now lupus. Lupus is a chronic (long-term) disease that can cause inflammation and pain in any part of your body. It's an autoimmune disease, which means that your immune system attacks healthy tissue instead.

The immune system is the body system that usually fights infections. In the case of lupus, healthy parts of the body are constantly under attack. Lupus can affect any part of the body, but the most common parts are skin, joints and internal organs. Since lupus affects so many parts of the body, symptoms run all over the map. This is one of the reasons lupus is so hard to diagnose. There is not one specific complaint that points to it. Most lupus patients, on average, take about six years to get diagnosed. Anyone can develop lupus. But certain people are at higher risk for lupus, including women ages 15 to 44, and certain racial or ethnic groups. The highest being people who are African American, Asian American, Hispanic/Latino, Native American, or Pacific Islander. Lupus is also genetic. Therefore, people who have a family member with lupus or another autoimmune disease are more prone to a lupus diagnosis.

No one knows what causes lupus. We do know lupus and other autoimmune diseases run in families. Researchers also think it may develop in response to certain hormones (like estrogen) or environmental triggers. An environmental trigger is something outside the body, such as any form of stress that can bring on symptoms of lupus or make them worse. This was all beginning to make sense to me. I was not crazy! I spent time going from doctor to doctor only to be misdiagnosed for nearly 10 years. After a while, you truly believe it is all in your head. I had given up looking for what was wrong with me in my early 20's. I could not believe that at 28 years old I finally had my answer thanks to routine pregnancy blood work.

For years, I tried every holistic treatment I could get my hands on. I have never been on any medications and just did my best to get through my days for my family. I suffered silently, refusing to ever let anyone know the pain I was feeling. As the years went on, I began to push myself to extreme limits pretending I was ok and like everyone else. I ran half-marathons, participated in extreme sports races and never took time to rest or care for myself. In August of 2017 it all went to hell. My family decided to move, both of my children were moving on to new schools and my husband was beginning a new job. The stress of all these things began to take a toll on me and I came crashing down.

I began to research, "Diet and Lupus." From this I found I was over working my body and eating foods that are inflammatory for people with autoimmune disease. I decided to put every minute of my day into finding out how to make myself healthier. The first thing I did was begin taking yoga classes. As my body and mind began to heal I became a new person. My passion to heal myself grew more and more every day. Yoga is about overall health - body, mind and spirit. After a few weeks my mind and spirit were becoming transformed so now it was time to work on my body. Inside and out. In October of 2017 I made the lifestyle change to a ketogenic/AIP diet. I removed all inflammatory foods from my diet and in a few weeks, I felt amazing and my energy level was through the roof. It is now over three years later and my lupus is in remission. I have no symptoms and blood

> ## "Life is way too precious to waste energy on anything that does not bring me happiness."

work shows no inflammatory markers. My doctor cannot confirm or deny that this way of life has anything to do with my remission, but told me not to change a thing. I feel absolutely fabulous and I am very healthy. My cholesterol and blood pressure are perfect! I have taken my yoga practice to a new level, becoming a Certified Yoga Instructor. I have my RYT 500, meaning my certification is globally recognized. I teach 3-5 times a week and practice about the same. What is most important is that I now function like a normal person.

Thanks to yoga I no longer sweat the small stuff. Life is way too precious to waste energy on anything that does not bring me happiness. I live every single day grateful for my body and mind. Like the song says, "Life is short, make it sweet." Don't give up. Keep researching and find the thing that works for you. I have found that the best medicine is a positive state of mind. This disease is terrible. I totally get that. I suffered for many years, but didn't give up. I researched and fought until I found what worked for me. I am aware my lupus can come back at any moment. Until then, I will live my life to the fullest.

# Brandon Mouw

Huntington Beach, CA, USA

**Published Author & Motivational Speaker**

*"Every day is a gift no matter how big or small. Never give up or be afraid to make the ask."*

## About Brandon:

*Brandon was just three-years-old when he was diagnosed as a Juvenile Type 1 Diabetic. His journey with diabetes is a survivor story. Growing up in a chicken farm, Brandon became a high school social studies teacher and law school graduate before becoming a brittle diabetic. He underwent nine surgeries, lost a kidney, was told that death was imminent, and even raised the funds to pay for his life-saving pancreas only transplant via Gofundme, in a short amount of time. Brandon can now be found catching waves in Southern California or hiking with his diabetic alert dog Boone.*

\* \* \*

*IG & FB: @brandonmouwofficial*

*Website:*
*www.brandonmouw.com*

My health was never an issue. I was so well managed on my own that I only needed blood work once a year with an appointment. My trusted doctor knew that if anything seemed off for me that I'd call and it would get handled. However, in my late twenties I had such a bad pain in my left side that I needed to go to the hospital. This was my second time having to go to the hospital in my life. Something was definitely wrong with me and it took me almost a week fighting the pain to admit that I needed to seek out help.

Being vulnerable is a terrible feeling. The fear of having someone know my weaknesses and using them against me is real. It has happened before, and I learned from that mistake. So years ago, I built walls that no one could get through, or climb over, to make me be vulnerable ever again.

I hid my Juvenile Diabetes the best I could for 28 years. I wasn't ashamed or had a victim mentality about my diagnosis, but it was no one's business to know what, if anything, was different or going on with me—and it made me look weak in the eyes of others that did not understand. When cohorts found out I was a diabetic, I would be chosen last to play kickball, less was expected of me, and I was seen as an oddball. It was better that no one knew because I could hide my illness.

There are really so few Type 1 Diabetics that people get it confused with other illnesses and think diabetes is caused from doing something wrong to yourself. That is not something I wanted others to think about me, so I made sure I was as normal as possible and doing a spectacular job at maintaining my health while reinforcing and making my protective walls stronger and stronger with each day.

However, that comes at a cost...there is a cost to everything, I suppose, and over time, I hid the part of me that made me seem less than in the eyes of others. By doing so, I also began to self-isolate from others: Not on purpose, but I was stronger on my own—less people to see me in a negative light. Instead of focusing on being social, I dedicated everything I had to my health, wellness, and climbing the financial ladder. I was happy, so I thought, and all was going swimmingly well until I had a terrible pain in my left side that wouldn't go away...

## "I was told all went well and I could get back to normal life as soon as I felt up to it."

My name is Brandon Mouw and I was diagnosed with Juvenile Type 1 Diabetes at age three. Type 1 Diabetes is an autoimmune disease that attacks the pancreas making the body dependent on insulin to control blood sugars. There is no cure, reversal, or diet that changes the fact that insulin is required for the body to break down food and function. I'm a former high school social studies teacher, law school graduate, motivational speaker, author, and advocate trying to raise awareness about chronic illness.

Turns out the pain in my side was from two kidney stones in my left kidney—completely unrelated to autoimmune diseases and diabetes. They needed to be removed surgically. I was told all went well and I could get back to normal life as soon as I felt up to it. And, I began getting back to life right away, but I didn't feel like my normal self. I wrote it off as my body healing; after all this was my first surgery. I saw the surgeon for my follow-up appointment and said I felt great, but that wasn't true. I had my stent removed and was told that all looked well. So, I didn't think twice about it and started right back up where I left off.

I never truly felt good after the kidney surgery. I was always lethargic, like my mind was foggy and I lacked the energy to get through the day. Additionally, I was in law school and I could feel, for the first time, the toll it was taking. My memory and short term memory had always served me well, and all of the sudden I would find myself having to write notes to help me remember basic facts when it had never been an issue before. This was very concerning to me as well. So, I asked my primary doctor what was going on. She ran some lab work and everything returned normal. After all, I was always the perfect specimen of health and I'd tell someone if anything was wrong.

A few weeks later, I made an appointment with my endocrinologist because I knew something was not right. I felt like total crap. I only felt like this when my blood sugars were off, and, to me, they were not off or out of my control. The endocrinologist said I was having more low blood sugars than normal, which was true but I wasn't noticing it to be an issue. So, we adjusted my insulin and I agreed to eat more often. Problem solved, right?

Wrong! I continued to feel worse and worse. I made another appointment with my primary doctor because the nephrologist (kidney doctor), surgeon, and endocrinologist all said things were normal, so it had to be something else. Deep down, I knew I could no longer ride on the coattails of being healthy and acting like everything was fine. I was not fine and no one believed me.

My primary doctor ordered more blood work and on my follow-up appointment she told me that feeling what I described was just my new normal and likely psychosomatic and I had to accept it.

## "The most difficult thing for me to overcome in life was to let down my walls of protection and allow others to see me in need with my illnesses."

However, I felt so good until the kidney issue, so I knew that simply couldn't be the answer. Being told, "to accept it," started a fire inside me. It burned up all the doubt I had about myself that I was doing something wrong in my care and made me realize that this time the doctors were doing something wrong. They were missing something. I realized that no one was going to speak on my behalf, SO I HAD TO. I had to learn to become my own advocate.

I googled doctors, specialists, surgeons, western medicine, my symptoms, and made appointments with everyone that I could. Soon, I walked around with a folder full of my health records to every appointment. If I asked a doctor a question about something they didn't know and they were dismissive about it, then I'd move onto the next one. Something was wrong with me; it was getting worse. My blood sugars were going too low for me to truly function. I would pass out at work, and not remember full days. Things were tail spinning way too fast, and I knew that no matter what happened I was giving it my all.

A low blood sugar is also known as hypoglycemia. It means the body doesn't have enough energy or sugar to function properly. The body needs sugar to function because it turns it into energy with insulin. When you don't have enough sugar in your body, then you start having low blood sugar symptoms and you begin getting confused, logical thinking stops, and the body begins shutting down non-essential functions to preserve enough energy for the heart and lungs to function in order to live (think of the Energizer Bunny running out of batteries), and I was having a low blood sugar episode a few times a week. This wasn't normal for me since I could control my low blood sugars by taking less insulin and eating the right foods. However, all treatments did not work. The disease of diabetes began to get it's cold grip of power over me.

Until now, I had never been in a situation where my doctor didn't believe me. I thought I knew myself well, that my doctors knew I knew myself well, and were on my side fighting and looking out for me. These ideals were shattered and so was my trust. Doctors were someone I always held in high esteem, who knew and would always do what was best for me, and I trusted them implicitly. I was very naïve in my view of my doctors being infallible and completely in my corner. Why wouldn't they be?

This sudden change in perspective destroyed my peace of mind because I no longer had anyone to trust with my health and I couldn't be trusted either. Normally, I would have retreated back and did my best to hide behind my walls because someone I was vulnerable with and trusted, my doctor, said I was the cause of me feeling sick, didn't want to work with me as a patient, acted like I was wasting her time, and gave me no options. This time, however, I did not retreat. I knew something was wrong and, while I couldn't put my finger on what was going on, I knew that I would need to start speaking up and asking for things.

So, now I was sitting there and things had gotten out of control. I went from a well-controlled diabetic with no secondary issues for my entire life, and I started a downward spiral, was told that I was psychosomatic, bounced from doctor to doctor, and it was clear to me that no one was taking my health seriously. What was I to do? No one knew about my illnesses. No one had known I was so sick and not working and was hardly able

> "As time went on, I was given less than two years to live, found out that I needed a pancreas-only transplant that wasn't covered by insurance, I technically died twice, and had to fundraise a large amount of money to pay for a lifesaving surgery."

to get out of bed. So, I needed to ask for help. The most difficult thing for me to overcome in life was to let down my walls of protection and allow others to see me in need with my illnesses. I don't want to be seen differently or less than because of it, but being vulnerable isn't at all what I expected it to be.

After all, vulnerability is a form of weakness; it's letting others have power over you, and giving yourself away. To state it more simply: being weak. At least that's what I thought it meant.

However, being vulnerable allowed me to be a self-advocate in ways I didn't know were needed. Once I allowed myself to ask for help, my worst fear was over. I was now allowed to speak up and ask more questions, call out health care professionals for unprofessionalism, follow-up with the pharmacy, insurance, and front office staff at doctors' offices without worry of offending anyone. I wasn't an asshole about things, but I did hold everyone to a higher standard in my care. I began to know what I needed and took a bigger role in my health all by making the ask, speaking up, and making sure that my voice was heard.

As time went on, I was given less than two years to live, found out that I needed a pancreas-only transplant that wasn't covered by insurance, I technically died twice, and had to fundraise a large amount of money to pay for a lifesaving surgery. Surviving this was only possible through self-advocacy.

I love my strong will and dedication to myself. I love my new passion for living life and living it to the fullest. Before I discovered that I couldn't rely on being healthy at all times, I used to live my life searching to satisfy my American Dream. While it is possible to achieve this dream, it no longer has the allure it once did because my experiences taught me that life is not guaranteed and every moment is a gift.

Because of my new passion for life, I love that I am more easy going. This allows me to worry less about the small things and focus on what matters. I love my willingness to be adventurous. This allows me to not be afraid to say yes to new things. I love that I am able to be more spontaneous. This allows me the opportunity to drop everything to be hospitalized for a rejection treatment or book a next day trip to go swim with manatees. I love that I don't have to plan out my future and life. This allows me to set short term obtainable goals. I love that I am willing to meet new people. This allows me to connect with others—specifically chronic illness warriors—when I likely wouldn't have before.

I love that I'm not afraid to take risks. This means that I am not afraid of the what ifs: Not afraid to make mistakes. It allows me to learn when something doesn't go as planned. I love that I can be an advocate. This means I can share my experiences without being afraid of being vulnerable, and show the path I took for others to learn from and expand on. Finally, I love to speak up on my own behalf. This allows me to express how I feel without worry.

If I could do anything, it would be to advocate for others, show that being vulnerable isn't a weakness, and the importance of self-advocacy. In addition, because of this newfound love for adventure and life, I am not scared to make new friends or meet new people, talk about my chronic illness, and not waste a single moment second guessing myself. I am doing what I didn't think possible before, like deep sea fishing, scuba diving, and having hopes and dreams. I no longer think this is something I would do once I reached a certain life goal, I now just do it. Sure, health and finances are taken into consideration, but I am free and living a dream I didn't know was possible to have.

Every day is a gift no matter how big or small. Never give up or be afraid to make the ask. Even in your darkest of times, know that the sun will rise tomorrow. That is something you can count on when everything else has failed you, and most importantly, be a self-advocate; no one is going to be able to know what is going on or happening with or in you, so tell your family, friends, and doctors. If no one listens, find new people to listen to you. Find online communities for support and to learn from, find new doctors and specialists, google things and find new ways to rephrase what you're asking, and don't be afraid to make the ask. Vulnerability feels like weakness, but it is required to have the best health possible. You know your body best, so be your best advocate!!! I didn't choose to have an invisible illness that turned into the worst case scenario. I also didn't do anything to cause it. However, I did choose to do all I could and can to keep moving forward and conquer it. What seems impossible can be possible!

216

CHRONICALLY
Empowered

Allison Tennyson

Amy L. Burk

Louisa Rüggeberg

Samantha Moss

Maria De Leon

Katya Kozary

Misti Blu Day McDermott

# I AM
# Ever-
# Evolving.

**Stories of chronic illness warriors learning to start over.**

# Allison Tennyson

Minnesota, USA

## Peer Recovery Specialist

*"You are not alone. You are worth fighting for."*

## About Allison:

*My name is Allison Tennyson, and I am disabled and proud. I am from Minneapolis, Minnesota, and I have my degree in Marine Biology from the University of San Diego. I am also a Minnesota board certified Peer Recovery Specialist. I was born with connective tissue disease (CTD), and as a child, I knew that my body just did not feel quite right. I am now diagnosed with over 24 chronic illnesses – none of which have a cure. I am constantly relearning how to live my life with every new diagnosis. The truth is that chronic illness take a toll on your body and mind. I expierienced medical gaslighting sine my childhood – I was blown off and my symptoms were dismissed for years. Finally at the age of 31, I received a Nutcracker Syndrome diagnosis in August of 2020. This rare vascular compression disease has been wreaking havoc in my abdomen since I was a little girl. This disease is now opening doors to exploring CTD, and it aided in my Postural Orthostatic Tachucardia Syndrome diagnosis (POTS). Let me tell you my story!*

\* \* \*

*IG:* @microcatmachine

My name is Allison Tennyson, and I would like to share with you my story of how I managed the adversity of chronic illness. I am hopeful that by sharing my story, I am able to help at least one other person from suffering as I have. Let me begin by stating that I am disabled and proud. My chronic illnesses have empowered me to pursue a career in social service and advocacy. I am currently an Administrative Specialist for a nonprofit social service organization in Minnesota – I specifically work in disability services. I am also a certified Peer Recovery Support Specialist, and I have my bachelor's degree in Marine Biology from the University of San Diego. My illnesses have gifted me with empathy, understanding, and unwavering strength. My illnesses have also taught me perseverance, adaptation, and self-worth. I am happy to share my chronic illness story in hopes of empowering other chronically ill individuals to keep fighting, never give up, and love themselves wholly.

I suffer from more than 20 chronic illnesses, and the list continues to grow. I was born with connective tissue diseases – I am suspected to have Marfan syndrome and hypermobility Ehlers Danlos syndrome and will be evaluated by a geneticist in a couple months. My connective tissue disease has predisposed me to bilateral femoral acetabular impingement syndrome, postural orthostatic tachycardia syndrome, tendinitis, costochondritis, arthritis, peripheral neuropathy, asthma, near-sightedness, IBS, cyclic vomiting syndrome, and more. I suffer from many rare diseases, but there is one, in my opinion, that truly lacks awareness, research, and understanding. That one illness is nutcracker syndrome.

Nutcracker syndrome is a rare vascular compression disease, in which the left renal vein is compressed between the aorta and superior mesenteric artery. This compression stops blood from leaving the left kidney. Blood is diverted from the left renal vein to the ovarian vein, which stops blood from backing up into the left kidney. The ovarian vein is not equipped to take on this extra load of blood flow, so the ovarian vein grows into an enormous web of thumb-sized abdominal varicose veins. It is the abdominal varicose veins that cause the pain and congestion involved with nutcracker syndrome. The symptoms of nutcracker syndrome are left flank pain, pelvic congestion, and overactive bladder. Nutcracker syndrome can occur secondary to abdominal trauma, or it can occur at birth. I was born with my left renal vein completely compressed.

At 17 years old, I saw my first urologist to evaluate my overactive bladder and pelvic congestion. I could feel a mass in my abdomen, but my urologist gaslighted me. He performed a bladder ultrasound, diagnosed me with an overactive bladder, and prescribed me oxybutynin. The medication gave me horrible stomach pains and discomfort, so I discontinued it after a couple months. I was told to work on holding my bladder and to see a therapist when the medication failed. I believed that it was all in my head and just dealt with the discomfort for 13 more years.

I was finally diagnosed with nutcracker syndrome at 30 years old, in August of 2020. The finding was accidental. I had developed POTS (postural orthostatic tachycardia syndrome) in March of 2020 and then C. diff (Clostridium difficile) in July of 2020. The C. diff flared my cyclic vomiting syndrome for weeks. Finally, after vomiting everything that I ate for five weeks straight, I was forced to be hospitalized. The doctor at the hospital ordered an abdominal CT scan, chest x-rays, and loads of blood work. He told me that everything was normal and sent me home. When I was sitting in the parking lot after leaving the hospital, I decided to read my lab results. That is when I saw it on my abdominal CT scan - I have nutcracker syndrome.

My primary doctor referred me to an experienced vascular surgeon. He told me that my left kidney would not fail, but that the abdominal varicose veins would continue to grow. He never pushed surgery on me -

## "The medication gave me horrible stomach pains and discomfort, so I discontinued it after a couple months."

I decided that surgery was right for me on my own and with the help of my family. On Friday, November 6, 2020, I had left renal vein transposition surgery. In my vascular surgeon's forty years of practicing vascular surgery, he had only performed this surgery three times before mine - I was his fourth left renal vein transposition surgery. It was an open-abdominal surgery that involved rolling my left renal vein down on my aorta and ligating off my ovarian vein at the left renal vein and ovarian vein junction. It was

a six hour surgery that required three days of recovery in the hospital, two weeks off of work, and months of recovery at home.

The surgery was a success. My back pain, pelvic congestion, and overactive bladder have been completely resolved. I have a giant scar from my rib cage to my pelvic line, and I am still recovering from the surgery, but I could not be more grateful to have had it done. The first week after my surgery, I began to experience relief. I do not think that I fully understood how much discomfort I was in, until my left renal vein compression was resolved. I remember thinking, "So, this is how everyone else feels." My surgery was truly life changing. I could not be happier about my decision.

Nutcracker syndrome affected me physically and mentally throughout my life. The medical gaslighting increased my depression and anxiety. Doctors made me feel like I was crazy. They blamed my anxiety and hormones. It diminished my self-worth and destroyed the trust that I had in myself. This distrust spilled over into my professional and social life. I lacked self-confidence. I was scared, ashamed, and embarrassed. I felt like if I cannot even feel normal in my own body, then my mental health must be severely poor. These emotions left me chained to the prison of my own mind and unable to escape for years. I used drugs and alcohol to mask my physical discomforts and to numb my mind. I felt broken, wrong, and dirty. I survived molestation, domestic violence, sexual violence, and suicide - all experiences that I could have avoided if I would have known my self-worth. Unfortunately, I was blown off, minimized, and invalidated for so many years that I felt undeserving. The gaslighting was devastating.

It was not until August 24, 2020, the day that I received my nutcracker syndrome diagnosis, that I finally felt validated. I finally felt that I was not crazy. My nutcracker syndrome diagnosis gave me the strength that I had lacked for so many years to advocate for myself. Since receiving my nutcracker syndrome diagnosis, I have also received a POTS, fibromyalgia, and FAIS (femoral acetabular impingement syndrome) diagnosis. It led me to my current rheumatologist who explained to me that I was born with connective tissue disease (suspected Marfan syndrome and hypermobility Ehlers Danlos syndrome) and that all my illnesses are connected – they all make sense. I finally feel like I fit in. I finally feel like I can trust myself. I finally feel worthy and strong.

Being born with nutcracker syndrome forced me to learn how to adapt to the discomfort early on in life. I just peed constantly. I would wake up 5 to 8 times every night to pee. My life was just a series of pee breaks. I always knew to pee right before I left my house, right before I went to bed, right before anything I ever did. My constant urination is how I relieved the bloating and congestion from my nutcracker syndrome. I also learned at an early age that I could relieve my symptoms by stretching out my lower back. I reach forward and pop out my lower back – pretty much the opposite of what any chiropractor would tell you, but, with the arthritis and impingement syndrome in my hips and my nutcracker syndrome, this motion has always been very helpful to me. Essentially, I spent my life in the restroom and popping out my lower back. I never knew any different, so I never let it stop me from living my life.

My illnesses make my life difficult, but they do not define me. I have so much to offer life, and there is so much to love about myself. It has taken me a lifetime to truly start to love myself. I love my empathy, understanding, and compassion for other people and animals. I love my dedication to education and advocacy. I love my genuine warmth. I have experienced a lot of adversity in my life on top of my chronic illnesses, and I am proud of myself for putting in the time and effort to recover and thrive. I have had to start over so many times that I have learned to no longer fear change and the unknown. Instead, I trust that I am strong enough and determined enough to adapt and evolve to anything life brings my way. I love my ability to pivot and adjust as needed. I can thank my chronic illnesses for learning how to adapt, regroup, and carry on.

I also love my creativity and love of learning new things. I love to crochet, macrame, knit, embroider, make pressed flower frames, sketch, write poetry, shibori, make videos, and make music. I am a total sucker for all things crafts! I am always looking for new crafts! I have been hand-making my family's gifts since 2011. My first homemade Christmas gifts were shark tooth necklaces – I collected the shark teeth from the shark tank at the marine laboratory that I interned at after I graduated university. My family loved them, and I loved making them! I also love my cooking and baking skills. I no longer eat wheat, soy, dairy, corn, or sugar – essentially, I follow a 'paleo' or low inflammatory diet. My diet greatly helps to reduce and quiet my symptoms. I have become an excellent paleo cook and baker! I can cook or bake almost anything while still adhering to my low inflammatory diet, and I am super proud of that! I can make paleo food taste great.

Since developing POTS (postural orthostatic tachycardia syndrome) in March of 2020, I have become physically disabled. I use a mobility aid to get around now, and there are many things that I physically can no longer do. I once dreamed of being a wildlife conservationist, veterinarian, or scientist, but, after a lifetime of excitement and a now disabled body, I look forward to a simple life. If I could be doing anything, I would be taking care of a small hobby farm and my family! I have traveled to 30 countries, I have worked in veterinary medicine for nine years, I have worked with everything from sea turtles, dolphins, and lions, to cats, squirrels, and songbirds, and I have shifted to a career in social work. My life has been very exciting, and I am ready to make a home and a family. I cannot wait to be a mother, and I never thought that I would be saying that. But, I dream of the day that I can be a mother and a wife with a small hobby farm with plants and animals while I write, craft, cook, and bake all day.

I have learned so much about managing symptoms and living with chronic illness that I would love to share. My advice to anyone who can relate to my story is to trust yourself and never give up. I tried seeking answers and treatment for my pains and discomforts as a child, but I gave up in my late teens after being told that it was just in my head, that I was attention seeking, and that I was fine for so many years. I am 31 years old now. I have had to suffer without answers for 31 years. My connective tissue disease is still undiagnosed, which is now limiting my care. Until I receive a diagnosis for my connective tissue disease, my doctors will continue to treat me as a person without connective tissue disease. So, I urge others to never give up. If you do not feel right, then trust yourself and get answers. I wish that someone would have told me to trust myself and ignore other people's thoughts and opinions. I wish that someone would have reminded me that this is my body. That I am the only person who will ever inhabit this body. Pain and discomfort are not normal – chronic illness is normal. If I am hurting, then I should be able to know why and receive treatment.

You should not be suffering in pain and discomfort. You deserve to know what is wrong with you and what you can do to feel better. My advice is to prepare for appointments – do your research and show up to your appointment with your questions, your suspected illnesses, tests that you want done, and your past lab results. If your doctor gaslights you – that is, if your doctor minimizes or completely blows off your concerns and dismisses them as psychological or completely made up – then you need to go find another doctor. I wish that I would have known that medical gaslighting is not to be tolerated when I was younger. It is important to recognize medical gaslighting and to not let it stop you from getting the care that you need.

My chronic illnesses have empowered me to be strong, to be adaptable, and to recognize my worth. I am proud of all the things that I can do, regardless of my illnesses and

## "My chronic illnesses have empowered me to be strong, to be adaptable, and to recognize my worth."

disability. I am not defined by my illnesses. I am so much more than a chronically ill, disabled person. I am a crafter, a friend, a lover, an animal mother, a daughter, a sister, a student, a worker, a writer, a singer, a dancer, and a warrior. I fight unimaginable battles every minute of every day – I fight these battles on the inside. They are invisible battles. I have to work twice as hard to get half as far. However, when I take a minute to really look at what my chronic illness has done for me, I am left seeing my strength, my determination, and my ability to evolve. My disability has given me the opportunity to dream again. My chronic illnesses have never closed doors for me, they have only opened them. I hope you know that you are not alone. I hope you know that you are worth fighting for. I hope you know that you are a warrior.

## Keep fighting, warrior, and never give up.

# Amy L. Burk

Huntington Beach, CA, USA

*Encourager of Hurting Hearts and Minds*

*"It's not foolish
to still have hope..."*

## About Amy:

*Amy is a fighter that loves Jesus with all of her heart! She finds deep joy fulfilling her dream of being a wife and mama! Life has thrown curveballs gifting her a unique perspective to share with the world. It is her hope to be a person who makes invisible sufferers feel seen and encourages through her writing. She is grateful for the sunny days that Southern California has to offer where she, her husband, and their daughter have made a home. Amy believes you can never really go wrong with a good struggle and an episode of "I Love Lucy.".*

\* \* \*

Hi! My name is Amy. I'm 32 years old, I'm a wife to an amazing man, a mom to a miracle sunshine girl, and I love interior design and writing. Welcome to my story! It's full of peaks and valleys as I've been living with chronic and mental illness for over a decade. I hope my story resonates with you and encourages you to press on.

In November of 2009, when I was 21, I got pregnant and became so sick that my baby and I both almost died. I had hyperemesis gravidarum and I spent the next nine months almost completely bed ridden and throwing up. About halfway through my pregnancy we found out that our baby girl had two very severe heart defects that would require multiple open heart surgeries and she only had a 20% chance of survival if she made it to birth. I was devastated.

Over the next three years (2010-2013) I had three surgeries and our daughter had seven heart surgeries. There were some close calls, moments of overwhelming joy, and moments of deep grief. We also moved, had to end multiple toxic relationships, and lost a close friend to suicide. It was also during this season that I was diagnosed with fibromyalgia, severe treatment resistant depression, anxiety, suspected endometriosis, gastroesophageal reflux disease, acid reflux, gastritis, irritable bowel syndrome, two inguinal hernias, pectus excavatum, hyper mobility and postural orthostatic tachycardia syndrome (POTS). I battled daily with extreme fatigue, a super high heart rate just from standing, every night I had nightmares, I never fully recovered from my C-section or from my hernia repairs. I was extremely isolated during this time and I could barely do anything around the house. I spent a lot of time laying on the couch feeling like a failure. To say it was a difficult season would be an understatement. The heaviness of that season broke me both physically and mentally. Complex post-traumatic stress disorder (CPTSD), depression, anxiety, watching my daughter endure so much, heavy grief, constant surgeries and hospital trips, tests, failed treatments, pain... my body had just had enough.

> **"I would let myself feel the grief of another dead end and then I would dig for the strength to find another doctor and new hope."**

In August 2014 I had a mental breakdown of sorts which I now know was OCD (I was diagnosed with OCD years later). Over the next several years I was in the trenches fighting for my own life while also helping our daughter through two more heart surgeries. I was physically unable to leave my bed most days. When I had to leave the house I was often carried to the car and needed a wheelchair to get around. The pain from fibromyalgia was slowly spreading over my whole body, the tachycardia from POTS would cause my heart rate to jump up near 200 after only a few minutes of standing causing me to pass out or feel like I was going to pass out every time I got up, I was weak and shaky from the muscle atrophy. I couldn't even take a shower or brush my own hair. There were times I needed help feeding myself. On particularly hard days I even had to be carried to the bathroom from my bed. I was severely depressed and tormented by OCD.

> **"I was slowly gaining more strength and independence to do things that I hadn't been able to do in years like taking a quick shower and walking short distances."**

I spent years seeing dozens of specialists, trying every medication and treatment under the sun to treat my ever-growing list of symptoms. I was promised relief so many times and yet the waves of sorrow in mental and physical illness kept coming and the doctors were left scratching their heads. I was devastated every time. I would let myself feel the grief of another dead end and then I would dig for the strength to find another doctor and new hope. Each time it seemed to get heavier and harder to pull myself back up. Nobody hears about the people in this community that fight hard to be seen, to be helped, to be validated! We fight for research, we fight for tests and treatments, we spend tens of thousands of dollars looking for help when insurance won't cover us. We take the

medications promised to help us only for our bodies to reject them and have severe side effects that leave us feeling even more broken and confused and lost than before. Yet, we keep fighting.

In March of 2017 I spent two months at the Mayo Clinic getting detailed testing. I was diagnosed with central sensitization disorder, bicuspid aortic valve, and inappropriate sinus tachycardia. While I was there my depression was so severe I couldn't even speak at times. They started electroconvulsive therapy (also known as electric shock therapy or ECT used to treat severe depression). In typical fashion my body had an unusually hard time with the treatments. Each treatment caused severe migraine headaches that would last the whole day and night. Halfway through my treatments I aspirated while under anesthesia and ended up getting pneumonia and going septic. Due to pain medications I was also extremely constipated to the point of needing a colonoscopy and colon biopsy. Once I was discharged I resumed my ECT treatments. Finding the courage to go back and continue treatments was so hard but I did it. I still have large chunks of my memory missing over a several year time period as a side effect. It's a very unsettling experience to have black holes of your own past. The ECT treatment results did not last.

I then turned to transcranial magnetic stimulation (TMS). When my first round of TMS finished and I was still struggling we packed up and moved halfway across the country to sunny California. We thought the shock of change would do me some good.

We started our new chapter in September of 2017. We knew I needed a stable climate for my fibromyalgia pain and sunshine for mental pain that was worsened by the dark grey winters. The move renewed my hope and purpose. I was slowly gaining more strength and independence to do things that I hadn't been able to do in years like taking a quick shower and walking short distances. I was learning how to socialize again in the evenings on the lawn with neighbors. I found a place to continue TMS and we started that again in hopes of it helping me more in this new, healthier environment. I was still struggling both mentally and physically but I was full of hope. A few months later we learned that another close friend had died by suicide. It was so heavy and my depression and physical condition started to decline again.

> ## "The silence of others in the midst of your suffering is one of the most painful things in the world."

We decided to move into a condo we could rent long term. The change helped me find purpose again. I still had a super long way to go but I was full of cautious optimism that one naturally develops after a life of obstacle after obstacle. About a month later in April 2018 I got a call from someone I considered to be one of my closest friends and it shattered me. Overnight our friendship of nearly a decade was over because of the lies of the man that was manipulating her. I was heartbroken. I found myself spiraling into yet a deeper depression, a level I hadn't experienced before and for the first time the suicidal thoughts became my constant companion. I cried everyday. I was so physically ill. I leaned heavily on my faith and I clung to my therapist's words. The betrayal and the rejection of that small circle of friends strengthened the voice in my mind that said "this world doesn't want you," "your life only brings pain and confusion," "even when you open up and love people and allow them into your story they don't believe you and they don't love you," "you will always be misunderstood." The pain was overwhelming. For the next year and a half I was the loneliest I had ever been and I was facing the darkest depression I had ever faced. During all of this I got a few more diagnoses. I found out I had severe hormonal imbalances, vitamin deficiencies, candida yeast overgrowth, high levels of mercury in my blood, Epstein Barr virus, and adrenal insufficiency. At the end of November 2018 I was starting to build some of my strength up yet again but in December I got the flu and it was a terrible setback mentally and physically. It took me about a year to physically recover.

In 2019 I was diagnosed with a mitral valve prolapse and suspected periodic paralysis. I was still doing TMS but because of insurance restrictions every eight weeks I'd have to have a three month break without TMS before I could start up again. Each break was scarier than the last. The depression was suffocating me. I couldn't speak, I couldn't feel any connections. I was only crying and staring off and I knew I wasn't going to make it much longer. I was sure I wouldn't survive the next TMS break. I was coming to the end of that treatment round. The loneliness of that season coupled with the deep grief and trauma of the last ten years overwhelmed me. It felt unbearable. I wept over the end that I was sure was coming. My mental illness was winning and that made me so angry and sad. I didn't want people to remember me that way. I had so much more to me than illness.

The people in my life seemed eerily, painfully silent. The silence of others in the midst of your suffering is one of the most painful things in the world. The overwhelming voice of our culture shouts with its silence to the chronically ill "You aren't worth the extra effort," "I'm too busy to make time for you," "Your heaviness and difficulties make me feel sad and uncomfortable so I'd rather be in denial that it exists," "You aren't trying hard enough," "You are so dramatic." Yet when the chronically ill and the mentally ill die by suicide, the world says "if they had only reached out and asked for help." I don't know if they say that to just make themselves feel better or if they are really truly that naïve about how absent they have been in the lives of the suffering close to them. Don't wait for them to ask for help; reach out and offer support. Chronic illness means being sick with no end in sight. I never really get used to it even though I've learned to accept it. I have often felt so alone, so isolated, so judged, and so misunderstood on my journey of illness; therefore, the opportunity to share my story

along with other fellow fighters is such an honor.

> ## "Some days I just get through by taking it one second at a time and all I do that day is breathe...that's okay."

Finally, in December of 2019 I started a new treatment called Alpha-Stim. I use it to help my depression. I use the device every single day and I also do TMS as often as I can. The two of these treatments together are helping to keep my depression at a manageable level and I'm more stable than I have been in over 6 years! I'm so incredibly thankful that I never gave up. I still have a long way to go and as of September of 2020 I have started dealing with yet another new diagnosis, chronic urticaria. The hits may keep coming and I don't know how my story will end yet but I'm so proud of my fight thus far. One of my favorite things I've discovered about myself through this last decade of struggle is that hidden beneath my body's frail exterior, my difficulties have produced an inner strength to press on in the midst of invisible suffering while fighting battles in my mind that no one else can see. It takes more than most people will ever know. I pray my story will bring encouragement to anyone who feels alone in their suffering.

My best advice for people fighting battles is to find hope in Jesus. Suffering is more tolerable if it is temporary and has a purpose.

As a Christian, my faith has propelled me to press on and find the resilience to keep fighting time after time. I still get knocked down and face new obstacles but I'm continually evolving and learning more about myself. I know that in God I have someone who gives me strength. Life still has so much to look forward to. It takes a shift of thinking and there is a grieving process for the life you had imagined and dreamed about. Acceptance isn't giving up or losing hope that you can improve or have a better quality of life but it gives you the freedom to explore your body's current boundaries and abilities. I'm so excited that in September of 2020 I started a jewelry making business from my sick bed. I make and sell jewelry created to bring hope and awareness for other fighters! It takes time but you can adjust and adapt and find joy and purpose again! I still have moments of grief for the things I've lost and the things I long for and yet there is still so much joy and fulfilment in a life with disabilities. I can still shower my family and friends with encouraging words and love. I can still laugh and make memories. If I could be anything in this world I would want to be a person who loves and encourages the suffering who feel abandoned and invisible! To speak truth to them, to lead songs of encouragement and strength with them.

I won't sugarcoat chronic and mental illness. It is hard. Some days I just get through by taking it one second at a time and all I do that day is breathe...that's okay. My life hasn't been easy but I can say honestly I believe it has made me a better, stronger, wiser, more compassionate person and in the midst of suffering and pain I have still found joy and purpose. I'm learning to adapt and accept myself. I'm allowing the people around me to accept me and I'm not clinging to who I used to be. I know I still have value and I have a lot to offer to the world. I always try to celebrate the little things because I think the little things are actually the big things. When I feel weak, broken, and lost, I hold on tight because I have hope that the light will shine again. In the Bible I love Romans 5 where it says that we can actually even rejoice in our sufferings because "suffering produces endurance, endurance produces character and character produces hope and hope does not put us to shame..." So when I'm struggling to find hope after each setback or closed door, I'm reminded that it's not foolish to still hope because hope will not put me to shame especially if my hope is in God. Keep fighting, friends!

# Louisa Rüggeberg
Berlin, Germany

*TBD*

## About Louisa:

*The last time I was on stage as a dancer was over 6 years ago. A feverish infection usually subsides after a few days, but sometimes the body does not recover completely. In my case, I am still struggling with the consequences of the infection years later, or rather with my chronic illness that developed from it. I had to adapt my life completely to my physical possibilities, but I am proud of what I managed to do despite the illness.*

\* \* \*

*IG: @lounanuit*

*"No matter what you are going through, or if you feel alone – especially then – you should never forget that you are not alone!"*

Hi, my name is Lulu and I am 23 years old. I have been chronically ill since I was 17 years old. In 2018 I was diagnosed with ME/CFS and POTS.

ME/CFS is a still largely unknown neuroimmunological disease. It is associated with severe fatigue, worsening of symptoms after exertion, pain, and a wide range of other symptoms. When I got sick, I was training to be a ballet dancer. I developed a fever during a performance, but I didn't want to take a break. It was only one evening, and I wanted to make it. I collapsed at the airport. Since then I have not been able to stand on a stage.

Instead, my mother drove me from doctor to doctor. I would never have thought that after six years I would still not be healthy. It never occurred to me that my life could change like this. In the following weeks, months and years, I also had to realize that not every doctor is willing to help.

## "Some days I can't even get out of bed."

From one day to the next I was no longer independent, my entire life had changed. I was dependent on the help of my family, because I could hardly leave my bed. I had severe pain that exhausted me so much that I spent many days waiting. I waited for it to get better, for the day to be over and for me to get through another day.

Three years passed before I was diagnosed.

I was allowed to try out several therapies and my condition actually stabilized a little. I was able to leave my bed more often, I was able to finish school and I was able to start studying. Now I have been studying biology for almost three years. My illness was one of the reasons why I chose this subject. I want to be able to understand what is being talked about in research.

However, due to the disease, I cannot go to the lectures. I am still dependent on help. I study (whenever possible) at home.

Since all my energy goes into studying, I can't do much else. I can't just meet up with friends, do something with my boyfriend or go on vacation. Some days I can't even get out of bed. Very often I had to cancel my plans spontaneously because my body suddenly broke down. But, I won't give up. I am very proud that I have always found a way to do something I love. I am proud that I have found someone who loves me as I am. I am proud that I have not lost my positivity and continue to fight no matter how many stones are in my way.

But if I could just do whatever I wanted to do, without limitations, I would love to travel. I would want to be spontaneous without having to think about the deterioration of my condition.

Now I would like to tell you that no matter what you are going through, or if you feel alone - especially then - you should never forget that you are not alone! You are worthy and you are strong!

# Samantha Moss

Brisbane, QLD, Australia

## Writer, Blogger, Podcaster and Founder of Online Support Forum

*"Don't let your happiness be defined by what has been taken away from you."*

## About Samantha:

*Sam medically retired from a successful Executive Management Career in Financial Services, in 2014 at the age of 49, She has a rare disabling bone disease, Rheumatoid Arthritis and a permanent colostomy. Sam lives in Australia with her husband who is both her soul mate and full-time carer. As Sam's disabilities progressed, she started a blog. She also set up an online support forum for anyone wanting the hand of friendship, as they journey an often lonely and difficult path, living with the effects of chronic disease. Both her blog, and global Facebook online support group, are a place to laugh, cry, share and vent together". Sam is also a member of the Chronic Illness Bloggers Network and a regular contributor to online publication The Mighty. She is a passionate patient advocate, raising awareness of what it is like living with chronic disease and how it is possible to find new ways to live a full and rewarding life. She also volunteers as an online support forum administrator for not-for-profit organization Arthritis Queensland. You can follow more of Sam's story at her Blog.*

\* \* \*

*IG & FB: @mymedicalmusings*

*Facebook Forum: Medical Musings and Friends*

*Website: mymedmusings.com*

## My Story

In 2010 I was in my mid 40's, at the height of my career as an Executive Manager in a major Bank.

In April of 2010, I was getting ready to take six weeks long service leave to spend some quality time with my beautiful husband. We were going on a road trip, through South East Queensland down to the Hunter Valley in Northern NSW, and I was so looking forward to having a break.

On the way home I started feeling really unwell and I just couldn't shake off extreme tiredness, joint pain like I had never experienced and abdominal pain. My hands were so sore that even the slightest touch was excruciating. I couldn't hold my husband's hand or pick anything up. My hips were so painful walking normally was becoming difficult unless my husband supported me. We knew something was not right.

### A Long Road Ahead

As soon as we got home we headed for my GP and a whole list of specialist appointments followed. Long story short, two months later I was diagnosed with Rheumatoid Arthritis (RA) after being first diagnosed with Q fever, Ross River Virus and a list of other false positive diagnoses.

My body was not behaving normally and my doctors and I were to discover, over the next six years, just how abnormal it actually was. I had no idea what lay ahead.

With RA medication on board, I continued to work for another 12 months

> *"I have been called 'special,' 'unique,' and 'one of a kind,' but really they all believe overall, aside from Rheumatoid Arthritis, I have a rare idiopathic disease (a disease of its own kind)."*

before my body began to basically break down bit by bit. My last day in the office was Melbourne Cup Day 2011. I was trying to push through the day, getting ready to judge my Departments "Fashion on the Fields," when my Personal Assistant found me in agony in the ladies bathroom and rang my husband to come and pick me up.

From that day my life was never to be the same again.

In 2011, I was diagnosed with a prolapsed rectum which refused to mend despite 3 attempts at conservative surgery. By mid-2013 we knew we had no choice but to accept I needed a permanent stoma.

In November 2013, I medically retired and became the "proud" owner of a permanent colostomy. It has been quite a journey with my medical team including a Clinical Immunologist, Colorectal Surgeon, Endocrinologist, Orthopaedic Surgeon, Gynaecologist, Ear Nose and Throat Specialist, Infectious Disease Specialist, Neurologist, Dermatologist, Gastroenterologist and an Opthamologist, all trying to work out what is causing my health issues.

I have been called "special," "unique," and "one of a kind," but really they all believe overall, aside from Rheumatoid Arthritis, I have a rare idiopathic disease (a disease of its own kind).

I have lost count of the number of times I have been hospitalised over the past 10 years. I have had 14 surgeries since October 2010, with the prospect of more ahead.

I thought Rheumatoid Arthritis and a permanent colostomy would be an end to what my body was going to challenge me with. I hoped I could settle comfortably into medical retirement with my husband, but I soon came to realise my life was going to be an ongoing medical adventure.

## An Unexpected Surprise

In October 2014 my left femur (thigh bone) broke spontaneously. Yes, all on its own, I didn't fall from a great height or have a major car crash, which is apparently the type of accident I should have been involved in having the strongest bone in my body break. Mine just broke as I was opening my bedroom door!

It is called a pathological break and my specialists believe I have a rare genetic bone disease. My bones are extremely dense and marble-like and my bone turnover is almost non-existent. We also now know that my bones are dying and much of the soft tissue around my bones is also dead tissue.

Twelve months after my left leg broke, my right femur was also showing signs of disease on MRI with bone marrow involvement, so a rod had to be placed in that to prevent an imminent break. We didn't need a repeat medical emergency like we had with my femur break in 2014.

I am constantly dealing with multiple foot fractures and none of my broken bones in my legs or feet will heal. My bone pain is excruciating on a daily basis. My left femur which snapped in two is still broken nearly 6 years later and has been diagnosed as a non-union break. I have been on two crutches or a walker since the femur broke and also use a mobility scooter.

## Finding Ways to Live with the Unknown

I have a long and unknown journey ahead and surgery after surgery keeps me in a constant recovery state. My bone disease is also attacking my spine and causing severe stenosis and nerve compression. This has resulted in two major spinal surgeries three months apart. I still remain hopeful that we will eventually arrive at a more settled way of life, even if my prognosis is unknown.

> **"We can laugh because we know life can be and is good, even if it is learning to live at a different pace and in a very different way from what is considered "normal.""**

I have been approved for the highest level Home Care Package which includes life long approval for Permanent Residential Care whenever I need it. I am so grateful for this provision and the peace of mind it brings.

In 2015, I decided to start blogging to reach out to others, who have found themselves suddenly physically disabled, and medically retired from a normal way of life.

Despite my health issues I still choose to have a happy fulfilled life, different yes, but fulfilled all the same. Seven years ago I would have thought a stoma was the end of the world. Today I am so relieved to have a functioning bowel.

Ten years ago I was facing the fact that Rheumatoid Arthritis was causing radical changes to my life, the biggest being saying goodbye to my Executive Management career and the team I led and loved. My company was so fantastic to me throughout the whole medical retirement process, which was such a blessing and I remain forever grateful for their support.

Today I am medically retired, on a permanent disability pension and my husband is my full time career. My original plan was a healthy retirement, full of travel and volunteering and fulfilling a lifelong goal of writing a book. I may not be able to have such an energetic retirement, my leg break and subsequent bone disease diagnosis has brought the travel idea to an end for the moment, but I am blessed that I can still write.

I'll have difficult days like we all do and days when plans and dreams are restricted by health but one thing I know, if I can focus on counting my blessings on those days, the clouds pass much more quickly.

My biggest blessing is my amazing husband who has walked this journey with me and stands side by side with me today. We have laughed and we have cried over the past six years as each health episode has thrown up new challenges.

We have even managed to laugh at the unpredictability of my health. We can laugh because we know life can be and is good, even if it is learning to live at a different pace and in a very different way from what is considered "normal."

## Chronically Content

Despite all my body has thrown at me, I still have an overarching feeling of being "Chronically Content."

So, how on earth can I feel content, even happy, in the midst of all this?

## What's my secret?

The simple answer is I love my life. My health is just one part of it and my chronic diseases have actually brought chronic contentment in multiple areas of my life.

**Let me share some of them with you:**

- I spend quality time chatting and laughing with my husband every day.

- I spend quality time writing, something I love to do. I have a blog called "My Medical Musings" and I write articles for "The Mighty."

- I spend the majority of my day reaching out to others through my on-line Facebook forum, Medical Musings with Friends. Connection with people is so important for my overall well-being, and the Medical Musings with Friends forum gives as much to me as I give to its beautiful members.

- I get excited about any achievement in my life no matter how small. Making the bed each day and making it look pretty brings me joy....even if I mess it up an hour later as I have to collapse onto it in sheer exhaustion. I still did it and that counts for a lot in my book.

- I don't dwell on what I can't do, I dwell on what I can do.

- I have a strong faith in God. I see His hand on my life in so many remarkable ways...the main one being that I'm "Chronically Content" despite my crazy health. My faith brings me a sense of peace in my darkest hour that really does pass all understanding!

Whatever your chronic disease or grief circumstances, don't let your happiness be defined by what has been taken away from you. Think upon the things that make you smile. Grab hold of those happy thoughts and ponder upon them until ideas form you can realistically put into action.

You may love to travel but health prevents it. Get travel DVDs or look at travel books or brochures and dream you're there. It saves the effort of packing and unpacking so there's an immediate bonus from my perspective.

You may love to eat out but find cafes difficult to access. Take a drive in the car and park in a beautiful spot to have a picnic with your loved one or friend. I've done this with my husband many times and it's been just a perfect date.

Above all try not to worry about things that may never happen. Life is too short to go there and when chronically ill, finding ways to be chronically content is a much better way to use your energy. I hope and pray my story encourages others who are facing an uncertain future and change in life's direction. I hope it helps you to find the courage to not give up, but over time learn to accept a new way of life and be brave enough to share your own experiences.

# Maria De Leon

Nacogdoches,TX, USA

## Neurologist, Medical Writer & Professional Dreamer

*"Having a passion in life and getting involved in other people's lives is vital to living a full life."*

## About Maria:

*Maria is a world-renowned speaker and author of "Parkinson's Diva." Due to her extensive and unique experience as a person living with Parkinson's Disease, she trained as a Parkinson's specialist. Fashion brings years of experience into a a living well as a woman with chronic illness (PD), despite the illness. And her Chronically Empowered story she shares her knowledge and life experience in order to and empower all women living with Parkinson's, and any with chronic illness, to find the best version of themselves, along with the beauty within to be warriors.*

\* \* \*

*IG: @drmariade*

## Parkinson's Diva Beyond the Illness

A few weeks after receiving a diagnosis of Parkinson's disease (PD) and still reeling from the loss of my grandmother (who also had PD), I found myself sitting in my car in front of my office trying to muster enough strength to go in and continue to see patients as if nothing had happened. For the first time in decades, I found myself wondering what I would do if I could no longer practice my medical profession. I felt winded, accompanied by a deep pang in the middle of my chest as I considered the thought of giving up what I had worked so hard to achieve. Until this moment, it had never occurred to me that this could happen, especially now as my life was just beginning to unfold. I had sacrificed, persevered and done without, with one goal in mind, for as long as I remembered. Once I had decided to become a doctor to care for Parkinson's patients there was no going back. All my energy and focus were spent on that goal. Since that time, every step had been carefully planned. The irony now was that I had the one disease I had strived to cure. Now I found myself struggling to even put on my shoes and bathe. Living one day at a time was an understatement.

Before the diagnosis, I felt exhausted. I spent a good part of nearly two years seeking medical advice from various specialists. I believe I ran the gamut of medical subspecialties and had every test under the sun short of a brain biopsy. Why did it take so long you may wonder? This was because despite the usual symptoms of Parkinson's including constant bladder issues, REM behavior (acting out dreams), stiffness, slowness, balance issues and rest tremors, I had other atypical symptoms not commonly known at time as being part of PD, particularly not at the onset of illness. These included excruciating pain which began in my left foot then progressed to both sides of my body, along with fatigue and visual problems. During this time, I was finding it difficult to focus on my work. I was ill-tempered all the time which was out of character for me and staff and patients noticed. I was having an even worse time at home trying to raise a toddler. As bright children often are, my daughter was particularly inquisitive and energetic which only served to clash with my lack of enthusiasm and energy, and challenged my already fragile cognitive status at every turn. My nerves were frail and on edge since I could not even hug my daughter without sending searing pain down my arms. This had to be one of the worst moments in my life as a mom, to not be able to cuddle my own child for fear of triggering excruciating pain. I did not want to scare her off so I would still try to hug her briefly despite the tears. After the diagnosis and initiation of treatment things did not go as I hoped initially. Yes, my vision was better as was my pain, but I traded them for constant stupor and emesis. Because of this, I had to close my practice. I could no longer juggle work and family, as well as care for myself.

For the first year the struggle was real. I could barely walk. I had to use assistive devices to avoid falling and I could no longer drive because of severe sleepiness from medication which would cause me to fall asleep while at the wheel. I relied on friends and family to run errands for me and take me to doctors' appointments. Morning drop offs at daycare were easy since my husband would drop our daughter off on his way to work, but retrieving her was another matter, and I was too weak and sick to keep her at home with me. Thank God for good friends, otherwise I would not have survived those days. It truly does take a village when dealing with chronic illness. I wish we had Doordash back then. I am not sure how I managed to feed my family back then; some things are still a blur. Once I began to slowly come out of the fog and become more independent again, I realized it was hard to multi-task and forget doing any mathematical functions. I nearly broke into tears one evening at a restaurant after throwing a dinner party for a friend because I could not figure out the bill.

Over the years, my memory mishaps have caused many 'wow' moments, both embarrassing and amusing. Fortunately, I finally discovered the right dose of medication to avoid such "open mouth, insert foot" moments or at least to keep my mouth shut if not sure and feel fuzzy in the head. One example of an amusing anecdote which my daughter and husband often regale others with is the time when I was trying to get my daughter to school. It was a particularly bad

**"Despite the years of hiding my physical flaws and disabilities, I now fully embrace them."**

morning. I had been dizzy and nauseated and stumbling all over the place, and I was unable to get dressed. Still wearing my pjs, I was hell-bent on getting my 6-year-old daughter to school before I passed out. As I was driving like a mad woman because we were running late, my daughter asked me what the names of the three musketeers were. In my stupor, I guess because she was so into the Ninja Turtles at the time or who knows why, I said with such conviction "Michelangelo, Raphael, and Leonardo." My daughter said something just like the turtles and I nodded.

Lo and behold she wrote a story about this at school which made all the teachers laugh but got a bit worried when they found the source of the information. Over the years she made many of her teachers laugh with my antics like when I accidentally blinded the beta fish she had because when I cleaned the tank with Clorox I forgot to rinse before I filled it up with water again. I discovered when he could not swim upright and kept banging his head on the glass of the tank. I am happy to say I rehabbed him and he lived for another couple of years. After that, my daughter learned not to ask me many thinking questions if I was not well or had not taken medication. Even now when there is something important to discuss, she always starts by asking, "How are you feeling now mom?"

Through the years, I have had to relearn new ways of doing things and adjust my way of dressing, cooking, and even the way I interacted with my toddler early on. I found ways to play in bed together, color, watch cartoons and read together without aggravating my pain. We maintained our routine of sitting in the "thinking chair" to read and cuddle. As she grew up, because I could not drive a lot or have enough stamina to do a lot of activities, my house became the central place for the gathering of her friends. Throughout everything I strived to maintain a normal childhood for her. I prioritized her needs and activities. For instance, if I knew she had an activity with the band that evening, I rested and did nothing else so I could have enough stamina to be present. I am proud to say that I only missed one piano recital because I had just had back surgery and it was difficult to sit. I was a medical officer in her Girl Scouts' troop for 15 years, And during that time they planted tulips at assisted living facilities among many other projects which I was extremely grateful to be part of. She is now 20 and I am proud of the caring and compassionate young woman she has become.

As I have traveled on this journey with Parkinson's, I discovered a few things about me. I am a lot stronger and more resilient than I thought. Despite the years of hiding my physical flaws and disabilities, I now fully embrace them. I bought a shirt that says I make Parkinson's look sexy and never looked back. Hence, the 'Parkinson's Diva' title. I wear my scars like a badge of honor for everything I have gone through and conquered. I discovered how much I love being a mom and I am thankful for the illness that let me enjoy all the important milestones in my daughter's life since sometimes being a doctor means sacrificing family for others. When I was growing up, I was very shy and did not like to be in the public eye. Now I have become the voice of women with PD all around the globe. In that capacity I discovered my own creativity, and multiple ways of using my medical knowledge and training. I rediscovered the power of love, faith and hope and the freedom and blessings of second chances.

It's funny, me and technology have never been friends. Yet, over the years I find that I depend on it more each time especially during this pandemic. Although I am extremely dystonic and slow when typing, I have managed to publish three books and write several blogs including Parkinsonsdiva.org. The joke at home with my husband is that he married a doctor who turned blogger turned writer and model.

> "I love beautiful shoes, but most beautiful shoes are neither comfortable nor practical when someone has balance issues."

I found that there is life after Parkinson's which has brought me many friends but also has taught me to be more patient (I was never very patient) and kinder to others. Having this disease has reinforced and strengthened my willful spirit. With God's guidance I have learned never to back down from any challenge. I am optimistic about the future and excited about living and continuing my advocacy work for women with PD. So, they too can find their inner 'divas' to be empowered to keep fighting each day.

I wish that I could own a fashion magazine for women with PD and other chronic illnesses. Just because we have a chronic illness does not mean we don't like to be pretty, sexy, and glamourous. We still like to buy nice clothes, shoes, and other accessories. However, the difference is that we now must think about our limitations and needs. Being a fashionista at heart it was difficult to adjust my wardrobe meshing both my taste with my needs. I love beautiful shoes, but most beautiful shoes are neither comfortable nor practical when someone has balance issues. When I first got diagnosed, I threw away most of my shoes because of the pain in my feet. This nearly broke my heart. Initially all the shoes that I could find that would not exacerbate my pain looked like something my 90-year-old grandma would wear and I am sure not even she would like. These were not fitting for a young, thirty-something woman. I now have tons of fine jewelry given to me by my husband over the years which cannot be worn because of the clasps or need for fine motor coordination which I have lost.

So, in my search, I went for jewelry that I could wear with ease. I have found many nice pieces, but all are costume jewelry because fine jewelry is not made with women with limitations in mind. The same goes for nice undergarments and dressy clothing. I can no longer wear most of my nice dresses because I cannot zip them up or take them off by myself. Forget wearing boots. I cannot put them on and if I do, I cannot take them off without feeling I am going to have a coronary. I have found gadgets to help, but it would be so nice to have nice clothes. I have been blessed to have been given the opportunity several times to have a photoshoot for article layouts.

I believe every woman should have the chance at least once to be fussed over. I would love to see gorgeous women with chronic illnesses who are doing extraordinary things for themselves, their families and for others be featured on the cover of this magazine. In this magazine, I would have women with chronic illnesses discuss not only fashion tips but also provide information and how-to strategies for salient women on issues like health, finances, and relationships.

In the end, I did not think it was possible to reinvent myself and start anew. Yet, my name, once synonymous with doctor and neurologist, is so much more. I am fierce, am bold, I am strong, and I am 'The Parkinson's Diva.'

Having a passion in life and getting involved in other people's lives is vital to living a full life. For me it includes God, my family, and helping empower other women. I feel I can face anything with the right shoes and my red lipstick on.

My recommendation for any woman on this journey is to find the beauty and strength that lies within. No matter where you find yourself, remember you are not alone. Many women have faced the same challenges and have come out victorious on the other side. Begin by embracing your disease, and open your hands and heart to new experiences and challenges. To those that want to help, give to others what you wish you had been given - things like understanding and compassion; and never ever give up or lose faith, because one day this too shall pass.

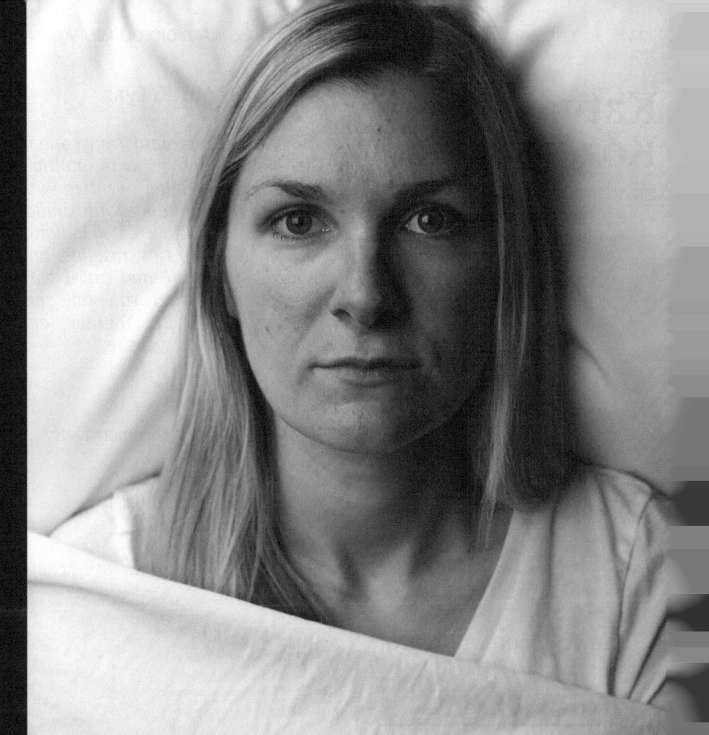

# Behind the Visible

*The unbelieved, dismissed, and chronically ill*

A film by Ashley & Cort Rippentrop

www.behindthevisiblefilm.com

# Katya Kozary

London, United Kingdom

*Digital Content Creator*

## About Katya:

*Katya is a content creator from London who was diagnosed with multiple chronic illnesses in her twenties. With a mission to help others with similar chronic illnesses, she created a digital platform to share tips, insights, and resources about life and travel with chronic illness. You can find her resources on IG, FB, Youtube, and across her detailed website.*

* * *

*IG: @positivelychronictravels*

*Facebook: @positivelychronictravels1*

*Website: www.positivelychronictravels.com*

*"APPRECIATE your body and embrace what it CAN do."*

My name is Katya, I'm a content creator, aged 26 and from London. I have multiple chronic illnesses, that I was diagnosed with two and a half years ago, including; hypermobile Ehlers Danlos syndrome (hEDS), postural orthostatic tachycardia syndrome (POTS), chronic migraine, atlantoaxial instability, allergies/mast cell issues, fibromyalgia and chronic fatigue.

The cause of most of my chronic illnesses is likely Ehlers Danlos syndrome, which is a connective tissue disorder, affecting the collagen in my body. Connective tissue is everywhere in our bodies, from around our joints to our organs, and so symptoms can be extremely widespread.

On a daily basis, symptoms are extremely unpredictable and can affect me in the following ways:

- All of my joints can sublux frequently; therefore my mobility varies extremely unpredictably.
- Migraines (pressure headache, neck pain, light sensitivity, sound sensitivity, nausea, facial pain); we know these are caused by atlantoaxial (neck) instability.
- Fatigue; a lot less energy.
- Brain fog; difficulty concentrating or thinking.
- Widespread body pain (fibromyalgia).
- Dysautonomia; lightheadedness / fainting.
- GI issues (IBS, nausea, suspected gastroparesis; trouble digesting so many foods and motion sickness).
- Allergic responses to many triggers such as foods, animals, beauty products, perfumes, chemicals, etc.
- This is due to probable MCAS; which is where cells excessively release chemical mediators resulting in allergic type attacks.

These symptoms mean that daily life is affected by a huge range of very basic triggers, making it often very disabling. For example, anything that involves bending down / forward, turning my neck, walking up stairs or up a hill, lifting anything heavy, standing after prolonged sitting (POTS), jumping/dancing/high impact exercise, opening heavy doors or the car door and SO many foods or environmental stimuli can trigger responses! I can never know how I'm going to feel from one day to the next and so daily life is simply focused on management strategies that ease symptoms and slightly improve my quality of life.

Before diagnosis, I always experienced symptoms but they were assessed in piecemeal visits to the GP and were never connected into a handful of causal conditions. I was diagnosed when I was 23, because my health slowly deteriorated over a period of a few years whilst I was working in a high stress environment at a film production company. I had been working in a role that they later divided into seven! I ended up working there for 3.5 years. I realise in retrospect that being a perfectionist, a people pleaser and being unable to say no to tasks, are what led to my condition worsening as much as it did.

After just five weeks working there, my appendix ruptured. My body was clearly trying to tell me something, right? A month after I had gone back to work, I had to have ANOTHER laparoscopy as I had adhesions (scar tissue that heals wrongly, which we now know is due to EDS). After the second surgery, I wasn't given any advice to do any essential physiotherapy to regain muscle, and continued to work very long hours with little to no energy for self care.

> ## "There are SO many more factors to consider when you have chronic illness, that the unpredictability of travel suddenly made us uncertain if we'd ever be able to do so."

Another year on, and I had a chronic daily migraine that at the time was undiagnosed for eight months. I would sit with my head in my hands in agony at intervals at work, but felt as though I couldn't stop working. I even got promoted at this time so I was under even MORE stress. In the summer of 2018, for the first time ever, my coccyx subluxed (it now just wiggles...) I asked for a referral to rheumatology but kept walking on it despite the pain for another four weeks until my left AND right hips both subluxed to the point that I had severe sciatica shooting down both legs and couldn't walk. I ended up going privately to the rheumatologist (an essential at the time, when the wait list for NHS rheumatology ended up being a further nine months and my work needed an explanation for my illness). He diagnosed me with the conditions I mentioned above. But what led to me getting to this point was the combination of stress, deconditioning of muscles (meaning they weren't supporting my joints and allowing them to sublux) and the perception of being ignored and gaslit by medical professionals all my life that I felt the only way was to continue despite the immense pain.

When I first found out, I was certainly relieved to know that there was an explanation for all my symptoms. I definitely went through the common stages of grief, and not necessarily in an exactly linear order. I find when new symptoms pop up, the grief cycle repeats itself over again.

- **Denial** - It took a long time till I focused on my symptoms - I tried to ignore them, especially coming up to my diagnosis. I continued working (from home) yet didn't take one sick day apart from going to doctors appointments and tests. I wanted to be healthy again and I thought that not focusing on it could make it go away. I was very wrong!
- **Anger** - at my body for being incapable of so many tasks, for constantly having endless symptoms and being in constant pain, which definitely became a cycle!
- **Bargaining** - I believed I was going to heal and be 100% able bodied again, (as if it was a broken leg). I expected healing to be linear and was hoping for certain therapies to fully cure me, when I realise now it's about constant daily management of symptoms.
- **Depression** - it was definitely a dark few months questioning the future; if I'll be able to have a family, how I will be from one day to the next - there is a huge sense of lack of control over symptoms.
- **Acceptance** - it took me a while, but by realising that it's not going away per-se, there is no cure, however, that I CAN slightly alleviate symptoms daily through management strategies and do my best to

feel good and improve my quality of life, is where my mindset is now. It was a long period of focusing on these daily strategies and altering my perspective of my reality to change my lifestyle in general and once I got to this point, I finally felt like I wasn't "battling" my illness but accepting things as they were and embracing my body as it is. I stopped hating myself and my body and its issues and started to love myself despite it. Yes, my chronic illness may have shaped many aspects of my personality; making me much more health focused, organised, anxious, analytical and also shaping my hobbies or the places I want to visit into things/places that are less sports/activity focused and more sedentary - but it doesn't or shouldn't fully define "me" and I am (although perhaps shaped by it) MORE than just my chronic illnesses.

When I was diagnosed, my partner and I had been planning on a long term trip, traveling around the world. Diagnosis halted our plans, and I wasn't sure if it would ever be possible. There are SO many more factors to consider when you have chronic illness, that the unpredictability of travel suddenly made us uncertain if we'd ever be able to do so. I searched for a place online that would confirm that I could, yet I couldn't find that. So I researched every day for over a year to research, plan and prepare our trip to make our travels as suitable and accessible as possible. Finally, after years of waiting, we departed on our (meant to be 18 months+) travels in December 2019.

After a few months of travelling in a way that is perhaps different to how people would conventionally travel, and learning the most suitable ways to travel with chronic illness, I realised that all my research and experience could maybe help someone else with chronic illness to do the same. I wanted to streamline the process for them to make their journey a little easier than mine has been. So, I created the platform Positively Chronic Travels; creating tips, insights and resources for life and travel with chronic illness. After just three and a half months, the global pandemic cut our trip short. I had thought the only possible thing that could bring us home would be an issue with my health and of course no one could have envisioned things as they are at the moment with the pandemic, but once travel is safe again I will be back out slowly travelling and visiting beautiful places and beaches. In the meantime, I'm continuing to create free content to help (hopefully!) even just one other person in a similar situation to me, to make planning a trip and just living with chronic illness a little easier for them!

What advice would I give to someone who relates to my story? I'd say to avoid stress, know your boundaries / limits, assert when you're overworked or anything that is not beneficial for your wellbeing/symptoms, focus on a change of lifestyle and management strategies, and to APPRECIATE your body and embrace what it CAN do.

# Misti Blu Day McDermott

Rockledge, FL, USA

## Published Author, Health Advocate & Entrepreneur

*"Never stop advocating for yourself because by doing so you are also advocating for others.
We are all worthy."*

## About Misti:

*Misti Blu lives in Florida with her three kids, husband, and golden fur nugget. She is an author and has her own apothecary self-care product line called Wildling Apothecary. She is a Biomedical Science student and plans to be involved in research. Misti has Ehlers-Danlos syndrome, Wolff-Parkinson-White syndrome, Dysautonomia, a pacemaker, and she is an open-heart surgery survivor. She loves to travel, create art, and listen to music. Misti is passionate about advocating for chronic illness, self-care, and mental health. She has a digital magazine and podcast called Blu Dream Health Collective. She is the President and Publisher for ImagineWe Florida Division. Her goal is to publish several books and to also help others to share their story.*

\* \* \*

IG:
@mistibluday
@bludreamhealth
@wildlingapothecaryus

FB:
@mistibluday
@bludreamhealth
@wildlingapothecary

My name is Misti Blu Day. I was named after Jimi Hendrix's song, "One Rainy Wish." My soul had always resembled a blue, gloomy day. I was very attached to my name because in a way it really did represent me. Now that I am married, I added McDermott to my name but I still held on to my identity. I was born in California and grew up in Missouri, just before finishing my junior year in high school in Florida.

I always felt like it was me against the world. I had this strange, dark luck that loomed over me. Whether it was my health or just simply ordering food and getting the wrong dish every time, something always went wrong. This is just how my life works, and still does. The only difference now is that my perspective has changed. I went from being a wounded civilian to a warrior. I hit a point in my life, or a fork in the road, where I had to choose: do I keep dragging my wounded life around or do I get up and fight? I chose to fight and I didn't stop there. I choose to pave the way and let my fire shed light on the path for those who feel like I once did. I think of it as: I am taking one for the team. I always felt lost and alone. Now, I realize none of us are ever alone because together we have created this community where we all have each other's backs. We are all also in different places in our lives, from newly diagnosed to the hardcore advocate. Together we help each other and grow together. We teach each other more than any patient pamphlet ever could.

I was born with many health issues, but it has taken my lifetime to unravel each diagnosis. I do not remember a time where I didn't have heart issues (and other health issues). I remember being around 5 or 6 years old and playing hide and seek with my cousins. I stopped and told the nearest adult that my heart was going so fast."That's normal, silly. You are running around!" My heart felt like a hummingbird and as if it would fly out of my chest. This is normal, I reminded myself. That's what everyone always told me. My face would be red for hours. This continued on throughout my childhood and into my teens. At the age of fifteen, I was finally diagnosed with supraventricular tachycardia. My heart rates would go into the 250s and even reached the 300s. These episodes were daily and I was told I would simply just outgrow this.

At the age of nineteen, I had these episodes up to fifty times per day. I never outgrow it. Some episodes lasted for a few seconds and some for up to thirty minutes. I could just be sitting there eating my lunch and with the blink of an eye switch from 60 to 260. I would hold my breath and try to convert the rhythm, all day every day. I had my first catheter ablation to help treat my arrhythmias. A procedure that normally takes up to an hour and a half took six hours. The doctor discovered that I had a disorder of my heart's electrical system, called Wolff-Parkinson-White syndrome, which is from an accessory pathway in the heart. The ablation was unsuccessful due to the area of the pathway being in a complicated spot. We tried again a second time. It was still unsuccessful and when I went to my follow-up I learned that my doctor had relocated to a practice out of the area.

Over the years I had two more ablations, all of which were unsuccessful. In my 20s, not only did I still have these fast rhythms but I also had low rhythms, as low as 30 beats per minute. When I stood up my heart rate went from 40 to 150. I was constantly fatigued. I was always dismissed. How could my doctors let me live this way for so long? Why couldn't anyone help me? I was given medication to slow down my heart but what about my slow rates? My doctor insisted that I didn't need a pacemaker. After trial and error I realized I could not take medications without making other issues worse. I was left untreated for a very long time.

## "My exes all thought I was a hypochondriac and that I 'always complain about something.'"

At 26 years old I ended up having open-heart surgery to repair a tear in my aortic heart valve. For several years, my aortic valve was missed as the main focus was electrical, not the plumbing. Finally when an ER doctor took a deeper look, he discovered I had severe aortic insufficiency with an echocardiogram. No doctor wanted to touch my heart and I spent a good amount of time being short of breath and miserable. Some doctors think the aortic valve tear was from my previous ablation, but no one really knows how it happened or why. Eventually I found a surgeon who cared and wanted to take on a complicated patient like myself."Wow! I can't wait to get in there and fix what's going on. When is it good for you?" my surgeon said, after years of doctors telling me they didn't want my family to sue them for malpractice

if I died on their table. I will never forget when I was admitted to the hospital for over a week because the doctors didn't know what to do. One surgeon said, "You aren't a car. I can't just pop open the hood and fix you. You are young, unlike my elderly patients. If you die on my table then your family could sue me for malpractice." I never felt so hopeless as I did in that moment. Having this new surgeon was a breath of fresh air. He was going to pop open the hood and fix me. Thank you, Dr. Kevin Accola!

After my valve repair, I felt a little relieved. I had more energy but the arrhythmias were still a thing, as well as the low rates and the daily presyncope feeling. Fast forward to the age of 32. I had 52 ER visits in less than two years and every time was dismissed for anxiety. After finally getting a new electrophysiologist, I found someone who listened. I had a heart monitor on for thirty days. During some of my ER visits, I wasn't even put on a heart monitor because I was dismissed as having anxiety. Fortunately, I had a monitor under my clothes and it caught everything. At one point we were trying to rule out seizures so after an EEG, I left the room and walked down the hall to exit my doctor's office and I fell to the ground. The nurse witnessed it and called my new electrophysiologist. My heart monitor picked up that my heart rate had suddenly plummeted. My tilt table test showed that I had a severe cardioinhibitory response and suggested neurocardiogenic syncope. Having sick sinus syndrome, dysautonomia and neurocardiogenic syncope, I finally got my pacemaker. For the first time I could take medication to treat my high heart rates and had a safety net that would not allow me to drop under 60. The pacemaker changed my life and I can't believe it didn't happen ten years sooner.

I have many other health issues that would take an entire book to explain, which is in the works. To keep it short, I am mostly sharing my heart story. Soon after my pacemaker, I finally saw a geneticist and was diagnosed with Ehlers-Danlos syndrome. No one sent me to a geneticist ever. I sought after one myself. I needed answers. Looking back at medical records, at the age of 16, I often saw, "the patient has many unusual symptoms," along with a long list of ailments. I even found a diagnosis of POTS (postural orthostatic tachycardia syndrome) but it was mistyped as "potts syndrome" which is actually related to tuberculosis and nothing like POTS. It is interesting to me how a little typo like that can make such a difference. I was never educated on how to manage my health issues and no one I knew had to deal with these issues. At the time, the Internet was not what it is today so forget about online support groups. Finding a geneticist really put the puzzle together. I am grateful to have found Dr. Atwal, who specializes in Ehlers-Danlos syndrome. That appointment fulfilled everything the teenager and twenty-something-year-old in me needed. I left with validity, education, and someone who believed me. That ticket opened the doors to management and care that I was starved of my entire life.

Relationships were a nightmare for the longest time. My exes all thought I was a hypochondriac and that I "always complain about something." This common trait in significant others eventually trained me to feel like a burden and therefore keep everything to myself. There were times when I would go to the ER and not mention it. I was very alone in my chronic illness world for a long time. I did not feel worthy. My doctors didn't even believe me back then either. No physician could help me, for so long. All I wanted to do was give up. And I did give up, for a while.

## "My life is like Madonna's music career, a constant reinvention of myself."

After I turned 30, I had gotten over the worst break up. I spent about six months being a mess over it. One day I looked in the mirror and hated the person I had become. I didn't recognize my body. The eyes staring back at me were so hurt and broken. I was wasting my life being miserable. It was me against the world. I decided to make some big changes and only focus on myself. I quit drinking alcohol and cut out toxic friends. I made healthier choices in every aspect, both mentally and physically. I told myself that I was worthy and that I deserved the best. I think it is so important to spend time in your life alone to just focus on yourself. I am so grateful that I gave myself that time to heal and love myself, the person that I once hated for so long. I was able to become a better mother and when it was time to meet someone, it would be different. It was. Everything I trained myself to do was undone. My husband always wants to know how I feel. I never feel like a burden because I am not; I never was. I only allowed myself to give my heart to others who didn't see my worth, because I didn't see it either.

My life is like Madonna's music career, a constant reinvention of myself. I adapt and then something happens, remember? It always does--but it's okay. What else can I try? What is next? I chose not to dream one single dream. I follow where each dream takes me. One dream falls apart and another turns into something else, but I ride each wave and see where it takes me. I am currently in school working on my Bachelor of Biomedical Science. I have made it ten years since I had my sternum cracked and had open-heart surgery. It is only a matter of time until I get on the cold, hard operating table again. I will need a new valve soon and in a few years it will be time for a new pacemaker. This is my life. It is my normal. My health is a dream-stopper but it's okay, because instead I am a dream-hopper.

> ## "Flowers, puppies, and chocolate can make you smile but true happiness is what you allow yourself to experience, despite what life has handed you."

I don't know where I will end up but I adapt by modifying my dreams, being patient, trusting the process and where I am headed, and being accepting of where I end up. As long as I am trying and having fun, it's all that matters. As we grieve having a chronic illness, we must find a way to cope. Many of us cope by finding our purpose in life. We advocate for ourselves because no one else did. We educate ourselves because we are fighting for our lives. We shed light because we have been in the dark for so long.

Despite my illnesses and mixture of bad genes, I love how resilient I am. I am strong, I am worthy, and I am determined. I have turned my anger and frustration into fuel. I am getting my foot in the door to contribute to medical research so that the next generations can have a better experience, more answers, and more understanding of rare diseases. I have my own digital magazine and podcast so that I can share my story and others'. My kids are now teenagers and I never want them to feel how I felt. I never want anyone to not feel worthy. I truly believe that together, we are changing the world. One of my professors, Wayne Brown at Eastern Florida State University said, "It's up to all of you to change the cracks in our healthcare system." That's when I knew I had to get involved and make a difference myself.

If I could be doing anything in my life, it would be exactly what I am doing now. Looking back, getting to where I am today was like climbing Mount Everest. Just to even get back into school, it took me two years to pay off old tuition debts and retake classes I failed as an 18 year old. If I could give any advice it would be to start small. Take life day-by-day, step-by-step. If you have a big goal, that is great! However, sometimes it feels impossible if that is your only goal. Break that huge goal down into little crumbs. One by one, tackle each crumb until you get to where you want to go. Be patient with yourself. We all fall down, but with a chronic illness, we fall more often and harder. Decide if you are going to be that wounded civilian who drags yourself around or if you are going to be a warrior badass. Take your time.

You will have days where you feel hopeless and that is okay. Give yourself a break. Rest. Take care of yourself, even if you have to take care of others. Make yourself a priority, especially your mental health. Know that you are not a burden, even if you have to tattoo it on yourself to remember. Do not put up with anyone who makes you feel like you are not worthy because it's them; they are not worthy to be in your life. Love yourself. Why do you only see beauty in anything other than yourself?

When I stopped drinking and surrounding myself with fake friendships, I was able to find myself. I was distracting myself with relationships and numbing the pain by drinking and "having fun." Oftentimes we don't realize we are numbing our pain and distracting ourselves from the hurt buried inside. It gets old being numb and you make no progress doing that. The saying, "the only way out is through," is something that resonates with my mental health story. I was diagnosed with severe major depressive disorder when I started seeing a therapist. I had to go through acknowledging my traumas, depression, and self-worth in order to save myself from drowning. I kept my depression to myself for so long because I was in denial and thought I had control. I also hid it because I did not want it used against me as I was trying to find a diagnosis. This needs to change. I can't count how many times ER doctors joked and dismissed me, saying that I was in there to get a break from my kids. I wasn't just dismissed once or twice; I was dismissed by more doctors than I can count. I am forever grateful to the ones who listened to me. Speak up and don't be afraid to find a new physician if you aren't feeling heard. You are allowed a second or even third opinion.

Even though my health continues to progressively decline, I am happier than I have ever been. Happiness depends on you and no one else. No one can make us happy. One of my greatest lessons was to learn that we can't rely on obtaining happiness from anyone other than ourselves. It is just too much pressure to put on someone. Flowers, puppies, and chocolate can make you smile but true happiness is what you allow yourself to experience, despite what life has handed you. I am in chronic pain every day and I worry about how long I have left on this planet, but despite that I choose to live my best life (rain or shine). You don't have to conquer the world or know exactly what you are doing. Don't compare yourself to others or feel like your journey has to be aligned with everyone else. We are all at different points in our lives and at different places. Not everyone is transparent so know that what you see is not always reality. We all have our own battles and we are all in this together.

Keep fighting your battle and know that there is a community that is fighting with you, even if you haven't found it yet. It is absolutely okay to cut people out of your life for the sake of self-care. Don't ever give up because you never know what is around the corner. Never stop advocating for yourself because by doing so you are also advocating for others. We are all worthy.

# Vitassium®
by SaltStick

**saltstick®** Vitassium®
Buffered Electrolyte Salts

Vitassium® is a medical food made specifically to provide sodium and potassium for the dietary management of Dysautonomia, POTS, EDS, CF, and more.

Join the Vitassium Club for exclusive savings at Vitassium.com.

NON-GMO    VEGAN    GLUTEN FREE    PRESERVATIVE FREE    ALLERGEN FREE    STARCH FREE

This product should only be consumed under the guidance of a physician.

# I'M STILL KICKIN

## OVERCOMING THE IMPOSSIBLE WHEN YOU'RE MAD THE WORLD

### WRITTEN BY BRANDON MOUW

**Buy Now!**

At the age of just 3-years-old, Brandon Mouw was diagnosed as a Juvenile Type 1 Diabetic. Over his lifetime, he underwent a series of surgeries before he was told a pancreas-only transplant was the only thing that could save his life. Unfortunately, he needed $250,000 to afford it. In this book, you will learn about how Brandon went on to raise a quarter of a million dollars online and lived to not only talk about it but to become an advocate for those facing similar challenges.

Helping women with autoimmune disease to take back control of their health and happiness

www.ketolupie.com

**Danielle Turco CLC**

Instagram:@ketolupie

#CEREBRALPALSYAWARENESS

**BUY NOW!**

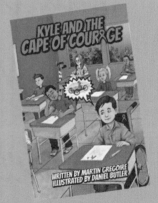

WRITTEN BY MARTIN GREGOIRE
ILLUSTRATED BY: DANIEL BUTLER

Kyle is a typical kid, who loves typical kid things. There is one thing that sets Kyle apart from the rest of the kids. Kyle has Cerebral Palsy and dreams of one day doing things like riding a bicycle. One day a surprise arrives in the mail that inspires Kyle to be happier, stronger, and face his fear. Join Kyle as he takes a whole new ride on this new adventure!

Brought to you by

FOOTSTEPS of WNY

Victoria F. Burns

Amanda Osowski

Wendy Meyeroff

Ella Balasa

Kay Mimms

Madelyn Saner

Amy Courtney

# I AM
# *Determined.*

## Stories of chronic illness warriors accomplishing things despite their barriers.

# Victoria F. Burns

Easley, SC, USA

## University Professor, Researcher, and Writer

## "Let go of the shame and find meaning in your chronic illness."

### About Victoria:

*Victoria Burns, PhD is a registered social worker, writer, and university professor. She has a BA (psychology) (University of New Brunswick), BSW, MSW and PhD in social work (McGill University). Drawing on over a decade of social work practice, and her own lived experiences with chronic illnesses and addiction, her research focuses broadly on the areas of home/homelessness, stigma, addiction, and recovery. Dr. Burns combines her research interests with her passion for storytelling and the arts, including documentary film, to raise awareness and combat stigma for marginalized populations.*

\* \* \*

*IG: @betesandbites*

## The Sober Professor:

## Recovering from Chronic Illness, Addiction, & Trauma

*"The body holds what the conscious mind wants to forget."*

-Bessel Van der Kolk

As instructed, I arrived at my first trauma therapy session 15 minutes ahead of schedule. Clipboard carefully perched on my lap, ballpoint pen in hand, I read question 1 from the three-page intake form: Summarize in one to two sentences your situation: your physical, psychological and/ or emotional illness (es) or conditions. After hemming and hawing for several minutes, I answer the question as concisely as possible:

*I am a 38-year old woman with type 1 diabetes, celiac disease, and polycystic ovarian syndrome (PCOS). Sober from alcohol for seven years, I am recovering from diabulimia, adrenal burnout, and complex post-traumatic stress disorder (PTSD).*

Seeing "my situation" in black and white feels instantly overwhelming. I think to myself, "Where am I going to start with that rat's nest of problems?"

As I reread the summary, the word "traumatic" stands out from the rest. Over the years, when asked by health care professionals about my trauma history, I have answered reluctantly because of narrow ideas of what constitutes legitimate trauma.

Feeling as though my trauma was not "traumatic enough," has paradoxically been retraumatizing. Like my half rape. Trauma researcher Van der Kolk, MD defines trauma as "the holes in the soul that result from not having been wanted, not having been seen, and not been allowed to speak the truth." Put that way, I have had plenty.

On paper, I had a normal childhood. The middle child of two sisters, I grew up in the suburbs. We didn't go without anything material. As an adult, I had the diplomas, the husband, the house, the car, the dog, the job. But there were plenty of other holes. Craters created by early childhood trauma, sexual violence, and years of fat-shaming. Subtle holes too, shaped by more socially acceptable behaviors, like work binges, repressed anger, and saying yes when I wanted to say no. Holes that I filled with drugs, alcohol, food, accolades, work; you name it. So many holes are hidden under a veneer of "normalcy," "niceness," and "success," I was stuck in a battle that should have ended decades ago.

*"Trauma makes the immune system oversensitive to threat so that it is prone to mount a defense when none is needed, even when this means attacking the body's own cells"*

- Gabor Maté, MD

In the fall of 2011, shortly after my 30th birthday, I was diagnosed with type 1 diabetes (T1D). Formerly known as juvenile diabetes, T1D is a chronic, autoimmune disease that requires 24/7 attention. In contrast to type 2 diabetes, your body no longer produces insulin, because the beta cells have been destroyed by the immune system. Diet, exercise, or other lifestyle changes cannot reverse the condition and you are dependent on insulin for the rest of your life. It is a difficult disease to manage because everything affects your blood sugar: food, sleep, exercise, temperature, menstrual cycle, stress, medication, infections, you name it. T1D is also a very expensive disease to manage. People with T1D require multiple daily doses of insulin to survive, and its high cost, particularly in the United States, prevents ready access to this life-sustaining therapy.

> "When addiction lives with you, it sprouts many vines."
> -Sarah Hepola

For the past 10 months, I've been on long-term disability from my 70-hour per week university professor position. It's been a long time coming. The year preceding my T1D diagnosis of type was filled with a number of good and bad stressors. I got married, bought a home, started a Ph.D., and adopted a two-month-old puppy. In between the puppy training and home renovations, I had cobbled together three research assistant jobs to help make ends meet. I was also sexually assaulted. Two weeks after the attack, I started to get all the classic symptoms of T1D: constant hunger and thirst, frequent urination, yeast infections, and rapid weight loss.

That entire semester I was in total shock. Full of shame, I told very few people. I grew up in an alcoholic home, where the rule was if it's not discussed, it doesn't exist. I did what I usually did, repressed, put on the happy mask, and pretended everything was fine. But as Van der Kolk, MD writes, my body was keeping the score and shutting down. I ignored my symptoms, buried myself in my doctoral work, and anesthetized with alcohol.

For the first six months following my diagnosis, I followed my diabetes treatment plan like a true academic. But no matter how hard I tried, I couldn't get my numbers right. I was extremely sensitive to insulin; one unit off would take me into unsafe highs and lows. I'd eat a normal dinner, take the required insulin injection, feel full, and then need to eat again two hours later to make it through the night. I started to put on weight and was getting more and more frustrated, angry, and depressed. I blamed myself for being a "bad diabetic." No matter how hard I tried, I felt like a failure.

It didn't take long to figure out that omitting insulin was not only an effective weight-loss tool, compared with vomiting, it was a much less violent way to purge. Having a history of bulimia nervosa, I thought I had found the holy grail. Coined "the world's most dangerous eating disorder,"1 I had developed diabulimia, which is characterized by the omission of insulin to lose weight.

Within no time, my glycated hemoglobin (HbA1c) level crept back up to the dangerous range. I was fortunate to be connected to a diabetes team, but no one seemed to know about diabulimia or ask me about my relationship with food and/or history of eating disorders. It was easy to keep my diabulimia secret—it was largely invisible. I was a "normal" weight. I didn't look sick. I blamed my double-digit HbA1c level on being someone with "brittle" or labile diabetes, meaning I am prone to large swings in blood sugar, which was true. I had figured out the right amount of insulin I needed to keep my weight down and avoid diabetic ketoacidosis. This behavior carried on for eight years.

> "Wake up, be aware of who you are, what you're doing, and what you can do to prevent yourself from becoming ill."
>
> – Maya Angelou

Adapting to my limitations hasn't always been simple. I had a hard time accepting my T1D diagnosis. I was suffering from PTSD, and every injection was a painful reminder of being raped. Having struggled with drinking since my teens, I thought my T1D diagnosis would be the cure to my alcoholism. I was told by my endocrinologist that my body could no longer tolerate large quantities of alcohol, that it would kill me. Unfortunately, addiction doesn't work that way. It defies all logic. By the grace of God, I had my last "drunk" on November 23, 2013. I am grateful for my T1D because it brought me to my bottom sooner and ultimately saved my life. With alcohol out of the picture, I was finally able to start addressing the underlying issues fueling my chronic conditions.

Through intensive therapy, I awoke to the reality that alcoholism and eating disorders were mere symptoms, and my chronic illnesses were mere consequences of the root issue: trauma. Repressed trauma that I numbed with addiction. Repressed trauma that was destroying my body and ultimately eroding my True Self. In order to put an end to the addiction whack-a-mole game and stop adding more chronic conditions to my growing collection—I had to heal deep trauma wounds that left imprints at the cellular level. I also had to start living authentically; the masks had to come off once and for all.

To this end, I have been doing somatic EMDR (eye movement desensitization reprocessing) therapy. EMDR is an evidence-based trauma therapy backed by a robust body of scientific research, that is helping me work through triggers, reconnect with my body, and regulate my nervous system; all of which enable me to better manage stress and my chronic illnesses.

Social support has also been central to my recovery. Getting active with the T1D, diabulimia, and addiction communities have not only been validating but have provided me with practical resources and hope. Until recently, I remained private about my history with addiction and a growing collection of chronic conditions. I was advised by more senior academics and mentors to remain tight-lipped. I wore the mask of a capable, accomplished scholar very well. I am a firm believer that we are as sick as our secrets; shame and stigma prevent people from getting the help they need. In April 2020, as a quarantine project, I started an Instagram account @betesandbites. It started as a platform to share tools that have been helpful on my recovery journey. It has turned into an advocacy platform to combat stigma and raise awareness about chronic illness.

> ## "Living with chronic illnesses means that you are constantly dealing with grief, so be gentle with yourself."

When I think about what I love about myself, despite my illness/disabilities, I've always loved to write. I am fortunate that writing has never been overly laborious for me. It was something that carried me through graduate school with relative ease. I was gifted my first diary at age four and have consistently kept a journal ever since. I love the puzzle of writing. Figuring out how to express what I want to say in a sentence.

Like a game of Jenga, taking one word out can make the whole idea collapse.

Writing is also my medicine. The page is my container for all the noise and emotions; putting pen to paper allows me to express complex situations and see them in a new light. It's expansive, in the sense that the more I write, the more I learn about myself. Seeing an idea expressed in black and white gives it new legs to stand on. Having a conversation with the page gives me distance from the painful emotion, which in turn diffuses its power. Importantly, writing has been a tool to lessen the grip of shame. Even if it is sharing my thoughts and emotions with an inanimate object, such as a piece of paper or a word processor, it pulls away from the cover a bit, which has been an essential step of healing.

Despite my chronic illnesses, I managed to finish my Ph.D. ahead of schedule, complete a post-doctorate, and secured a full-time tenure-track professor position. I have a wonderful husband, who I have been partnered with for 14 years and counting. We are the proud parents to Pinot, our 9-year old Poodle-Bichon.

I am fortunate to have my dream job as a university professor. This position provides me with opportunities to conduct research, supervise students, publish, and teach. I firmly believe my experience with chronic illness makes me a better professor and social worker. It has allowed me to cultivate more compassion for myself and others.

My diagnosis of T1D and recovery from

addiction have also shaped the trajectory of my research. I recently received a grant to begin studying the impact of addiction stigma in higher education settings. My goal is to continue chronic illness advocacy work, in order to raise awareness about the role of the environment, and especially toxic stress and trauma, in developing and treating chronic illnesses.

Living with chronic illnesses means that you are constantly dealing with grief, so be gentle with yourself. One of the most memorable conversations I had in the early days of my diagnosis was with my family doctor. He was the first person to normalize the frustration, anger, and sadness I was feeling. He went as far as to refer to what I was feeling as grief; he indicated that I would need to grieve over the loss of what my life no longer was. The coupling of grief and diabetes seemed strange to me—but he was right. Kubler Ross (1969) famously conceptualized a five-stage model of grief in her book On Death and Dying to explain the complex emotions experienced by survivors of an intimate's death: denial, anger, bargaining, depression, and acceptance. Over the last five years, I have gone through all five stages—and not in a linear fashion. About three months after my diagnosis, I wrote the poem [included in the beginning of this book] that is titled "My Invisible Fear." When I wrote it eight years ago, I was obviously stuck somewhere between the shock and anger phase of grief. By naming my feelings, and seeing them in black and white, I have been able to move through a lot of my pain.

Since my T1D diagnosis, I've worked through Kubler Ross's five stages of grief. This process has not been linear. I've only recently moved to the sixth stage – what David Kessler refers to as "meaning-making." I've been able to find meaning by letting go of the shame and sharing my story openly, conducting research on the mind-body connection, and specifically the role of trauma in developing chronic conditions like T1D.

My main advice would be to let go of the shame and find meaning in your chronic illness. You did nothing wrong. Your story is your superpower and can benefit someone.

Finally, if you are struggling, know that you are not invisible. I see you. You are not alone.

# Amanda Osowski

Hoffman Estates, IL, USA

**MPH, CD, CPLC, Infertility & Postpartum Doula, Bereavement Preparation & Loss Specialist, Certified Professional Life Coach & Patient Advocate**

*"Today is not forever and there is more in store for you."*

## About Amanda:

*Amanda Osowski is an infertility & postpartum doula, a wife and mom living and working in Chicago, IL. Her passion for advocacy, community, and writing along with her experiences of becoming a parent have made her both a fierce advocate and a pillar of knowledge.*

*Amanda was diagnosed with Crohn's disease in January 2016, after suffering for more than six years with disease-related symptoms. Her path to diagnosis was incredibly trying and drastically impacted her mental health & her support system. Amanda has spent the last decade sharing her experiences and tirelessly fighting to help patients of all types assert their own voice, advocate for themselves, and ultimately see an improvement in their quality of life.*

\* \* \*

*IG: @amanda.osowski*
*@heartfeltbeginnings*

*Facebook: @amandabosowski*
*@heartfeltbeginnings*

*Website:*
*www.heartfeltbeginnings.com*

Hi, I'm Amanda! If you know me in person, or follow me on social media, you know a few things about my life, in no particular order. I'm an Enneagram 2, a creative writer, an infertility and postpartum doula and a fierce advocate for mental health. I'm a wife, the mother of a sassy toddler conceived via In Vitro Fertilization (IVF), and we have a super snuggly pup named Ollie (after Oliver Queen on the TV show Green Arrow). The song "Brave" by Sara Bareilles is my anthem, the book "If You Feel Too Much" by Jamie Tworkowski is my bible, and I believe we are the ones we've been waiting for. I also manage Depression and Anxiety while living with Crohn's disease.

## "Living with chronic illnesses means that you are constantly dealing with grief, so be gentle with yourself."

Crohn's disease is a form of Inflammatory Bowel Disease (IBD), an autoimmune disease which causes inflammation in the digestive tract leading to uncomfortable, unfortunate and significant GI distress - in the form of unbearable abdominal pain, severe diarrhea, crippling fatigue, and overwhelming nausea and vomiting, to name a few. Crohn's disease inflammation can involve different areas of the digestive tract - anywhere from the mouth to the anus - and can also cause extraintestinal manifestations (complications of the disease/inflammation outside of the digestive tract). I lived with these symptoms for a long time before I knew they were caused by Crohn's disease, and my journey from there to here has changed me in all of the ways.

Before I jump into sharing my story, I want to note one thing. There are parts of this journey that I'm not proud of, but I truly believe I had to walk through all of it to end up where I am now. Crohn's disease has taught me that I'm resilient and determined to be ever-evolving, and I hope this story shares all of that with you.

My pathway to diagnosis was both not the typical journey for Crohn's disease patients, and also incredibly common in the IBD community. From onset of consistent symptoms to diagnosis, I walked through 6.5 very long years, saw provider after provider after provider, struggled to manage my daily life, was in and out of the hospital, and after enough time, lost hope and direction. My mental health and credibility as a person and a patient were questioned and challenged over and over again when test results came back inconclusive or without answers, causing me to doubt myself and my experience on an intimate level.

I was 23 years old in 2009 when my GI symptoms required that I pause my life. I was a young professional, trying to navigate my workday while in and out of the restroom, unable to eat much food, and constantly exhausted. I fought with debilitating abdominal pain, constant, frequent and urgent diarrhea, persistent nausea, regular vomiting, and crippling fatigue, along with headaches, joint pains, and dizziness. It was really hard to continue being a person every minute of every day! Initial testing said nothing catastrophic was wrong with me, but what I hoped was a virus or infection never went away. I took leave, worked from home, adjusted to my "new normal," tried medication after medication to manage my symptoms, and worked with both Eastern and Western medical providers, but my symptoms stayed present, varying with intensity in different seasons but never leaving me alone.

> ## "Having a diagnosis meant that I could understand, finally, what was happening inside my body, and where the malfunctions were occurring."

Hoping that I could manage my health in the ways I'd come to understand, I moved away for graduate school in the fall of 2011. I established care with new providers, began classes and was thriving - until I wasn't. What started as one really painful night led to multiple ER visits and admissions to the hospital away from my family. Losing weight and strength over time as I spent more and more of my days in bed or being sick forced me to pack up and move back home.

The next two and a half years were the lowest of the low for me. As I physically felt like garbage every single day, it wasn't a surprise when my mental health really began to suffer.

Although I finished my Masters Degree, my ambitions faded and I struggled to find my voice or a way to engage professionally in my community. I was miserable. I doubted the reason for my existence, what my future would look like, and if I would ever find happiness again. Without a diagnosis or a treatment plan, I had no way to control my symptoms, manage my expectations, or take back my life. I was stuck in every single way. If you passed me then, you knew this, because it's all I could talk about. That's all I knew.

Looking back, it's evident that the darkest season led to the best dawn. Through my struggles, I met a friend of a friend who changed the rest of my life. Six years ago when I was introduced to my now husband, I was so unsure of everything - including who I was or how I was going to survive. As a friend, and then a boyfriend, he encouraged me, supported me, researched with me, went to appointments with me, stayed overnight in the hospital with me, and advocated for my physical and mental well-being. He believed that the abdominal pain and GI symptoms that monopolized my life were not the end of my story. He believed in my passion for helping others, and knew that I needed help and hope to continue onward.

I began working with a new doctor, and he was persistent. Although the typical diagnostic tests for GI disorders (colonoscopy, endoscopy, CT, MRI, bloodwork) had not previously given me the answers I was hoping for, he believed in my symptoms and he believed in better days for me. Eventually, a new diagnostic test - the pill cam, or the capsule endoscopy, provided the evidence we needed. I was diagnosed in January 2016 with Crohn's disease in my small bowel - something that other tests had previously alluded to but were unable to confirm. As an autoimmune disease, Crohn's currently has no cure, just a variety of treatment options to manage symptoms and mitigate the inflammatory disease process.

After finally receiving a diagnosis, after giving up hope and trying to re-learn it, after being unsure if there was a reason to stay alive, I walked through a season of finding acceptance. I faced denial knowing my life would never be the same, that I would always be "sick," I struggled with anger at why this happened to me, I grieved my "before" - my healthy life, and finally, I found a space where I could come to terms with my new life - one that would forever involve managing my Crohn's disease.

It took about two more years to find a treatment option that really managed my disease and improved my quality of life, but during that time of trial and error I found myself again. Having a diagnosis meant that I could understand, finally, what was happening inside my body, and where the malfunctions were occurring. It helped me to better predict how things I ate or did would impact how I was feeling, both short and long term. I was still a regular patient at my local hospital, my GI doctor's office staff knew me by name, and the infusion center carried my favorite snacks, but my approach to life was different than it had been. Before diagnosis, I felt like everything was a guessing game, and

I was the losing contestant time after time. I felt unsure of if, or when, or how I would ever feel better. Knowing we were managing Crohn's disease enabled my doctor and I to establish a plan, and to modify it as time went on and things changed.

During those years, my boyfriend and I got engaged, planned a destination wedding, and exchanged the most beautiful vows. We settled into life as newlyweds and found a rhythm that always involved managing my Crohn's disease. The names and doses of my medications were on cards in both our wallets, my hospital bag remained packed and easy to grab, my doctor's phone numbers were saved on both our devices, and every meal we ate was in the context of how my stomach was feeling at the time. We talked endlessly about having a family, and began trying to become parents. My Crohn's disease wasn't in remission, but it was better managed than it had previously been, and that gave us hope.

As chronic illness life often comes with curveballs, the fall of 2017 again changed my life as a patient and as a person. During a hospital admission, I wasn't taken seriously by staff, which almost led to fatal consequences. It became of paramount importance that both my husband and I became my best, fiercest, and loudest advocates. It also became an unfortunate necessity that I leave the doctor that I trusted most.

With new medical care came new options, and the challenge that almost took my life empowered me to find and do better. I began an infusion medication called Remicade, one that eventually gave me a sense of health again.

I found remission, and with it, a deep and profound sense of hope and determination. I began engaging with and then writing for some health-centered and IBD-focused patient communities, I started working in patient recruitment for clinical trials, and my husband and I began fertility treatments. Each month, I celebrated another milestone of not being admitted to the hospital or not presenting in the ER, and each month I reflected with gratitude on the routine that kept me feeling well.

Even on my best days, it's important to note that Crohn's disease is still on the top of my mind. The limitations of life with Crohn's disease in remission are two-fold. First - it's working around the underlying disease, and doing what you can to manage stress and diet is only a brief start. For me, it means taking my oral medication every day, twice a day, without fail. It means remembering to schedule routine blood draws, follow up doctor's appointments, and monthly infusions - and not missing a single one. The second part of the limitations I live with include the waiting - the knowing that at any moment, remission can be a memory and active disease (and symptoms) can again rule every moment of my life. It means being prepared, having as-needed medication available in case of emergency, backup plans in place, and expectations that reflect reality - that remission is a gift, on a timer, without a known expiration date.

Living with Crohn's disease means that symptoms can start at any moment, and they may pass quickly, or they may linger for an unknown amount of time. Trust me, they both cause worry, but that worry can increase symptoms in a flash - so I've learned to moderate my feelings, to take each day and each symptom in stride, and to look at the big picture as often as possible. Living with Crohn's disease also means that the way I think of my body, and my life, has changed and evolved several times over the last decade. I might be biased, but the most recent changes have been my favorite.

My body is one I resented for a very long time. It was broken and it was scarred and it was barely surviving. Even after I began to feel better, and have a better quality of life, I was unsure I could ever trust my body in the ways I'd always hoped to. 2019 was the year it proved me wrong. That May, I gave birth naturally to my daughter. My body carried and grew her for nine months, and her entrance to this world was everything I could've hoped for and more. This body also afforded me the opportunity to breastfeed, nourishing my daughter as she grew strong. I wasn't sure if I'd be able to do any of those things, and I've spent the last year since praising my body and speaking my gratitude out loud. Despite my illness, I love my body for allowing me to become a mother. I love my determination and intentionality, for believing even on the worst days that I could reach this milestone.

> **"If you're in a hard season, just know it will pass.."**

Through this journey, I've learned that my experiences are not unique, but the ways in which I've grown from them are. As a forever patient, I have become a fierce advocate in the healthcare space for both chronic illness patients and for mental healthcare as well. Combining these passions with my journey into parenthood, I've spent the last year building a business as a doula - providing guidance, support and advocacy for those walking through infertility, pregnancy and the postpartum period. This is everything I never knew I was meant to do with my life until each of my experiences converged and led me here. The way I'm working professionally and personally in this space is everything I could've dreamed of.

Another thing I have learned and relearned along the way is the need for me to ride the wave. Whether it is an emotional wave building inside me, a resentful wave of rage that momentarily crests when a provider is not listening to what I am saying and would prefer speaking at me than to me, or the physical wave when the medications you have on-hand are not enough for the next few hours of the night; to the other end of the experiences when things go right for a change and I notice the gratitude of a daily ritual, the wave of appreciation I feel for getting through an activity or a day without running to the bathroom, the wave of relief I feel when labs remain stable, or the wave of emotions I experience when I think about how far this journey has taken me - each wave rises and falls in time. That metaphor is also a very literal way that I think about my Crohn's disease - the challenges come and go. Finding my footing in the chaos, finding my way to swim through the waves - it's what's kept me grounded and allowed me to grow and change.

I want to add one last thing. If my story resonated with you - first off, I'm sorry. And second, I'm grateful. The life I'm living today, as someone who has Crohn's disease, is full and beautiful and I hope that means that yours is too. And to other patients fighting through undiagnosed symptoms or chronic illness diagnosis, I'd say this - every moment, even the worst ones, are part of your story. You will one day look back and thank yourself for your strength, your persistence, your determination, your grit and your grace. I promise. If you're in a hard season, just know it will pass.

# Wendy Meyeroff

Pikesville, MD, USA

**Ghostwriter & Marketing Consultant in Health & Tech Communications Worldwide**

*"Understand and encourage anyone you love with epilepsy."*

## About Wendy:

*Wendy Meyeroff says her husband figures she became a health reporter 'cause it was the only way she could force a doctor to answer her questions. That's what she's been doing since the early 90s for tons of print and online materials, including magazines, social media, even eBooks. Among collaborators you'll recognize: NIH, Sears, Merck, Johns Hopkins, and CBS.*

\* \* \*

*Facebook: @ghostwriterbizgrabber*

*Website: www.wmmedcomm.com*

*Linkedin: @wmeyeroff*

## Julius Seizure: King of Stigmas

First, let me give you a specific word's definition: "seize upon." And not just seize, but to do so through an oracle. That is, to choose one human body, take control and make that human an Oracle, so as to communicate the gods desires/warnings to fellow humans.

In some ways, it sounds as if a human's received a blessing, even an honor. I mean, think about--or look up--the Oracle of Delphi. Delphi's a location in Greece that reportedly had an oracle liaison connecting with the amazing god, Apollo.

You would think, then, that "seizure" would have at least some positive meaning.... but no. Fast forward a few centuries and you'll discover that during the Renaissance a seizure became an evil thing. It was Satan, not God, grabbing hold of you.

Ever since, the word has had a terrible stigma, so much so that not only in America, but worldwide, we cannot discuss seizures. That's 50 million people, "many of [whom] suffer silently...[and] alone." We especially can't chat specifically about one of the main medical conditions with which they are equated: epilepsy...which is the word that actually translates into "seize upon."

### Sounds of Silence

So you want to talk about mental health issues? How about growing up with a disorder that could not be discussed? One that meant--even in the middle of the 20th-century--being "cured" with lobotomies? (At least you were quiet and no longer a family embarrassment.) Or how 'bout being locked away in a mad-house before mental health was discussed more kindly...at least to some degree.

I partially missed both disastrous treatments of epilepsy...but not totally. When I was three years old, I ran a 106-degree fever and went into convulsions, the only word I would hear for almost 50 years.

### Early Suffering

For years I was put on medications and seemed stable. 'Course once I was old enough to tell the docs, "I still don't feel well. I'm getting nauseous. I'm getting dizzy" and similar statements (I mean, how accurate can you be at age six?) they didn't believe me. Even after getting older and more sophisticated linguistically I was still dismissed.

While outsiders didn't see seizures, I became an outcast for most of my early life. You know all those pants-wetting commercials you see now? Imagine doing it when you first get into school. I would sneeze, cough, laugh.... and wham! Clothes wet, school floor or chair damp. (Took a half-century before I heard epilepsy could cause a neuro-urology issue.)

And constant teasing! The cruelties lasted more than a decade, since the same class stayed together for years. They called me "Wettie pants" and then "Crybaby," since I wept as they verbally tortured me about it. (We didn't talk about bullying back in the day.)

I ended up living on one glass of water daily, so I wouldn't be wet. I stayed mostly solo, with my nose in a book. Thank God I got to sing in high school, and even performed a solo knockout edition of "Who Will Buy?" from the movie Oliver! But that waited 'til high school.

Meantime, I'd been a klutz (probably 'cause of the old meds' balance effects) from the beginning, but that was ignored. And I remember having visions. I swear to God (or whatever force you believe in) I'd have these moments (usually a few minutes, maybe just seconds) where I was in another time, another place. And gosh darn it, it was never someplace cheerful...like one with floral smells and rainbow colors.

> ## "When I was finally conscious, that was the first time that I actually heard a doctor say I had epilepsy. And I found out I nearly died from it."

Oh no. I was always on the battlefield. Seeing smoke, smelling terrible odors. And what the heck could I know about battles as a six-year-old, ten-year-old, and even 16?

### So Why Should You Be Scared?

But the docs didn't believe me. Nor did they tell me about small (petit mal) seizures. In fact, I remember the main reaction from all of them: "There, there, sweetheart. Don't worry. Just do what we tell you." (Very often with a pat on the head as accompaniment.)

After all, while on meds I didn't have any major seizures, like the kind you see on TV. You know, the falling to the floor, thrashing around kind. That's the kind that used to be called "grand mal" (great sickness). Now they have highly clinical, politically correct designations that I won't even get into.

So what if I'm lonely, sad...even afraid?

I mean, this is before the 'Net, folks. I had no real way to do medical research. I didn't hear the word "seizure," let alone epilepsy, 'till I was 21. And that's 'cause I almost died.

### The Death Factor

Nearly died, you say? Yep, I do. Anyway, fast forward to age 21. To further redeem myself, I had just knocked myself silly getting good grades in college. I had just graduated magna cum laude--and I'd just met a guy. We were scheduled for our third Saturday-night date...but I didn't make it.

I'm not clear why. Yes, I was nauseous all day, and it was the kind of nausea that scared me. But every time I told the doctors about it, they dismissed it. Anyway, I got home from school and since finals were over, I had fun. Put on the stereo (yes, I remember stereos) and started singing and dancing.

Next thing I knew, I was in a hospital. When I was finally conscious, that was the first time that I actually heard a doctor say I had epilepsy. And I found out I nearly died from it. If my younger sister hadn't found me not long after I went down, I might not have made it to the hospital quickly enough, where I had seizure after seizure after seizure for hours. I'd faced what's called SUDEP: Sudden Death from Epilepsy.

But somehow, I'd not only escaped it, I'd come back whole. My communications skills, consciousness, and other things are still in place.

Including the guy I'd just met. And there a problem arose.

## Talk About Embarrassment!

The Vietnam veteran (from a medical unit no less) was worried about me. Yes, Mom had called and told him I was ill and wouldn't make our date, but she tried not to elaborate.

He finally said, "Look, Mrs. Smith (I won't give you my maiden name, though you can probably find it somewhere), if you don't want to tell me anything, that's up to you. But I'd like to visit and cheer up Wendy." At that point she confessed I was in the hospital and where, but that's all she told him.

Well, next thing I know the guy comes to visit. No phone call saying he's coming, of course. And there I am, no makeup (though back in the day I had great skin!), hair a mess, red eyes from crying, in the glamorous hospital scrubs. The visit goes something like this:

Him: "Hi! You look good. How are you feeling?"
Me: "Fine."
Him: "Well, I'm glad to hear that. What happened?"
Me: "No big deal. Don't worry."

It sort of went like that for a few more Q's and A's and then he finally said something like:

"Look, Wendy, if you don't want to tell me anything, that's OK. But I've been in military medical units both here in the USA and then in 'Nam. I've seen things, stuff that even shows like M*A*S*H, barely whisper at replicating. I'm sure I can handle whatever you tell me."
So, I whispered: "I have epilepsy."
"What did you say?"
I whispered again, "I have epilepsy."
"Wendy, I can't hear you. If you don't want to

tell me...."
"I HAVE EPILEPSY!" fills the room. And I wait.
Him: "Oh. So...do you feel OK?"

And that was it. 'Course, it was the last time I told anyone (beyond family and doctors) that I had epilepsy for close to half a century.

## Where's the Media?

It's not like I didn't TRY to tell the rest of the U.S. (and later, through the 'Net, the world) about epilepsy. My husband joked early on that I must have become a health writer 'cause being a reporter meant I could finally force a doctor to answer my questions--at least in an interview.

First, I wrote on the clinical side, then healthcare business, and then in consumer magazines. (Trust me; not all clinical writers can write "consumer-speak.") If this is published, it'll be a miracle. That's because even though epilepsy was this country's major neurological disorder 'til Alzheimer's finally eclipsed it, I've never gotten a single well-known outlet to cover it. (A few articles in lesser known, but good, publications.) TV neither. Oh, that outlet started covering HIV/AIDs in the 80s. Oprah helped Michael J. Fox talk about Parkinson's disease (PD). Ellen was allowed to "confess" to being gay in the 90s. (Not a disease of course, but many still hide sexuality.) And, as our 21st-century war began and troops came home with very aggressive brain wounds, news folks started reporting on "Traumatic Brain Injury (TBI)."

Now, let's be clear. I'm not dismissing any of these issues. It's wonderful that I saw/heard all of them being finally talked about openly in my lifetime.

## America's Last Stigma

But not epilepsy. Did you know there are approximately twice the number of people with epilepsy in this country than with Parkinson's? Over 3.5 million (an "all-time high") vs. 1.5 million. Yet in that 3+ million can you think of any celeb that's admitted to my condition?

Did you know the Epilepsy Foundation is almost always lacking really good dollars, for research, for advertising? When was the last time you saw a local fundraiser that helped epilepsy the way folks help Alzheimer's, depression, and other issues in your neighborhood?

Oh, I wrote to Oprah, asking her to help this shame go the way of others. Later I wrote to Ellen. I even sent an email to a major news anchor pointing out a whole slew of ways epilepsy in adults could be news items.

How 'bout these:

• Getting a concussion--Remember all the football talk? Well, be it a kid or pro player, seizures can develop through this kind of brain injury...and a host of other falls and accidents.

• In our country's service--When have you heard of our military coming home with a permanent seizure disorder?

• Car and other motor accidents--I met a lady who'd been in a minor car accident who--for reasons never figured--developed major seizure issues every day.

And I told you about my fever-inspired event, known as "febrile" convulsions. We later found it had left a scar in the left front temporal lobe; that is, the front upper left side of my brain.

These are just a few of epilepsy's causes, BTW. Of course most can affect any of you-- or anyone you love--any minute.

## So Where's Our Help?

So why should this disorder be hidden? Why should we feel as if we're doing something shameful? Why can't we get media coverage?

Why can't we educate our doctors to look for all the clues? Do you know how often patients are patted on the head and told they're imagining issues? Even when they're believed, they're misdiagnosed! About 75 percent of folks in decent areas do not get the right treatment, let alone in poorer areas, or areas with few neurologists (let alone epileptologists).

## As for My Big Mouth....

So here I am, finally "cured." As my seizures escalated in 2010 (for a variety of reasons) I said, "The heck with this. It's time for surgery." I took my reporter's skills, did my research and was blessed to discover a clinical trial for a surgery related to exactly my type of epilepsy at the special neuro division of the National Institutes of Health (NIH).

You know the Institute, folks? The one that Congress is always figuring can be dismantled, underfunded or otherwise punished? Well, trust me. You'll never know when they might save you, someone you love, or even someone you sort of know. Look at how they've helped during the pandemic. Most Americans have no idea how much NIH's seven separate divisions (besides neuro, they include "homes" where diabetes, arthritis, and even aging issues are targeted) are fighting, including some truly scary issues.

Anyway, I had brain surgery in 2014. Now my MRI shows I have a totally white area on the left side of my brain! Yet here I am. Haven't had a seizure since, my medicines have been reduced, I can drive again, and yes, as you can tell, I can communicate. (I couldn't remember words like "dog" and "ketchup" for a while!)

And for the first time in my life, I finally admit to living with this disorder. Oh, my depression still sinks me many days (and with my meds I can't take anti-depressants). My hubby's been too old to hire for 10 years, even when he got his first degree—in cyber

> ## "Did you know if you're smart and not totally disabled and working, you can still be fired if the boss finds out you have epilepsy?"

networking!

Apparently now so am I. I figured what with yet another economic downturn, why not get a steady income (and health coverage, maybe even a pension) while I still had the chance.

But there was no chance for me either. Somehow I've been rebuilding my health and tech communications biz, which I had to give up during an extensive recovery, but it's been tough going. And maybe we're crazy but with rental fees escalating we decided—nearer the last quarter of our lives no less—to assume home ownership's responsibilities. Of course we fret constantly on how we'll maintain a mortgage plus condo fees, the car,

my healthcare...and then other expenses.

Which is why I'm telling anyone with epilepsy (or seizures, or strange visions: consider honesty!) Come on out. Even if it's not in public, come out at least with doctors. Bang down the doors, find ones that will listen and get help earlier, not later.

Yell at Congress and local lawmakers about how impossible it is to get disability support for epilepsy. The one lawyer I knew who helped folks with epilepsy get disability told many stories of battling for support for nine years, even for those who spent their days in endless seizures.

Did you know if you're smart and not totally disabled and working, you can still be fired if the boss finds out you have epilepsy? Did you know in some states technically you can't get married? Seizures start becoming common after age 60...and we've got an aging population. Think we're prepared, or will we just diagnose small seizures as Alzheimer's? (That does happen, BTW.)

Above all, understand and encourage anyone you love with epilepsy. Help them disintegrate the shame and stand tall.

After all, maybe the gods are seizing upon them. But it's to make them leaders, whether battling this disorder or other injustices.

Get moving folks!

# Ella Balasa

Richmond, VA, USA

## Patient Advocate & Health Consultant

*"Keep looking for ways to feel accomplished and motivated."*

## About Ella:

*Ella Balasa is a patient advocate and a person living with cystic fibrosis. Diagnosed at 18 months old, having countless hospitalizations since being a child, and despite having 28% lung function, she's never let it be her excuse. Having a biology background, she is an advocate for the development of novel therapies for the treatment of antibiotic-resistant infections including phage therapy, as well as speaking publicly about the value of patient voice in research. She serves as a member of research committees for the CF Foundation and is a director for the US Adult CF Association. She also has a passion for writing about her health experiences as well as introspectively about the hardships yet triumph that comes with living with a chronic illness. She has been published on MedPage Today, HuffPost, and Pulmonary Therapy Journal to name a few. Through these opportunities, she provides a scientific voice and hopes to encourage empowerment in patient communities. In her free time, Ella enjoys cooking, drawing, spending time with friends, and traveling when she can. More of her work and experiences can be found on her website.*

\* \* \*

*IG: @thisgirlella, @ellabalasaadvocacy*

*Website: www.ellabalasa.com*

Fulfillment to me means achieving a dream, pursuing a passion, striving to be happy every day, and finding joy in what I do. To say I did my best and made every moment count. I believe having those dreams and feelings of fulfillment comes from motivation. Motivation to do and be better in whatever parameters one sets for themselves. My motivation for life comes in the most innate form — the will to live. To live the fullest life I can, in the time I am given to live it.

My name is Ella Balasa and I was born with a genetic, chronic, progressive, and rare lung disease called cystic fibrosis. It causes the buildup of thick sticky mucus primarily in the lungs, and overtime the cycle of bacterial infections that grow in the lungs causing inflammation leads to scarring and lung function decline and eventually respiratory failure. Having cystic fibrosis has shaped me to want to live each day to its fullest. My motivation to have this attitude has grown with each passing year, though it's taken time to gain the maturity, experiences, and confidence to find my identity and purpose.

## "I started accepting who I am, and I wanted to share it with others."

Growing up, I was always a quiet child, especially around strangers. It terrified me to even think about having to talk to somebody I didn't know. I stayed this way through high school, a time that I was more insecure with myself than at any other point in my life. Having CF, the insecurities that come along with being a teenager, and being somewhat introverted by nature I call it a "situation" because it was always something I wanted to leave behind. I wanted to be social and make friends easily, but it never was easy. Having CF was a huge obstacle. I was always thinking about what others were going to think when they knew I was different.

After my first year of college, during a pulmonary exacerbation of infections my doctor stated "It's time to consider a lung transplant." Those words, uttered from my pediatric CF doctor eight years ago, made me, in an instant, think about all the joys of life I hadn't gotten to experience yet. Not only was I terrified of dying, but I was also afraid of dying before I had started living. I was scared of departing, not having lived the life I wanted. This was the lowest point in my life thus far from an emotional aspect.

I've seen articles and videos where they interview elderly people on their deathbeds who are asked what they regret in life. Most people regret not having lived passionately, fulfilled, and happy. I believed I would be one of them if I didn't make a change.

It was a slow transformation, but I began to tire of the feeling that life was passing me by, and I wasn't living it the way I wanted to. I began being more open about CF with peers and finding others dealing with similar challenges within the CF community. I also advocated for myself with my doctors and educated both those in the medical field and strangers about this disease. I began to be more comfortable in my own skin. I started accepting who I am, and I wanted to share it with others.

Fortunately, the lung transplant program doctors at the time still thought I had some life left in my lungs. It's been 8 years since that first transplant referral and I am still hanging on with my native lungs.

I began writing to inspire and motivate others, and feel satisfied. I'm able to express the words that I can't exactly think of when I speak. It brings me a sense of accomplishment and satisfaction.

But my writing stemmed from the experience of another one of the most difficult times in my life. My first piece was a pained and confused reflection of being stuck in a position where my body was starting to fail me but ambition kept me reaching for the next rung to climb the corporate ladder. I had decided to turn down my first big girl job a year after college. Having cystic fibrosis, my life had other plans in store, and keeping up, in that sense, wasn't in the plan. At the time, already only having 30% lung function, realistically, I wouldn't be able to maintain 8+ hour work days and take care of my health to keep infections away and stay out of the hospital.

In our society, so much emphasis is placed on the origin of our success through our careers, and I felt this pressure too, despite being aware that I was someone with a chronic illness who didn't know what even a few months might bring. Whenever we meet a stranger, one of the first questions we ask is "What do you do?" It was one of the hardest decisions in my life – feeling like I was giving up a part of my identity.

I vowed to find my success in other ways, but I didn't know what that would look like, or whether I really would find it or just feel like I was floating through life. Little did I know, that first article I ever wrote, when all I wanted to do was vent frustrations and reach others that may have been going through the same things, ended up igniting a passion for writing that has provided me fulfillment and other opportunities to use my skills and biology degree simultaneously.

As time has passed, some of the microbiology work that I have done has had an intersection with CF, as common infections in CF lungs and antibiotic resistances they acquire are also commonly found in the environment. Having this background knowledge has allowed me to explore and understand CF research and be involved in various research related advisory committees tasked in providing patient perspectives on research questions as well as working with researchers and professionals and helping them and the general public communicate and relate to each other.

## "Don't be fearful to love to the fullest."

My background in science and my self-advocacy efforts paid off about a year ago when I became very ill with the worst lung infection I had ever had. I was using supplemental oxygen constantly; my lung function was 18% and it was even difficult for me to take a shower because of how short of breath it made me. I was coughing constantly and producing thick green mucus for weeks, despite being on intravenous antibiotics. The antibiotics had stopped working and my infection had become completely antibiotic resistant. That's when I knew I had to try something else. I had heard about an experimental treatment called phage therapy. In early January of 2019, I traveled from my home in Richmond, Virginia to receive this treatment at Yale University. The treatment worked, and looking back, I don't think I would have been able to clear that terrible infection without this intervention. Soon after, I decided to share my experience publicly to raise awareness about the dire need for novel therapies to treat devastating antibiotic resistant infections and since then I have spoken at the FDA, the Milken Institute, and other conferences and congressional meetings to bring about changes to policies and inspire researchers to pursue this research.

Despite my relief in symptoms from that infection, my lungs remained very weak and I was referred for transplant once more. This time, I relocated to Durham, North Carolina to begin the transplant process at Duke University in the summer of 2019. For a few months every weekday, I exercised for pulmonary rehabilitation for 3 hours a day and attended transplant classes to learn about what my life would be like after undergoing a lung transplant. But, after a few months in the program, I was granted compassionate use access to a new drug called Trikafta that treats the underlying cause of the disease, relieving me of the burdensome symptoms of constant thick green mucus, and gives me the ability to breathe just a bit deeper. In a short period of time, it changed the trajectory of my transplant journey and once again the doctors and I decided I had recovered enough to put the transplant on hold for a while longer. I was able to move back home to Richmond.

These days, I still feel the effects of my disease more than even two years ago, but with Trikafta, and my will power to focus my daily efforts on treatments, exercising, and nutrition, I hope to push through more years without needing a transplant. I've grown to have an even greater will to go on and to have an appreciation for the life I have, for however long I have it. I've become an advocate for phage therapy and have been able to share my story about my treatment as well as push for development of novel therapies for treating the relentless bacteria that plague CF lungs. My lung function still stays at 30% but I hope to again travel as much as I can. My next big adventure will hopefully be visiting my family in Hungary and attending my cousin's wedding.

I want to reassure those dealing with difficult circumstances and complex obstacles outside of their control, to keep looking for ways to feel accomplished and motivated. For some of us the inability to plan for our careers or our futures in general can be viewed as a negative thing, but it can allow us to pursue avenues we never thought possible.

Things in life work out. As long as we have the drive, determination and ambition to put our best into whatever we do, and to gain fulfillment from that task or accomplishment, we are successful, each in our own way.

Don't be fearful to love to the fullest, to be bold, speak your mind, and let others experience who you are. I fight every day, for one more breath, to accomplish one more thing. Living, that's my motivation.

# Kay Mimms

Matteson, IL, USA

### Educator, Author & Lupus Warrior

### "Do not merely survive. Thrive."

## About Kay:

*In 2004, Kayrene Mimms, retired after working in education for thirty-plus years: four months of teaching home economics to physically handicapped teens at Spaulding High School in Chicago, Illinois; twenty years of teaching home economics, Home Economics Related Occupations (HERO), and psychology at Bloom High School in Chicago Heights, Illinois; and twelve years serving as a counselor at Rich South High School in Richton Park, Illinois. About one year after retirement and after years of suffering various symptoms— for which no definite diagnosis was given—Kay almost died from a serious lupus flare. After months of rehabilitation and years of volunteer work to increase lupus awareness, she developed a strong desire to share her story and the stories of others who suffer the chronic and potentially devastating effects of the cruel, mysterious, and unpredictable disease called lupus. Because of her strength, resilience, and determination, FIGHTING LUPUS BATTLES – Hope for a Cure was born. Later Kay wrote a sequel, FIGHTING LUPUS BATTLES – Living, Hoping, Searching, Climbing, Researching for the Cure. Kay is excited about participating in the Chronically Empowered Project and having this exceptional opportunity to promote awareness and support for the lupus community...*

Sometimes, I am still jolted awake by dreams of the weeks I spent in the Rehabilitation Institute of Chicago after a near death lupus flare. I would wake up around the same time each morning and wait to hear the sound of the blood pressure cart being pushed down the hall. As the sound got closer and closer, I would try to judge how long it would be before the aide reached my room. I knew that even if I tried to call before she reached me, I probably would not get a response. (You see I could only whisper, and most times people at the nurses' station would forget that fact and, I guess, think that someone was just playing with the call button). I knew the aide would have to take my blood pressure and administer my Synthroid (thyroid medicine) by 6:30 a.m. I would just lie there and hope that I could hold out until she arrived. I had a catheter, but I did not want to take a chance on dirtying my diaper.

I see myself as a walking miracle, a living testimony of God's amazing grace, love, and care. My name is Kay Mimms, and I am a lupus warrior. Coming back from a near-death flare helped me to become stronger and more determined to fight and win lupus battles.

Systemic lupus erythematosus (SLE), or lupus, is commonly described as a complex, chronic, incurable, mysterious, unpredictable, and potentially life-threatening autoimmune disease. It can affect any part of the body, including your blood and blood vessels, brain, heart, joints, kidneys, lungs, muscles, or skin."Lupus happens when the immune system, which normally helps protect the body from infection and disease, attacks its own tissues. This attack causes inflammation and, in some cases, permanent tissue damage." (https://www.niams.nih.gov/health-topics/lupus - 2021).

According to MedlinePlus, lupus can have many symptoms, and they differ from person to person. Scientists agree that some of the more common ones are: pain or swelling in joints; muscle pain, unexplained fever; butterfly-shaped rash, most often on the face; chest pain when taking a deep breath; hair loss; pale or purple-colored fingers or toes; sensitivity to the sun; swelling in legs or around eyes; mouth ulcers; swollen glands; and feeling very tired. Diagnosing lupus can be difficult and may take months or even years. Symptoms may come (flare) and go (remission), and they can change over time (LFA). Some symptoms mimic other diseases. There is no single test for lupus; doctors may use medical history, physical examinations, and laboratory tests to make a lupus diagnosis (LSI).

## "I discovered later that I didn't have enough markers (symptoms) to determine a definite lupus diagnosis."

It's reported that the exact cause of lupus is still unknown. Some studies suggest that a number of different genes may determine one's risk for developing the disease. However, having certain genes is not the whole story because other people who have similar genetic backgrounds may not develop signs or symptoms. It is apparent that some environmental factors, like sunlight, stress, and medications, also appear to play a role in lupus (NIH and LSI). There is no cure for lupus yet. Many scientists are involved in research aimed at finding more efficient diagnostic procedures, more effective treatment plans, and eventually a cure.

For years, probably my whole life, I suffered with various symptoms that could have been related to lupus. I remember having sore spots in my mouth at age four. I've had cold hands and feet and sensitivity to cold since I can remember. During my teen years, I experienced painful, sore, and swollen joints and muscles and low blood counts. Extreme redness of eyes started when I was in my twenties. Later in life, other lupus-like symptoms included itchy and discolored blotches on my skin, blistering after short exposure to the sun, and chest pain with each deep breath.

Doctors suspected that I had lupus. My dermatologists and ophthalmologist even recommended evaluations for lupus twice. I followed their recommendations, but the results were negative. I discovered later that I didn't have enough markers (symptoms) to determine a definite lupus diagnosis. All those years, doctors did an excellent job of treating my symptoms; however, many times the old symptoms reappeared, or I'd get new ones. Since I had excellent and caring doctors, along with good insurance plans, I was able to successfully complete a 33-year career in education as the doctors tried to keep my symptoms under control.

When I first retired in 2004, life was beautiful. Though I suffered with mild flares at times, I was still able to spend my days being involved in many activities. I exercised four days a week, had breakfasts and lunches with my retired buddies, took advantage of free seminars and workshops, participated in two book clubs, started singing in a community gospel choir, and began traveling more.

## "I was admitted to the hospital where I almost "bled out" the same night.."

In 2005, my symptoms became more pronounced: extreme cold, throbbing pain, itchy and flaky scalp, hair loss, no appetite, and extreme fatigue. My primary care physician was able to narrow possible diagnosis to sarcoidosis or lupus. He researched both diseases and thoroughly reviewed my medical history, my symptoms, and my laboratory results. At age 59 and after 55 years of suffering, I finally received a definite diagnosis - systemic lupus erythematosus (SLE), or lupus.

I didn't like the lupus diagnosis, but I was relieved and hopeful that I would get the help I needed. I arranged an appointment with the rheumatologist, but before I saw her, things got even worse. I experienced nausea, more pain and swelling, difficulty in mobility, and deep coughing that produced pinkish mucus. Those additional symptoms led me to the hospital emergency room where attendants discovered problems with my lungs and heart. This made them suspect pericardial and pleural effusion (fluid around heart and lungs). I was admitted to the hospital where I almost "bled out" the same night. I ended up in ICU, intubated and sedated off and on for 65 days. That means that I was hooked up to various machines and tubes including a breathing machine, a trach in my windpipe, a feeding tube in my abdomen, a catheter in my urinary tract, and a PICC line -a thin, flexible tube inserted into a vein and was guided into a large vein above my heart and used to give intravenous fluids and to take blood samples (https://pubmed.ncbi.nlm.nih.gov). My treatment plan included high doses of prednisone and Cytoxan (chemotherapy). Doctors presented a very grim picture; they didn't think I was going to make it. I almost died, but I think God had a different plan for me.

When I was finally weaned from the ventilator and feeding tube, I was moved from ICU to a regular hospital room. The unusual length of my stay in ICU resulted in extreme losses. I was unable to walk or talk and had to complete three weeks of intensive in-patient therapy (occupational, physical, respiratory, and speech). There were also months of in-home and outpatient physical and speech therapy.

During my rehab stay, I learned to walk with a walker, to use techniques that helped my speech, to go up and down two steps (steps, not stairs), to cook from a wheelchair, to walk on carpeting, to transfer from the bed to the wheelchair and from the wheelchair to

the car. Basically, I had to relearn many things that we take for granted. After less than a month in rehab, I could walk with a walker, but still had to use a wheelchair most of the time. Then I moved to using only a walker and cane. For several months, I did more therapy at home and then at an outpatient clinic. So, on February 13, 2006, I walked into the hospital emergency room. In April 2006, I was rolled to the rehabilitation center on a hospital bed. Then on May 17, 2006, I left the rehab in a wheelchair, being able to use a walker for short periods of time. Finally, in October 2006, I was free of the wheelchair and walker; I only needed a cane. I still have the cane, but I haven't had to use it in years. Thanks to God, my husband, daughters, family, friends, primary care physician, and hospital and rehabilitation staff, I survived a near death situation.

In the process of learning to deal with lupus, I discovered a new "calling:" to work toward increasing lupus awareness. My experiences have inspired me and my husband, Cecil, to do volunteer work with lupus organizations, participate in area lupus support groups, distribute lupus materials at health fairs, and speak at meetings of local organizations and churches. We also help to host the Southern Suburbs Illinois Lupus Walk during Lupus Awareness Month in May. I am the Captain of team K's Hope for a Cure. Some of my volunteer work involves serving as a participant in several lupus research projects and raising funds for research that we hope will lead to more efficient diagnostic procedures, better treatment plans, and eventually a cure. We are very committed to supporting the lupus community.

I've been blessed to share my story on three talk shows: Christian Coaches Huddle - Blog Talk Radio with Donna Brumfield, Senior Talk with Clara Hubbard, and WVON's Community Health Focus Hour with Susan Peters. Parts of my journey were included in newspapers - Southtown Star, Chicago Defender, and the Chicago Tribune. The Community Team of PatientsLikeMe spotlighted my story for their members. I participated in a television news segment about the possible shortage of Plaquenil for lupus patients if it gained approval for the treatment of COVID - 19. Justin Parks developed a lupus video where we share our stories on YouTube. Recently, I participated in a discussion of my first book, FIGHTING LUPUS BATTLES - Hope for a Cure with the Lupus Spoons Support Group and another one with Gamma Pi Rho Lupus Sorority. Cecil and I have been invited to participate in Gamma Pi Rho's discussion of dating and marriage relationships for lupus patients. In March, I will attend LFA's 2021 digital Lupus Advocacy Summit.

Articles that I have written include: Fighting Lupus Battles for iPain Magazine (International Pain Foundation), I Am Still Alive for Lupus Society of Illinois, Living Well with Lupus for Story Sharing Project, Living In Spite Of Lupus for Dynamic Healthcare Newsletter, Living With Lupus for the Illinois African-American Family Commission, Living With Lupus for WEGO Health, Rare Disease Survey also for WEGO Health, Shadows Of Death for The Well Magazine, Still Alive - National Education Association for Today for Retired Members, and also Treasured Relationships for the Coleman Family Reunion Newsletter.

I tell about my struggles, fears, losses, and victories in my first book - FIGHTING LUPUS BATTLES - Hope for a Cure, published in 2015. It includes more than twenty true stories about real people who are living with the effects of this mysterious and unpredictable disease called lupus. With medical commentary from two of my doctors, as well as general educational information about lupus disease, the book was written to help raise awareness, broaden knowledge, encourage understanding and compassion, improve provider/patient communication and relationships, and promote research. In 2019, I published my second book - FIGHTING LUPUS BATTLES - Living, Hoping, Searching, Climbing, Researching for the Cure. It includes updates from the first book, stories from more lupus patients, and information about lupus research. Both books are available at hiltonpub.com and amazon.com.

"If you have lupus, you may have times of illness (flares) and times of wellness (remission). Lupus flares can be mild to serious, and they do not follow a pattern. However, with treatment, many people with lupus can manage the disease" https://www.niams.nih.gov/health-topics/lupus (2021).

**I use the following strategies to help manage my condition.**

1. I won't give up. I try to learn as much as I can about lupus.
2. Search for health care providers who will listen to me and address my concerns.
3. Actively participate in my care. Pay close attention to my body, mind, and spirit, and keep a list of concerns and questions that Cecil and I present to the healthcare providers at each visit. Taking these actions makes it easier for providers to see the whole picture, and it helps me remember what I want to discuss.
4. Maintain a good support system of family, friends, medical professionals, community organizations, faith-based groups, and support groups.
5. After discussions with my health care team, I use appropriate stress management techniques such as exercise, relaxation, and meditation. Plan for adequate rest and quiet.
6. Try to follow guidelines for a healthy diet.

What I would like people to remember after reading my story:

Today, my condition is fairly stable. I awake each day being thankful to God for three main reasons: I am still alive; I can usually function independently; and I have loving, caring family members and friends who support me. Even though I have painful and sore joints and find it difficult to walk sometimes; even though my voice is raspy and I am not able to sing like I used to; even though I still have a mild productive cough; even though I fatigue easily; even though I forget or may not fully understand things at times; even though I second-guess most things I do; even though I have to take lots of medications, I am still alive and learning to live with lupus in a positive and productive way. As a lupus warrior, "My mission in life is not merely to survive, but to thrive; and to do so with some passion, some compassion, some humor, and some style." (Maya Angelou) I try to do what I can to stay as healthy as possible, and I leave the rest to God.

You may find more information about lupus by searching online at:

**Lupus Foundation of America (LFA)**
**www.lupus.org**

**Lupus Society of Illinois (LSI)**
**www.lupusil.org**

# Madelyn Saner

Rochester, MN, USA

*Advocate and Artist.*

## About Madelyn:

*Madelyn is a chronic illness and disability advocate from Minnesota. She has been sharing her story online in hopes of bringing light to the experiences of young, chronically ill, and disabled people. In her free time, she enjoys art and music, from painting and digital art to playing ukulele and guitar. She's only been an advocate for a few years, but she wants to continue her advocacy to make the world a more accessible and accepting place.*

\* \* \*

*IG & FB: @chronicallymadelyn*

*"You are worthy. No matter what illnesses, disabilities, or struggles that you have."*

My name is Madelyn, and I'm chronically ill.

I was diagnosed with postural orthostatic tachycardia syndrome (POTS) with orthostatic hypotension when I was 12 years old, after being misdiagnosed with anxiety for a year. At age 17, I was diagnosed with hypermobile Ehlers-Danlos syndrome (hEDS), a diagnosis I spent a year searching for.

Both POTS and orthostatic hypotension are forms of autonomic dysfunction, also called dysautonomia, which is when dysfunction occurs in the autonomic nervous system (ANS). hEDS is one of 13 different types of Ehlers-Danlos syndrome, a group of syndromes that affect the connective tissues.

## "Taking control of my own health wasn't easy."

My life since my POTS started at age 11 has been very, very different from the "normal" and expected path of a teenager. The path that I took was, for a while, defined by some things that certain doctors of mine told me that ended up being untrue. Doctors told me that, since I got POTS so young, I would grow out of it by my early twenties. This lie became so ingrained into my preteen mind that I lived my life by the standard that I just had to ride this out until I was twenty and then I would be okay again.

That was my mindset for over three years. During those three years, I ended up having to cut down to half days at school when I attempted a pain program that caused me and my family trauma - a pain program that continues to be recommended to me to this day, no matter how many times I explain how deeply it traumatized me. After seventh grade, my body could no longer handle being in school, so I had to leave. And when this happened, I ended up losing all of my friends.

It wasn't until after eighth grade that I started doubting what those doctors had told me. I continued to get worse even though I was doing everything they told me to do. My stomach started getting really bad, to the point where some days I couldn't eat. While I didn't know it at the time, I started advocating for myself when I was 15. I have always been a shy person, especially around doctors, but I started getting tired of the life I was living. I was falling behind in school, was constantly nauseated and in pain, and I was over it.

Taking control of my own health wasn't easy. The first appointment I wanted was a gastroenterology consult, which I ended up missing because I had a panic attack in the car. My appointment was rescheduled and I forced myself to go. But the tests that were scheduled following that appointment I ended up canceling. I was scared.

There was one appointment that was a result of that appointment that I went to. It was with a pain doctor who thought he could help my stomach pain. So every few months for the next year, I got steroid injections into my abdominal wall. Their point was to numb my abdomen so it didn't cause pain when touched. Whether they helped, I don't know. If they did, it wasn't enough to make a big enough difference in my life, so I stopped getting them.

Throughout my five years (at the time) of living with chronic illness, I had never felt so sad and angry at all of the struggle and pain that my body had put me through. And the reason that I had never reached that point before is because I had never had so much hope either. I had finally realized that I am worth more than the life that I was living, that I deserved better.

This was when my depression started. Even so, I had never yet been more empowered. My life and the quality of it had never meant so much to me. I was having panic attacks and episodes of derealization every day, but when I felt okay enough, I started researching.

I first started watching videos about POTS and people with POTS. For the first time since being diagnosed, I heard other people's stories. I was finally able to feel like there were people out there that understood what I was going through, and it was almost soothing. I wasn't alone anymore. My world had been opened up to people like me, a feeling I hadn't experienced since I was a little kid.

As I kept watching more and more videos of people with POTS, I noticed that many of them also had something called Ehlers-Danlos syndrome. I had never heard of it before, but, being the curious person that I am, I started looking into it. I realized I had some of the symptoms, like hypermobility and unstable joints, but I just thought it was a coincidence. Doctors had told me that POTS is more common in people with hypermobility and that my instability was due to deconditioning, so I believed them.

For weeks I watched as many videos as I could find. As the days passed, I slowly became more and more comfortable in my body, finally identifying myself as a chronically ill person. I became more confident, so much

so that I decided to start using a wheelchair anytime I left the house.

My relationship with needing a mobility aid didn't start out well. The first time I used a wheelchair was on a trip to Walt Disney World, but at the time I thought it would be a thing that I would only use on trips. The next time I used a wheelchair was for a doctor's appointment. I was feeling very sick that day, but when the doctor saw my wheelchair, he told me that I wasn't doing what he told me to do. That I wouldn't need a wheelchair if I was doing my POTS treatment program correctly. He was blaming me, a 14-year-old at the time, for not doing good enough. He then forced my parents to not let me use the wheelchair to walk back to the car. I ended up crying the entire way back, embarrassed and ashamed, blaming myself for being sick.

"Sharing my vulnerabilities with the world was terrifying. But I knew that if my story could help anyone, even just one person, it would all be worth it."

That experience scared me out of using a wheelchair for years. I stopped leaving the house because I physically couldn't handle walking around a store or eating at a restaurant. And times when I tried to go out without a wheelchair would end in me being the person needing to end outings early. The scenario that sticks out the most to me is when I made my sister leave the line to meet Miranda Sings early, because I was feeling so sick. She's never complained, but I've always felt bad.

For nearly three years, I rarely left the house for something that wasn't a doctor's appointment. I was scared out of using a wheelchair for some idea that if I used one, I was a failure. That I didn't try hard enough. But no doctor would help me get better. Most would blame me. Some didn't believe me. One doctor misdiagnosed me with something I don't have, but did it without telling me or my parents.

So, when I decided to regularly use a wheelchair, it was a big change for me. My first outing after making this decision was to my cousin's graduation party. As someone who hates drawing attention to myself, it took a lot of strength for me to get over it and use my wheelchair in public. Since it was a graduation party, not only was all of my family seeing me in a wheelchair - most for the first time - but a bunch of people my age that I didn't know would also be seeing me as well. I was scared that I would be judged, pitied, or looked down upon. Some people asked questions, and I got some weird looks, but I made it through, and I was proud of myself. For the first time, I was no longer held back by the barriers that my illness had created around my life. I had finally broken free.

I would have never gotten to that point if there weren't people who posted videos and wrote on social media about their chronic illness experience. I was inspired by them, so I decided to create my own Instagram to document my chronic illness under the moniker chronicallymadelyn.

My hands were shaking with the first post I made. I had never shared any part of my story with anyone besides my family. Sharing my vulnerabilities with the world was terrifying. But I knew that if my story could help anyone, even just one person, it would all be worth it.

From there, I started sharing my life online. After a few weeks went by, I finally gained the courage to write to someone who shared the same diagnosis as me. And for the first time, I finally spoke to someone else who was chronically ill.

There's a feeling of understanding among people with chronic illnesses that you will never find anywhere else. You'll never find other people who joke about their symptoms or bemoan terrible doctor's appointments. But you'll also never find any other stronger people.

I began learning more about patient advocacy and disability advocacy. Even though I had been for years, I finally realized my disabilities and the extent of them. It had been put into my mind that disabilities are a bad thing, a thing to pity; but I became proud of mine. Societal standards were no longer controlling me. I had grown into who I am today: a proud, disabled woman.

The more and more I followed and spoke to people with POTS, the more I realized that many of them also had this thing called Ehlers-Danlos syndrome, specifically the hypermobile type. And as they talked about their EDS symptoms, I realized that I also had many of them. Joint pain, joint instability, hypermobility, easy and unexplained bruising, along with digestive problems and dysautonomia, possible comorbidities of EDS. I'm not one to self-diagnose, but the number of symptoms that lined up seemed like too much of a coincidence to me.

That summer I saw doctors of gastroenterology, allergies, rheumatology, had an endoscopy, and had a seemingly endless amount of blood drawn. In the end, they all decided I had a pain disorder.

I ended up seeing a pain doctor in October of that year. He called me "loosey-goosey" and was so shocked at how much my kneecap could move, that he told the resident in the room that she had to feel it, and was amazed by the hypermobility in my elbows and hips. But in the end, he gave a full lecture, including a slideshow, about the pain disorder he believed I had.

The only good thing about that appointment was he gave me a prescription for physical therapy. After a few weeks of feeling lost, I picked up that prescription and found a physical therapist.

I had had bad physical therapy experiences in the past, but this was nothing like them. With all of the physical therapy patients, they teach them the science behind chronic pain. They have a set of flashcards and everything. Not only did my physical therapist give me a better explanation than any previous doctor for my pain, but she also created a plan on how to lessen my pain, something no doctor had done before.

The thing that made me feel the most comfortable though, is that she worked with people with POTS. She understood how my body works and how to avoid overdoing it, one thing that I struggled with.

Even though my physical therapy was going great, I still felt like I had to try one final time to see about an EDS diagnosis. I decided my last attempt was going to be with the people who should know about EDS the best: genetics. I wrote to my primary doctor - who is amazing, asked her to send a referral to genetics, and she did.

When I got my appointment booked, I told my physical therapist. Since she isn't a medical doctor, she can't give medical advice, but when she said "I think that's a good idea," I knew I was on the right path.

My appointment was the first week of February. I was terrified since all of my previous appointments had been awful. A woman came in and collected my family medical history and then told me that the doctor I was supposed to see had a change in appointments, so I would be seeing someone else. This only did more to raise my nerves. The doctor walked in, shook my hand, sat down, and asked, "Why're you here?" My heart sank.

## "You have... Ehlers-Danlos syndrome. I knew from the second I shook your hand."

After going through my medical history, checking my hypermobility, checking for skin hyperextensibility, he was done. He turned to me and said, "You have Ehlers-Danlos syndrome. I knew from the second I shook your hand."

A weight lifted off my shoulders. I finally had the validation that I had spent years looking for, and it was almost surreal.

Of course, I wasn't cured. I have a genetic disorder. But I take pride in my diagnosis. I will have hEDS for the rest of my life, so I'm going to be proud of the life that I live as a disabled person. No one is going to take that away from me. A few years ago I never would have thought that I could feel so empowered while being chronically ill and disabled, but I am. And I'm proud of myself for that.

I do have some personal hopes for myself. Because I was so sick, I wasn't able to graduate from high school. As of writing this, I'm working towards getting a certification that is a high school diploma equivalent so I can go to college - or university, something I've wanted to do since I was a kid.

*Lastly, I want to give some advice if you're in a similar situation as me. First and foremost, you know your body the best. Don't let anyone - especially doctors - tell you differently. I have spent way too much time doubting if my pain is real or if I'm creating it in my mind, just because I have had doctors that made me believe that. Second, you are your own best advocate. Don't be afraid to speak up. I'd rather have a doctor who thinks I'm annoying than a doctor who gives me medications or tests that I don't need. And finally, you are worthy. No matter what illnesses, disabilities, or struggles that you have, you are worthy of happiness, help, and love. Society is inherently ableist, so people might tell you differently, but they are wrong. My story is nowhere near finished, but thank you for reading up until now.*

# Amy Courtney

Las Vegas, NV, USA

## About Amy:

*Amy Courtney has struggled with endometriosis for over 20 years. She started advocating for herself when she realized no one else was going to. After years of incorrect information from physicians, failed surgeries, and countless hours doing her own research on the disease, she knew she needed to help others. She started a support group helping other women and families who struggle with endometriosis and adenomyosis. She has an amazing support group which includes her husband and two daughters. They are always helping her promote and spread awareness as well as giving menstrual hygiene products to those in need.*

\* \* \*

*IG: @lasvegasendosupport*

*"Doctors don't know what they don't know."*

My name is Amy Courtney and I have endometriosis, adenomyosis, pelvic floor dysfunction and pelvic organ prolapse.

Endometriosis is tissue that is similar to, but not identical to, the lining of the uterus, that is found elsewhere inside the body. This rogue tissue creates lesions that become irritated, bleed, and breakdown resulting in pain, scar tissue and inflammation.

Adenomyosis is a condition of the uterus that occurs when the tissue that normally lines the uterus (endometrial tissue) grows into the muscular wall of the uterus.

Pelvic floor dysfunction is the inability to control the muscles of your pelvic floor.

Pelvic organ prolapse refers to the prolapse or drooping of any of the pelvic floor organs, including, bladder, uterus, vagina, small bowel, and rectum.

My story began when I was only 13 years old. As long as I could remember, I had bad cramps and intense pain that I was always told was normal. My mother did not think anything was wrong or out of the ordinary because I was always the "different" one in the family. This pain was normal right? Well, that is what I was told. I am odd, full of anxiety and neurotic.

In 2000, when I was a sophomore in high school, my pain got intensely worse and one day while watching a school play, I collapsed to the ground and I could not move nor get up.

My sister and mother managed to get me to the emergency room where the hospital staff thought my appendix burst. The hospital was preparing me for surgery.

After some time, the physician decided that it couldn't be my appendix and I just waited and waited. That is all I could do was wait. A few hours had passed, I had random testing and I still had no answers. I ended up with no definitive diagnosis. We were upset and scratching our heads. My mother and I were about to leave when another emergency room physician mentioned the word that would change my life forever, "Endometriosis." She mentioned that she was unsure if this was what I had, but all my symptoms pointed to this diagnosis. She recommended a referral to a local gynecologist. We now had hope to get answers as to why a young girl was in severe pain.

Within the week, I was able to see the gynecologist that she recommended. It was very awkward for me, a young girl, who was also a virgin, to see a male doctor. No one at the point in my life had seen anything I had to offer. If I even had anything to offer at that age.

This gynecologist agreed with the emergency room physician that it could be endometriosis. Within the week, I was scheduled for my first diagnostic laparoscopy, or what my doctor called surgery- a surgery to see what he would be able to diagnose me with.

My operative report stated the uterus and ovaries appeared normal, however in the Pouch of Douglas along the uterosacral ligament were gooey endometrial implants that were biopsied. It was confirmed, and I was diagnosed with endometriosis. Shortly after, I started six months of Lupron, as a junior in high school.

Soon, my health started to deteriorate

294 • CHRONICALLY EMPOWERED: A CHRONIC ILLNESS WARRIOR COLLABORATION

and life started to fall apart. Despite multiple visits to the emergency room, inpatient stays, and waiting weeks at a time to get first, second, and third opinions from physicians, I still had no answers as to why I was experiencing pain. I knew my body, and deep down I knew there was no relief. I was worried that this was how my life would be every day for the rest of my life.

## "My hysterectomy was 100% the best decision that I could have ever done for not just me but for my family."

I didn't have any answers. I was told by multiple physicians that I would not be able to have children, let alone carry them. On so many levels, I honestly lost hope and did not know what to do.

I decided to take matters into my own hands. I started researching and reading everything that I could find about endometriosis. I even started a support group both online and in person. After all my research, I finally found a true endo specialist that accepted my insurance out of state. I finally found the hope that I was looking for. By this time, I was a 32 year old woman who had experienced pain for almost 20 of those years.

After reviewing my lengthy medical records, the endo specialist knew my case was complicated and agreed to see me. I was ecstatic. No words were able to describe how I felt. This physician finally acknowledged all the pain that I'd been

experiencing and that it was not in my head.

The specialist informed me that along with endometriosis, I also had a rectocele, cystocele, descending uterus and adenomyosis. On January 25, 2017, I had excision surgery, a sacrocolpopexy and a hysterectomy.

My hysterectomy was 100% the best decision that I could have ever done for not just me but for my family. After a year of my hormones feeling like a human teeter totter, I finally had my life back. I felt amazing. For the first time in my life, I did not have to take pain pills. I actually recovered from my hysterectomy pain pill free. I finally had what I was searching for the past 20 years. Relief.

It baffles me that from my first surgery in 2000 to 2016, I had exactly 15 surgeries for endometriosis as well as numerous biopsies, gallbladder and appendix removal, and a hysterectomy.

I say I am not fully 100% pain free. I feel relief from my adenomyosis but not from my endometriosis. Due to the fact that I kept my ovaries, I still have cyclic pain that I struggle with, but luckily, I am able to time my ovulation and plan around the pain which I have never been able to before. Some days are worse than others, but I manage to get by.

Despite everything that I've been through and my struggles, I had to adapt. Adapt daily. Realize that I can't always make plans because I can't always keep them. I manage though. I have a great support system. My family understands what pain I go through and have helped me every step of the way.

Despite having endometriosis for more

than half of my life, I love that I am able to overcome any obstacle that I encounter. I was able to successfully deliver two beautiful and healthy daughters. In 2019, I was finally able to complete college and graduate with my associate degree. Life isn't always easy. Life with endometriosis is even harder. But I never let endometriosis win. I am bigger than this horrible disease and I will overcome it.

*If I could provide advice to another woman experiencing the same symptoms that I had or are told that they have endometriosis, I recommend finding an excision specialist. The earlier, the better. This may not always be feasible, but if you can, do it. If you are unable to due to finances or insurance restrictions, research your local physicians and determine which ones are familiar with the disease, which ones will provide the most adequate care. I always say, "Doctors don't know what they don't know." No one knows what is best for you other than yourself. You must be your own advocate and find a physician who believes you. Your pain is real and is not in your head. Believe in yourself. Believe in your body. If something feels wrong, there could be something wrong. Stay strong and most of all, do not give up.*

Johanna Vekara

Stacey La Gatta

Kate Henry

Kelly

Sarah Golden

Kristen Lewis

Becca Blanckenberg

# I AM
## *strong.*

**Stories of chronic illness warriors learning about their strength.**

# Johanna Vekara

Finland, Europe

## Quality Auditor in Technology industry

*"You are not alone, we are here with you!"*

## About Johanna:

*I am Johanna, 33-year old woman living in Finland, Northern Europe. I'm M.Sc. in Business administration, auditor, sister, friend, fitness athlete and multiple chronic illness warrior and advocate. When I first got sick, I would have given anything for a community and people who I could relate to with these often harsh experiences. Therefore I find it so important to share my story, so someone else out there might get comfort in knowing they are not alone. My multiple diagnoses include ankylosing spondylitis, reactive arthritis, IBS, asthma, epilepsy, fibromyalgia, burnout and depression. Took me years to figure out, that I have to look at myself as complete person, consisting of not only physical health but also mental health. This all takes a strong survivor, you are one too!*

\* \* \*

*IG: @chronicallyjohanna*

Hello everyone! My name is Johanna, a Supply Chain Management specialist. I'm 32 years old and from Finland. My chronic illness story is long, dates back to early childhood, but what really has had an impact is ankylosing spondylitis. Ankylosing spondylitis (short AS) is a form of inflammatory autoimmune disease, where the cells of the body attack itself. Symptoms can be numerous, but most often lower back pain, joint pain, inflammation, iritis/uveitis, and vast pain symptoms all over the body. AS is a chronic illness, which means that you can have better periods but there is no cure. Therefore I've found throughout my illness journey, it is extremely important to be persistent in finding ways to take care of yourself.

> **"Eventually I figured out that until I had dealt with all my medical trauma backlog from past years, I could never truly make myself feel better."**

For me, ankylosing spondylitis has mostly had an effect on mobility and joint inflammation. I got my diagnosis eight years after initial symptoms, when my neck was so inflamed, I couldn't turn my head to either side more than 20 degrees. That was finally enough to convince the doctors to start me on biological medication, which has ever since stabilized most of my symptoms, so that I can function most of the time like a normal person (if we don't take into consideration the fatigue and tiredness). I still have pain and especially stress that induces more symptoms, a.k.a. flares. This manifests in pain, anxiety like muscle and joint pain all over my body, headaches and bloating, stomach symptoms, etc. Every person is an individual and no two persons even with the same diagnosis have the same symptoms or how they can relieve their pain and condition.

As we are all so unique, I've tried almost everything, but what I've found most helpful over the years is exercise and diet, these two as a combination have helped most! Even one of my first rheumatologists suggested diet (gluten and dairy free) as treatment for AS, since inflammation resides in our bowels and that is also where our immunity is based. Therefore, for over 12 years I've had a very limited diet, and recently had to add FODMAP foods to restrictions, like onion, dates, corn, yeast etc. Sugar in large amounts also increases inflammation and makes my stomach upset. It's really difficult to like yourself when you are blown up like a balloon. Stomach problems also affect mental health, since our bowels are our second brain.

This brings me up to my second point where my illness has had a major effect: mental health. I never really stopped to think about it, that illnesses like this don't only affect our physical wellbeing, but human beings and we as individuals should be looked at holistically from every aspect. Everything is connected. Even though I ate perfectly according to my diet and exercised regularly at the gym, I would still get flares and feel worse. Eventually I figured out that until I had dealt with all my medical trauma backlog from past years, I could never truly make myself feel better. I don't believe that any kale juice will heal autoimmune diseases, but it is possible to dial down the symptoms and reach a state called remission. This is where the inflammation is so reduced, that symptoms are almost non-existent for a longer period of time.

Resilience is needed to figure out the combination of mental, physical, etc. holistic aspects of health in the bigger picture to manage wellbeing. Each of us has our unique history and genes. My experiences can give a hint about what generally might help (diet and exercise) but figuring it out, everyone has to, unfortunately, do that for themselves. The journey is hard but worth it in the end.

I truly learned my limitations through burnout in 2019-2020. Before that, I had treated myself as a normal healthy person, ignored my boundaries and didn't recognize my body signaling for me to rest, at all. I was disassociated from my own body, and only after I had high blood pressure did I notice to stop. Limitations of this illness come in a variety of ways; not only in physical (some jobs are forever banned like pilot, trucker, flight attendant) but also mental (chronic fatigue and inflammation of the body takes also mental strength, as you never feel truly rested, but still have to carry on and the same things are expected from you especially in working life). After my burnout, I had to

really listen to my body on a whole new level. I still sometimes go overboard, push myself too hard at the gym for example, but now if I can't sleep as my heart rate is elevated, I recognize this as my body signaling to slow down.

Despite my illness I am determined not to be discouraged, but am pursuing my first ever fitness competition in Autumn 2022. It

## "I'm happy just as I am."

was supposed to be already spring 2021, but we pushed the plans with my coach due to my burnout. If nothing else, this hobby demands strong mental health and clarity, willpower, perseverance, and persistence. And we, as chronically ill, are exactly that. Through years of trials we are hardened diamonds who have gone through so much, but we are still going strong. Giving up is simply not an option.

These personality traits about me, not giving up in the face of adversity, are what I have grown to love about myself. Battle scars are there, but they only made me stronger to advocate for those who are still in the early years of their battle and don't have the strength to battle for themselves.

At this exact time, I'm happy just as I am. I've found a desk job with supportive employers, I'm free of toxic relationships, I have come to know my boundaries better, and with continuous learning I believe I can truly be happy. I feel joy! I wouldn't want to be anything else at this moment in life.

My first advice to others, especially in

the early days before diagnosis, is to practice self-empathy. I was so hard on myself earlier. I was so disappointed I wasn't like everyone else. I didn't accept my illnesses and thus lived in denial of them for over a decade. Only in therapy did I finally accept that these illnesses are part of my reality.

My second bit of advice is to get therapy. I once saw a great meme on Instagram which said, "If your doctor doesn't refer you to a therapist with your new diagnosis, find a different doctor." I couldn't agree more. Even if finally receiving a diagnosis is a relief, that you finally have a name for this thing that is "wrong" with you, it is still a big adjustment. And I wish I had done the grieving at that time, and not denied it for so long. As this then had major implications in my mental health.

My third bit of advice is not to stay alone in all this. What I later discovered is that there are so many people like me struggling with these same thoughts and experiences, and I found the chronic illness community online in Instagram. And you know, although the COVID-19 year has been rough on many fronts, I have not felt lonely, as I get such amazing peer support from chronic illness advocates from all around the world! It truly makes a difference knowing that you are not alone. That there are other people out there who are wondering the same things. What kind of medication would suit me? Am I ever going to find relief? Will this go on forever?

## You are not alone, we are here with you!

# Stacey La Gatta

Easley, SC, USA

## Teachers Aide for Students with Disabilities

## About Stacey:

*Stacey is a 27-year-old from New Jersey who was diagnosed with colitis two and a half years ago. Since becoming diagnosed she strives to raise awareness about colitis and help those who have it know they are not alone. In her free time she enjoys exploring new places and going to the beach. She also likes to bake and spend time with family and friends.*

* * *

*IG: @colitiswarrior18*

*"I have learned to find joy in the small things in life I once took for granted."*

Hi, my name is Stacey and I want to share with you my journey of battling colitis. Never would I have thought that at age 24 I would be told that I have a chronic illness. More so I thought, who gets a colonoscopy in their twenties? Surely this procedure was only for people over the age of fifty. At first, I did not know what colitis even was so I was not too concerned about it; it was not until I researched this illness that I was instantly filled with fear. Colitis is a chronic, inflammatory bowel disease that causes inflammation in the digestive tract. There is currently no cure for this illness. This inflammation usually is only in the colon and can range from mild to severe. It is seen as an invisible illness since a person with colitis may look "normal" on the outside but internally their body is very sick.

When I first found out I had colitis I only had it very mildly but slowly it became progressively worse. It got to the point where I could barely eat or sleep. I would constantly be crying from being in so much pain. I got down to a weight where my bones began to stick out of my body. Finally, I decided I needed to be admitted to the hospital. I thought it would be a brief in and out trip for the day but it was not. I was there for over a week and it was such a traumatic experience. I was poked and prodded on the hour. I hated needles but just got used to the fact that I needed an IV stuck in my arm. Days after I was admitted I finally got some relief. I finally got to go home but I was not out of the woods yet. I experienced intense joint pain from the medication and I became depressed. I felt so defeated and just laid on the couch for days like a withered vegetable. If it were not for my family and friends, I do not know how I would have survived that month. Thankfully the steroids started to kick in and I began to feel some relief. I even had to take a month off of my job as a teacher's assistant since I was unable to walk more than 10 steps without feeling exhausted.

"It is honestly difficult, especially as a woman, to have to share with someone you are romantically interested in that you have a disease"

Colitis has not only affected my career but has also impacted every aspect of my life. Mentally this illness has challenged me in so many ways. Having colitis brings bouts of anxiety for fear of another flare-up and also depression of accepting my life will never be the same. Colitis has also affected my social life. During a flare-up I could barely have the strength to hang out with people for a long time. When I am feeling better I can see people but I have to be sure to be in a place with a bathroom nearby. I sometimes have to leave social events early because of feeling sick. This disease has also been difficult in finding a romantic relationship, as I often feel like a burden. It is honestly difficult, especially as a woman, to have to share with someone you are romantically interested in that you have a disease that comes with bloody diarrhea and rectal bleeding. I have learned though that if someone truly loves and cares for me they will want to be there to support me. Physically this disease has also impacted me. I lost 20 pounds in just a few weeks while in a flare. Some people told me I even looked good with all the weight I lost, but little did they know I could barely even nourish myself. These comments made me have a negative view of my body image. My hair is now falling out in clumps, so I may need to get extensions. I also experience frequent joint pain that makes it difficult to exercise.

## "I just want to be a light for those who feel they have no hope."

In order to adapt to my illness, I have learned how to make some changes in my life. I now eat gluten and dairy-free to try and alleviate some symptoms. I have learned to bring some food options to social gatherings so I always have something to eat. I have found people on Instagram and Pinterest who make yummy, colitis-friendly recipes. I carry around an extra pair of underwear just in case I have an accident. I make sure to always bring my heating pad to every overnight trip. I also have implemented some stress relief practices. This includes yoga, walking, and journaling to help reduce my anxiety. I have learned the importance of speaking up to others about my illness and telling them what I need.

What I love about myself despite my illness is that I can still find joy when living in chronic pain. Though some days are really hard, I know that God will give me the strength to make it through. I have learned to find joy in the small things in life I once took for granted. This includes enjoying a meal with friends and not feeling sick after, being able to sleep without pain, and going for walks. I also love that I am able to love others well, despite being in pain.

If I could do anything in my life it would be to advocate for those who have colitis. I want to inform those outside the colitis community about this disease and how they can help. I want to advocate for better medical care and a cure for colitis. I would love to be able to walk alongside those who are suffering from colitis and encourage them. I just want to be a light for those who feel they have no hope.

*Some advice that I would give to someone who may relate to my story is to never give up. Though you may go through some really dark days there is hope that one day things will get better. Look around you and find a community of people that will support you through this. More often than not people want to help but just don't know how. Let them help you and never think of yourself as a burden. This illness is not your fault. Try the very best you can to stay healthy but understand that no matter how hard you try you may still experience pain. Give yourself grace and take rest when you need it. You are not weak when you need time to heal. This illness will make you more resilient than you ever were before. You can have empathy now for those who are walking through similar things. Keep fighting, warrior; you are stronger than you know.*

# Kate Henry

Christchurch, South Island, NZL

### Bachelor of Design, Photography Student

## About Kate:

I'm Kate, a 19-year-old from New Zealand. I have lived with multiple chronic illnesses throughout my life. I am the founder of Princess Poorly, a community of chronically ill youth

\* \* \*

IG: @princesspoorly

Website: www.princesspoorly.com

*"Use your voice, because you are worthy of everything you need."*

As I sit here beginning to write one of the most relevant stories of my life, the last four years are flashing right before my eyes. The hospital admissions, the IV's, the needles, the doctors appointments, the surgeries. Everything. The very things that have shaped who I am today, the very reasons why I am sitting here writing this. But that's getting ahead of myself, so let's go back to the start.

I'm seven. I'm sitting on a hospital bed with my mom's arms wrapped around me. I'm weak, my eyes are filled with tears and I'm being tested on. An unfortunate but very normal reality to me. I'm always uncomfortable, I struggle to digest any food, and I have a cold most days of the year. I am sick. After years of testing I am finally diagnosed with Selective IgA Immunodeficiency, which is when your body doesn't produce IgA antibodies and this can affect many aspects of your health such as autoimmune disease and recurrent infections and illnesses. Alongside severe gluten intolerance which wasn't very common back then. I very quickly became the kid who can't eat anything at birthday parties, the kid with the weird lunches and the kid who couldn't go on sleepovers due to my pain levels. But finally I found some relief, a relief that every kid deserves, that allows me to actually enjoy my childhood again.

But then well... high school happens. My body changes and so does the state of my health. I go downhill quickly and all of a sudden I'm collapsing during class, I can't stomach any food, and I feel unwell all of the time. At the age of 14, is when everything changed. My life got flipped upside down and I didn't know who I was anymore. I was replaced with constant anxiety of when I was next going to be sick, in severe pain, have severe weakness and suffer with chronic fatigue. So here I was, seven years after my first bout of health concerns, reliving all of what seemed to be my past life experiences and more. The testing began again. The disbelief and undermining of the doctors began again. The loneliness began. Again. And all whilst I was fighting for answers, I started to lose weight, missed most days of school, never saw my friends and was struggling through every single day. Because of this my mental health began to decline, and I was left with severe anxiety and disordered eating. I spent my days inside the four walls of my bedroom, grieving my past life, wishing I wasn't in the situation I was in and struggling to come to terms with my new self.

## "My story has made me strong, determined and most of all in a strange way, positive."

Slowly but surely we began to make progress. I switched doctors and found one who truly cared. I pushed for more testing and I went through surgeries, MRI's, endless amounts of blood tests and more. With most things coming back clear I was diagnosed with IBS, and worked with a dietitian on that. I suffered mostly with chronic bloating, nausea, and debilitating pelvic pain. I found some relief from lifestyle changes and I put my absolute everything into taking control of what I could, including seeing a psychologist for the mental toll chronic illness was having on me. But I was still unwell and was progressively getting physically worse, which resulted in not being able to sit for my final school exams, as my cognitive function was nowhere near healthy. I couldn't go to my final prize giving, and I couldn't enjoy all of the last day of high school experiences. I was at a point where I was so fatigued that I slept at least 15 hours a day and my head constantly hurt alongside my whole body. When I got to this point I was sent to do thyroid tests, which showed I have Hashimoto's disease in which hypothyroidism was occurring. Hashimoto's disease is an autoimmune disease where the immune system mistakenly attacks the thyroid gland, therefore the inflammation may prevent the thyroid from producing important hormones that affect your main organs including your brain, heart, digestive system, reproductive system and more. Receiving this diagnosis made so much sense, all of the random symptoms I was experiencing pieced together like a puzzle. The brain fog, cognitive problems, chronic fatigue, temperature irregulation, hair loss, weakness and a puffy/swollen body and face were all signs that my thyroid wasn't okay, and we had finally listened to it. It's now been over a year since my Hashimoto's diagnosis and like many I haven't seen much improvement once starting my medication, so to this day I am still struggling with my treatment. Because I was still ill it meant that the testing continued and around 6

months ago I was finally diagnosed with Postural Orthostatic Tachycardia Syndrome also known as POTS. This condition affects my autonomic nervous system and I struggle with the symptoms it brings daily. I'm currently still figuring out how to manage this complex body of mine, but I know I will get better, because I have to. I want to.

## "I'm still sick daily, but the little amounts of progress that I've made have added up and now I've been able to take a huge step forward in my life."

So that's me and my story so far. A very complex part of my life, but a very important part of me. My story has made me strong, determined and most of all in a strange way, positive. I have my down days as does everyone, but my body has chosen its own path for life. And over the last four years I've struggled with coming to terms with the idea of changing my plans. Now I am okay with the path life is taking me down, and I truly mean that because I know my pain has a purpose. Don't get me wrong, no one wants to be sick, no one wants to be in pain, but sometimes our bodies choose our paths, not ourselves. Sometimes we simply cannot control everything, like the way we think we can. So everyday when I wake I tell myself that although this situation is uncomfortable, I cannot control it. All I can do is find some kind of comfort in the chaos, and do my best to work with the situation I have been given, in whatever way that may be.

So where am I now? I've just managed to make the move to start my degree, after taking time off work and studying I have allowed my body the rest it needed. I'm still sick daily, but the little amounts of progress that I've made have added up and now I've been able to take a huge step forward in my life. I'm also constantly building my strength and a community alongside it and am dedicating most of my energy into my brand Princess Poorly, a safe place for those with chronic illness. This community is the reason my pain has a purpose. A family member once told me "it's hard enough being a teenager, let alone a sick one" and that single sentence has stuck with me over the last four years. In amongst all of the craziness that comes with being a teenager, we also have our health and for those who are chronically ill, our health interferes with every single normal teenage experience that everyone else around us is having. When we are sitting at home in bed unwell scrolling through Facebook, Instagram and Snapchat comparing ourselves to our peers, it can be easy to feel left out, or like we're not good enough. But when I was confronted every single day of "missing out on the normal experiences" it pushed me to grow, to find that although my life experiences are not the same as everyone else's, they are just as important and I am so strong because of them and my mission is to show the chronically ill youth just that - through Princess Poorly. This is also something that every single one of you needs to remember. Your illness does not define you. You may miss out on normal

> **"I often think about what life would look like if I wasn't ill. What decisions would I have made, how would I have lived my life differently."**

experiences, and sometimes it's not fair. But you are strong, you are brave and most of all you can and will have a fulfilling life with chronic illness.

Chronic illness affects you in ways unimaginable. Every choice I've made has been impacted by my illnesses. Every decision, big or small. When you're a teenager you're faced with making big decisions everyday. I often think about what life would look like if I wasn't ill. What decisions would I have made, how would I have lived my life differently. Truth is sometimes I wish for it. But I know deep down, I have been given a voice for a reason. A voice that can help so many, a voice that can change the way chronically ill individuals are viewed in society. Chronic illness took a lot away from me, but it also gave me so much. It gave me a strength I didn't know was possible, a voice that can be heard, experiences that can help others and a community filled with kindness. So for me, it's given me a chance to stand up and be strong. And if anything, that's all I want to do in life. I think it's important to remember that everything depends on the choices we make now. So my advice. Let Go. Grieve if you need to grieve, but once you're ready just let go. Let go of society's expectations of what your life is meant to look like, let go of your own expectations. Your chronic illness will affect the decisions you make, but it can also lead you to amazing experiences, meeting amazing people and being the strongest version of yourself.

One of the biggest parts of living with chronic illness is being able to adapt, anytime, anywhere. Adapt plans, meals, situations, everything. And because chronic illness impacts the choices we make, we need to try and adapt to our new situation, something that is much easier said than done but is so important. Changing the way we live after receiving a chronic illness diagnosis can be painful, but it is important for our bodies to know we are listening to them, by adapting and making our lives that tiny bit easier.

For me personally, I began to know my limitations after a few years of struggling with chronic illness. I guess you could say I was a bit stubborn about the situation. I forced myself to stay in school, continuing to hold high standards with my grades which put a lot of added pressure and stress onto a body that was already struggling. I tried to keep my illness a secret for a long time and I continued to play sports for the first year when I was ill. So many of these decisions ended up meaning I was pretending everything was fine, which only resulted in a lot of anxiety and trauma due to the things I put myself and my body through. If only I had accepted my life was changing earlier on, I wouldn't have gone through so many of the things I did. In saying that, it's hard to let go of parts of your life that make you...you. But after I struggled my way through high school and

had finally finished, I made a huge decision that was just for me, that went against all of society's and my own standards. I didn't go off to university straight away like I had always planned to, and I stopped working as well, which meant a huge lifestyle change. But I've never regretted it. I made a decision solely for me and my body, and now I've been able to make the move to study like I had always hoped to. Adapting our plans can be scary, but know you aren't alone and everyone's time lines are different. Everyone is different.

Spending the past year reflecting on myself, has been an emotional roller coaster. I have pushed myself to go through many different tests, many different appointments and have fought for action to be taken. The last 12 months have shown me the drive I still have in me, the want to get better, it's still there.

*So if you are sitting, reading this story, thinking it relates to you, then I have one thing to say. I believe you. I see you and I care about you. For many with chronic illness, we go for years not being believed, being judged and not receiving the help we deserve. We are told it's in our head or it's not real. But I am sitting here telling you, I believe you. Continue to fight for your answers, be your own health advocate and get the help you deserve. And whilst you're doing that, use your voice, because you are worthy of everything you need. And I will continue to fight for you too. My battle is nowhere near over and I accept that my health is something I will continue to struggle with forever. But I know I will be okay, because I know I am strong. And you are too.*

# Kelly

Denville, NJ, USA

**College Student**

## About Kelly:

*My name is Kelly and I live in New Jersey. I have had ulcerative colitis for twelve years and have had five surgeries. I had my colon removed nine years after my diagnosis and I now have a j pouch. I am currently in college and studying nursing.*

\* \* \*

*IG: @kellys.uc*

*"It feels like I was given a chance to slowly learn to love the parts of my life again that I had missed for so long."*

My name is Kelly, I am 21 years old, and I am a college student. I was diagnosed with ulcerative colitis when I was nine years old, but have experienced issues with my bowels since kindergarten and had my first actual flare up a year before my diagnosis. Ulcerative colitis is an autoimmune disease that causes inflammation in the colon and rectum. The defining characteristics of my flare ups have always included bloody diarrhea, uncontrollable bowel movements about fifteen times a day, and extreme pain, all lasting for around two to three months, with IV and oral steroids typically putting me into remission. While I had a flare up almost every spring for my last few years of elementary school and a flare up later in eighth grade, I was able to achieve five years of remission until the flare up that left me with more than a few challenges for two years.

## "I adjusted to living away from my family, started meeting a lot of new people, and started dating for the first time."

Being sick with this disease when I was young meant that I experienced a large amount of anxiety walking into my elementary school knowing that just a flash of stomach pain could lead to me needing to run to the bathroom, or worse, having an accident in front of my peers. I felt a constant fear surrounding that possibility and can remember certain moments where I frantically panicked in my head, trying to "control" my stomachache in class and hoping it would just subside. I missed a lot of school back then; I would do homework in the hospital and my classmates would send me cards, and when I returned to school after months my peers were excited to see me back.

They'd poke my steroid "moon face" and ask why my cheeks were suddenly so chubby. The vice principal once visited our classroom to say goodbye on the last day of school, and I remember her coming up to me and saying to me, "you're so strong." I could see just how different things were for me in my situation than they were for my classmates. When I entered high school, I was in remission after a previous flare up I had in eighth grade. For the next four years I was taking my regular six mesalamine pills a day, and somehow I experienced little to no health issues; my parents were almost convinced that I had "outgrown" the disease.

Starting college felt like a shift in the gears of my normally laidback life. I adjusted to living away from my family, started meeting a lot of new people, and started dating for the first time. I went to my first parties, and while I never drank due to my own fears about my health, I watched my friends drink alcohol freely. While college was enjoyable that year, it was also my first time really dealing with relationship and friend issues.

Coming home for the summer, I remember having this feeling that the amount of stress I had been experiencing throughout the year was going to send me down a spiral. I felt all the hurt in my stomach, and could almost feel myself getting sick physically over how emotional I felt. Even after the hurt had faded, my body was still processing it.

I spent my nineteenth birthday that year in the hospital. Within a month of my flare up starting, it had escalated so fast to the point where I had not responded to my usual treatment of steroids and was now trying Remicade and an experimental cocktail of four different types of antibiotics at once (around 18 pills a day). We met with a surgeon to discuss my colon removal at the advice of my gastroenterologist, and I had to lay down halfway through the consultation because I was so weak. Still, my parents and I decided that we would try whatever we could to get me into remission before considering surgery.

Fast forward to October - I was doing a little bit better and was able to go back to school, but things went downhill quickly. After experiencing an accident in my dorm room that left me laying down and crying on the floor, I called my mom begging her to take me home, and not soon after that I realized that this surgery was inevitable.

Waking up from the first surgery was a blur. The only thing I remember really was my surgeon showing me a picture of my colon on his phone. I wasn't surprised with just how sick and inflamed it looked upon being taken out; it looked like the pain I had felt so many times had been brought to the outside of my body for a visual. I don't even remember looking at my ileostomy for the first time. I think I was just so relieved to the point where the idea of the bag on my stomach wasn't

scaring me as much as it used to.

In the hospital the first few days after surgery, I would get sick from eating my meals and felt weak and exhausted. I would have a fever every night, and then one night I had the chills so bad that I couldn't stop my body from shivering or my eyes from rolling back. I was given a big pile of blankets, and the residents on call continued to order fluids for me. I watched as my nurse pumped fluid bag after fluid bag into me. I was sent from the pediatric wing to an adult wing after that, and soon we noticed that my arms, hands and legs were all swelling. Fluid started leaking out of my wounds, and I ended up so swollen that I couldn't walk. I watched the nurses struggle to put a catheter and IV in me, and I remember my room filling up with person after person. One of my nurses was telling others in the room that I needed to be put in the ICU, and eventually I was sent there.

*"I spent a lot of time feeling an anxiety I had never felt before. It was as if I was trapped, and I couldn't see life outside of the hospital."*

The next day almost feels like a dream now. I remember having a PICC line put in and after that barely being able to stay awake. They then brought me to surgery to place a drain in my abdomen, due to an antibiotic-resistant infection that had most likely occurred from the leakage in my colon prior to it being removed. The next couple of days,

I was on oxygen and monitored as the fluids continued to pour out of my wounds. I lost the forty pounds I had gained in water weight from the swelling in a matter of a few days, and was left with big stretch marks all over my hips, legs, and even a few on my left arm.

In the next week while I was still in the hospital, a blood clot was discovered in my abdomen, as well as one in my lung that was referred to as a possible "over-read." I was put on a heparin drip right away, which led to massive bleeding in my rectum, since the blood thinner had aggravated the UC that was still present there. I remember blood pouring out of my rectum while I was laying in the hospital bed. It would continuously flood out of me for minutes, and I would attempt to use a bedpan to catch the blood that was coming out. After the first time it happened I needed a blood transfusion from the amount I lost, and I was so fearful of it happening again. Of course, it happened again and again. It would get all over the sheets, the floors, my shoes. I remember feeling so scared as doctors and nurses congregated in my room in the middle of the night all trying to figure out how to help me, and the same nurse who had fought for me to go to the ICU came over to me and told me that everything would be okay.

My third week in the hospital would involve another drain placement surgery for an abscess in my abdomen. As I continued to recover from all three surgeries, had physical therapy in the hospital hallways, and spent time resting, I was the most unmotivated I have ever felt in my life. Getting up was hard. Walking was hard. Doing anything besides

listening to music or watching TV was hard. Most days I was crying on and off, and I felt useless most of the time. I spent a lot of time feeling an anxiety I had never felt before. It was as if I was trapped, and I couldn't see life outside of the hospital. I knew the road to recovery would be a long one, and it hurt to think about how much this whole experience was going to change my life going forward.

After 23 days, I was released from the hospital. The night I got home I couldn't stop crying because I was feeling so unfamiliar with my life. Nothing felt normal anymore, not even being home. I remember thinking that my life had turned into a nightmare and that I was trapped in a body that I didn't know anymore.

The next week involved changing my wound bandages, taking care of the drain I still had, and learning how to change my ileostomy bag on my own. Everything felt like a challenge. I had at-home infusions of antibiotics that my mom had to give me every morning and night through my PICC line. I would have a home nurse come every few days and a physical therapist come once a week. I had to practice doing simple movements like lifting my legs and bending my knees again. I felt so far from ever recovering fully.

In time I got better, and life started to feel normal again while I adjusted to having a bag. Eventually I found myself preparing for my next surgery to switch my end ileostomy to a loop one and create my j pouch, a pouch created from my small intestine so I can use the bathroom again. With this surgery came an abscess and another drain, and this time it was placed while I was awake. The pain of the needle and tube being shoved so far into my body is something I won't ever forget.

A few months later I had my reversal surgery, and this time I woke up crying uncontrollably. Since the moment I woke up from it, something felt off with me. I looked down at my stomach, still crying, and saw where my small intestine had been sticking out before; it was now only a big bandage covering the wound where it had been. For the next week, I was told that my stomach hadn't woken up yet, meaning I would get sick after eating anything. It got to the point where I was hardly eating, and the doctors told me I could only go home if I was able to keep food down. My anxiety was so bad this time, as I remembered my first surgery's traumatic hospital experience that for the most part took place in the same wing I was now in again. I felt scared and uncomfortable all the time, continuously asking for something to help with my anxiety. When I got home after that week, the anxiety followed me, and I couldn't fall asleep at home either. Nowhere felt comfortable, and I was right back to those feelings of helplessness that made me resort back to my "living a nightmare" mentality. Soon I was back in the hospital for another abscess, and after another drain being placed in my abdomen I was mentally exhausted from all the issues I had to deal with. It took a long time to feel right again.

After recovering physically and mentally that summer, I went back to school at a community college in the fall. I had to take the previous year of school off to get my surgeries done, and it was hard to watch most of the people my age going to school and getting ahead with their degrees. My life finally felt somewhat normal now that I could go back to school, despite still adjusting to this new circumstance of going to the bathroom with my j pouch and finding myself running out of energy more easily. Things started to get worse with my energy, and we found out that I was very anemic and needed a blood transfusion immediately. Apparently, the small amount of blood, which I was told was normal to see after the reversal surgery, had added up without me realizing.

Then one day, after walking up a hill to get to class, I noticed a pain in the back of my leg suddenly come on. I figured I must've pulled a muscle walking up the hill. For the next few days, I kept feeling the pain, and eventually it spread to that entire leg and the bottom part of my other leg. After having an MRI and a CT a few days later, it was found to be a blood clot in my pelvis that was pushing on my sciatic nerve. This blood clot, being the third one we found, would lead to my next challenge of being on blood thinner medication regularly after it was found that I had genetic predispositions to clotting, along with ulcerative colitis being a big factor in blood clots forming as well. This would aggravate the small amount of colitis still left in my cuff, causing me to bleed again.

In the next year, I had several blood transfusions and iron infusions. After consistently losing blood with no clear explanation besides the small amount of colitis left, we finally found out what the blood thinner may have been aggravating: ulcers in my j-pouch along with an ulcer higher up near the ileostomy surgical site. To finally have some answers was such a relief.

A lot of times people tell me they would take my struggles for me any day if they could, and I have to remind them that who I am allows me to get through them. I have also grown enough through these experiences that, when more issues present themselves, I am able to take what I've learned and attempt to conquer them like I have before. There's no manual on how to do life, and there's definitely no manual to guide anyone through severe illness. The way you heal and cope is your way of reacting to your own experiences. You do what you need to do in order to survive, heal, and move on.

> **"It feels like I was given a chance to slowly learn to love the parts of my life again that I had missed for so long."**

I decided to switch from studying psychology to nursing when I went back to school. I would love to be able to help others who may be at their lowest like I was. I can't explain how great the nurses who have all taken care of me have been. Many have inspired me to choose this career path myself, from the nurses who took care of me during my first hospital stay in fifth grade to those who helped me recover from surgeries.

Adjusting to life without a colon and learning to live with a j pouch is something that will probably take a long time for me. From all of the complications I've experienced, I've developed anxieties over the possibility of more health issues presenting themselves. However, this illness has taught me that I need to live in the present. After all of the hopeless days, surgeries, and scary moments, I now feel like my perspective on life has been renewed. Something I genuinely love about myself is how I took these experiences and allowed them to show me that life needs to be appreciated. It feels like I was given a chance to slowly learn to love the parts of my life again that I had missed for so long. I think about how much I've missed so far: how many friends I had to drift from when I left my first college; how many celebrations or holidays I've spent sick or resting; how many days I've spent in a hospital room, missing normal life so bad that I would do anything to have it back. The hopes I have for myself and my future feel amplified. I'm inspired to take each day that lies ahead of me to enjoy life and find more of what makes me happy.

# Sarah Golden

Chicago, IL, USA

## About Sarah:

*Sarah is a recent college graduate currently working as a text technologist and a large accounting firm in Chicago, IL. She studied industrial engineering at the Georgia Institute of Technology in Atlanta, GA, where she is originally from. Her parents reside in the nearby suburbs with their dog, Zeke. She would like to express her full gratitude to her parents, brother, grandparents, aunts, uncle's, cousins, friends, and doctors. Without them, life would be so much dollar and none of this would be possible.*

\* \* \*

*IG & Twitter: @sarahgoldenn*

*Facebook: @sarahgoldennnnn*

## *Management Consultant*

## *"You deserve happiness and success."*

As my eyes flutter open and my consciousness returns, my instinctive first thoughts go directly towards the pain. Physical pain, thinking about how badly my bones ache upon awakening and how difficult it's going to be to get through today. Is my vision okay, or am I going to spend the entire day both frustrated with and grateful for the partial vision that I have been left with? Will my stomach be calm for once, or will I spend the day putting on a fake smile as I severely restrict my diet and face sharp aches? Mental pain, thinking about how hard it can be to continue pushing through the exhaustion while everyone else seems oblivious. How many times will I consider calling into work sick or canceling whatever plans I have made to instead lay in bed and rest? Emotional pain, wondering what I have done to deserve this and why I feel so alone in the battle.

My name is Sarah, and I am a 23-year-old female. I work in tax technology at a major accounting firm, consulting on a variety of wealth and asset management, banking, and insurance clients to improve their tax functions. At my core I am an engineer, trained to think critically and solve problems. On the side, I am just another spoonie trying to fight the battles of chronic illness one day at a time.

Upon my illness and subsequent diagnosis, it was easy for me to move my thoughts directly towards solutions. I believe this is due to my educational background — in STEM, there is no emphasis on feelings and emotions, with the only focus on solving critical problems efficiently and effectively. I did not stop to consider the fact that I would potentially lose my vision completely or never feel healthy again. Instead, I only thought about how I would fix this and bring myself back to normal. After realizing that I may never feel the same, no matter how many pills I take or injections I am given or doctors I see, I was forced to define a new normal for myself.

> ## "My illness affects me deeply and personally. Whether I like it or not, it is a part of my life."

In November 2018, I was at a southern restaurant in the heart of Atlanta, GA celebrating Friendsgiving. I had been feeling a little bit off all day, even skipping lunch at our college football game's tailgate — a first for me. I still wasn't hungry by dinnertime, but ordered regardless, figuring it would be important to eat. Just before the food was served, I was struck with sharp pains across my stomach. My friends took me home and, with the help of my family, looked over me for the next few months. I was barely able to eat; the simple act of drinking water, which I previously took for granted, caused excruciating pain. Group project meetings were held in my bedroom as I struggled to sit up in bed for more than 15 minutes. I went through various scans, had dozens of vials of blood drawn, and underwent the dreaded endoscopy/colonoscopy combination, all to be told that nothing concrete could be found. My stress heightened as I began feeling even worse, wondering if I would be forced to live in pain forever. I woke up one morning with black dots in my vision; however, I was unconcerned, as this seemed to be the least of my medical issues.

One month later, on March 15, 2019 at a routine eye exam, I casually mentioned that I had developed black floaters and was having trouble seeing from my left eye. After briefly looking into my eye, I was immediately sent to a retina specialist, who diagnosed me with pars planitis that afternoon. Pars planitis, a subset of intermediate uveitis, is an eye disease characterized by inflammation of the pars plana, the narrow area between the iris and choroid. It generally leads to blurred vision, dark floating spots, and progressive vision loss. While the cause is technically unknown, it is thought to be an autoimmune disorder, where the inflammation is caused by an autoimmune reaction.

My illness affects me deeply and personally. Whether I like it or not, it is a part of my life. It is something that I cannot stop thinking about and is on my mind plaguing my thoughts daily. Every time there is a place I can't drive to or a menu I can't read or a sign I don't see, I am reminded that my vision has failed me. Furthermore, I am led to believe that this is my own fault — I put my body under so much stress, consciously or unconsciously, that it was forced to attack itself.

Over time, I have learned to change my patterns of thinking and avoid the negative blame. I accept the fact that there are activities I can no longer do, simply because it is just too difficult for me to see. Instead of letting this ruin my day and leave me feeling defeated, I remind myself to embrace change and be grateful for the remaining vision that I still have. These changes in thinking certainly are not achieved overnight, and by no means is this successful 100% of the time. I face a mixture of good days and bad days, as does the remainder of the world. And while it may be difficult, I find that sometimes the best way to foster positivity is to simply stop thinking about my health and distract myself with something more promising. At the end of the day, there is nothing more important to me than my strong relationships with my friends and family, and that is something I will always maintain regardless of how well I can see.

I love my sense of urgency and constant desire to make the most of every opportunity. Regardless of the happenings of my day, I can almost guarantee that I will be plagued with impending fatigue and exhaustion by nighttime. Therefore, I feel obligated to seize every moment and pass the time with activities that truly make me happy. This may look very different depending on the day — some days we move mountains, and others we are lucky simply to make it outside for a walk around the block. No matter what my definition of victory is, any day that I get out of bed and do something that makes the world a better place is a successful day in my book.

It is difficult in nature to surrender to control and accept the fact that you no longer have a handle on your own body. More than ever, I have had to learn how to rely on others and accept help when needed. Both physically, such as asking what something

> **"As a child who despised going to the doctor even for routine vaccines and fainted more than once while getting blood drawn, I had no clue how I would combat my fear of needles and somehow begin injecting myself."**

says or admitting that I can't read something, and mentally, admitting that I am tired and feeling helpless. To some it may feel like an exclamation of weakness, but I personally believe asking for help when it is needed is the greatest signal of maturity and acceptance.

Recently, I was caught in the middle of a series of battles between my insurance company and my doctor's office. As a patient of a top 10 hospital in the United States serving some 600,000 patients annually, I imagined a seamless insurance department designed to help patients efficiently and effectively. At an appointment with my doctor in summer 2020, an abundance of inflammation and clusters of white blood cells were found in my left eye, the cause of major vision loss. She recommended an Ozurdex implant, a common steroid treatment for non-infectious uveitis patients. The implant is injected into the eye in the doctor's office and is designed to treat swelling and reduce inflammation, lasting for about six months. At the end of the appointment, the next steps were for the team to submit the implant for approval by my insurance company and then to work with me to schedule the injection. This was followed by weeks of daily phone calls in which I uncovered issues such as submission of the case to the wrong insurance company, files with incorrect diagnosis information, and the incorrect treatment plan outlined in the request for approval. Weekly, the doctor's office would schedule my injection, believing they finally had the case under control, only to call me just hours before the appointment to cancel, admitting they had made yet another mistake. This left me in tears multiple times, unable to comprehend how a top-ranked hospital could somehow be so incompetent.

Once finally resolved, I received a phone call from the doctor's assistant asking me to come in that afternoon. Unfortunately, it was too late — we had waited too long and the window of opportunity passed. There was too much inflammation to do an injection; so much, in fact, that I was diagnosed with anterior uveitis on top of my intermediate uveitis. I now had inflammation in two separate parts of my left eye, known as panuveitis. While there was simply no choice but to accept it, this additional diagnosis left me angry. Every morning I was scared to open my eyes, afraid not of what I might see but instead of what I might not be able to see. The most difficult part was coming to terms with the fact that this could have all been avoided under a healthcare system that was not so deeply broken.

After enduring this series of events, I have become motivated to help others facing similar difficulties. In my future, I hope to begin a new career helping others with chronic illnesses learn the ins and outs of the insurance industry and understand how to help themselves. I truly believe there is nothing more important than being your own biggest advocate, mainly because no one cares about you as much as you care about yourself. Therefore, I want to teach others who find themselves in a similar position how to fight for themselves against a system where patients are often seemingly destined for failure from the beginning.

To combat the blurred vision and swelling,

> **"I never fully grasped the true meaning of courage, defined as the ability to do something that frightens someone, or strength in the face of pain or grief, until this very moment."**

my doctor recommended I begin taking a biologic designed to bind to and block TNF molecules, ideally reducing inflammation. Once again, the insurance approval process was longer than ideal, riddled with confusions about the exact diagnostic code and prior screenings required and the correct pharmacy, just to name a few. I found myself alone on the radiology floor of the hospital with contrast agents flowing through my veins, thinking that my childhood self never would have imagined something like this happening at the young age of twenty-three. As I entered an MRI machine for brain imaging, I wondered if yet another organ had failed me or if my body was just playing tricks at this point. That's the ironic thing about chronic illness — sometimes not having any answers is even worse than the actual answer. At the end of the day, regardless of the diagnosis or lack thereof, the patient is still facing the same symptoms and likely desires relief.

I lay completely still, and slightly claustrophobic, in the scanning tube, allowing myself to consider the potential outcomes and the corresponding consequences of my choice going forward. Depending on the results, I would either be forced to accept yet another autoimmune diagnosis, or I would move forward with bi-weekly injections of a medication designed to suppress my immune system (amidst a global pandemic).

As a child who despised going to the doctor even for routine vaccines and fainted more than once while getting blood drawn, I had no clue how I would combat my fear of needles and somehow begin injecting myself. I spent weeks worrying about how big the needle would be, how much it would hurt, whether or not the side effects would somehow be worse than the actual disease. Furthermore, success is not guaranteed — would I be going through all of this trouble only to see no improvements? When you are a child, the main fear is the unknown and lack of control, with no way to know or plan for the exact moment that the nurse is going to press the trigger. In this case, it's the exact opposite. You are in complete and total control, with the only thing stopping the needle being your own finger.

I never fully grasped the true meaning of courage, defined as the ability to do something that frightens someone, or strength in the face of pain or grief, until this very moment. Pain, as in the stab of the needle, and then the uncomfortably cold medication coursing through your body, and then the subsequent exhaustion and muscular fatigue. Grief, as in mourning the loss of Sunday nights as you know them, now reserved as the dreaded "injection nights." The stark realization that your life may never be the same after taking these harsh new medications; the even starker realization that your life was never the same long before this therapy was introduced. Bob Marley so beautifully sang,

> **"You never know how strong you are until being strong is the only choice you have."**

While it gets harder to get out of bed every morning and put on the facade of a normal life, it becomes even more important to continuously remind yourself that you deserve happiness and success. It may require a new definition of those words, but regardless, your illness should never be the limiting factor in chasing your dreams.

As Demi Lovato famously said,

"You can take everything I have
You can break everything I am
Like I'm made of glass
Like I'm made of paper
Go on and try to tear me down
I will be rising from the ground
Like a skyscraper"
I may feel fragile, but I am
nonetheless destined for greatness."

# Kristen Lewis

Fort Lauderdale, FL, USA

## Nonprofit Program Manager
### &
### Small Business Owner

*"Do not shy away from the moments that may not have been on the roadmap we originally charted for our lives."*

## About Kristen:

*Kristen Lewis is a passionate advocate of chronic illness and equity. She currently manages a literacy program for a nonprofit while using her downtime to build a small lip balm business. Kristen lives in South Florida with her 18 year old toy poodle, Elijah. Her philosophy on managing her chronic illness is all about listening to her body and practicing self-care.*

\* \* \*

*IG: @misskristenL*

My name is Kristen Lewis and I have struggled with my health throughout my life. In my pre-teens, doctors blamed a poor immune system for my constant bouts of illness. My report cards show the story of a child who would never have perfect attendance, but kept herself on the honor roll, nonetheless.

My medical chart was a thick folder full of medical visits that ended in diagnoses of strep or tonsillitis. I frequently struggled with asthma during these bouts of illness and would often spend the evening in the ER waiting room or crouched on the bathroom floor while a hot shower was run for the benefit of the steam.

I had a favorite over the counter and prescription medication. The pink meds tasted like bubble gum and the chunky white meds made my stomach churn. The orange flavored over the counter meds were preferable to anything grape flavored.

## "He thought my complaints were just laziness or lack of enthusiasm."

I had achy joints at the age of 12 and my softball coach would often take me out of the game because he thought my complaints were just laziness or lack of enthusiasm. I learned to entertain myself during sick days and soaked in hours of daytime TV. Somehow, these coping strategies forged in my childhood have helped me greatly to this day.

My mother, who suffered from similar chronic illness symptoms, died suddenly from a heart attack the Christmas of my first year of college. I was 18 years old. Even as she struggled with her own health, she did not see the signs and symptoms of her child's monthly flare ups. The stress of grief only made my flares worse and it was not uncommon for me to have a straight week or two of being sick. Once, I had to take a math final with a 103 degree fever – although I still managed to get an A.

It wasn't until I was 26 years old that I was diagnosed with an unnamed autoinflammatory condition within a group of illnesses called Periodic Fever Syndromes. At this time, I had pushed myself halfway through my master's degree in Social Work while holding down three part time jobs. Periodic Fever Syndromes are a class of autoinflammatory conditions that cause cyclical flare ups of systemic inflammation. These flares often, but not always, involve a high fever; mouth/genital ulcers; swollen lymph nodes; and a variety of other forms of chronic inflammation throughout the body.

At the time, I was sick for over a month before finals one semester and my kind primary care physician decided that something just wasn't right with my health. She was the first doctor to ever take my health seriously and I truly owe so much to her. But, a suspected diagnosis is not the end of the journey for anyone with a rare chronic illness. Over the past six years, I have had to tumble through trying medication after medication to see what will work. I am still not at the end of this journey.

This is not an abnormal story for a patient with a chronic illness. This is not unique. But outside of the obvious symptoms and pain that my body went through, my chronic illness kept me in a safe bubble as a child. In sixth grade I was pulled out of all sports - dance, gymnastics, and softball - because my aches and pains were blamed on "growing pains." Instances of excitement can also occasionally cause flares and I was often sick around holidays and on vacations. My family once took a trip to Lancaster, PA to visit Amish Country and I got so sick they had to bring me to an Amish healer -which was a pretty unique experience.

I lived my life, but parts of it felt a little bit muted. Outside of the physical symptoms, unbeknownst to me, the inflammation was also taking a toll on my mental health. At 32 years old, I now know that I often dip into a depression when the inflammation in my body starts to rise. As a 14 year old, mixed with all of the hormonal fluctuations and changes happening at this age, I was often an emotional mess. I was not suicidal, but suicidal ideations were very present in my thoughts.

The one aspect of my personality that truly saved me was my ability to adapt. In my teen years, the idea that "it gets better" really helped propel me through the difficult moments. But, as an adult, my ability to roll with the punches - which comes from my experience with illness - has really saved me. I have adapted and thrived. While my physical body may be weak, I have learned to problem solve and think smarter in my work and life.

I currently manage an early literacy mentoring program at a nonprofit and utilize all of the skills I have cobbled together through my experience with chronic illness. I have learned to take breaks and give myself time to rest or risk a long stretch of debilitating symptoms.

"There are definitely moments in life where I am in awe that I have made it to where I am today."

It truly sucks, but I love that my own experience has given me a lens to view the world through in order to point out inequities for the disabled community. Although my illness is invisible, I try my best to use my voice to advocate for those who live with chronic illness. The trauma of chronic illness has also given me a wicked sense of humor. I really love that aspect of my personality, even if it is often perceived as too dark or too risky.

On the downside, my health has definitely put a bit of a ceiling on my career aspirations. High stress jobs are an easy way to land myself in the hospital. I truly feel that the perfect balance for me can never be found in a traditional 9 to 5 job; but, at the moment society seemingly requires me to hold down a full-time job for the health benefits.

In the perfect world, I would make money from a small business - like writing or an online boutique - and make ends meet with short term contract work. This is the dream

- so I will continue to make small steps in that direction and work to keep my health as stable as possible along the way.

There are definitely moments in life where I am in awe that I have made it to where I am today. I may not be wealthy, but I am a chronically ill female making my life work. I have made many choices in my life for the benefit of my health and continue to try my best to advocate for myself and my well-being.

I feel so very far away from the woman I was just a few short years ago, where my condition was out of control and I would often find myself so sick that I could not walk or do much else other than lay in bed and shiver myself to sleep from fever. I made a definitive decision in 2017 to quit my stable job in Boston and move to South Florida in hopes that the warm weather would soothe my joints. This was a dangerous move, but I am so grateful to not be struggling through winter. My body is still deteriorating from the inflammation, but I truly believe it is at a much slower pace than it would be if I had stayed in New England.

*Life is never a straight line. We all have to make choices for our own well-being that may not have been on the roadmap we originally charted for our lives. As scary and disappointing as it can be sometimes, there are moments where we have to make big changes in order to truly improve our lives and give ourselves a bright future. My two cents would be to not shy away from those moments. My chronic health issues have taught me many things over the years – including that so much of life is not guaranteed.*

# Becca Blanckenberg

Cape Town, South Africa

## Ceramic Artist

*"Don't allow this illness to stop your life and stop you from living!"*

## About Becca:

*South african-born renal transplant recipient, Rebecca Blanckenberg, is currently battling chronic renal failure for a second time. She is a ceramic artist with experience in photography and jewelry design. She enjoys Reading, Writing, and the outdoors. But her favorite and most important role is being a full-time mother to her one-year-old son, Liam Bodhi.*

\* \* \*

***IG:*** *@beccablanckenberg*

I remember waking up one morning with unusually clouded vision. One week later my vision jumped from bad to worse and I was starting to lose my eyesight. I felt extremely anxious and afraid because I had no idea what was wrong with me. I went to see an optometrist to examine my eyes, only to find that no problems were detected. I went to see a Doctor immediately after and he found my blood pressure to be unusually high for a 19 year old. I was referred to a local hospital called Victoria hospital. I went home to pack my bags in case of an overnight stay and off I went, not knowing just how much my life was about to change.

I was transferred to Groote Schuur Hospital where I did a series of tests and spoke to many doctors. This was all new to me as I had never stayed in the hospital before and had never been seriously ill before. The specialists eventually told me that I have congenitally abnormal kidneys which means that my kidneys stopped developing and could not support my body anymore as I grew older. This meant that I needed to be placed on dialysis immediately. In the public healthcare system, due to financial constraints and lack of resources, not everyone is afforded the equal opportunity to access dialysis. Your personal case needs to be presented to a panel of doctors and specialists who decide whether you can access this treatment or not. They analyse your lifestyle, they consider your age, your background, and everything about you determines whether or not you will receive this life saving treatment. I was very confused at the time as this was all new to me and I don't remember being particularly sad about it. I was young and I took everything as it came. They returned to me with good news. I was accepted and was able to start the much needed renal dialysis immediately.

For the first few months I was put on peritoneal dialysis but later the doctors decided that I could be put on haemodialysis. My eyesight improved the minute I started dialysis. While all of this was happening, my mother, sister and brother were getting tested to see if any of them were a match to donate a kidney to me. It turned out that my sister was the closest match and in a short few months we were scheduled to have our transplant.

Our successful transplant happened on December 5, 2007. My sister was hospitalised for a week and I was there for nearly one month. I remember our rooms were next to each other and we called one another on the telephone because we couldn't walk yet. When we eventually saw each other face to face we kept cracking jokes but laughing was really hard with our brand new scars. This transplanted kidney was a beautiful, selfless gift that would keep me alive for longer.

The journey with a transplanted organ is not always easy. I have had countless hospital stays over the years, regular check-ups and many needles but I would choose this over dialysis any day.

In my second year of studying, teaching, and being married for seven years, I found out that I was expecting. After trying to have a baby for years and crying out to God to bless us with a child, He had given us a tiny growing miracle. We were over the moon when we found out; we had to let the doctors know and we were told to come in immediately. Still on cloud nine, we entered the doctor's office, expecting to be welcomed with a warm congratulations but the mood quickly dampened. The doctor began explaining everything that could go wrong and then he recommended that we terminate the pregnancy. Everything became hazy and I broke down right there. I couldn't stop crying, I went in excited and left heartbroken. He told us to think about it over the weekend and to return on Monday with a decision. I cried so hard that entire weekend. We prayed about it, we spoke to our support system and by Monday we concluded that this pregnancy was Heaven sent and God gave us this blessing for a reason, we decided to go ahead with the pregnancy.

> **"I did everything I could do to try and save my kidney but unfortunately that was out of my hands."**

I had to do a biopsy at ten weeks gestation. Thereafter my journey at the maternity hospital began where I saw doctors and professors every single week. They told me the same thing as the renal doctors, they strongly recommend terminating the pregnancy. I spent most of my pregnancy crying and praying. It was tough, I spent so much time in the hospital away from my husband. I had to be monitored closely as I was a high risk patient due to my kidney transplant. With all of this, my kidney function was quickly dropping and getting worse each week. So many trials but we remained faithful no matter what the medical professionals threw at us. We were warned that I could lose my only working kidney if I carried on with the pregnancy but we had faith that the baby and I would be fine.

On October 23, 2019, I gave birth to a tiny little premature baby boy. At 34 weeks, Liam Bodhi, my miracle baby, was born in perfect health. Only God could make that happen, our munchkin beat the odds.

I did everything I could do to try and save my kidney but unfortunately that was out of my hands. There was nothing the doctors could do anymore and I was put back on dialysis after getting very sick seven months after I had given birth.

So here I find myself again, thirteen years later, my new chapter begins. Back where I was but this time everything is different. Physically and mentally it is more challenging. This is hard, I won't lie. So far I've been dealing with it as it comes, but some days I can't stop crying. Some days I feel normal and other days I feel like I can't even hold my son because I'm that weak. Severe anaemia and hypertension makes things so much worse too. I can't stand the thought of being on dialysis three days a week, four hours a day and I have a love/hate relationship with my dialysis machine; but at the same time I am thankful for the opportunity to once again be receiving this life saving treatment.

One thing I have learned this time around is

that it's so easy for me to spiral into depression when I give this too much thought. I have to keep looking at the good in everything and find the light and that is how I get through my days. I have also been speaking more openly about it and how it affects me, even sharing on social media because not only does it help me but it can help someone else battling with chronic illness. I have learned that every single emotion I feel in this process of healing inside and out, is worthy of acknowledgement. I can't stand it when people say "you should be grateful to be alive" or "there are other people who have it worse than you." As true as those statements are, my feelings are still valid no matter what they are. That is how we heal, by feeling our way through our experiences. Being a young person on dialysis feels paralyzing in so many ways but there is always hope. I know that God has healed me before and He can do it again. I have a few family members who are being tested to see if they are a match to donate a kidney to me. The other issue we currently face is the COVID-19 pandemic. Transplants are currently on hold which is a bit sad but I know everything will happen in God's perfect time.

People close to me constantly tell me how strong I am and I know that is true but I also know that everyone suffering from chronic illness has it inside of them to be stronger than they think they are. Our bodies go through so much and we need to respect them. I love my body now more than ever for what it has brought me through, a transplant, childbirth, numerous operations, I have never respected my body more. Another part of me that I love is my scars. My storytelling scars, from my surgeries, blood draws, dialysis, fistula, tests, etc. These scars make me a warrior and they are a constant reminder of my strength. I look forward to seeing what my future holds. I remain creative in pursuit of my dreams of teaching art and having my own ceramics studio someday.

To all the young people out there fighting the same battle, please don't give up. Don't allow this illness to stop your life and stop you from living! It is a really hard journey, one of many trials but it certainly does not have to mean the end of the road for you. Speak about it, write about it, and be open about it because it helps. Keep your faith strong and on days when you need to cry, cry! Feel every emotion because you are worthy! Reach out to people who have gone through what you are going through; their world of knowledge and experience is a huge comfort. Lastly, remember that you have a purpose in life, do not allow your illness to define you or make you feel like your life is worth nothing. God created you for a beautiful purpose and you owe it to yourself to push through this.

anchor.fm/bludreamhealth

@bludreamhealth

bludreamhealth.com

**WRITTEN BY AMY CROCKFORD**
**ILLUSTRATED BY: DANIEL BUTLER**

**Buy Now!**

Amy is a deaf 10-year-old girl who loves to swim and play with her friends. Her friends learn a valuable lesson about deafness. Find out about how they come up with a way to embrace it. Amy learns the true meaning of friendship.

**RAISING DEAF EDUCATION & AWARENESS FOR CHILDREN**

## Your health story has the power to make a difference.

WEGO HEALTH

Join a community of patients and caregivers who are getting paid to change healthcare using their real life experience and insight.

www.wegohealth.com
@wegohealth

# CHRONICLES OF ZAZZLES'
## CONNECTIVE TISSUE ISSUES

**BUY NOW!**

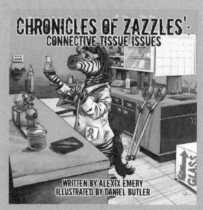

WRITTEN BY ALEXIX EMERY A.K.A ROBIN POWERS
ILLUSTRATED BY: DANIEL BUTLER

Zazzles is a beautiful zebra who loves to rhyme, solve problems, teach, and do science things. She grew up suffering from many things, but never let it stop her from achieving her dreams. Find out about how Zazzles adapts to her Connective Tissue Issues in this very first children's book in the Chronicles of Zazzles series!

**RAISING EHLERS DANLOS SYNDROME EDUCATION & AWARENESS FOR CHILDREN**

Emily Natani

Tessa Hansen-Smith

Brandy Haberer

Samantha Bowick

Eliška

Cydni Fried

Oliver Collins

CHRONICALLY Empowered

# I AM A
# *Warrior.*

**Stories of chronic illness warriors paving the way for the rest of us to impact our world.**

# Emily Natani

Easley, SC, USA

## *Chronically Ill, Survivor, Mom, Advocate, Empath*

*"Never give up."*

## About Emily:

*I'm Emily and at 26-years-old, my life turned upside down from chronic illnesses. In the 11 years following, I've been searching for answers, doctors (whether Eastern or Western) who can help. I am a mom of 2 and wife first, but all of my dreams have been shattered by sickness. I used to be in public relations, wanted to travel the world and have a successful career, but this was taken from me. I long for the day when my kids can see me healthy and they do not have to bear witness to this anymore. One of my main goals in life is to be a writer and I am grateful for this amazing opportunity to share my story. I hope to Advocate and raise awareness for these invisible illnesses.*

\* \* \*

*IG: @emilynatani3*

I have been chronically ill for 11 years. Some of my diagnoses are ME/CFS, vestibular migraine, dysautonomia, pots, fibromyalgia, as well as constant chronic infections and viruses, specifically a resistant bacteria called pseudomonas.

Throughout my journey I have seen most of the top doctors in the NY and NJ area and each has a differing opinion as to what has caused my health to deteriorate. By the end of my treatment plans, I am passed on to yet another specialist, whether in the functional or medical realm. Sometimes, I find that doctors expect my reactions to procedures, medications, supplements, dietary changes, and anything else they throw my way to be the way in which all of their other patients have reacted. When the doctor looks at me, perplexed, like he has just seen a unicorn with three heads, I know our time is up.

It all began with the onset of my first pregnancy twelve years ago, where episodes of presyncope dominated my life. Falling down an elevator shaft or being in a rocking boat became part of my daily vestibular issues. I would wake up to seeing just white or black dots and quickly close my eyes tightly, praying the feelings would cease. I worried for my baby and myself as my health took a turn for the worse. I contracted IUGR, where my son was no longer getting any food from my umbilical cord and he was at severe risk for breathing problems. I was induced immediately and luckily was blessed with a healthy baby and avoided the NICU by a hair.

## "I was told by close family and friends that my illness was in my head.

Postpartum, I remained positive that my hormones would somehow shift back to where they were prior, but they never did. I was in a constant state of dizziness and searched desperately for relief. At first I was diagnosed with orthostatic hypotension and sought treatment from cardiologists. This remains a current issue I have to this day that I cannot control, from lying down to sitting and then standing, my blood pressure and heart rate waver.

Then, I went to four endocrinologists and was told by two of them I definitely had PCOS and two others vehemently disagreed. I took PCOS medication for a year and a half with no improvement, realizing I was falsely put under the umbrella that too many women are. I went to a naturopathic doctor simultaneously, who advised me to go off gluten, dairy and maintain a low sugar diet. I have been on the diet for 11 years and it has not made a dent, even though it has been applauded for its anti-inflammatory effects. Acupuncture, Chinese herbs and meditation were all suggestions that I took seriously. For several years of my life, I was told by close family and friends that my illness was in my head. I needed to learn mindfulness, be positive, change my frame of mind, seek therapy, meditate, do yoga and learn to accept it. I was much younger, caring for a newborn, and alone. I felt I could trust these people so I went to a psychiatrist who put me on antidepressants and told me this was the answer. She chalked it up to postpartum depression and familial issues. I knew I did not have any postpartum depression and my heart was broken because the body I had depended on was now betraying me. I knew something was very wrong and dedicated all the time I could to research. I continued on despite the naysayers and went to see nephrologists for vascular testing as well as various cardiologists to address my extremely low blood pressure.

By the time I became pregnant with my

> **"I used to run and exercise with ease and now getting up in the morning without falling over was a mere miracle."**

second child, I was still at square one while somehow remaining hopeful that this new life might reverse my vestibular problems. However, I quickly learned that the health problems would only multiply. I immediately developed what seemed like allergies and pregnancy rhinitis. Debilitating migraines, sinus pressure, and severe tmj pain were now added to my list of symptoms. During my delivery, I could not stop shaking, jaw chattering, and my disequilibrium and dizziness were at a record high. I could barely walk, held onto the bed constantly, but was

blessed to have yet another healthy child in my life. As I looked at my two beautiful children all I wanted was to feel the happiness and joy that I was supposed to. But, I could barely see straight, let alone walk in a balanced way. I fought every single day jogging, but attempting to make it around the block seemed like a New York City marathon. I used to run and exercise with ease and now getting up in the morning without falling over was a mere miracle. All my blood tests were normal and every single doctor told me I am so lucky nothing is wrong with me, I am a healthy individual. The insanity of the constant doctor visits, testing, and no real treatment plan began to bleed into my mental health. I was no longer a human. I was a pincushion with arms and legs just trying to care for two young children that needed my attention 24 hours a day. I would not give up. After a horrific dry needling experience, where I blacked out and lost all functionality, I was recommended to see a neurologist who diagnosed me with vestibular migraines and autonomic dysfunction. He immediately prescribed Zoloft and Clonazepam, which I dreaded taking because again, this felt like another failure. I was giving into medicine that I knew would be impossible to wean off of and doubtful of it even being the least bit effective.

During this same time period, I also developed a strong mucosal cough that showed evidence of strong bacterial infection. This pregnancy rhinitis morphed into something entirely different. My allergist put me on antibiotics, inhalers, steroids, nasal sprays, nebulizer treatments, and immunotherapy. My cough was so strong I needed frequent chest x rays, regularly bruising my ribs badly and coughing up blood from the intensity of exertion. I had CT scans which showed mucosal thickening, but nothing that anyone could or would act on.

My next stop was the pulmonologist who put me on heavy doses of antibiotics mixed with prednisone for almost a year. She believed this was a chronic infection but it could not be resolved. I then saw an infamous otolaryngologist in NY who performed several endoscopies in her office revealing LPR and GERD "off the charts". The next step was invasive testing, including manometry and 24 hour ph monitoring. I will never forget the feeling of the tube inserted through my nose and then reaching down into my stomach cavity. I had to eat and sleep with this and kept praying it would yield answers. I was put on a PPI, Zantac, Amitriptyline, Gaviscon, Prevacid, and Gabapentin, but the side effects were becoming unbearable. Since none of her anti reflux and neurological medications were improving my condition she told me a Stretta surgery was necessary to close "a gaping hole" in my lower esophageal sphincter. Post surgery, my dizziness was significantly worse and this doctor's answer was that the surgeon accidentally cooked my vagal nerve. So I could now add permanent burning of my vagal nerve to my list. I tried not to dwell on it and moved onto functional neurology,

where I tried an innovative program of 24 sessions in one week. I began neurological exercises and rehabilitation, took VNG testing, which showed low brain function as well as difficulty with eye movement. This functional neurologist had me continue exercises at home for about a year, but this did not prove helpful in any way.

## "I still did not want to give up so I sought after doctors that were integrative in nature."

I went back to the drawing board and focused my sights on black mold. After realizing that I was exposed to black mold as well as others, I was convinced this was the answer. I sought help from an infectious disease doctor, who confirmed that mycotoxins were in my blood and urine. She put me on Amphotericin as a nasal irrigation tool and Itraconazole, an oral antifungal. I was prescribed a number of supplements and was told it would take at least a year for this infection to detox out of my body. I gave it exactly 12 months with these medications and followed every protocol, however the improvement was little. My dizziness and disequilibrium persisted and I began to have vertigo spells as well. With a cough as severe as mine, I could no longer eat or drink around anyone. I remember getting coughing attacks, running away from people and spitting large green mucus balls into tissues. It was embarrassing and humiliating.

I felt like a constant failure. If I wasn't in the middle of a horrible coughing attack, I was about to pass out, fall or be so dizzy that I could not function normally.

Acting and faking joy, pleasure, happiness, really anything became a full time, exhausting job. No one really knew the level that my illnesses had reached. I hid it so well."You look like you're doing well," "I am assuming you're feeling better, then?" "Did you ever try

## "I felt so wronged by the medical community, abused in a way, passed on like a piece of garbage and then blamed by doctors when their genius treatment plans didn't work."

drinking more water or taking deep breaths?" "I am happy to see you've put on a bunch of pounds and that you are all better. How could an illness even last that long?" "What is your illness again, I mean, it just doesn't make sense." My head was spinning from all the toxic positivity, unwarranted commentary, unnecessary questions and statements posed as challenges for me to prove what is wrong with me.

I still did not want to give up so I sought after doctors that were integrative in nature. I took gamma globulin shots, IV vitamin therapies, saw GI specialists, rheumatologists, and then started searching

for any doctor who helps solve medical mysteries. I found one who confirmed pleurisy in my lungs, no surprise there, but also found fungal growths on my tongue, multiple active viruses in my blood, including M. pneumonaie, parvovirus, and coxsackie. He put me on antiviral pills which didn't stop the constant infections and viruses. I sought after another doctor, pioneering for invisible illnesses and she diagnosed me with ME/CFS and POTS. Her testing showed active EBV, herpes, and I always had a high positive ANA. She recommended Valcyte and Cypro to treat the bacteria and viruses and believed that they had entered my bloodstream, requiring a more aggressive approach to eradicate them. Nothing was working so I felt I needed to go back to my pulmonologist and get my sputum re-tested. It produced a highly dangerous bacteria, pseudomonas. The doctor told me that I likely have an immunodeficiency because my body is unable to fight these infections and they keep reactivating. She sent me right to an immunologist and infectious disease specialist who prescribed a midline to treat my pseudomonas, with IV infusions of ceftazidime every eight hours.

This was one of the worst 17 days of my life. The midline was aggressively pushed through my veins and the pain never subsided. Every infusion felt like pieces of glass were passing through my body, shivering and shaking as my eyes would roll to the back of my head. The level of fatigue was unreal and when I told the doctor what was happening, I was again put into the complex case file. There was nothing he could do. The midline was clearly a horrible mistake. He took it out as I lay in his office non-functional, retested my sputum and as luck would have it, the pseudomonas was heavier than it was prior to the midline. I thought I was in the twilight zone. I felt so wronged by the medical community, abused in a way, passed on like a piece of garbage and then blamed by doctors when their genius treatment plans didn't work. It was my fault that I could not be fixed. I needed to go on more neurological medications after this midline procedure because it destroyed my body, immune system, and entire being. I was beyond weak

> **"I have tried about a million holistic options and remain just as debilitated, just as lost, just as alone and just as lonely."**

or fatigued. I felt accomplished if I could even survive another day. Since that time,

I have tried about a million holistic options and remain just as debilitated, just as lost, just as alone and just as lonely. I wish I had a happy ending to my medical journey of eleven years, but I might as well be pregnant with my first child twelve years ago. I know nothing and I honestly believe I never will.

# Tessa Hansen-Smith

Fresno, CA, USA

## Content Creator

## About Tessa:

*My name is Tessa and I have a chronic condition called aquagenic urticaria (AU). This is an allergy to water, which includes sweat, saliva, tears and other bodily fluids. AU Can present itself as both external and internal symptoms, although external are the most common. I have both external and internal reactions. I used to hide my condition from people for a very long time, but now I use my voice and my experience to be an advocate for rare and invisible chronic illnesses.*

\* \* \*

*IG: @livingwaterless*

*"Self-worth comes from yourself and not some external source."*

My name is Tessa and I have a condition called aquagenic urticaria. Simply put, aquagenic urticaria means I'm allergic to water, which includes sweat, saliva, tears and bodily fluids in general. The most common form of this illness is having external symptoms, however there are also people who experience internal symptoms. I am one of those people who have both external and internal symptoms. Aquagenic urticaria gets progressively worse over time, so when I was first developing symptoms at age eight it was much easier to manage. Now at age 22 it has grown into a debilitating condition. I am not able to support myself anymore because of this and have been forced to give up a lot of my goals and aspirations. To cope with this rare condition, I created an Instagram page to document and reflect on my experiences. Since doing so, my page has grown into so much more, and now I create content to advocate for aquagenic urticaria, raise

## "My bright future as a successful medical professional who could support oneself quickly fell apart within weeks."

awareness, and spread education.

Throughout high school and college, I was working towards my goal of working in a medical profession, but unfortunately chronic illnesses have a way of dismantling all of one's plans and hopes. Because of all of the obstacles my condition has given me, I've been constantly learning how to start over. For a long time, I was your stereotypical good student and teacher's pet. I always worked really hard and would sacrifice hours of sleep to study, because I was in an environment where academics came above all else... including one's health. I was able to put my health low on my priority list when I was younger, but once I was in college, I started seeing the cracks forming. I was taking the maximum amount of credits I could each quarter and I was working two jobs, but my body and mind could handle it because academics came first. Within two years I started showing signs of burnout and simple willpower wasn't enough to overcome my health. In my last two years of college, I was pushed to quit both of my jobs, I was taking the bare minimum amount of credits, and my condition was forcefully making itself top priority over academics and my life in general. As someone who was used to overcoming health problems, I was suddenly losing my identity as a good student. For a long time, all of my self-worth came from how good of a student I was, how good of an employee I was, and I was losing that source of worthiness. I was barely passing and sometimes failing classes, I was constantly calling in sick to work, and I didn't recognize who I was anymore.

My bright future as a successful medical

professional who could support oneself quickly fell apart within weeks. Years of work went down the drain, and I was faced with the reality of my situation. I ended up moving home to live with my family and could not work because of how debilitating my condition had become. I had absolutely zero self-worth, no direction in life, and was stuck with the thought that my condition will continue to progressively get worse. So, I had a few choices to make. I could either give up completely and just sink further into depression, or I could push to find a new path in life for myself that emphasizes my

> ## "Living with aquagenic urticaria is not easy whatsoever, and even while taking medications to reduce the effects of the condition, it is incredibly debilitating."

health and taking care of myself. I chose the latter.

Now I use my experiences with my condition and all of its hardships as a way to raise awareness and educate about aquagenic urticaria. Now I am an advocate and work towards paving the way for others who have the same condition I do. Because it's a rare condition that not many people know about, not even most medical professionals know about, people who have aquagenic urticaria are often met with doubt and sometimes

even hate. In my journey of rediscovering my own worth and purpose I came into contact with a bunch of other people like me, which is truly incredible because for over a decade of having my condition I had never spoken to anyone else who experiences what I do. These people are part of my purpose now. I share incredibly raw and honest parts of my condition, regardless of how vulnerable it is, so that all of the other people with aquagenic urticaria don't have to. Which I am always happy to do because being an advocate was my new starting line in life.

Living with aquagenic urticaria is not easy whatsoever, and even while taking medications to reduce the effects of the condition, it is incredibly debilitating. For me personally, this is how it affects my life. I cannot drink water because I have both external and internal symptoms. When I drink water my tongue and throat itch, and my stomach and intestines will cramp and cause such overwhelming pain that I will cradle myself in the fetal position while I wait for the water to leave my system. Before I go any further, I want to explain why I can be internally allergic to water even though the human body consists of 70% water. The digestive tract in humans is considered "external skin" because it is technically a tube with each end open to the environment. The skin has to have the same properties as the skin on the surface so that not everything can be absorbed into the body. Because I cannot drink plain water without excruciating pain, I rely on whole, dairy milk to maintain some level of hydration. My normal is everyone else's form of dehydration, which means I'm not able to consume enough water, even through drinking milk. If too much water enters my system it will overwhelm my body. So my body will absorb the bare minimum amount of water needed to support the body's metabolic functions.

This also extends to foods with high water content. Fruits and vegetables are very difficult for me to eat, but not impossible! The sugars in fruits help buffer my digestive tract so it isn't just being overwhelmed by water. Vegetables are a little harder because they don't have the same levels of sugars in them as fruits do. Macronutrients like fats and proteins are also why drinking milk—which has water in it—is a good solution for me. Think of it this way: have you ever eaten something spicy and drank water afterwards and it still hurts? Now have you ever eaten something spicy and drank milk afterwards and it no longer hurts? This is because the macronutrients in milk coat the receptors in the digestive tract, so that those pain signals from something spicy (or in my case, from water) are reduced. Because my diet is so restricted due to water, I have to rely on supplements to help make my body function better, but that only does so much. This leads to cognitive function issues, problems with my muscles, and overall my body just isn't in good shape health wise. People say to treat your body like a temple and give it what it needs to thrive. Unfortunately, I am

> **"I do not swim, but I love to paint. I do not exercise, but I love to listen to music. I do not live a normal life, but I love to raise awareness about what it's like to live with aquagenic urticaria."**

only able to give my body the bare minimum needed to survive.

Water is an unavoidable part of life, which is what makes this kind of allergy so unbearable and debilitating. Constantly medicating and constantly encountering allergic reactions everyday takes its toll on the body. I have multiple chronic rashes on my body that are always there no matter how many medications or precautions I take. I always have to be careful when regulating my body's core temperature, such as avoiding wearing layers even in the winter and keeping constant airflow on myself. This makes summers really difficult, the rainy season impossible, and lots of the world's activities a challenge. I cannot swim in the ocean. I cannot dance in the rain. I cannot run and play to my heart's content. I cannot do a lot of things. I limit showers to once every two months, I limit the amount of yummy fruits I can eat, and I limit some of the best and some of the most mundane activities in life. Adapting to limitations

346 • CHRONICALLY EMPOWERED: A CHRONIC ILLNESS WARRIOR COLLABORATION

is really difficult, because I can't just use willpower to overcome my issues and find a workaround. Instead, I limit myself and find other things in life to love.

I do not swim, but I love to paint. I do not exercise, but I love to listen to music. I do not live a normal life, but I love to raise awareness about what it's like to live with aquagenic urticaria. I've learned to turn my bad allergic reactions and difficult experiences into positives, because I can share these things with the world and be a part of the chronic community and educate. Now whenever I have a really bad day, I write up my story and I share it with the world; find a silver lining in everything I go through. A nasty rash after a shower is an opportunity to teach people about what it's like to take a shower when you're allergic to water and explain everything from the mental distress it causes to the bodily reactions I deal with. I am not living the life I wanted and once worked towards, but I am living a life I love and am proud of. I can still use the knowledge I gained in school about the human body, psychology, and public speaking to engage with my community, spread awareness, and be a mental and physical health advocate.

## "I found love and happiness as an advocate for chronic conditions."

Even though I love my life and am happy with where it is headed, I often think about what I could do if I didn't have aquagenic urticaria. The first things that come to mind are scuba diving, playing in the snow, and running as far as my body will take me. I miss the feeling of swimming and having water just completely surrounding me. I miss being able to do everyday tasks and experience big milestones without the worry of how my body will react and what precautions I need to take. However, these things are never the final answer I reach when I think about the one thing I would do in life if I could do anything. I'm actually working towards that one thing. I want the entire world to be aware of Aquagenic Urticariaaquagenic urticaria. I want every family member, friend, stranger, and medical professional to know it is a real condition. As of right now, lots of people with aquagenic urticaria have a similar story. Most of us spent many years of our condition having never met anyone else like us. We've all encountered doctors telling us we're lying about our symptoms and that our own experiences aren't valid. A lot of us have had to deal with family members and friends ignoring our medical needs and telling us to just suck it up. Some of us have even had people threaten to throw water at us or have even had that actually done to them—I've experienced this multiple times. Therefore, the one thing I would do if I could do anything in life is to make aquagenic urticaria a well-known condition, so that when people open up to others about having this illness it isn't met with doubt and hate but love and support.

For anyone who's experiencing rashes or hives in response to being exposed to water, I would tell them to get on medications that work to suppress the immune system and reduce the allergic reactions, and to start learning your limitations and precautions that will help you avoid water as much as you possibly can. This advice is something I would hate to hear, and is something I still hate to follow, but these are all things I've had to learn the hard way because I didn't have anyone to look up to or ask about their experiences. It is not easy to one day realize you have to start saying no to some of the best things in life. Once I started working on accepting my life the way it was, I was able to start looking for the positives in life that I can still experience. I found love and happiness as an advocate for chronic conditions. I listen to the sound of rain and close my eyes and smile as I hear each raindrop fall. I pour all of my support and encouragement into friends for following their dreams and find joy in seeing them succeed. I learned new skills like digital illustration as a way to occupy my time without exerting too much energy and hurting my body. Even though I still face hardships every day and still get sad when I think about my life before my condition became too overwhelming, I am happy and look for the positives in every situation.

My name is Tessa and I have aquagenic urticaria, and at age twenty-two I have had to restart my life, give up on my hopes and dreams, and lose my source for self-worth. Now I am letting my health determine my path in life, and I look for positives and new goals every day. I have learned that my self-worth comes from myself and not some external source.

# Brandy Haberer

Easley, SC, USA

## Community and Social Media Manager at Hiki, Disability and Autism Activist, Illustrator, & Podcast Host.

*"Never to stop advocating for yourself if you think something is going on with your body."*

## About Brandy:

*My name is Brandy Habererand I'm a disability and autism activist, podcast host, and illustrator. I manage an Instagram where I educate and advocate for autism, chronic health conditions, and mental health through my writing and art. My husband and I are a late-diagnosed autistic couple, both with ehlers-danlos syndrome, a connective tissue disorder that can affect a lot of autistic people. We started sharing our journey to help others and share valuable insights to our podcast in hopes of bringing more awareness to under-diagnosed conditions and help change the stigma around autism and mental health.*

\* \* \*

*IG:* @the.chronic.couple

*Facebook*: @TheChronicCouple

*Podcast:*
anchor.fm/the-chronic-couple

My name is Brandy, and I've spent most of my life as a medical mystery. Lots of debilitating, life-threatening symptoms that would come and go, and a gut feeling that I was different from everyone else. Until 2019, at age 38 when I found out that I was autistic and I was diagnosed with Hypermobile Ehlers-Danlos syndrome, a connective tissue disorder that affects the bones and joints, and mast cell activation syndrome (MCAS), an immunological condition in which mast cells inappropriately and excessively release chemical mediators, resulting in a range of chronic symptoms, sometimes including anaphylaxis, neurological and respiratory problems. These are the formal definitions of my conditions. It sounds so strange.

> ## "It wasn't until I was referred to a specialist at a very prestigious hospital that I slept my first night without feeling like my body was on fire."

I've lived my life since birth with an invisible illness that no one could figure out. So when I finally got an official diagnosis, I looked at these words as vindication for every weird symptom or strange medical thing that has ever happened to me. I've always felt this need to prove myself to friends or family members who questioned if I was just "too sensitive" or "lazy." But a diagnosis meant that it was all real. It wasn't in my head; there was actually something going on with my body.

When I was a child with asthma, anxiety, unexplained weight gain - despite eating the same as my family, pain, fatigue, and food allergies, I knew I was different. My anxiety was so bad that I would throw up from the smallest amount of stress. I couldn't go to school or function like the other kids. The pain was so bad at times that I thought I was dying. Fits of rage or anxiety over nothing, insomnia, fear of going in public, and thoughts of impending doom. My family, who had their own issues to deal with, bore the brunt of a teenager with a chronic health condition.

When I was 16 years old, we moved into an older house. I was excited about having a larger room in the basement. Little did I know the mold in the basement, that didn't affect anyone else in my family, would trigger my first official "mast cell attack." I woke up one day before school covered in hives. My eyes were swollen and completely shut; my lips were triple their size. And nothing could explain the searing, burning pain of full-body hives. I went into anaphylactic shock and had to be given an EpiPen shot (adrenaline) to keep me from dying. This happened almost every day with anaphylactic reactions every few months for the next three years.

Several doctors, medications, and diets were tried, from steroids to even the suggestion of chemo when nothing really worked. It wasn't until I was referred to a specialist at a very prestigious hospital that I slept my first night without feeling like my body was on fire. They put me on a new drug at the time for organ transplant patients, which just so happened to stop hives for some reason? I didn't care what the side effects were (and there were plenty) I just wanted to be an average teenager.

That first night (sleeping on my parent's couch because I couldn't go near the basement), I slept like I'd never slept before. For a few years, I could go to college, work, date, and have friends. I could even function to the point where I could hide any issues that I had without anyone knowing I had a chronic illness. I was eventually even able to come off the medication. The crippling anxiety never left, though, like an old friend that was always in the background to remind me that I wasn't the same as everyone else. And sometimes that was hard to hide.

Stress from school or a breakup would send me into a space where I couldn't stop my emotions. I felt like I was drowning, and I eventually tried to end my life. The pain was so much; I felt like I had no control. I was sent to an inpatient facility for teens. When the doctors saw I was on steroids and several different medications, I was sent home after two days and told to get a hobby.

When I came home, it was almost more frustrating. Because now I was looked at as mentally ill. I was put on antidepressants and told my illness was all in my head. It made me question myself. Was I really just "crazy?" Something deep down inside of me knew I wasn't.

Working and navigating relationships is already tough in your twenties, this didn't help, but I managed to go to college, hold

## "I remember crying out, 'Please don't take this away from me, not now!'"

down a job, and get married despite it all.

I found an absolutely wonderful husband who supports and loves me no matter what. When we met, I glazed over my health issues. Partly because I didn't want to scare him off and also because I didn't fully understand them myself, it all came to a head about three months into our relationship when I had another one of my "mysterious flares" of pain where I couldn't move. He wasn't bothered by our lives being put on hold because of my health. He looked at me in a way that I had never had a partner look at me. He held my hand when I cried and told me he was there for me no matter what. Eight years later, and he's still here. Loving me on my good days and loving me even more on my bad ones.

At that time, my chronic health symptoms came and went, but I could live a somewhat healthy life despite moments of flares during stressful times. For example, I was covered in hives and in pain on the most special day of my life, my wedding day. But it was my standard, I put it away and pushed through the pain still not knowing that I had a chronic condition that explained everything. Even after several miscarriages, I sometimes thought it was me, not my body. I was crazy or made bad decisions; I stressed out too much and brought this on myself. I had an excuse to blame myself for everything.

I managed my mysterious illness for years until I reached a point where my hives came back in my early 30's, full force. I panicked, all the horrible memories from my past came rushing back. My life was stolen from me by this disease, and I had finally gotten it back.

I was happily married and lived in a beautiful house, I had my dream job as a lead vocalist in a band, I was a professional background singer at a record label, and I had an album on iTunes, I even owned my own business as a stylist! I remember crying out, "Please don't take this away from me, not now!" I started researching alternative treatments, and I was able to manage my symptoms with a more "holistic" approach. But chronic illness was always there, lurking in the shadows, waiting for me to stress out.

## "Looking back, this was a pivotal moment and one of the best things that ever happened."

When my husband and I bought a brand new house in 2016, my body finally gave out. I could use my will to fight through the hardest times, and you would never even know underneath my smile. But a brand new house full of the chemicals that come with new building materials was the last straw. I became bedridden, unable to work, breathe, or barely walk from severe pain. I had once again lost everything due to my body. My beautifully furnished brand new home with brand new furniture was now my enemy, and I was in another severe mast cell flare from something out of my control. After only living there for six months, we put it up for sale and moved in with my parents to help take care of me.

After that, I wasn't the same, and it terrified me, the smell of anything set off a list of symptoms. My body was protecting me by telling me everything was a threat. If I went into public, I felt like I was dying. One of the neurological symptoms after someone sensitive like me is exposed to high levels of chemicals, was a severe emotional reaction. I would cry and shake uncontrollably. My throat would feel as if it were closing, and my sense of smell was unreal! My mom disinfected her entire house and made a safe room for me that I couldn't leave for months.

I went to my Doctor, who had no idea what was happening to me because my routine blood work was normal. Luckily she was wearing perfume, and it caused a reaction, so she was able to see that something was wrong physically. My body turned bright red, my face felt like fire, and I started to pass out. She had to speak to me through the doorway. She still had no idea what was going on with me and had no real suggestions on how to help.

This left me with more questions; why did this happen to me? Looking back, this was a pivotal moment and one of the best things that ever happened. It started my search for answers, and it made me realize that I couldn't keep living like this. I had something seriously wrong with me that I could no longer push through.

That summer, we were finally ready to move into our own house in our favorite place on earth, Asheville, NC, where we could look for more answers.

The stress from the move sent me into a horrible flare. I was devastated. It's inconvenient for others when their shampoo or cologne sends you into symptoms of pain, dizziness, and nausea for days. I couldn't expect them to understand or change their way of living. I felt trapped. This year of my life was a dark one. I lost friends and close family members. People don't understand when you don't get better. It's an inconvenience to their lives.

It's during times like this that your real friends and family step up and those who love and respect you are apparent. The people who are left after a life-altering event are the really special ones.

After we settled in Asheville, I finally made an appointment to see an allergy and immunology specialist. It was confirmed that I had MCAS. I started proper medication and began to have a few good days. When you've been sick for so long, sometimes having a taste of what health is like, is just cruel. Because you know it won't last. You wake up and feel like a human again. So you do everything you used to do. You go to the gym, run a couple of errands, take your dog for a walk. Only to realize, you're not going to be the person you once were without paying a price. By doing the things you used to do so easily, even if only halfway, you end up on the couch, exhausted and in pain from even attempting it.

Good days are amazing, but sometimes they're sad. They make you forget about chronic illness for a moment. Only to be harshly reminded that you'll never be the person you used to be. So you spend your days searching for answers and trying different doctors, googling until your head hurts, spinning with symptoms of which you have most of them. When the doctors won't listen, and you have nowhere to turn, you have to turn to yourself.

> **"It's during times like this that your real friends and family step up and those who love and respect you are apparent."**

My diagnosis took a lifetime. But I never stopped advocating for myself until I found the answers that I so desperately needed. One diagnosis leads to the next. I noticed a pattern on social media of people with MCAS also having Ehlers-Danlos syndrome. After pleading with several doctors trying to convince them that I had this extremely rare condition that they could barely pronounce, I finally found one who listened to me and sent me to a geneticist for confirmation.

My intuition was right, and I was then diagnosed with Ehlers-Danlos syndrome hypermobility type, and according to my doctor, "The worst case of mast cell activation I have ever seen."

There's still a lot that's unknown about EDS, and there's no cure, only just management of symptoms. But now I know what to focus on managing. That has been life changing. Later that year, I also found out that I'm autistic. Learning I'm autistic made me extremely aware of just how misunderstood autism is in society. When faced with reevaluating my own view of autistic people, I felt ashamed and embarrassed.

When all you've seen are portrayals of autism on television that don't represent the full spectrum, the topic is rarely discussed and your only interactions with autistics in real life were children who also had an intellectual disability, your view of what autism actually is becomes limited and incorrect.

After my diagnosis as an adult, social media become my greatest source of information from other #actuallyautistic adults. I then realized that autism isn't just the stereotypes I had been led to believe. It's not a modern epidemic to cure, but a different way of processing the world. It made me believe that being autistic wasn't inherently worse than being non-autistic. It made me believe in myself.

Realizing that I used to pity the very community that I belonged to.out of ignorance, in large part due to an ableist society, made me sick. It made me want to change that, so people can see what I see now. That requires more openly autistic people to break the stereotypes, so others feel safe to do the same. I no longer think that being autistic is something I need to fix or some horrible tragedy. But not knowing you're autistic and living your whole life thinking you're broken, definitely is.

Shortly after my diagnosis we found out my husband is also autistic and has hypermobile EDS. What are the odds that two people found each other that had no idea they were both on the spectrum, and both with the same connective tissue disorder? It was then that we started noticing a connection with Ehlers-Danlos syndrome and the autism community.

Many autistics have joint hypermobility-related disorders, even though a link between them is rarely discussed. My husband Matt and I started a podcast to talk about our journey for answers called, "The Chronic Couple." We want to encourage others never to stop advocating for themselves if they think something is going on with their body.

I no longer hate myself for not being like everyone else. Receiving the answers I had desperately been seeking my entire life made me realize, all of those things I used to tell myself were lies. I wasn't lazy; I wasn't crazy; it wasn't all in my head or something I could just push through or ignore. And most importantly, I wasn't weak. In fact, I was quite the opposite.

# Samantha Bowick

Aiken, SC, USA

**Owner of Chronic Illness Support, LLC, Author & Patient Advocate**

*"Do as much research as you can about your chronic illness so you can make the most informed decision that's best for your body."*

## About Samantha:

*Samantha has a Master of Public Health degree. She is the founder of chronic illness support, LLC, and a patient ambassador with the Chronic Disease Coalition, @chronicrights. With her business and patient advocacy, she works in the office of a local restaurant. Samantha has a blog, guess blog, and podcasts; which can all be found at her website. She is the author of four books: 1) "Living with Endometriosis", 2) "Living with Alpha-1 Antitrypsin Deficiency", 3) "Living with Endometriosis: Workbook and Daily Journal", 4) "Living with Kidney Stones."*

\* \* \*

*IG & Twitter: @skbowick*

*Facebook: @samantha.bowick*
*@ chronicillnesssupportllc*

*Website:*
*www.SamanthaBowick.com*

# Overcoming Endometriosis

Endometriosis occurs when tissue similar to the uterine lining is found outside of the uterus in other places in the body. There have been cases of endometriosis found everywhere in the body. Symptoms of endometriosis include pelvic pain, irregular periods, debilitating periods, painful intercourse, nausea, constipation, and diarrhea as well as others. The only true way to diagnose Endometriosis is through laparoscopic surgery. Endometriosis can be microscopic and should be excised by an endometriosis specialist as they are the most skilled in the disease and recurrence decreases greatly when the disease is cut out rather than burned. At least 200 million people worldwide suffer with endometriosis and there's no cure. Endometriosis has comorbidities or other illnesses that can arise. This means most people with endometriosis have at least one other chronic illness, most likely more.

When I was 13 years old, I started my period. I, just like most girls, was so excited because it meant I was getting older. However, that was short lived. Shortly after my first period, I started having cramps that would leave me missing days of school and later work. I had heavy periods that would last anywhere from seven to ten days. I couldn't wear tampons because they increased my pain and had to be changed frequently. In middle school, I tried wearing a tampon and had to call home because I had bled through to my pants. One time I had a period that lasted for three weeks, but my gynecologist at the time wasn't concerned. I was nauseous all of the time and my weight fluctuated at least ten pounds from bloating. I felt like I was a different person when I was on my period. I took dance from the time I was five until right after I started my period. I decided to quit dance because it was taking so much energy out of me and when I was on my period I would have to miss class, which wasn't fair to anyone involved. It was something I loved, but I felt like I needed a break. I had to go to school; I didn't have to go to dance even though I wanted to so badly.

At 16, I went to my first gynecologist and was put on birth control because of my cramping. By 19, I was having pelvic pain even when I wasn't on my period. I was falling asleep while I was studying in undergraduate pre-pharmacy classes either from pain, fatigue, or the pain medication I was taking. This led me to have my first laparoscopic surgery in 2009 that diagnosed me with endometriosis. My gynecologist used ablation (burning) instead of excision (cutting) the disease. At the time, I didn't know the difference between ablation and excision. My gynecologist told me she burned all of the endometriosis she could and that I still had some close to one of my ovaries. She also drained an ovarian cyst. I was still having pain weeks after surgery and she told me there was nothing else she could do for me.

This led me to seek help from other gynecologists, gastroenterologists, urologists, a pelvic floor physical therapist, a counselor, and an endometriosis specialist. I have had five other surgeries related to endometriosis. My fourth surgery, in 2014, was a complete hysterectomy. I decided to have a hysterectomy even though I knew it wasn't a cure for endometriosis because I was desperate to be out of pain so I could try to get on with my life. By this time, I had already had to leave pharmacy school once and had just been accepted to a second pharmacy school in hopes of becoming a pharmacist.

I had my complete hysterectomy at 23 years old and hoped it would be my last surgery. However, it wasn't my last surgery. My next surgery was with an endometriosis specialist a year later that found endometriosis and excised it even though both ovaries, cervix, and uterus had been removed. This is because the gynecologist didn't remove all of the disease. Since then, I have not had pain directly related to endometriosis.

Endometriosis has affected every aspect of my life. Along with leaving pharmacy school twice, I have had to deal with feelings of being unable to get pregnant, lost friends because I canceled plans, and have been to more than 20 doctors and health professionals trying to find answers and get pain relief. I have had my appendix, both ovaries, uterus, cervix, and gallbladder removed because of endometriosis and chronic pain. Endometriosis was found on my ovaries, pelvic area, and colon. I was unable to work from 2013 through most of 2019 because of endometriosis and other chronic pain. It was extremely difficult for me to stand on my feet for long periods of time because my pain would intensify. This has left me relying on my parents to help me financially. Thankfully during my time of investigating endometriosis, I had health insurance. I spent many days lying in my bed sleeping or studying because I was exhausted and extremely nauseous from the pain.

Besides laparoscopic surgery, birth control pills, pelvic floor physical therapy, and Lupron, I have tried other treatments like pain medications such as Norco and Percocet, and changing my diet. I tried all of these things because I was desperate and felt like there had to be something that would give me some type of relief.

## "I knew this is what my body needed even though I knew it wasn't a cure."

Lupron is a drug that I honestly wished I would have never tried. There is a limit of twelve injections, which should be an indication and red flag. I have had a total of three injections; two in 2011 and one in 2013. Essentially, Lupron shuts down the ovaries so that the patient doesn't have a period anymore. This is medically induced menopause. Some medical professionals believe that periods can cause endometriosis to continue growing. However, I and so many others are proof that endometriosis persists during menopause without a period. I was diagnosed with osteoporosis after a knee stress fracture from running at 24 years old and have had a tooth chip. These are all side effects of Lupron and there are far more. I blame Lupron, but a doctor hasn't come out and told me it was the cause of my osteoporosis or chipped tooth. Many people have had terrible side effects from this drug, but it still remains on the market as a treatment for endometriosis and doctors receive kickbacks (money) from the drug company for prescribing the medication to patients. When I tried this drug, I trusted my doctors and wasn't told about side effects. They assured me I wouldn't have problems getting pregnant from Lupron.

When I was on Lupron, I experienced horrible hot flashes and night sweats even though I was on add back therapy, which is low dose estrogen. In 2013, my pain actually worsened, which led me to switch gynecologists and not receive my next injection. The gynecologist that gave me this Lupron injection did an ultrasound and actually told me that my uterus looked like a 70-year-old's, like that was a good thing. Lupron is an injection that can be given in monthly increments or every three months depending on the dosage the doctor uses. It was initially and still is used as a chemotherapy drug for people with prostate cancer. It is believed that the ovaries will "wake up" and function as they should once the drug is out of the system, but nobody can tell you when that will be as everyone is different.

One of many obstacles that I have encountered because of endometriosis and chronic illness was scheduling my hysterectomy. At the time of scheduling, there was apparently some disconnect between my gynecologist at the time and me. I had an appointment where we discussed a few different treatment options including a hysterectomy and presacral neurectomy. Before leaving that appointment, I said that I wanted to do my own research to make

sure a Presacral Neurectomy was something that I wanted. I went home and researched and decided that I did not want a presacral neurectomy because of the risks of uterine and organ prolapse. Presacral neurectomy involves cutting nerves so that the patient doesn't have as much feeling to their uterus in hopes to decrease their pain. It has helped patients, but I didn't want to take a chance on prolapse so I called the office back and told them that and said I wanted to schedule a hysterectomy.

A few days before my hysterectomy was scheduled, I received a phone call from the hospital to go over all of my demographics and the procedure I was having done. They told me that I was scheduled for the presacral neurectomy. I immediately got off the phone and called my gynecologist's office. I explained to the person I was talking to what was going on and that I should have been scheduled for a hysterectomy. I was told they would figure out what was going on and call me back. I didn't have a problem going to counseling. I had a problem with being treated like I wasn't capable of making my own decisions; like reproduction was my only purpose because I'm a woman.

I received a phone call from the office and was told the only way my gynecologist would perform a hysterectomy on me would be if I went to see a therapist to talk about my feelings and decision for a hysterectomy. I was hysterical to say the least. This meant I would have to wait. I was a few months away from moving to a new city and starting pharmacy school. My family and I had been preparing for this for weeks. We had made plans to travel as this doctor was two hours away from home. I had taken the time off work for surgery and recovery. I had come to terms with my decision before I ever discussed it with my doctor. I knew this is what my body needed even though I knew it wasn't a cure. I didn't have any children at the time of my decision and was fully aware I wouldn't be able to have any after a hysterectomy. Did I want to get pregnant and have children? Absolutely. I grew up with everyone telling me that I was great with kids and that I would be a great mother. But, I wasn't able to live my life outside of my bed/bedroom because of endometriosis. I wasn't able to do the things I enjoyed doing. Endometriosis was taking so much from me.

I decided to find another gynecologist. I went in prepared as much as possible. I spent time making a list of every treatment I had been on/tried and when, the names of doctors that prescribed these treatments, the tests and procedures I had done, specialists I had been to, and my symptoms. I took this with me and gave it to the new doctor to make my case of having a hysterectomy since I felt like I had to prove myself from my previous experience. This doctor understood and appreciated what I did. He saw that I had tried every treatment (or at least we knew of),that I was tired of being in so much pain and that it had taken over my life. When he did my hysterectomy, the gynecologist told me I made the right decision to have both ovaries removed because they were covered with endometriosis. He said this even though he wanted me to keep an ovary prior to surgery for hormone purposes.

Pelvic floor physical therapy can be extremely beneficial for those who have pelvic pain. A trained pelvic floor physical therapist uses different techniques to work the pelvic floor muscles to try to help them relax rather than contract and spasm. This involves working abdominal muscles and vaginal muscles. I live in a small town and the closest pelvic floor physical therapist to me at the time was three hours away. Now, there are more physical therapists and they may even offer telehealth appointments. There are stretches and things you can do on your own in between appointments. I saw a pelvic floor physical therapist for several months and did find relief in many areas, but my ovary pain was still there, which led to my hysterectomy decision.

Counseling is something that I think everyone needs to at least try. It can be extremely helpful to talk to someone who is outside of your circle of friends and family about your feelings and what you're going through. Usually, therapy sessions are 45 minutes to an hour and you can talk about anything. If needed, they can refer you to a psychiatrist who can prescribe medication if you both think it's needed.

Along with endometriosis, I have been diagnosed with vitamin d deficiency, irritable bowel syndrome, polycystic ovary syndrome, interstitial cystitis, osteoporosis, pelvic floor spasms, kidney stone, and sphincter of Oddi dysfunction and I am an alpha-1 antitrypsin deficiency carrier.

## "I have still found a purpose in life.."

I'm now 30 and have had six abdominal surgeries that required incisions, lithotripsy for a kidney stone, endoscopic retrograde cholangiopancreatography (ERCP) for sphincter of Oddi dysfunction, countless CT scans, several MRIs, two colonoscopies, a barium enema, and countless pelvic exams.

After having a dream that I was writing a book in 2013, I decided I needed to write a book about endometriosis, including medical information as well as what I had been through and was going through, to help others. When it was first suggested I do pelvic floor physical therapy, I had never heard of it and had no idea what it would entail. I wish I had known about it much sooner, and want others to know all of their treatment options before they make a decision about their health.

I want to share my story to help others in their health journey, help educate the public, and let others know they aren't alone. I wish I would have known that I could get myself in to see an endometriosis specialist instead of relying on a gynecologist to admit they weren't capable of performing or treating endometriosis with excision, and then referring me to an endometriosis specialist anyway. I encourage everyone to be their own advocate. Do as much research as you can about your chronic illness so you can make the most informed decision that's best for your body. I'm glad that I'm able to use what I've been through to help other people. It has been a hard road, but one I needed to take in order to be able to do this. Even though I didn't get to finish pharmacy school, I went on to get a Master of Public Health Degree on-line and graduated in 2017. Had I found a true endometriosis specialist sooner, I may not have had a hysterectomy, but everything happened in the order that it did for a reason. I believe this happened for a reason even though I didn't understand it at the time.

If I could do anything, I would be a medical research coordinator helping to study and find cures for illnesses. I want to help people as much as I can to not go through what I and so many others have/are going through with endometriosis and chronic illness. Even though I don't have any children, I have still found a purpose in life. I do still struggle with feelings of never being able to carry a child and know I can adopt. The feelings aren't as persistent and I know I made the right "choice" for myself in having a hysterectomy. I say "choice" because at the time I didn't feel like I had a choice. Do I live in fear of endometriosis rearing its ugly head? Yes, but I hold on to the fact that I have received the gold standard of care (excision) for endometriosis and that I haven't had pain or surgery directly related to endometriosis in six years. Did my life turn out how I planned in high school? No. Even though it didn't, I have been able to find a new way forward.

I'm extremely thankful for my family and friends who have stayed by my side throughout my journey. They and my faith continue to give me hope.

# Eliška

Prague, CZ, Europe

## About Eliška:

*My name is Eliska and I'm part of this book because I'd like to raise awareness about my rare spine disease – Tarlov Cyst. I'm obviously much more than just my disabilities, as every other person with some form of chronic illness and/or disability, but it's part of my life which cannot be cut out. People with rare and/or chronic illnesses and/or with disabilities have to face so much stuff we need to talk about and many things need to change! That's also why I started a Blog and an Instagram account.*

*\* \* \**

*IG: @wanderingpatient*

*"Remember that you don't need to always be the strong one."*

I'd never believe that I'll be a part of something like this - mainly because I'd never believe that I would fall under the labels disabled and chronically ill. It's so weird how things can change. My name is Eliška and I have a Tarlov cyst. As with many people who are chronically ill, my doctors are not quite sure what's all wrong. Due to my hypermobility, other diagnoses and issues, my geneticist suspects a connective tissue disorder, but we don't really know. Tarlov cyst is a rare spine disease (these cysts are fluid-filled nerve root cysts and they're most commonly at the sacral level of the spine) – and it's the reason why I started with writing. At first I wanted someone to talk about it. I waited and hoped that there would be more people – especially in my country – talking about it openly. Spreading awareness, connecting with other patients, pointing out the struggle with doctors, trying to change something so people with Tarlov cyst can receive support when needed... and then I realized – while I'm waiting for something, I could at least have a blog and share my experiences with treatment for others (because some time ago, I would have appreciated that myself). I shouldn't wait for someone to do it. If I want to change something, I need to start the change myself, even though I have fear of not having enough privacy. So I challenged myself and I started.

My Tarlov cyst affects me in many ways. Problems with standing and walking due to back pain and nerve pain (leg burning, stabbing pain, etc.), problems with sleep due to the chronic pain, leg twitching and weird sensations in legs, inability to have sex, because...it affected basically everything from my waist down (bladder, bowel, genitals, legs). I would never believe that one thing can cause so many problems. One day it started with sudden loss of sensation. To be honest I totally freaked out when it was not going away and I felt like I'm losing touch with parts of my body. I remember that I was once crying in the bathroom, wishing and hoping that whatever it was, would eventually disappear. The pain and other symptoms started occurring and getting worse and my life changed completely. It definitely turned my life upside down pretty fast. Especially with the lack of treatment and doctors not believing or not understanding my disease.

We didn't know what was wrong for months. Doctors were insisting that it's anxiety, that my relationship just must be unhappy because "women tend to have sexual dysfunctions in unhappy relationships," that I should care about my mental health more and take antidepressants, and that I'm simply overly sensitive and that it's all psychosomatic. That I'm too young to be sick and that I'm a woman, so I must be just overly emotional and not really in pain. And you know what? Even though I knew that something was horribly wrong, I started to doubt myself under that pressure. It can be so hard to stand up for yourself when someone older and educated who is supposed to understand your body is trying to convince you that everything that you feel and struggle with is not real.

One doctor accidentally found a tumor on my spine and they wanted to make sure that it was benign. And to be honest, I believe that this pretty much saved me and otherwise we wouldn't know my diagnosis to this day. I would probably be labeled as hypochondriac, attention seeker or notorious liar. A CT scan wasn't enough to confirm the tumor was benign, so they had to send me for a MRI (first time in my life, even though I've struggled with back problems since my childhood), even though they looked like they really don't want to send me there, you know, I'm young and it could be a waste of resources. After the magnetic resonance imaging, we found out that my issues weren't "just in my head," because a large cyst showed up, reported along with bone erosion and nerve pressure. I was surprised...but at the same time not surprised at all, because it hurt like hell, so it was a bigger surprise to others. Honestly, I hope I won't trust others more than myself and my body anymore, because I did it too many times and it was always wrong. By the way, my second lucky thing was that the radiologist was shocked by the size of the cyst, so he reported it and sent the CD to us so we could look at it - the doctor who was supposed to tell me the MRI results said "nothing is wrong with your spine, have a good day." Only after we said that we already got the CD and a medical report from the radiologist, did he admit that there was something wrong. A few doctors later, someone finally said – this has a name. It's Tarlov cyst.

> **"To be honest, I've not accepted my life the way it is now. I don't want it to be like this and I can't even imagine it to be like this forever – I'm hoping that surgery (under a specialist) will help me."**

The doctors couldn't deny that something was wrong anymore, but still some of them have been...acting poorly. Saying things like "if it was serious, I would know about it, so therefore it isn't a real problem." Seriously, some doctors laugh at me to this day, while others within the same hospitals are shocked at how this can be happening. I'm still anxious about it, but after almost three years, I know I don't have to and don't want to put up with behavior like this, so I started bringing all my medical records and few official studies everywhere to be on the safe side and I'm learning my best how to respond to the comments. I should probably also add that I underwent one procedure under non-specialists and it didn't help at all – in fact it made me worse, some symptoms got worse, new symptoms appeared and my cyst got even bigger than before. Now, I can never believe a doctor who says that I'm his first patient with this. Not everyone – even in the right medical field – who has a white coat, is the right person who can and should treat you. And I'd never let others laugh at people who are caring about their health and searching for other patients and their experience, searching for another doctor's opinion and googling official studies. Researching can help prevent mistakes (bad decisions) from being made. If I hadn't done that, I wouldn't have undergone that procedure.

To be honest, I've not accepted my life the way it is now. I don't want it to be like this and I can't even imagine it to be like this forever - I'm hoping that surgery (under a specialist) will help me. I won't say that I'm full of self love and that I completely love everything in my life the way it is and how I wouldn't change a thing. I wouldn't choose this, I would be better without my health issues and I struggle with self love and self acceptance a lot.

## "I have a hard time listening to my limits. I had to learn that things that may be healthy to others, aren't necessarily healthy for my body (like lifting weights, yoga, etc.)."

And it didn't make me stronger, I didn't need to "become stronger" in the first place, it made me exhausted and traumatized. People just have this weird imagination that coming through something bad is really cool, that it must be a nice character development after all and that experiences and knowledge are always beneficial. It's normal that it didn't make me stronger or fearless. This is reality and not a movie – it's neither romantic, nor fearless. It's okay that I struggle with self love and self acceptance. It doesn't mean that I'm not trying enough and it doesn't mean that I'll struggle with it forever. My adaptation is basically acknowledging my limits, because I have no other option anyway. It has been few years now and I'm still learning to listen to my body, because I don't want to damage myself even more and the line between "I'm just healthily trying my best" and "I'm overworking myself to prove something to myself and I shouldn't have done this" is really thin. I think because I was masking and suppressing many of my struggles through life, I was trying to

ignore them and not to show them to others so as not to be commented on and seen as "weird" or "problematic." I have a hard time listening to my limits. I had to learn that things that may be healthy to others, aren't necessarily healthy for my body (like lifting weights, yoga, etc.). I'd probably struggle with self love even without my illness due to my mental health. But I love that I didn't lose my humor and I love my body for pushing through it all. And it's quite superficial, but I'm happy that it didn't change how I look so nobody would ever bet what I'm going through (but it's then harder for people to believe me because "I look normal").

If I could do anything in my life, I would like to live a "normal" life, enjoying things that I'm not able to enjoy right now because of my problems. I would enjoy living pain free and not being exhausted. Doing things without fear of falling on my back like horseback riding. I'd ride a bike and I'd love to learn how to roller skate on the retro skates. I'd definitely start to exercise because I don't feel good when I'm weak and have no stamina; it scares me and makes me feel old and fragile. I'd maybe go skiing, ice skating or just playing in the snow for days, because I'm realizing more and more how much I love winter. I wanted to do ballet when I was younger, so I'd maybe do that too if my joints weren't problematic, because I have good abilities for ballet - I'm not just flexible, I'm hypermobile.

I'd tell others that are in a similar situation, to find more people with the same struggles to talk to. Tips and tricks from others who are going through the same thing can be helpful and it just feels good to know that there's someone who understands you.

Learn how to listen to your body, don't be so harsh on yourself and allow yourself to rest. Care for your mental health and if you need a therapy or a psychiatrist, reach for help - it's not a shame, the emotional toll of being chronically ill isn't talked about enough and it's completely normal to feel bad mentally when you're constantly affected by your illness. Basically if you need any kind of help, learn how to ask/apply for it, because no help will come to you unless you start trying to actively get it.

> ## "Remember that you don't need to always be the strong one and if you feel bad, you shouldn't need to pretend that you're always happy and have "good vibes only" to be accepted."

Don't be ashamed to seek the opinion of a different doctor, definitely find a specialist (and if you deal with chronic pain, try a pain management center) and don't feel bad for googling stuff - especially when you have a rare disease, it can help you a lot if you use it wisely. Remember that you don't need to always be the strong one and if you feel bad, you shouldn't need to pretend that you're always happy and have "good vibes only" to be accepted. Allow yourself to be sad or cry, because holding everything inside is harmful. Don't fall for toxic positivity. Remember that you don't need to achieve something special to be valuable, you don't need to do extraordinary things to be likable. You don't need to be active in the community and actively advocate if you don't feel like it; but if you do, don't be afraid to speak up for yourself. Just be yourself. You're enough and you should be loved the way you are. Don't forget that there's no right way to live with chronic pain, that you know your body the best and you don't have to put up with people that are downplaying your struggles and constantly commenting on your health related stuff or making fun of you. You have it hard already, you don't need mean people in your life. Also - there's a difference between not understanding and not wanting to understand. If someone left you behind because of your illness,

I know it's hard and it hurts,
but remind yourself that in hard times
people show their true colors and at least
you know that it wasn't a strong bond
anyway. To be honest, my life would have
been much better if I stuck to my own
advice! I think that sometimes we know
what's the best for us, but it just feels too
hard to achieve, too hard to change.

# Cydni Fried

New York City, NY, USA

**Part-time Student & Professional Writer**

*"We are all a warrior in our own stories."*

## About Cydni:

*Cydni Fried is a student at John Jay College of Criminal Justice in New York City, pursuing a major in Human Service and Community Justice with a minor in Counseling. Cydni earned her associates in arts degree in 2019. She is a member of Phi Theta Kappa International Honor Society, and was also on the executive board of the student government Association. Cydni's interests include gymnastics, art, photography, and social media advocacy.*

\* \* \*

*IG:* @IBSpositiveasican

*Blog:* ibspositiveasican.tumblr.com

My name is Cydni Fried, I'm 21 years young and I live in New York City. I am a senior at John Jay College of Criminal Justice and here is my story! In March 2015, I had my first appointment with a gastroenterologist, better known as the GI Doctor. I was having really bad abdominal pain and was nauseous often. I thought it was acid reflux or something easy to resolve. I would take Mylanta, Pepcid, Pepto Bismol, and Tums. In the short term, some of these medications worked but in the long term, I was in pain and nauseous. This GI doctor was very dismissive and minimized how I felt. She gave me a prescription and sent me on my way.

I went on for months in severe pain. I worked as a gymnastics coach after school and it helped take my mind off the pain for a bit. Until this happened. On a Thursday afternoon in December 2015, I had a bad pain in my stomach when I got home from school. What I thought was a gas pain ended up being a toilet bowl filled with blood, and I did not have my period. Terrified and shaking I screamed for my mom. Quickly my mom called the office of the GI I had previously gone to but asked to see a different doctor. She explained what had happened and they miraculously had an appointment for the next day at 2:30 p.m. We took it.

We went to the doctor's appointment the next afternoon. He asked me and my mom many questions. When he heard my story and blood was involved, he did a quick test in the office to see if blood was still there and it was.

Off to the Emergency Room we went for poking, prodding, and many tests. Everything came up negative. The final test they wanted to do was a stool test. They were looking for parasites and Clostridium Difficile, better known as CDiff. The doctors kept saying it was just to rule out these things and they didn't think any of these tests would be positive. They just needed to be thorough.

The next day the GI doctor called and low and behold I was positive for CDiff. Everyone was in shock. I was not in a high-risk group for this type of infection. I wasn't old or in a nursing home or hospital setting where this was prevalent. The doctor told us the good news was that an antibiotic will cure it; so for 14 days twice a day I took a strong antibiotic. Then two weeks later I had another stool test. I was so happy, it was negative. We thought this was all behind us. Boy, were we wrong!

I was a junior in High School (2015-2016), I tested positive for CDiff three separate times. On the third time, the GI doctor put me on an antibiotic for 42 days, three times a day. I would be taking this through the end of school. We had to tell my school and they suggested I stay home until the doctor cleared me to come back. They were worried because CDiff is contagious. Thankfully, no one at school, work, or in my family ever got it. Meanwhile, at the gym where I was coaching, colleagues were starting to worry about me because I was losing weight and it was obvious. At the same time, my GI doctor had mentioned wanting to send me to a CDiff specialist in Philadelphia at CHOP (Children's Hospital of Philadelphia). We made an appointment when school ended in June.

During the summer I planned to work at a camp for kids with cancer and their siblings. I was kick-starting the gymnastics program and very excited. Because of the CDiff, I had to miss the first three days of camp. The camp doctor wanted to be sure I wasn't contagious because the kids at camp have compromised immune systems.

School ended two weeks before the beginning of camp, and I was on my way to the doctor in Philadelphia for a consultation about CDiff. When we got there, I was so impressed with how beautiful the offices and the hospital were. The surrounding area was the University of Pennsylvania's campus and I was in awe of the buildings. The doctor was really nice and made me feel very comfortable. My parents were both with me. She explained that because of the number of times I had a recurrence, she wanted to see what happens after the end of my 42-day stint on antibiotics. If CDiff reappears then her thought was, I would need to have an FMT (Fecal Microbial Transplant). After 42 days of grueling antibiotics, I had another stool test and it was negative, YAY!! Unfortunately, this is not where this story ends... I went through the entire summer and even fall of my senior year of high school CDiff free. But, by the spring it was evident that I would need an FMT. Not only was I getting an FMT, but I was going to be part of a study. It was scheduled for July 21, 2017, at CHOP. My life changed forever on that day.

So, for the first few months, I felt great, and I was considered a success. I was gaining weight, eating and all was good. In October 2017, I started not to feel good again, with stomach pain, etc. By February 2018, I started to have CDiff symptoms again. When I called my doctor, he said to be safe he would like to do a stool test. It came back negative for CDiff, but with a positive marker for colonized cells. I went on a short seven-day antibiotic regimen, just to be sure, and just continued to do what I do.

I was a freshman in college at this point and was having a tremendous amount of pain in my stomach whenever I ate, and the food would "go right through me." I started losing weight again. The GI told me I needed a colonoscopy/endoscopy to rule out Crohn's Disease or Ulcerative Colitis. That was my fourth time having the test done. Thankfully, there was no evidence of either disease. Between that point and the time of this writing, I had yet another colonoscopy/endoscopy and yet again ruled out Crohn's and Colitis. The pain and discomfort I have experienced are unbearable at times. I am battling my IBS ( Irritable Bowel Syndrome) and we cannot get it under control.

## "I continue to work my hardest at meeting the milestones I have set for myself."

During Thanksgiving 2020, I had just finally come out of a nine-month depression and realized all of a sudden, "Damn, there's been a pandemic happening!" I obviously knew this, but my depression made everything very cloudy; I couldn't feel anything but sadness and hopelessness. All of a sudden, I realized my food choices were narrowing. I used to have at least ten go-to foods, at this point there were only five, and then within a short period, I couldn't eat at all. I couldn't drink anything either, not even water. My mom had to feed me to get me to eat.

Three days later, I was admitted to the hospital, severely dehydrated and malnourished. I needed a feeding tube. While I was in the ER waiting to be admitted they did an EKG, blood work, a COVID-19 test, and they hooked me up to an IV. After six long hours, I was cleared to go up to the floor and 3 Central was my home for the next six days. The doctors and nurses were, for the most part, very nice. They gave me a choice: to eat on my own or to get a feeding tube. With tears in my eyes and rolling down my face, I told the doctor that I couldn't eat and that I needed the feeding tube. I knew all of this was breaking my mom's heart, especially hearing me say it. I was defeated. I didn't want to disappoint her or have her upset with me, but I knew this was the only way to get better. I was diagnosed with an atypical eating disorder that was partially caused by my IBS. Being in the hospital was what I thought was best for me at that time. I didn't just feel awful, but I looked awful. My skin was pale, and I looked like skin and bones.

While I was there, I met some amazing nurses and Child Life Specialists who helped me get over the hump to start eating again. I was scared to get the feeding tube, but once I had it, I was relieved that I wasn't under so much pressure to eat. Then I was terrified once I started to eat again, to have the feeding tube taken out, because then it was all on me to eat and sustain myself. But I did it!! If it weren't for the amazing Child Life Specialists I would never have done as well as I did. They had so much patience and spent so much time with me to help me. The next big hurdle was going home. I was excited to go home, but nervous about it all at the same time. I needed to be in a program. I needed some sort of structure and I needed therapy ASAP! The doctors were pushing an in-patient program, and for about a half a second, I thought maybe that would be better for me, and then it hit me that I want to be in my house, and I don't want to go away, but I also didn't want to be in a virtual program. Then we found a program in Connecticut that was not virtual and would give me everything I need. I have therapy twice a week with DBT (Dialectical Behavior Therapy), food therapy, and art therapy. Because of the pandemic, I don't really go anywhere, so at least this is a way for me to get out of the house.

I continue to work my hardest at meeting the milestones I have set for myself. Eating and expanding my food pallet is something I have struggled with from a young age and I always strive to be the best me possible; but while in treatment I feel as if I'm not the best possible version of myself but better yet a work in progress. I do art therapy every Monday, which is a group session where I get to do a lot of expressing myself in the way of art and then we relate it back to my ED. I also have food therapy on Wednesdays, where we try to incorporate old foods that have been removed from my diet due to IBS. I have three sessions of therapy a week on Monday, Wednesday and Friday where I work on DBT coping skills. The milestones must be met because without them I can't go back to my old self, the gymnastics coach, or even just working in life. I have zero energy and although I have hit the first milestone at this point in time, as of February 8, 2021, it is crucial for me to continue to push through the difficult times to be able to come out on top. In September 2020, I started an Instagram blog about my journey, called @IBSpositiveasican, and it has reached over 1000 people. It raises awareness for invisible illnesses. Although I started my account based on me being diagnosed with IBS, it has ended up becoming so much more to me. I speak the words that most people don't want to speak. I speak on behalf of those who don't want to make others aware that they are struggling, and most of all, I have become a part of a community of people who all support each other. I never thought I would ever find people who have to go through the pain I go through on a regular basis. Most importantly, it's truly amazing and inspires me to want to get better, but also to speak out for those who don't have a voice. I hope by reading my story someone going through something similar will have comfort in knowing that they are not alone in their battle.

While I was in the hospital, I had the art therapist come to my room and I made a painting with a quote I made up.

The quote says,

## "Hard days are okay because it shows you have something to fight for!"

I also have always lived my life by saying

## "Don't forget to smile "

and

## "We are all a warrior, in our own stories"

Those are the three quotes I live by.

*I speak the words that most people don't want to speak. I speak on behalf of those who don't want to make others aware that they are struggling, and most of all, I have become a part of a community of people who all support each other. I never thought I would ever find people who have to go through the pain I go through on a regular basis. Most importantly, it's truly amazing and inspires me to want to get better, but also to speak out for those who don't have a voice. I hope by reading my story someone going through something similar will have comfort in knowing that they are not alone in their battle.*

# Oliver Collins

Brisbane, QLD, Australia,

## Lawyer

*"I get up every day, and I keep going. I am still fighting, long after others may have given up. And I am proud of myself for that."*

## About Oliver:

*Lawyer from Australia who's showing the world that even if you're born with a physically limiting disability, that doesn't limit the possibilities of what you can do in your life with hard work and perseverance. Anything is achievable with the right attitude, and we should all reach for the stars!*

\* \* \*

*IG: @imolliecollins*

My name is Oliver Collins, or Ollie, and I'm a lawyer from Australia. At 18 months old, I was diagnosed with a rare, neuromuscular condition called fibrodysplasia ossificans progressiva, or FOP for short. This condition causes my muscles, tendons and ligaments to turn to bone, and for bone to grow on top of other bones and throughout joints, essentially encasing my body in a second skeleton. This results in very limited movement. When I am at home, or walking around my office, or for other short distances, I can walk with a cane as I have a pronounced limp. For any further distances though, I require the use of a manual or electric wheelchair.

## "It's all about trial and error to find the new happy medium."

My motto has always been "if you don't move it, you lose it" so I do still try and always move around a little bit whenever possible. But any sort of physical exertion is quite exhausting for me, and so I have to rest when I can. I now work from home 3 days a week to give my body a bit more time to recover. Although I do enjoy going into the office from the point of view of interacting with my colleagues, I need to give my body enough rest so that I can handle the mental exertion that comes from working full time as a lawyer in a top-tier law firm.

The excess bone that has grown can also cause me severe, chronic pain. I don't like taking pain medications though, and try to avoid it when I can. My attitude has always been that distraction is just as good as taking a pill, as I find that if I can get my mind off the pain for long enough, then eventually I will stop noticing it and can properly get on with my day. Some of the best distractions, I find, come from spending time with loved ones. I am a social person, and I get a lot of benefits from spending time with my friends and family. I also find that spending time with others helps me to stop focusing so much on myself and my own problems. My loved ones are also a great support network for me, emotionally, in dealing with the many trials and obstacles that inevitably come when one is facing life with a progressive, chronic illness like mine.

Another way I distract myself is with new experiences. I'm a bit of a foodie and so I love going to new restaurants and trying out new dishes. This has been challenging for me the past year, as my condition has now affected my jaw and I am only able to move it a few millimetres. But I have just had to adapt the way I eat and adapt some of the things I eat so that I can still go out and enjoy myself. I can't eat steak anymore, sadly, but I can still enjoy lots of different things. It's all about trial and error to find the new happy medium. I also try to wear dark clothes as eating can now be a bit messier. But with dark, patterned clothing any stains are much less noticeable.

I also have a great support team of carers who help make sure my life runs as smoothly as possible (there are always a few surprises when it comes to dealing with a disability like mine). I am unable to get dressed myself, in order to go to work and be the best version of myself I can be. So they come in every morning and help me with this. They also help ensure that I am able to have a balanced and healthy diet, as even though I love cooking it is often too difficult now to move around the kitchen with a walking stick and make the things that I like to eat. I also have another person come in three days a week when I'm at work and do all my grocery shopping, cook some meals and snacks for me, and make sure all my clothes are clean and ready for work. They also help take care of my dog, and generally take care of all the other errands that I need to have done to try and take some of the pressure off myself. They are an amazing team, and I'm very lucky to have them. I also have an amazing family around me who have been there with me from the start and who have been invaluable in supporting me in all aspects of my life - physically, emotionally and mentally.

My family has also pushed me, which has been so great in helping me grow as a person irrespective of my physical ability. Even though I have a disability, my brain works perfectly and my family's attitude has always been that I should be treated just the same as my siblings and everybody else. They have not cut me any slack just because of my disability, and I had the same high standard I had to achieve at school and university and was expected to have the same ambitions in terms of my career. Because of them, I think I have a better appreciation of the hard work it

takes in making my life run smoothly and also making sure that I had the drive to succeed in my studies and get the job I have now. There aren't many other disabled lawyers that I know in their fifth year working at a top tier law firm. But I'm hopeful that by continuing to do what I do, I can help change people's perspectives so that a) other people with disabilities thinking about becoming lawyers will know that it is possible and that they should give it a go, and b) law firms can know that disabled employees can fulfil the role just as well as our non-disabled counterparts and so we should be given a chance.

"My body has been dealt a bit of a rough deal - with this illness and with the near constant pain and exhaustion it copes with - but I am still going despite it all."

I think, too often, people with disabilities are told no or people say "that will just be too difficult for you" and so they don't bother trying. We need to change people's attitude so that, instead, people with disabilities are told "yes, we just might need to do it a little bit differently." And this is the same in terms of careers, travel, living independently, and many of the other "normal" things that everybody strives for in their lives. These can all be achieved, for everyone, with the right adaptations and the right attitude.

That's one thing I love about my life. So many of the things I didn't think were possible, I have been able to achieve with hard work, perseverance, and with a little bit of luck and a good support network. I love that I live in an apartment that I own, just like so many other "normal" 27 year olds. I love that I am working at a top tier law firm. I love that I can put on the nice clothes that I like to wear and go out every day that I want to, and live my life just like everybody else. Sure, I might need to plan things a little bit further ahead, and there might be a few more factors that go into me planning things - like arranging for a support worker, and then finding out if there is an accessible entrance and bathroom, and whether the wheelchair will be able to fit under the table. But I have been able to achieve everything I set my mind to.

Another thing that I love is that despite all the bumps and lumps and weird bony protrusions I have around my body, my body is still going. My body has been dealt a bit of a rough deal - with this illness and with the near constant pain and exhaustion it copes with - but I am still going despite it all. I get up every day, and I keep going. I am still fighting, long after others may have given up. And I am proud of myself for that. Some days, the fight seems more exhausting than others. But I don't let that stop me.

Last year, I started seriously trying to advocate for people with disabilities on my blog and using my instagram page. I hope, by posting about my experiences and trying to be encouraging of other people with disabilities, that I can do my small part to help shift people's perspectives and encourage others with disabilities to set goals for themselves, and to get out there and crush them. I think that social attitudes still have a long way to go before we are closer to equality for people with disabilities. I think people with disabilities also need to change their attitudes though - we need more people with disabilities to get out of their comfort zone, and get out there and make people see us and make people change their perspective. It's not an easy fight, that's for sure. But if we have strength in numbers then eventually we will win.

This is what I would love to see. And this is something that I really love doing at the moment - advocating in this way. Everybody's experience with disability is different. If I can connect with anybody, even a small number, through my sharing and through my writing, then I am making a difference and that is making a valuable contribution to their lives. This is something else we need more people to do - the more people sharing a wider variety of disability experiences with the world, the more likely we will get to a point where every single person, disabled or not, is appreciated for being unique and different. We are all the same, in that we are all different. We are all perfectly imperfect, and it's high time we all realised and appreciated this.

# CONCLUSION

## A Closing Message from our Illustrator

Instead of going over and writing about my still developing journey with chronic illness I would instead like to leave anyone living this roller-coaster with a message.

To the person diagnosed with an incurable illness; the person who is grieving their future; the person who does not know if they can go on this way, who sees each new day as another day of suffering. I am here to tell you that it is okay to feel this way, and it will get better. I know you are in an immense amount of pain right now and life may seem valueless. Your world is crumbling around you, everything you knew and planned has been ripped from your grasp. You know that your future is filled with worse and harder things. That you will forever be a slave to medication and doctors and surgery rooms. This is all true, you will face such hardships moving forward, but with this truth there also comes another.

Think about the millions of little things that bring you joy. Seeing a cute dog walk by, squeezing your grandpa or grandma tight,

*Your world is crumbling around you, everything you knew and planned has been ripped from your grasp.*

hearing your best friend roar with laughter at a stupid joke. When the sun warms your body and you look up and watch the clouds breeze by in that big blue sky and you have the slightest feeling of the grass tickling your ankles. Think about all of the people who love you. Your parents, friends, pets, people you haven't even met yet. All of these things, they are all in your future. Yes there will be hard times and days you wish you

## This is your second truth; Your future is also filled with happy times and joyful moments.

hadn't woken up, but there will also be days when you watch an elderly couple hold hands as they walk through the supermarket and you smile to yourself thinking about how pure that love and happiness is. Days when you come back from the beach salty and a little sweaty with a burnt nose and a warm heart. This is your second truth: your future is also filled with happy times and joyful moments.

To the person diagnosed with an incurable illness, while your world may often feel like it is falling apart let me leave you with this: your diagnosis will make your future harder than you expected but these hardships will make you appreciate and value your happy moments more than you ever possibly could before.

# –Julia Bartow
@thechronicallyhonest